VICTORIAN SENSATIONS

VICTORIAN SENSATIONS

Essays on a Scandalous Genre

EDITED BY
Kimberly Harrison
and Richard Fantina

The Ohio State University Press
Columbus

Copyright ©2006 by The Ohio State University Press.
All rights reserved.

Library of Congress Cataloging-in-Publication Data

Victorian sensations : essays on a scandalous genre / edited by Kimberly Harrison and Richard Fantina.
  p. cm.
  Includes bibliographical references and index.
  ISBN-13: 978-0-8142-1031-4 (alk. paper)
  ISBN-10: 0-8142-1031-7 (alk. paper)
  ISBN-13: 978-0-8142-9108-5 (cd-rom)
  ISBN-10: 0-8142-9108-2 (cd-rom)
  1. English fiction—19th century—History and criticism. 2. Sensationalism in literature. I. Harrison, Kimberly, 1969– II. Fantina, Richard.
  PR878.S44V53 2006
  823'.809353—dc22
                                2006005531

Cover design by Laurence Nozik.
Text design by Jennifer Shoffey Forsythe.
Type set in Adobe Garamond by Jennifer Shoffey Forsythe.

The paper used in this publication meets the minimum requirements of the American National Standard for Information Sciences—Permanence of Paper for Printed Library Materials. ANSI Z39.48-1992.

9 8 7 6 5 4 3 2 1

Contents

ACKNOWLEDGMENTS   VII

INTRODUCTION: Richard Fantina and Kimberly Harrison   IX

Part One Sensation: Genre, Textuality, and Reception

1. "Highly Flavoured Dishes" and "Highly Seasoned Garbage": Sensation in the *Athenaeum*   ELLEN MILLER CASEY   3

2. "Judged by a Purely Literary Standard": Sensation Fiction, Horizons of Expectation, and the Generic Construction of Victorian Realism
RICHARD NEMESVARI   15

3. Censoring Her Sensationalism: Mary Elizabeth Braddon and *The Doctor's Wife*   CATHERINE J. GOLDEN   29

4. Mary Elizabeth Braddon and the "Combination Novel": The Subversion of Sensational Expectation in *Vixen*   ALBERT C. SEARS   41

5. "Of All the Horrors . . . The Foulest and Most Cruel": Sensation and Dickens's *Oliver Twist*   DIANA C. ARCHIBALD   53

6. Naturalism in Charles Reade's Experimental Novel, *Griffith Gaunt*
DIANNA VITANZA   64

7. Swedenborg and the Disintegration of Language in Sheridan Le Fanu's Sensation Fiction   DEVIN P. ZUBER   74

Part Two Sensational Representations of Corporeality, Gender, and Sexuality

8. "That Muddy, Polluted Flood of Earthly Love": Ambivalence about the Body in Rhoda Broughton's *Not Wisely but Too Well*   TAMAR HELLER   87

9. Sensational Hair: Gender, Genre, and Fetishism in the Sensational
   Decade GALIA OFEK   102

10. "What Could I Do?": Nineteenth-Century Psychology and the Horrors
    of Masculinity in *The Woman in White* ANDREW MANGHAM   115

11. "Chafing at the Social Cobwebs": Gender and Transgender in the Work of
    Charles Reade RICHARD FANTINA   126

12. Women Alone: Le Fanu's "Carmilla" and Rossetti's "Goblin Market"
    NANCY WELTER   138

13. One Sister's Surrender: Rivalry and Resistance in Rhoda Broughton's
    Cometh Up as a Flower LINDSEY FABER   149

14. "Personal Property at Her Disposal": Inheritance Law, the Single Woman,
    and *The Moonstone* JENNIFER A. SWARTZ   160

Part Three Class, Racial, and Cultural Contexts in the Sensation Novel
and on the Stage

15. "I Will Not Live in Poverty and Neglect": *East Lynne* on the East End Stage
    ANDREW MAUNDER   173

16. "The Threshold of an Open Window": Transparency, Opacity, and Social
    Boundaries in *Aurora Floyd* LILLIAN NAYDER   188

17. Sensationalizing Victorian Suburbia: Wilkie Collins's *Basil* TAMARA S. WAGNER   200

18. Political Persuasion in Mary Braddon's *The Octoroon; or The Lily of Louisiana*
    KIMBERLY HARRISON   212

19. Wilkie Collins's "Secret Dictate": *The Moonstone* as a Response to Imperialist
    Panic VICKI CORKRAN WILLEY   225

20. Wilkie Collins's Gwilt-y Conscience: Gender and Colonialism in
    Armadale MONICA M. YOUNG-ZOOK   234

WORKS CITED   247

LIST OF CONTRIBUTORS   267

INDEX   271

Acknowledgments

WE WOULD like to thank the many people who contributed to the publication of this book. The genesis of this project was a series of panels organized by Richard Fantina at the annual conference of the Northeast Modern Language Association (NEMLA) in Pittsburgh in March 2004. The panels were inspired by Kimberly Harrison's course on sensation fiction at Florida International University in the summer of 2003.

Our first note of thanks must go to NEMLA for providing a forum for these panels. A special note of thanks goes to our contributor, Tamar Heller, who supported the panels from their conception and offered many helpful comments along the way. Tamar went above and beyond any reasonable calls for assistance by reading and commenting on many of the papers presented here. A special note of gratitude goes to Catherine Golden, a panelist at NEMLA and a contributor to this collection, who suggested the book project before it ever occurred to either of us. And thanks go to all who answered the call for papers for the NEMLA Conference or were otherwise supportive along the way, including: Elizabeth Anderman, Ruth Anolik, Julie Barst, Sara Beam-Thomas, Rachel Bowser, Marilyn Brock, Marie Granic, Neil Hultgren, Kirstin Johnson, Stephanie King, Heidi Logan, Idilko Olaaz, Anindyo Roy, Eleanor Salotto, Judith Sanders, Madhudaya Sinha, Anne-Marie Sourbiran, and Aaron Worth. Thanks to Sebastian T. Bach for his article on the panels in the *Victorian Studies Bulletin* and to Monica Young-Zook for graciously hosting our closing party at NEMLA. This event cemented the already strong solidarity we had developed during our brief stay in Pittsburgh. Many thanks also to Jennifer Carnell for suggesting the cover illustration, "Past and Present I," by Augustus Egg, and to The Tate Gallery for permission to use it.

We would also like to extend sincere appreciation to our colleagues at Florida International University and the University of Miami. Kimberly would like to thank Elsie Michie and Sharon Weltman who introduced her to sensation fiction at Louisiana State University. At The Ohio State University Press, editors Sandy Crooms and Heather Lee Miller provided continual support and encouragement for the project. Our anonymous readers gave detailed and careful comments that helped us in revisions.

Kimberly would also like to thank Jeremy Rowan for his support and encouragement, and for reading drafts with a historian's attention to detail.

INTRODUCTION

RICHARD FANTINA AND
KIMBERLY HARRISON

VICTORIAN SENSATION fiction was the literary rage in mid-nineteenth-century Britain. Serialized in periodicals such as *Harpers,* the novels also enticed readers in America. Today, sensation fiction is showing signs of popular resurgence with Mary Elizabeth Braddon's *Lady Audley's Secret* airing on Public Television throughout the United States in 2000 and with film adaptations of Wilkie Collins's novels *The Moonstone* and *Basil* released in 1997 and 1998. Andrew Lloyd Webber's musical adaptation of Collins's *The Woman in White* premiered in London in 2004, and a $10 million Broadway production opened in fall 2005. These Victorian thrillers, often involving themes such as bigamy, illegitimacy, drug abuse, murder, inheritance scandals, and adultery, captivated Victorians and continue to interest contemporary audiences.

While today's audiences for sensation narratives, whether delivered in print, on the stage, or on television, are unlikely to be shocked by candid depictions of crime and sexuality, Victorian critics frequently viewed sensation fiction as an inherently scandalous genre.[1] They decried the controversial content along with the physical and emotional sensations such content produced upon the audience. For example, H. L. Mansel, in his often-cited 1863 review of the genre, notes the novels' effects upon the nerves and questions "whether the pleasure of a nervous shock is worth the cost of so much morbid anatomy." Likewise, other critics assailed sensation fiction as "violently opposed to our moral sense"[2] and likened it to a "virus [that] is spreading in all directions."[3]

Despite the outrage of Victorian critics and churchmen, sensation novels were frequently best sellers. *The Woman in White* (1860) was so successful that it spawned a host of commercial products such as bonnets and dressing gowns fashioned after the dress of its title character. Also Mary Elizabeth Braddon's *Lady Audley's Secret* (1861) became so popular that George Eliot envied its sales, admitting that she "sicken[ed] again with despondency" when comparing the commercial success of her recent novels to that of Braddon's.[4] Ellen (Mrs. Henry) Wood became a household name due to the stunning success of *East Lynne,* her novel of a wayward, and eventually repentant, wife. Charles Reade, Sheridan Le Fanu, and Rhoda Broughton also gained fame and considerable fortune through their fiction which also became labeled as "sensational."

While some sensation novels, notably the best sellers by Collins, Braddon, and Wood, have remained in print, many others disappeared from public view over the years and are only now being reissued. Within scholarly circles, even *The Woman in White* for many decades garnered little attention as critics considered sensation fiction the bastard child of classic Victorian realism, something to be read as a curiosity but certainly not to be taken too seriously. T. S. Eliot's famous appreciation of Collins, for example, amounts to little more than damnation with faint praise, as he refers to the author as a "man of talent," opposing him to Dickens, the "man of genius."[5] And among some guardians of the Western canon, the sensation genre even today remains critically suspect and inferior in comparison to "classic" Victorian realism.

In spite of such resistance, attention to sensation fiction within the academy began to grow in the 1970s and 1980s with the expansion of the canon, a result of the cultural upheavals of the 1960s. Kathleen Tillotson's 1969 essay, "The Lighter Reading of the 1860s," provides an early example of a scholar taking seriously the sensation genre. In another early work, P. D. Edwards (1971) analyzes the harsh critical response to the best-selling sensation novels of the 1860s to explore the reasons why these novels created a cultural phenomenon. Winifred Hughes's *The Maniac in the Cellar* (1980) celebrates the genre and also situates the novels of Collins, Braddon, Wood, and Reade within the nineteenth-century critical debates they sparked. Hughes also emphasizes the novels' often transgressive approach to issues of class, race, gender, and imperialism.

During the 1980s, an increasing number of scholars began to focus on cultural and gender-based interpretations of the novels, and they often questioned both the Victorian and present distinction between high and low art. Elaine Showalter in her well-known *A Literature of Their Own* (1977) argues that women's sensation fiction was a response to women's dissatisfaction with their limited gender roles. Showalter and Hughes's scholarship, along with Sally Mitchell's *The Fallen Angel* (1981) and Ellen Miller Casey's often-cited essay "Other People's Prudery" (1984), have become standard sources for feminist readings of sensation fiction. In addition to these revisionist readings, D. A. Miller, in a 1986 essay on *The Woman in White,* applies queer theoretical approaches to sensation fiction by noting the "homosexual component given to readerly sensation by the novel" (112), pointing to both male homoerotic and lesbian elements in the text. Sensation novels have inspired psychoanalytical interpretations and have been richly interrogated in postcolonial readings. In the 1990s, work by scholars including Tamar Heller (1992), Catherine Peters (1992), Lillian Nayder (1997), Lyn Pykett (1992), Ann Cvetkovich (1992), and others continued to further our knowledge of the genre, its authors, and the cultural contexts to which they responded.

Important recovery work continues to be done by scholars such as Andrew Maunder and Jennifer Carnell. Maunder's recent series, *Varieties of Women's Sensation Fiction,* recovers sensation novelists such as Florence Marryat and Felicia Skene who were renowned in the Victorian era but who continue to suffer critical and popular neglect. Carnell's Sensation Press similarly makes available the lesser-known work of Braddon and others. Sensation fiction continues to offer scholars a plethora of research questions as we work to better understand the fiction that generated both a strong critical and popular response.

This collection aims to build upon a rich scholarship. Contributors explore and expand the limits of the sensation genre, identifying ideological biases that have influenced critical reception and suggesting new influences on the novels and novelists. Recognizing the difficulty of posing firm genre definitions, the essays highlight sensation's hybridity—of form, of characterization, and of the political ideologies reflected in the narratives. While most collections have focused on individual sensation authors, notably Braddon and Collins, we bring together essays on the sensation genre as a whole. We include discussions of "canonical" sensation texts such as *Woman in White* and *Lady Audley's Secret* but also provide essays on works that are not so frequently analyzed such as the novels of Rhoda Broughton and Charles Reade and Braddon's penny press fiction. Additionally, contributors resist a focus on the novels of the 1860s, suggesting that the genre is wider in scope and broader in impact than at times assumed. They also discuss authors at times located in the margins of the genre, such as Sheridan Le Fanu, Charles Dickens, and Thomas Hardy, arguing that fluidity of genre boundaries invites such an inclusive analysis. As a whole, the collection aims to further previous efforts to destigmatize the sensation genre, showing it as an integral part of Victorian literature and not as the subgenre that it has too long been considered. The collection's broad editorial scope indicates the breadth and complexity of the sensation genre itself.

When conceiving this collection, we envisioned its use in university courses. Therefore, we have worked to provide some introduction to the genre and its critical reception. To this end, certain essays, such as Vicki Wiley's colonial reading of Collins's *The Moonstone,* highlight dominant critical conversations. To provide a historical sense of the genre's reception, we begin the collection with Ellen Miller Casey's descriptive survey of sensation fiction reviews in the *Athenaeum.* Essays are organized thematically into three sections: the first concerning issues of genre; the second dealing with sensational representations of gender and sexuality; and the third with the texts' complex readings of diverse social and cultural phenomena such as class, race, and empire. To provide an introductory framework, we situate these new essays within a larger scholarly context and in conversation with each other.

Complicated Sensation: Questioning the Limits of Genre

Works within the sensation genre have often been described as "novels with a secret." Involving mysteries, murders, and social improprieties usually within the respectable middle class or aristocratic home, the novels capitalized on the Victorian public's appetite for scandal. While the newly instituted divorce courts provided lurid content for the daily newspapers, many sensation novels followed suit with narratives that questioned the sanctity of the family and the stability of middle-class mores. They also frequently challenged the stability of individual identity and showed a person's outward appearance and social standing to be poor indicators of personality and motives. Victorian critics responded to these novels with moral outrage, dismayed at the public's demand for fiction that did nothing to "elevate or purify," the primary function of art, as expressed by many establishment critics.[6] Related to both sensational journalism and melodramatic theater, sensation novels are generic hybrids, exhibiting characteristics of genres including melodrama, romance, the gothic, realism, and Newgate fiction. Often seen as artistically (and morally) inferior to Victorian realism, they are also frequently described as being "plot-driven" as opposed to "character-driven."

When attempting to account for such a broad body of fiction, however, such genre characteristics do not always apply, thus opening avenues for critical discussion regarding what novels and which authors are indeed sensational. While many novels often labeled "sensation" exhibit the characteristics above, others do not. And some that do have such characteristics are not called sensational.[7] Such difficulty in defining the genre is not surprising, Jonathan Loesberg argues, because the genre "was as much a creation of the literary journals who grouped the novels together as it was of the novels themselves."[8] The novels, he contends, are "almost deliberately thematically indeterminate" (116). Andrew Maunder similarly warns that "to talk of sensation fiction as though it were all of a single type or of equal merit would be misleading."[9]

In this collection, Ellen Miller Casey shows that such uncertainty regarding the label "sensation" is not new; in the 1860s, *Athenaeum* reviewers also struggled over the definition of the genre. Casey's survey contradicts Hughes's earlier assumption that for the novels' original audiences, the genre "appeared blatantly recognizable [. . .] hardly in need of official critical definition."[10] A number of essays in this collection also show that while many critics focus on the 1860s as a high point for sensation fiction, a full understanding of the fiction requires that we look throughout the Victorian period and not just to the "sensational sixties."[11] To emphasize the longevity of the genre, Casey cites reviews that demonstrate its survival into the 1890s. Richard Nemesvari, in his contribution, also looks to the 1870s and beyond. Further exploring the roots of sensation, Diana Archibald analyzes Dickens's *Oliver Twist* (1838) as a forerunner of the sensation novel and as itself a generic hybrid that defies classification as realist, domestic, sensational, or Newgate novel. Also, Tamara Wagner focuses on Collins's 1852 *Basil* as developing a gothic vision of suburbia, which, she argues, becomes an important setting for later sensation novels. As these essays show, sensation fiction did not burst unannounced onto the literary scene in 1860 as some critical works suggest.[12] The label "sensation" itself was in use by literary critics before the 1860s sensation best sellers,[13] and at midcentury, it also was applied to the theater and used in newspaper reports, mostly those describing the reactions of courtroom audiences to lurid case details.[14]

To further expand our understanding of the genre, other essays included here complicate criticisms that sensation is plot-driven to the detriment of character development. In his critique of sensation, Mansel asserts that characters in sensation novels are "but so many lay-figures on which to exhibit a drapery of incident." Even Patrick Brantlinger in his important 1982 essay on the genre seems to endorse this point when he writes: "Perhaps the overriding feature of both melodrama and the sensation novel is the subordination of character to plot," and "descriptive detail and setting can deduct from character."[15] However, while this perspective has endured, it has not gone unchallenged. As Heller writes, such a critique was originally "as much an ideological as an aesthetic judgment" that became part of the inherited criticism.[16] More recently, Maria K. Bachman and Don Richard Cox, in their edition of critical essays on Wilkie Colllins, write that "Collins was not, in his own mind, a writer who placed plot and sensation above all, as the unfair stereotypes of him suggest."[17] Even some early reviews of sensation novels applauded the authors' characterization; for example, an 1862 review of *Lady Audley's Secret* in the *Times* praised the novel for "showing such *even* excellence of plot, of passion, of character, and of diction."[18] Likewise, Henry James dismissed criticism of characterization by noting that: "There are bad novels and good novels, as there are bad pictures and good pictures; but that is the only distinction in which I see any meaning."[19] In her essay here, Dianna Vitanza focuses on characterization in Reade's *Griffith Gaunt*, suggesting that the novel was informed by current scientific theories, especially those of Darwin, as Reade portrays characters who respond to circumstances on the basis of natural drives and instincts. Vitanza sees this work distinguished, like that of Émile Zola, by an incipient naturalism. Devin Zuber also looks to characterization as he discusses the influence of the eighteenth-century Swedish mystic Emanuel Swedenborg on Le Fanu's fiction which presents characters with often fractured identities.

Underlying most discussions of the sensation genre is the relationship of these novels to their more respected counterparts classified as works of Victorian realism. Several contributors address this distinction, exposing the artificiality of the genre hierarchy. In particular, Nemesvari contests the critical assumption that at midcentury, the Victorian realist novel was an accepted art form, asserting that "by 1860 the Victorian novel was on the verge of an epistemological crisis." Victorian realism, he argues, owes its critical acclaim to the sensation novels of the 1860s; as critics defined these popular novels against realism, they cemented the realist novel's reputation as high art, a distinction that still persists. To further complicate such labels, Nemesvari explores how the sensation phenomenon influenced the fiction of Thomas Hardy as well as his attitudes toward his work. Archibald's essay also takes issue with this hierarchy as she explores the relationship between sensation and realism in *Oliver Twist*. Such work exposes the ideological interests that are served by genre distinctions that seek to oppose popular and "high" literature.

The self-reflexive nature of sensation fiction is also a focus of this collection. Aware of the public appetite for, as well as the critical disdain of, their work, sensation authors at times subverted popular and critical expectations. Both Albert Sears and Catherine Golden focus on Braddon's desire to critique the genre to which she owed her fame. While previous scholars have argued that Braddon should be recognized as more than a sensation author, Golden and Sears suggest that Braddon's skillful manipulation of readers' and critics' sensational expectations should be applauded.[20] As she subverted genre expectations, she also solidified her place in the literary market. Golden reveals that in *The Doctor's Wife* Braddon censored her own sensationalism and also answered the charges of critics with her portrayal of Isabel who, despite her consumption of allegedly dangerous and sensational reading material, triumphs in the end, much like another avid novel-reader of an earlier generation, Catherine Morland in Jane Austen's *Northanger Abbey* (1818). Sears, in his essay on *Vixen* (1879), argues that the novel teases its readers by raising sensational expectations only to subordinate them to a romance plot, albeit a rather nontraditional one. Throughout section one of this collection, contributors emphasize the generic hybridity of sensation fiction. Focusing on reception and the Victorian literary culture, they urge an understanding of the genre's broad boundaries.

Gender and Sexuality: Theorizing the "Lurid" Details of Sensation Fiction

Since the early reviews, sensation novels' representations of gender, sexuality, and the family have been topics of discussion and often of heated debate. For

Victorian reviewers, the authors' private lives provided fuel for their criticism of social improprieties they found within the novels. Several of the sensation authors lived their adult lives outside of the parameters of the Victorian nuclear family. For example, Collins's first common-law wife, Caroline Graves, finally chose to leave him and marry another man. Collins gamely attended the wedding, then took up with another woman, Martha Rudd, who bore their three children out of wedlock. When Graves's marriage failed, Collins, apparently without a second thought, took her back and proceeded to support two households. Reade, although employed by Magdalen College at Oxford in a position that mandated celibacy, had fathered an illegitimate son with one woman and lived unmarried with another, the actress Laura Seymour, for over two decades. Braddon, however, received the most attention for living and having children with publisher John Maxwell while he was married to another woman who was incarcerated in an insane asylum. As Golden points out, contemporary critics attributed the "immorality" of Braddon's work to her "immoral" lifestyle. These authors chose to flout conventional morality in their personal lives, so it is little wonder that they did so in their work as well.

Time after time, sensation novels take as their subject the domestic sphere, almost gleefully hammering at the Victorian façade of the harmonious home. The institution of marriage in these novels is often seen as a weapon to be wielded for financial gain. Love, in the sensation novel, often has very little to do with it. Percival Glyde marries Laura Fairlie in *The Woman in White* solely to dispossess her. Magdalen in *No Name* weds Noel Vanstone to regain a purloined fortune. Braddon describes a marriage in *Lady Audley's Secret* as "a dull, jog-trot bargain."[21] In the same novel, another character, contemplating marriage, wonders how to judge which will be the "one judicious selection out of nine hundred and ninety-nine mistakes" (204). In both Collins's *The Dead Secret* (1857) and Reade's *A Terrible Temptation* (1871), women conspire successfully to deceive their husbands about their children's biological paternity. In Reade's novels parents occasionally falsely imprison their own children for the most venal of motives (*The Cloister and the Hearth, Hard Cash*). In Collins's *Man and Wife* (1870), one character attempts to kill his wife and another has murdered her abusive husband. At times, Collins and other sensation novelists portray loving "families" that do not fit the traditional norm. In *No Name,* for example, the Vanstones seem in the early chapters to be a charming and apparently traditional nuclear family. Collins, however, soon reveals this family as anything but traditional, as the parents are unmarried and the daughters therefore illegitimate. Collins's novel explicitly endorses non-traditional domestic living arrangements.

In addition to portrayals of marriage and the family, sensation writers probe gender roles and push the boundaries of the Victorian ideology of separate spheres. In nineteenth-century critiques, the portrayal of woman as a "monstrosity"[22] in sensation fiction was especially singled out for condemnation. The villainous female characters received (and receive) much critical attention as they raise the possibility that the "Angel in the House" was not an angel at all. Sensation fiction often takes the paradigm of the sensuous but weak-willed and intellectually naive young woman and turns her into a willful and indomitable social actress, whether she is a wayward heroine like Magdalen in *No Name,* or a villainess like Lydia Gwilt in *Armadale.* Also, the novelists create women characters who, without completely flouting convention, call it into question, especially as they are juxtaposed with male characters who are weak (at least momentarily) and often confused. Collins endows Marian Halcombe with "masculine" traits in *The Woman in White* as her strength in the first half of the novel supports the weakened hero, Walter Hartwright. Marian defines herself as her sister's protector and is only supplanted in this role by Walter later in the novel. In *The Moonstone,* Rachel Verinder sacrifices her reputation to act as her lover's protector. Valeria, in *The Law and the Lady* (1875), also takes on the role of detective to save her husband. In many sensation novels, women act boldly to accomplish their goals, giving little thought to questions of propriety.

Feminist readings of the novels often are situated within midcentury debates regarding women's roles, such as those surrounding the Matrimonial Causes Act of 1857, the introduction of the first women's suffrage bill to Parliament in 1869, and the Married Woman's Property Acts, passed in 1870 and 1882. Sensation novels are frequently seen as taking part in these discussions, either supporting reform or reflecting cultural unease with shifts in separate spheres. Numerous twentieth- and twenty-first-century critics have questioned whether the texts, either intentionally or not, subverted Victorian gender ideologies. Did the controversial representations of gender and sexuality and the broader critiques of Victorian society within the pages of the novels provoke broader social critique and erode Victorian values? Or did the narrative structure contain the criticisms, neatly wrapping them up so that the average reader was content to find that often the "moral" characters married, inherited wealth, and lived happily?[23] Even further, were such representations as shocking to the reading public as we might assume?

Showalter was one of the first to claim Braddon as a feminist author, and Collins is frequently credited with creating women characters who defy the Victorian ideal and with critiquing the dominant culture. In this collection, Jennifer Swartz contributes to the argument that Collins used his fiction to critique women's subordinate status. Reading the *Moonstone* alongside William Blackstone's eighteenth-century codification of British common law, she sees the novel as an exposé of the *feme sole*'s tenuous legal position. In contrast to those who read sensation fiction as urging gender reform or challenging sexual mores, a number of other scholars conclude that the literary works and/or their authors were, ultimately, not terribly progressive in regard to women's issues. For example, in a 1976 article, Jeanne Elliot finds Ellen Wood's *East Lynne* to uphold strict gender stereotypes. Casey in her frequently cited 1984 article concludes that Braddon succumbs to Victorian mores and provides limited political critiques. Similarly, both Cvetkovich (1992) and Nayder (2000) question Braddon's feminist status. Catherine Peters notes that while Collins "liked women who were intelligent and gifted and spoke their minds," he was ultimately "not in the least interested in female emancipation."[24]

In response to such critical conversations, contributors in this section emphasize the ideological "hybridity" of sensation fiction and the ideological conflicts faced by the authors themselves. Heller, writing here of *Not Wisely but Too Well* (1867), situates Broughton's novel within the feminist tradition alongside novels such as *Jane Eyre* because of its depiction of the female body and its desires. She notes that by presenting Kate Chester as a fleshy and voluptuous heroine, instead of the slender and delicate women of many Victorian novels, Broughton challenges contemporary notions of both feminine beauty and female sexual appetite. She recognizes, however, the novel's "generic hybridity" and its split between radical and conservative elements. According to Heller, the narrator moves from a celebration of Kate's ample flesh to "the language of moral contagion deployed by critics of sensationalism," and the novel both celebrates and then censures female appetite. Similarly, Lindsey Faber analyzes Broughton's anonymously published first novel, *Cometh Up as a Flower* (1867), a work criticized by Victorian critics for dwelling on the female characters' sensuality. Faber sees both the subversive and conventional in this novel of the rivalry between two sisters, reading it as "a resistant *bildungsroman*" with Nell's resistance, yet final surrender, to womanhood.

Both Andrew Mangham and Galia Ofek illustrate sensation novelists as participating in ongoing cultural discussions, suggesting that their use of certain sensational content might not have been as surprising for Victorian readers as we may assume. Mangham proposes that Collins's exposure in *The Woman in White* of the gap between appearance and reality was not as subversive as critics contend. Examining nineteenth-century psychological treatises, he argues that science had already made this topic a "widespread Victorian obsession" and that it acknowledged the psychotic impulses simmering under Victorian constructions of masculinity. Likewise, while Braddon is often credited with creating the "fair-haired demon" in Lady Audley, Ofek shows instead that Braddon skillfully contributed to the fetishization of women's hair that was already taking place in both the arts and trade at midcentury. While this focus on women's hair was not new, Ofek contends that Braddon, and to some extent Collins, engaged, through their use of women's hair, in a debate that allowed a challenge to expectations regarding both women's behavior and literary convention.

Some contributors to this collection show that though homosexuality had not yet become a medical and scientific category, same-sex attraction was one of the themes that sensation novelists explored, however elliptically. Previously, several scholars have commented upon the obvious female same-sex desire in Le Fanu's "Carmilla" (1872). In this tale, Laura relates, for example, how Carmilla "with gloating eyes . . . drew me to her, and her hot lips travelled along my cheek in kisses" (251). Le Fanu is, perhaps ironically, the most overtly sexual *and* the most conservative of the authors profiled here. The very airing of the transgressive behavior depicted in "Carmilla" and other sensation fiction would seem to preclude its containment as it is presented so seductively. In this collection, Nancy Welter compares "Carmilla" to Christina Rossetti's homoerotic poem "Goblin Market" (1862) and finds lesbianism veiled as sisterhood in Rossetti's poem and as vampirism in Le Fanu's story. Richard Fantina points to numerous incidents of homoeroticism in Reade's work, both lesbianism in *A Woman-Hater* (1877) and the posthumous "Androgynism" (1911), and male desire in *Foul Play* (1868) and *The Wandering Heir*.

Welter and Fantina build upon the work of critics such as D. A. Miller, one of the first to suggest both male and female homoeroticism in *The Woman in White*. Elsewhere Jennifer S. Kushnier and, in earlier work, Nemesvari have explored the character of Robert in *Lady Audley's Secret*. Kushnier writes that Braddon used "the popular genre of sensational fiction to depict Robert Audley's secret homoerotic desires," which, she asserts, were nurtured by his public school education.[25] Ellen Bayuk Rosenman identifies the same novel as "a trenchant study in masculinity, especially in its treatment of the homoerotic ties between Robert and George" (32).[26] And "undercurrents of homoeroticism," according to Natalie Schroeder, inform Lady Audley's friendship with her maid Phoebe (92).[27]

While the subversive impact of sensation fiction remains a focus of critical discussion, some sensation novelists did overtly attempt to write novels with a mission. In *Man and Wife*, Collins's portrayal of athleticism satirizes "muscular Christianity," and the novel also provides a powerful argument against domestic violence. Collins's *Heart and Science* (1883) critiques "the hideous secrets of vivisection" and *The Evil Genius* (1886) argues for women's rights in divorce and child custody. Reade targets brutal prisons in *It Is Never Too Late to Mend* (1856) and the abuses of private "lunatic" asylums in *Hard Cash*. While Collins and Reade were conscious of their roles as "reformers," other sensation novelists would have shuddered at the notion that their work might question prevailing values. Yet, even those authors with profoundly conservative (even reactionary) political convictions, such as Le Fanu, explicitly depict characters whose behavior critiques Victorian values, even while their authors often unconvincingly attempt to condemn their actions.

Sensational Responses to Class, Race, and Empire

As with critical responses to sensation fiction's portrayal of gender and sexuality, scholars have interpreted both radical and conservative commentary in regard to class, race, and empire in sensation texts. Also, attitudes toward these topics within the novels are frequently seen in relation to social change at midcentury. In addition to debates regarding gender roles, as discussed above, Victorian readers also faced challenges to conventional assumptions regarding national and class identity. The Indian Mutiny of 1857 along with other revolts throughout the empire, including the 1865 Morant Bay Rebellion in Jamaica, are often seen as increasing British unease regarding their imperial might.[28] Debates regarding class reform also marked the period, with the 1832 and 1867 Reform Bills expanding the franchise and with liberal revolts throughout Europe in 1848 causing national tensions and fears of such uprisings within Britain. In analyzing sensation texts, scholars often point to ways the narratives respond to unease about such rapid social change and either question, subvert, or perhaps uphold conventional assumptions.

With political and social reform at issue throughout much of the Victorian era, it is not surprising that class identity is a frequent theme of sensation fiction. For example, *The Woman in White* chronicles the social rise of Walter Hartwright. While beginning the narrative as a poor drawing teacher, Hartwright is, at the novel's end, situated within the gentry and father to the heir of Limmeridge estate.[29] More subversively for Victorian readers, in *Lady Audley's Secret* Lucy infiltrates the respectable Audley family, successfully playing the role of the lady despite her low birth. Another social actress, *No Name*'s Magdalen Vanstone, moves easily within the Victorian class hierarchy, winning the affections of the propertied Noel Vanstone without giving a hint of her illegitimacy and thus her social stigma. As well, Lydia Gwilt, a former servant and ex-convict, succeeds in the role of a respectable Victorian lady. When placed in the context of midcentury parliamentary debates regarding reform, such narratives can be seen to respond to Victorian concerns regarding class identity during a period of social change. Loesberg, for example, argues that "sensation novels evoke their most typical moments of sensation response from images of a loss of class identity" (117). A fear of the loss of class standing, he points out, was "commonly expressed in the debate over social and parliamentary reform in the late 1850s and 1860s" (117).

The essays in this collection frequently seek further historical understanding both of Victorian reception of sensation's social messages and of literary representation of Victorian social hierarchy. Andrew Maunder points out that we have not yet explored how the working classes received the very popular sensation narratives. In his essay here, he shows that the stage adaptation of *East Lynne*, retitled *Marriage Bells*, that played at the East End's Effingham Theatre in 1864 focused much more heavily on class and the problems of poverty than does the novel. Social fluidity is the focus of essays by Lillian Nayder, Tamara Wagner, and Kimberly Harrison. In their discussions, both Nayder and Wagner focus on the often overlooked importance of architecture and geographical spaces in our analyses of sensation fiction. Nayder looks to the upper-class home in her analysis of Braddon's *Aurora Floyd*, illustrating that Braddon uses window imagery to "represent and test" social boundaries. Along with many sensation novels, *Aurora Floyd* demonstrates that class difference is not immutable, and Nayder identifies the character of John Conyers in the novel as emblematic of "class discontent and the blurring of social boundaries."

As Tamara Wagner looks to the newly developing suburbs in Collins's *Basil*, she shows how the novel promotes middle-class values while keeping the aristocratic ideal firmly in place. Kimberly Harrison's discussion of Braddon's pre–Civil War serial novel, *The Octoroon*, indicates that Braddon presented similar themes of social mobility in both her double-decker and penny press fiction but with different purposes. Harrison explores the simultaneous radical and conservative elements in this novel and demonstrates that while *The Octoroon* takes both abolition and miscegenation as givens, it also advises its audience to eschew revolutionary violence in favor of gradual change.

Studies of the sensation novel have also explored themes of empire, and a number of the novels portray or refer to colonial settings. *Lady Audley's Secret*, for example, is set in 1857, the year of the Indian Mutiny, and contains numerous references to that event.[30] In such discussions of empire, much attention has been focused on *The Moonstone*, as it begins and ends in colonized India. Some scholars see an incipient anti-imperialism in *The Moonstone*, and others find the Indian locales as mere exoticism which actually furthers the colonial project. While an anticolonial reading of some sensation fiction is certainly possible, one should keep in mind, as Nayder reminds us, that Collins authored the second chapter of Dickens's notoriously pro-imperialist "The Perils of Certain English Soldiers," which weakens any effort to locate his work as an unambiguous model of anticolonialism. However, Nayder also notes that Collins's contribution to that story "both complies with and resists Dickens's aims."[31] As Peters points out, Collins resisted the easy jingoism so prevalent in mid-Victorian society; she writes that *The Moonstone* "is remarkable for its serious treatment of the Hindu faith, at a time when the violence of the [Sepoy] Mutiny was still fresh in British memory" (309). And Anthea Trodd notes that Collins's 1858 article in *Household Words*, "A Sermon for Sepoys," comments on "the virtues inherent in the Moslem Faith."[32] This serious treatment of Hinduism and Islam stands in stark contrast to Collins's often sarcastic remarks regarding contemporary Christianity.

In this collection, Vicki Willey participates in current debates surrounding *The Moonstone,* agreeing with scholars who see the novel as presenting an antiimperialist message. However, even if we accept Willey's reading of *The Moonstone,* in most other sensation fiction we find, if not an endorsement, an easy acceptance of British imperialism. The Anglo-Irish Le Fanu, for example, enthusiastically supported British colonialism in Ireland. And Reade's work, often with settings in colonial outposts such as South Africa (*A Simpleton*) and Australia (*Never Too Late to Mend*), never questions the legitimacy of British rule.

While it might be gratifying for modern readers to argue that sensation authors frequently and compellingly critiqued colonialism, there is not sufficient evidence to make this claim for them. As Edward Said has written, what "the full roster of significant Victorian writers saw was a tremendous international display of British power virtually unchecked over the entire world" and "[i]t was both logical and easy to identify themselves in one way or another with this power."[33] Yet some sensation novelists appear more enlightened on racial issues than many of their contemporaries. Here, Collins takes the lead in his presentation of sympathetic mixed-race characters such as Midwinter in *Armadale* and Ezra Jennings in *The Moonstone.* In her essay on *Armadale* in this collection, Monica Young-Zook comments on the class, racial, and gender hybridity of Midwinter and Lydia Gwilt, suggesting that through these characters, Collins critiques social ideologies within the colonial sphere. The contributors in this section point to ideologically complex and often ambiguous representations of gender, race, class, and colonialism that indicate midcentury unease resulting from rapid social changes.

Situating Sensation in the Literary Tradition

At the heart of many sensation novels lies the recognition of the fluidity of identity. Rather than embracing essentialist notions of class, gender, race, and religion, the sensation novelists often complicate and at times defy them. Hughes writes, for example, of "Collins' scathing depiction of a hypocritical and venal society, in which the traditional moral categories have utterly lost their meaning" (150). The absence of any credible moral focus informs much sensation fiction and leaves its characters free to invent their own lives. The genre anticipates the loss of faith and the fragmentation of identity that would later characterize modernist fiction. The "crisis in masculinity" which became a hallmark of early modernism is already apparent in much sensation fiction with its strong female characters and uncertain, vacillating men. And the decentered narratives, especially in Collins's work, point ahead to postmodernism. With their characterization, narrative structure, and often subversive content, the novels invite various critical interpretations, as the essays in this collection demonstrate.

A generic hybrid—formally, thematically, and ideologically—sensation fiction is an integral part of Victorian studies. The themes developed in these works speak to our own era while the best of the novels deserve recognition alongside the classics of Victorian realism. By presenting essays on the genre as a whole, this collection highlights the complexity of both sensation fiction and the Victorian society which it reflected. While scholars continue to find engaging areas for inquiry within seminal sensation fiction, many of these works that have not yet received much critical attention provide fertile areas for inquiry. The essays presented here contribute to broadening the conventional understanding of the genre so that it is acknowledged as more than a handful of novels from the 1860s. Through its intricate narratives, memorable characters, and sometimes surprising responses to Victorian culture, sensation fiction intrigued the Victorian public, shocked their critics, and continues to resonate with readers today.

NOTES

1. See Ellen Casey's essay in this volume for detailed examples of critical responses.
2. Henry Mansel, "Sensation Novels" <http://gaslight.mtroyal.ca./sensnov/.htm. Subsequent references refer to this edition>. Unsigned, "Our Sensation Novelists," *Living Age*.
3. *Westminster Review*, quoted in *Wilkie Collins* by Lillian Nayder, 71.
4. George Eliot, *The George Eliot Letters*, 309.
5. T. S. Eliot, "Introduction" to *The Moonstone*, by Wilkie Collins, xi.
6. Cited in Norman Page, ed., *Wilkie Collins: The Critical Heritage*, 48, 52.
7. As Lynn Pykett points out in "The Newgate Novel and Sensation Fiction," Brontë novels, including *Jane Eyre* and *The Tenant of Wildfell Hall*, likely were not considered sensational only because of their early publication date. P. D. Edwards notes that in nineteenth-century criticism, the term was not applied to Anthony Trollope even though novels such as *Orley Farm* and *Phineas Redux* contained sensational elements. The reason, he concludes, is that critics applied the term only to authors of whom they held a low opinion (*Some Mid-Victorain Thrillers*, 6).
8. Jonathan Loesberg, "The Ideology of Narrative Form in Sensation Fiction," 115. Subsequent references will be cited by page in the text.
9. Andrew Maunder, "Introduction" to *Varieties of Women's Sensation Fiction*, 5.
10. Winifred Hughes, *The Maniac in the Cellar*, 18.
11. Like many critics, Loesberg focuses on the 1860s as the highpoint for sensation fiction, claiming that "by 1870 the genre itself seems to have lost definition and to have ceased to be controversial" (115).
12. Hughes, for example, states that the genre "sprang full-blown, nearly simultaneously, from the minds" of Collins, Wood, and Braddon (6).
13. Pykett, for example, has found the term used by Margaret Oliphant in her 1855 review of Collins's early novels ("Newgate", 33).
14. Thomas Boyle, *Black Swine in the Sewers of Hampstead: Beneath the Surface of Victorian Sensationalism*, 37.

15. Patrick Brantlinger, "What Is 'Sensational' about the 'Sensation Novel' ?" in *Nineteenth Century Fiction,* 12.
16. Tamar Heller, *Dead Secrets: Wilkie Collins and the Female Gothic,* 83.
17. Maria K. Bachman and Don Richard Cox, *Reality's Dark Light,* xiv.
18. Eneas Sweetland Dallas, "Lady Audley's Secret," *The Times,* 480–81.
19. Henry James, quoted in Walter M. Kendrick, "The Sensationalism of *The Woman in White,*" 18.
20. See, for example, Marlene Tromp, Pamela Gilbert, and Aeron Haynie's introduction to *Beyond Sensation* as an effort to claim for Braddon a reputation that extends further than the sensation genre.
21. Mary Elizabeth Braddon, *Lady Audley's Secret,* 6. Subsequent references are cited by page in the text.
22. Unsigned, "Our Sensation Novelists," *Living Age.*
23. Frequently, the sensation novelists themselves felt compelled to end their stories in a tidy Victorian manner, illustrating perhaps their hesitation to resist the tradition of the happy ending or at least the demonstration of some ultimate moral closure. Reade, for one, indicates his resistance to, yet compliance with, formal constraints, beginning the final chapter of *The Cloister and the Hearth* with the words: "In compliance with a custom I despise but have not the spirit to resist, I linger on the stage to pick up the smaller fragments of humanity I have scattered about" (439).
24. Catherine Peters, *King of Inventors,* 122. Subsequent references will be cited by page in the text.
25. Jennifer S. Kushnier, "Educating Boys to Be Queer: Braddon's *Lady's Audley's Secret,*" 69.
26. Ellen Bayuk Rosenman, "'Mimic Sorrows': Masochism and the Gendering of Pain in Victorian Melodrama," 32.
27. Natalie Schroeder, "Feminine Sensationalism, Eroticism, and Self-Assertion: M. E. Braddon and Ouida," 92.
28. For further discussion regarding the impact of such revolts on British national identity, see Jenny Sharpe, who makes a connection between resulting British colonial unease and their reliance upon "scientific" racial theories. See also Brantlinger's *Rule of Darkness.*
29. See Ann Cvetkovich's "Ghostlier Determinations: The Economy of Sensation and the *Woman in White*" (1989), which details Walter's rise in the social hierarchy.
30. For further discussion, see Lillian Nayder's "Rebellious Sepoys."
31. Lillian Nayder, *Unequal Partners,* 103.
32. Anthea Trodd, "Introduction" to *The Moonstone,* by Wilkie Collins, xviii.
33. Edward Said, *Culture and Imperialism,* 105.

-PART ONE-

Sensation

Genre, Texuality, and Reception

The essays in this section center on the emergence of the sensation "genre." Extending and sometimes blurring genre boundaries, these essays explore contemporary critical, popular, and authorial response. Introducing the section, Ellen Miller Casey discusses many of these reviews as they appeared in the pages of the *Athenaeum*. Richard Nemesvari identifies the ideological motives of establishment critics who sought to label sensation a lesser genre than realism, while Catherine Golden and Albert Sears analyze two novels in which Mary Elizabeth Braddon consciously tried to shrug off the "sensation" label, while continuing to evoke it. Extending Charles Dickens's relationship to the sensation genre, Dianna C. Archibald sees *Oliver Twist* as a forerunner to the sensation novel both with its violent elements and its social concerns. Dianna Vitanza and Devin Zuber examine literary and cultural influences on sensation fiction and character development, with Vitanza focusing on Charles Reade's *Griffith Gaunt* and its relationship to an emerging naturalism. Zuber finds the influence of Swedish mystic Emanuel Swedenborg in Le Fanu's syncretic use of the supernatural and sensation.

- I -

"HIGHLY FLAVOURED DISHES" AND "HIGHLY SEASONED GARBAGE"

Sensation in the Athenaeum

ELLEN MILLER CASEY

CONTEMPORARY critics generally agree that Victorian reviewers disapproved of and decried the sensation novel. Winifred Hughes, Ann Cvetkovich, Lyn Pykett, Patrick Brantlinger, Deborah Wynne, and others argue that reviewers condemned the genre for its overdependence on plot at the expense of character, its commercialism, its immorality, and its advocacy of female passion.[1] The anonymous reviews in the weekly *Athenaeum*[2] certainly demonstrated these judgments. But while they did attack sensation as "highly seasoned garbage,"[3] they also praised more than one "highly flavoured dish"[4] and acknowledged the power of sensation's transgressive subversion of Victorian artistic and moral conventions.

The *Athenaeum* reviewed virtually all major and many minor sensation novels, but valuable comments on both the genre and individual novels are also found in other reviews. Wilkie Collins's *The Woman in White,* for example, was inexplicably not reviewed but only included without comment in a "List of New Books" on August 11, 1860. Despite the lack of a review, comments on *The Woman in White* in other reviews reveal the novel's importance and the reviewers' response to it. Early in 1862, for example, Geraldine Jewsbury indicated that John Cordy Jeaffreson had imitated Collins's narrative method in *Olive Blake's Good Work.*[5] In his review of Mary Elizabeth Braddon's *John Marchmont's Legacy* the following year, Jeaffreson himself cited *The Woman in White* and Braddon's *Lady Audley's Secret* as the paradigmatic sensation novels (792). In his 1864 review of William Starbuck's *A Woman Against the World,* Almaric Rumsey asserted that *The Woman in White* presents "a dissolving view of the most startling character; but it is painted and adjusted with all the art that industry and mechanical skill can suggest"(804). In his 1865 review of Charles Felix's *The Notting Hill Mystery,* Jeaffreson complained: "In his anxiety to reproduce some of the mannerisms of *The*

Woman in White, Mr. Felix has lost sight of his master's finer artistic qualities." These comments make clear both the reviewers' continuing high regard for *The Woman in White* and their recognition of its innovative narrative techniques.

Though sensation is typically identified as a phenomenon of the 1860s, the *Athenaeum* reveals that it was vigorous through the 1870s and did not disappear until the end of the 1880s. The *Athenaeum*'s earliest use of *sensation* seems to have occurred in 1862, when Jeaffreson suggested that much of James Spence's nonfiction *On the Recognition of the Southern Confederation* was "mere 'sensation' writing" (233). As late as 1877 the *Athenaeum* still decried the "morbid taste of our time, in which the torpid imagination of the novel-reader must be incessantly stimulated by all sorts of ingenious mystifications."[6] The genre survived into the 1880s, though it was by then dismissed as old-fashioned. In 1886, for example, Katharine De Mattos labeled Denzil Vane's *Like Lucifer* a "genuine survival of an exploded type of fiction," and in 1889 an unidentified reviewer called Mrs. G. Lewis Leeds's *The Master of Rylands* "a sensation novel of a very old type."

Initially the reviewers struggled over a definition of the genre. Lena Eden's 1862 review of *Lady Audley's Secret* demonstrated both the "slippage" between economic and literary meanings for *sensation* noted by Cvetkovich (*Mixed Feelings* 20–21) and the early critical acceptance of the term to define the genre. Eden first used *sensation* in its economic sense, declaring that by publishing both its first and second editions on the same day and its third within a day or two, Braddon's novel "comes into the world determined to make 'a sensation.'" A few sentences later Eden used the term without quotation marks in a literary sense: "Strange to say, the book has some merit as a sensation novel, and, in spite of this puffery, will make its way" (525). In his review of *John Marchmont's Legacy* the following year, Jeaffreson acknowledged the reviewers' struggle with definition: "In the absence of an accepted definition of the word 'sensation,' as applied to prose tales, it is difficult to say whether this novel belongs to sensational fiction" (792).

Cvetkovich argues that reviewers identified sensation novels by their affect (14). The *Athenaeum* did define sensation novels by their bodily impact on readers, who find when reading them that "the flesh creeps."[7] These novels "curdle [readers'] blood, cause their hair to stand on end, give them 'pins and needles' in the region of the heart, and fix their eyes with a rigid stare for at least twenty-four hours."[8] They "alternately [freeze] the reader's heart and [cause] his hair to stand on end."[9] More commonly, however, *Athenaeum* reviewers used content to identify the genre. Jeaffreson hesitated to describe *John Marchmont* as sensational because it lacked a "strong element of mystery," a "grim secret vaguely hinted at," and "imperfectly shrouded horror." He finally decided that the novel was sensational, however, since it had "startling positions, sudden surprises, and a series of incidents rousing painful emotions" (792). Reviewers repeatedly identified sensation novels by plot devices: "a murder . . . an elopement . . . a gamekeeper knows some secret . . . secret marriages . . . a faint suspicion of bigamy . . . a detective";[10] "three murders, a death by self-slaughter, a case of wife-beating, a superabundance of drunkenness, and two or three instances of revolting cruelty to animals";[11] "deep-laid plots and conspiracies, and hidden wills, and spies, and mad-houses; and everybody . . . appears to have been married about six times over; and they all turn out to be the husband or wife of somebody else, at last";[12] "disease, secret murder, and open violence";[13] "murders and mysteries in ruinous manor-houses";[14] "hairbreadth escapes, trap-doors, disguises, personations, and surprises";[15] "monotony of murder, bigamy, and forgery."[16] Most succinctly, a novel was sensational if it manifested "murder, madness and mystery."[17]

However reviewers defined sensation novels, the genre framed their critical responses. Before the sensation novel was established as a distinct category, Daniel Owen Maddyn attacked Collins's *Basil* as an example "of the French School" (1322), while Eden praised Ellen Wood's *East Lynne* as a realistic novel for its "life-like" characters and "simple and natural" writing (473). Once the genre was established, however, *Athenaeum* reviewers resisted this "class of novels."[18]

One way the reviewers resisted sensation was by marginalizing it to what Patrick Brantlinger calls a "subliterary" category (143). Thus Arthur Butler described Henry Holl's *The Golden Bait* as "not far from being a very good novel, of the 'sensational' class, be it understood" (173), and Thomas Jackson recommended Collins's *Man and Wife* "as a sensation novel much superior to most sensational novels" (46). Repeatedly the reviewers qualified their praise of sensation fiction by this technique of marginalization, echoing the ways in which some of them limited women authors. Indeed, since Braddon reigned over "the realm of the sensational novel"[19] and Wood was "chief of the sensational school,"[20] many sensational novelists were doubly marginalized.

Another sign of resistance was the repeated declaration that sensation was a temporary phenomenon. As early as 1863 Eden found it "some relief to meet with a novel which contains no very startling incidents, no impossible and intricate plot, and only a very '*mild mystery*'" (emphasis in original).[21] Since the reviewers simultaneously recognized the popularity of "the 'vulgar sensational' line so much striven after at present,"[22] this "relief" seems to have been theirs and not the public's. One can, however, see them trying to persuade the public that it should share their opinion. John Doran announced that the public was "now weary of excess of sensation,"[23] and Jeaffreson was sure that "the present morbid taste for tales of thrilling horror will doubtless soon pass away."[24] Jewsbury hoped "that 'sensation novels' are running themselves to seed"[25] and complained: "Our sensibilities are fatigued by the strong sensation novels we have daily to encounter: even as the music of Verdi is said to wear out the voices of robust singers."[26]

By 1866 Jewsbury exulted that in *The Lady's Mile* Braddon had moved from sensation to "the didactic school of manners and morals," that in *All in the Dark*

Sheridan Le Fanu seemed "to repudiate all that is sensational," and that in *Common Sense* Emma Newby forsook "the sensational school of writing, in which her first novel was written." Despite these hopes that the sensation fad was waning, William Lush recognized that sensation was still "the order of the day."[27] Lush seems to have been right, since sensation continued to dominate the market. Lush complained that good nonsensational novels were scarce since "high literary talent content to settle down in a sublunary sphere of action is becoming daily a greater rarity."[28] Jeaffreson proclaimed that "writers of the sensational school have, in these later years, so often shocked the nerves and tried the patience of readers, that criminal romance has by this time ceased to agitate habitual devourers of prose fiction."[29] Henry Fothergill Chorley declared that Collins's *Armadale*, "a 'sensation novel' with a vengeance," was a product not just of an individual author but of "a period of diseased invention" (732).

Sensation continued into the 1870s as Frederick Cosens announced the English public was "weary of the sensation novel."[30] Candy declared "many novels of the season" sensational,[31] and Butler judged it unlikely that George Meredith's *Beauchamp's Career* would be popular since it was "anti-sensational" (18). In 1874 Butler announced: "We think, on the whole, we see signs of a re-action from the taste which refused everything less stimulating than bigamy and murder."[32] The caution expressed in "we think," "on the whole," and "signs" surely indicates that sensation still abounded.

One sign of the popularity of the sensation novel was Alfred Austin's three-part *Temple Bar* series of 1870 which defined contemporary novels as either "fast," "sensational," or "simple." These categories appeared in the *Athenaeum* through the 1870s, though with different names. The *Athenaeum* called the three types the snobbish, the sensational, and the commonplace when it suggested that novelists "who do not pander to the more hardened appetites for sensation and snobbery, have learnt to vie with Mr. Trollope in accurate reproduction of the details of commonplace existence."[33] The same tripartite system appeared when "most novels" were identified as "dreary, vulgar, or sensational,"[34]

Despite, or perhaps because of sensation's popularity, *Athenaeum* reviewers consistently opposed it, as Jewsbury reminded her readers in 1868: "We have never shrunk from avowing ourselves plainly against sensation novels."[35] Lush had taken the same stand earlier that year: "We have not minced words ourselves, on more than one occasion, concerning a good many of these [modern sensation-novels]."[36] These unminced words were directed primarily at the sensation novel's alleged artistic weakness and immorality. Chorley put this clearly in his review of Collins's *Armadale:* "Those who make a plot their first consideration and humanity the second . . . have placed themselves in a groove which goes, and must go, in a downward direction, whether as regards fiction or morals" (732).

The sensation novel's major weakness "as regards fiction" was felt to be its unrealistic focus on plot at the expense of character for, as Rumsey declared, "a book which is all incident is inartistic."[37] With a vivid metaphor, Jeaffreson complained that when plot overwhelmed character "the wild tangle of plot and counterplot is too much for endurance; the jungle rises far above our heads."[38] The reviewers valued character over plot, and realism over sensation. Lush suggested that "we would rather have a book like [Catherine Spence's *The Author's Daughter*] with its wholesome mediocrity than all the brilliant insults to experience, probability, and common sense, which the last year has brought forth." Edward Wilberforce praised Harriet Thynne's *Colonel Fortescue's Daughter* for "using its plot to excite a fair amount of curiosity, not to drive us breathlessly to the end, and making more of its characters than pegs on which to hang mysteries." Robert Romer conceded the "unexciting character" of Margaret Oliphant's *The Three Brothers* but praised it for its "resemblance to Nature." He argued that complexity of plot directly correlated with the probability of artistic failure, so that sensation novelists were doomed to "inevitable condemnation that their own want of judgment in the selection of their subject has entailed upon them."

Butler's review of *The Golden Bait* discussed at length the artistic weakness of sensation novels, which he defined as those "in which character is subordinated to incident and motive to action." He did not summarize the plot, for that would have removed the "only . . . pleasure obtained from reading a 'sensation' novel," unraveling a puzzle. He presumed that sensation authors began with incidents, then fit in agents, and lastly molded these characters to give them some appearance of probability. Unlike sensation novelists, "masters and mistresses of fiction . . . make the character their basis, and, starting from this, trace unerringly the consequences which result from its development, and from which the events spring." Although he relegated *Bait* to "a low class of art," Butler praised it for avoiding "gross improbability and absurdity."

Probability and realistic characterization were not the only values excluded by the sensation novel's focus on plot. Romer contended that because of the kind of plot that sensation novelists "waste their time upon," their novels omitted "delicacy of handling, knowledge of characters, a high tone of feeling and a sense of humor."[39] This position was echoed when the *Athenaeum* complained that the "ingenious mystifications" and "cunningly contrived" plot of the sensation novel routed "delineation of character, analysis of passion, [and] beauty of style."[40]

Another artistic weakness of the sensation novel was lack of originality, though the metaphors used to assail that quality confirm Brantlinger's suggestion that the sensation novels' status as a "mass-cultural commodity" contributed to their devaluation (*Reading Lesson* 163). Over and over Jewsbury asserted that the primary failure of sensation novels was that they were "machine-made."[41] She identified John Harwood's *Miss Jane, the Bishop's Daughter*, for example, as "a favourable average specimen of the automaton toy novel" (720). She complained that sensation novels were "manufactured by the score" in the same way as Nottingham lace or Balbriggan hosiery. This, she felt, was inevitable when "there is a large demand for objects which, in the first instance, were devised at some cost of invention and material."[42] Jewsbury was not alone in her judgment that many sensation novels were derivative of earlier models. Robert Collyer, for example, suggested that "originality is rarer than 'sensation,' and success in a limited sphere is better than following a multitude to do evil."[43]

As Collyer's comment reminds us, sensation novels were condemned not only for their weaknesses "as regards fiction" but also for those "as regards . . . morals." It was seen as "a triumph in its way if a novel could be both sensational and decent,"[44] and sensation novelists were repeatedly attacked for fishing "in filthy waters."[45] Again and again the reviewers lashed out at the novels' immorality, describing them as "effete and deathly,"[46] "impure,"[47] "morbid,"[48] "poisonous . . . and degrading,"[49] and "neither . . . natural nor . . . wholesome."[50] In short, sensation novels undermined morality because they were "pervaded by a vague, relaxing element, in which no brave or strong principle of virtue can exist."[51]

Victorian gender ideology intensified the resistance to sensation novels, for women authors made immorality especially reprehensible. Jeaffreson said that sensation, which "lowered the tone and deadened the moral perceptions," was worse when the author was one who should exhibit "feminine instinct" and "womanly refinement."[52] In his review of Braddon's first novel, *The Trail of the Serpent*, Jeaffreson had gone so far as to hope that "M. E. Braddon" wasn't a woman, for if she were, the novel would destroy the favourable impressions created by her book of poems, *Garibaldi* (393). He later acknowledged the success of Newby's *Wondrous Strange* but could not congratulate her for it since she was expected to produce "sound and wholesome work" (178). Doran suggested that if Florence Marryat's *For Ever and Ever* had been "from a man's pen," he could "give it more unqualified praise than we feel justified in now doing." As it was, however, there was "a vein of coarseness meandering through some of the descriptions which must be protested against" (427). Jewsbury's complaint was typical: "There is a low condition of moral health which will readily develope [*sic*] into specific vices. The female writers of fiction of the present day are, with few exceptions, doing their utmost to bring about this state of things."[53] That it was worse for women than for men to contribute to such moral illness is evident in Jewsbury's speculation that "it is curious that the most questionable novels of the day should be written by women."[54] Her admonition of "Leigh Spencer," whom she presumed to be a woman, is typical: Spencer should "purge her brain and cleanse her heart of all the morbid stuff which they have absorbed from 'sensation novels'" so that "she might produce a story worth the trouble of reading."[55]

Gender ideology formed the basis for criticizing immorality and also established the grounds for praising decency. When women avoided sensationalism, they often received extravagant applause. Doran gushed over Elizabeth Jenings's *Thyra Gascoigne:* "It is as a sweetening of the air to get into the company of good, honest, unsensational women, in works of fiction; and it is as satisfactory that more than one authoress of that sisterhood . . . are preparing other illustrations of the beautiful and the true" (639). Rumsey praised "George Graham," whom he presumed to be a woman, because "her experience lies in a respectable sphere. She does not drag us into irregular houses, where some Clytemnestra of doubtful origin has managed to gain the place which should be occupied by a genuine lady, and determines to hold it with dagger and bowl if need be."[56] He similarly rejoiced in Annie Thomas's *Denis Donne:* "It is pleasant to have a book from the hands of a lady novelist without the usual complement of dungeons and draw-wells, bombast and bigamy."

Yet despite these many illustrations of what P. D. Edwards calls the sneering and snarling of Victorian reviewers, *Athenaeum* reviewers also acknowledged sensation's attraction and power and praised a number of sensation novels.[57] Although they insisted that realism was the highest artistic value and wished that superior novelists like Le Fanu would write of ordinary life,[58] they acknowledged that many realistic novels lacked interest. While he praised William Harrison Ainsworth's *Hilary St. Ives* as a novel which "quite refreshes the reader after the fashionable sensational romances of the present day," Romer also called it "quaintly old-fashioned" and "a perfect model of the simple narratives which pleased an older generation." Lush acknowledged Newby's "usual laudable system of discarding sensationalism" but found *Married* only "a harmless, pleasant, fairly interesting little story." Even Jewsbury found Braddon's novel of manners *The Lady's Mile* "a little dull."

They admitted that sensation was a reasonable reaction to this dullness of realism. Jeaffreson, for example, said in 1863: "'Sensation' would not have achieved its brief and pernicious triumph, if public patience had not been over-taxed by writers not sufficiently mindful that the novelist's first, though by no means his only duty, is to amuse."[59] This was, of course, rather different from Maddyn's assertion a decade before that "the proper office of Art is to elevate and purify in pleasing."[60] Sensation novels were seen as an inevitable reaction against the innumerable "*panada*" or "water-gruel" novels of "the old, prosy, harmless school, in which, it was conceived, the manners and customs of the time were meekly portrayed for the edification of gentlewomen."[61]

True, the reviewers blamed some sensation novelists for merely pandering for popularity. Butler dismissed Lucy Walford's *The History of a Week* as comical because Walford did not belong to the sensational school although she used "the established ingredients of high-flavoured fiction." Rumsey derided Florence Marryat for aspiring in *Veronique* "to the honours of a 'sensation' novelist, without possessing the qualifications by which the perishable laurels of sensation novelists are earned" (368). An unidentified reviewer attacked Oliphant for her deference in *Young Musgrave* "to a morbid taste of our time," a deference which was all the worse since she was "not even at home in murder and madness." Unlike Collins and Braddon, she took no "heartfelt interest in triumphantly baffling the reader's curiosity" but only threw in mystery "like a sop to appease the public" (769). Too often such halfhearted attempts at sensation contained "the ingredients of a sensational novel, but, like damp fireworks, [they declined] to explode."[62]

More frequently, albeit reluctantly, the reviewers acknowledged the power of sensation novels. Despite his judgment that *Wondrous Strange* was "neither agreeable nor wholesome," Jeaffreson ranked it "amongst the most powerful tales of its kind" (177). He admitted that Le Fanu's *The Wyvern Mystery* "overflows with cleverness and force" (398). Bright allowed that "some writers of the adultery and bigamy school win a certain admiration by their powerful delineation of passion, even base and brutal."[63]

Later in this volume Richard Nemesvari suggests that Henry Mansel's identification of sensation fiction as a "loathsome dainty" signaled his lack of objectivity. Certainly more than one contemporary critic has noted the metaphors of disease and poison that were used by reviewers.[64] Another way to read reviewers' diction, however, is as a sign of their recognition that though they might praise sensation novels for probability and workmanship, the genre's real attraction lay in irrational depths. Eden called *Lady Audley's Secret* "just the sort of book to be read by everybody . . . having no end of plots and conspiracies for those who like plots, and plenty of light, easy, agreeable conversation for those who do not." Despite this rational praise, the description of Lady Audley as "one of the most beautiful and bewitching fiends ever met with in the annals of literature" and "a brilliant and incomprehensible anomaly" displayed another and more potent source of the novel's attraction (525). Eden's review of Braddon's *Aurora Floyd* demonstrated the same pattern. She declared that "the characters are more natural and the story more probable" than in *Lady Audley.* Despite this emphasis on realism, Eden repeated her extravagant language in describing the heroine. Aurora, with her "wonderfully brilliant eyes" and "dangerous beauty," forced the critic into sympathy "in spite of our better reason and judgment . . . by sheer force of fascination" (144). Chorley acclaimed Collins's *No Name* "a work of Art" for its "vigour and brightness." Though he found Magdalen "coarse" and her reformation unbelievable, he created a sense of her dangerous and attractive power by his use of such words as *indomitable, beauty, adroitness,* and *courage* and by his repetition of "*reckless* determination," "*reckless* of the agony she has caused," and "the penalty of her *recklessness*" (emphasis added) (10). Chorley criticized Charles Reade's *Griffith Gaunt* for being "too theatrical" and for fishing in filthy waters for its subject. His description of its hold on its readers, however, was emphatic: "the man cannot be a member of the Novel-Readers' Guild (which includes our best thinkers, our most imaginative writers, our sturdiest moralists) who could lay by this tale, once having begun it" (602). Jewsbury praised Collins's *The Moonstone* for "the carefully elaborate workmanship, and the wonderful construction of the story," but her eating metaphors describe its readers as being "in a state of *ravenous* hunger" and the novel as appearing in "*tantalizing* portions" (italics added). Over and over the reviewers praised or censured sensation novels for conventionally acceptable reasons while betraying in their diction the irrational basis of these novels' attraction. The reviewers were like the novel-readers they disdained "who, while they feel half-ashamed of themselves and boast of much pious indignation against sensationalism, are seduced by its fascinations nevertheless."[65]

Two reviews by Jeaffreson illustrate this simultaneous indignation and seduction. His review of *The Wyvern Mystery* suggested that the novel would be disliked by "mild and commonplace people" who think that a novel should raise rather than depress readers' spirits, "forbear to give pain which is not calculated to enhance the effect of its pleasurable representations," contrast "its illustrations of the evil" with "equally vivid exhibitions of the good of human nature," and at the end "leave the reader in the intellectual and moral condition of a man who has been listening to fine music, or contemplating a noble work of art." On the other hand, those readers who "delight in strong hysterical emotions" and think it appropriate that the novelist provide "pictures of eccentric vice and cruel violence" would like the novel for its "sensational inhumanity" (398). While it's tempting to read Jeaffreson's description of noble art as illustrating the Victorian resistance to sensation, it is important to note that he is fully satisfied with neither "mild and commonplace" nor "hysterical" readers.

This same ambivalence toward sensation is evident in Jeaffreson's review of *Wondrous Strange*. Jeaffreson correctly assumed that the anonymous author was a woman and regretted that she had been "unfortunately induced to imitate" the "objectionable artists" who wrote sensation novels which "disturb a sensitive breast with every kind of creeping horror, crawling chill, and hideous surprise." Nonetheless, though *Wondrous Strange* was "neither agreeable nor wholesome," Jeaffreson acknowledged its strong appeal to the emotions, indicating that it was "capable of carrying emotional readers through a succession of unpleasant feelings." He censured its heroine's "unnatural crimes" and "unholy love," but suggested the force of the novel by using such phrases as "*inflamed* with cupidity," "*splendour* [of] her envied beauty," "*marvelously* adroit application of chloroform," and "the lovely Jezebel *fascinates*" (emphasis added). These phrases describing one of "the most powerful tales of its kind" outweigh his more staid praise for the novel's "delineations of character" and "moral reflections."[66]

Butler declared that the world was not better off for sensation novels, but proposed that if it would take "its intellectual drams in this form, it is as well that the stimulant should be of good quality, as well as of agreeable flavour."[67] This drug metaphor simultaneously modifies the praise of the "good quality" and "agreeable flavour" of some sensation novels and suggests the genre's appeal to the irrational. Jewsbury had been similarly reluctant in her praise when she had announced: "One has often to admit good qualities in the most obnoxious acquaintance, and sometimes even to give his due to the Devil."[68] In the cookery metaphor in her *Moonstone* review, Jewsbury suggested that readers of the sensation novel "utterly ignore all delicate distinctions of cookery." Chorley used a similar metaphor in describing the "salad" of Emily Spender's *Kingsford:* the novel could be "partaken of without antipathy, though it cannot be said to enter into the domain of honest cookery." We can extend this metaphor. Contemporary reviewers are not wrong when they suggest that most Victorian critics disapproved of the sensation novel. Certainly *Athenaeum* reviewers did their best to dismiss sensation novels as "highly-seasoned garbage." Nevertheless, they were often captured against their will by a "highly flavoured dish" which was frequently more attractive than a realistic novel containing "neither food nor poison" and therefore "too feeble to be even unwholesome."[69]

NOTES

1. Winifred Hughes, 34–67; Ann Cvetkovich, *Mixed Feelings,* 14–23; Lyn Pykett, *The Sensation Novel,* 1–13; Patrick Brantlinger, *The Reading Lesson,* 2, 17–18, 142–65; Deborah Wynne, 1–14.

2. As many reviewers as possible have been identified using the two Web sites based on the marked copies of the *Athenaeum:* City University, London, *The Athenaeum Index of Reviews and Reviewers: 1830–1870,* and The University of Ghent, *The Athenaeum Index of Reviews and Reviewers (1872–1886).*

3. [Collyer], review of *Checkmate.*
4. [Jewsbury], review of *Stella,* 773.
5. [Jewsbury], review of *Olive Blake's Good Work,* 150. Henceforward no note will be provided when a reviewer and the novel being reviewed are identified in the text or when only one work is listed for an author. Page numbers will be provided in parentheses as needed.
6. Review of *Young Musgrave,* 769.
7. [Rumsey], review of *Gaspar Trenchard,* 781.
8. [Jeaffreson], review of *Wondrous Strange,* 178.
9. [Jeaffreson], review of *The Wyvern Mystery,* 398.
10. [Wilberforce], review of *Waverney Court.*
11. [Jeaffreson], review of *Wondrous Strange,* 178.
12. [Eden], review of *Which Does She Love?* 462.
13. [Jeaffreson], review of *Lady Flavia.*
14. [Jewsbury], review of *Guy Deverell.*
15. [Jewsbury], review of *One Against the World,* 179.
16. [Lush], review of *The Girls of Feversham.*

17. [Jewsbury], review of *Lynn of the Craggs*.
18. [Jeaffreson], review of *Wondrous Strange*, 177.
19. [Jewsbury], review of *The Lady's Mile*.
20. [Jeaffreson], review of *Lord Oakburn's Daughters*, 428.
21. [Eden], review of *A Point of Honour*, 291.
22. [Jewsbury], review of *Church and Chapel*, 46.
23. [Doran], review of *Thyra Gascoigne*, 639.
24. [Jeaffreson], review of *Janet's Home*.
25. [Jewsbury], review of *Altogether Wrong*.
26. [Jewsbury], review of *Emilia in England*, 609.
27. [Lush], review of *The Man of Mark*.
28. [Lush], review of *Never–For Ever*, 461.
29. [Jeaffreson], review of *Piebald*.
30. [Cosens], review of *Margarita*, 352.
31. [Candy], review of *Caught in the Toils*.
32. [Butler], review of *Vanessa*.
33. [Collyer], review of *Fernyhurst Court*.
34. Review of *Pauline*.
35. [Jewsbury], review of *Nature's Nobleman*.
36. [Lush], review of *Lucretia*, 527.
37. [Rumsey], review of *Sedgely Court*.
38. [Jeaffreson], review of *Foul Play*.
39. [Romer], review of *Gwendoline's Harvest*.
40. Review of *Young Musgrave*, 769.
41. [Jewsbury], review of *Dangerous Connexions*.
42. [Jewsbury], review of *Hever Court*.
43. [Collyer], review of *Jabez Oliphant*.
44. [Bright], review of *Halves*.
45. [Chorley], review of *Griffith Gaunt*, 603.
46. [Jewsbury], review of *Altogether Wrong*.
47. [Doran], review of *Alfred Hagart's Household*.
48. [Jeaffreson], review of *Janet's Home*.
49. [Lush], review of *Lucretia*, 528.
50. [Jeaffreson], review of *Lord Oakburn's Daughters*, 429.
51. [Jewsbury], review of *Miss Jane*, 720.
52. [Jeaffreson], review of *Viola*, 494.
53. [Jewsbury], review of *Miss Forrester*.
54. [Jewsbury], review of *Woman against Woman*.
55. [Jewsbury], review of *The Cabinet Secret*.
56. [Rumsey], review of *Percy Talbot*.
57. P. D. Edwards, *Some Mid-Victorian Thrillers*, 9.
58. [Jeaffreson], review of *A Lost Name*.
59. [Jeaffreson], review of *Janet's Home*.
60. [Maddyn], review of *Basil*, 1323.
61. [Noll], review of *Florence Manvers*, 777.
62. [Jewsbury], review of *Dacia Singleton*.
63. [Bright], review of *Mad Dumaresq*.

64. For example, see Brantlinger, *Reading Lesson,* 143; Deane, 69–70, 76–77; Cvetkovich, *Mixed Feelings,* 20–21; Hughes, 35–36; and Wynne, 4–5.
65. [Lush], review of *Mrs. Hardcastle's Adventures,* 566.
66. [Jeaffreson], review of *Wondrous Strange.*
67. [Butler], review of *Lady Judith.*
68. [Jewsbury], review of *Nature's Nobleman.*
69. [Bright], review of *Mad Dumaresq.*

- 2 -

"JUDGED BY A PURELY LITERARY STANDARD"

Sensation Fiction, Horizons of Expectation,
and the Generic Construction of Victorian Realism

RICHARD NEMESVARI

SENSATION FICTION was a provocative form of writing, so a provocative statement to begin: by 1860 the Victorian novel was on the verge of an epistemological crisis. At first such an assertion seems counterintuitive, since by that date prose fiction had become the dominant mode of literary expression in England. The foundation of popularity established by Walter Scott's *Waverley* novels early in the century had prepared the way for the even more extensive popularity of Dickens, whose *Great Expectations* began serialization in the very year I have chosen for my supposed moment of crisis. Further, the appearance of *Adam Bede*, in 1859, and *The Mill on the Floss*, again in 1860, suggested that the future of the novel was safe in the sure hands of George Eliot. Yet these authors can be used to illustrate my thesis, as much as they may seem to undercut it. By midcentury Scott's heavy reliance on romance and gothic conventions appeared increasingly antiquated, and while Dickens had managed to transform such elements into social commentary via the Newgate novel, it was these aspects of his writing that received the most negative critical commentary by Victorian reviewers. Because of Dickens's now-unquestioned canonical status it is sometimes forgotten that throughout his career he had numerous detractors, so that Margaret Oliphant, in the May 1862 issue of *Blackwood's*, could assert "Mr Dickens . . . has never ventured to depend for his special effects upon the common incidents of life. . . . [W]henever he has aimed at a scene, he has hurried aside into regions of exaggeration, and shown his own distrust of the common and usual by fantastic eccentricities, and accumulations of every description of high-strained oddity."[1] Of course Oliphant had her own agenda to advance, since she and writers such as Charlotte Yonge were central figures in creating, during the 1850s, what Winifred Hughes describes as "the ascendancy of the domestic novel, which centered on the familiar events and social interactions of everyday life."[2] Thus, although Dickens stood second to no one in his celebration of Victorian domesticity, there is little doubt that his commitment to the "common incidents of life" was quite often overwhelmed by "high-strained oddity," and that his fictional mode was very different from his critic's.

Eliot might be seen as the counter to Dickens's excesses, but her confidence in her method was less secure than it has subsequently seemed. Both the famous chapter 17 in *Adam Bede*, "In Which the Story Pauses a Little," and the Rhine/Rhone section of *The Mill on the Floss* are self-consciously intrusive defenses of an aesthetic which Eliot clearly feels needs to be explained, and indeed taught, to the reader. Each of these interventions in the plot, especially the second, demonstrates an anxiety about her audience's desire for "romance" that the author is worried may result in the rejection of her very ordinary characters and their realistic troubles. Clearly by this cultural moment, just under the surface of the novel's continuing popularity, roiled a series of unresolved questions about exactly what fiction was supposed to do, and how it was supposed to do it. This unsettled situation might have persisted for some time had not something happened to force it to a head: the explosion on the scene, once again in 1860, of *The Woman in White*.

Wilkie Collins's text was a cultural phenomenon. Aside from the astonishing popularity of the book itself, the appearance of *Woman in White* perfume, *Woman in White* bonnets, and of course the *Woman in White* dressing gown, all demonstrated a response to the text which, while no doubt gratifying to its author, did not contribute much to the aspiring dignity of novelistic fiction. Such extreme reader involvement might have been dismissed as an isolated fad had not Ellen Wood's *East Lynne* (1861) and Mary Elizabeth Braddon's *Lady Audley's Secret* (1862) caused almost equally intense reactions. The huge sales they generated could not be ignored, and what was now perceived as a trend initiated a literary debate unprecedented in both vehemence and duration. For close to a decade the conflict between sensation fiction and the realist novel was the constant theme of often overheated reviewer comment and analysis. Deborah Wynne has recently suggested that this "battle of the books" took place during a time when the novel was "well established as legitimate art form,"[3] but I find Hughes more convincing when she suggests that the debate "carried persistent overtones of the novel's presumed inferiority to the forms of serious art" (28), since this helps explain the often excessive rhetoric employed. The proponents, evaluators, and creators of a confident and mature art form would not have demonstrated the insecurity which runs rampant through the magazines, journals, and quarterlies of the period as they struggled to locate the novel in its proper relationship to Victorian society. That novelists had an increasing impact on their culture could not be denied: that the form they were working in had achieved enough gravitas to merit that influence was still in doubt.

Modern critics who have focused on sensationalism have been quick to note the ideological implications of the ensuing debate, and have produced a number of significant studies linking it to various Victorian apprehensions. Writers such as Hughes, Patrick Brantlinger, Jonathan Loesberg, Ann Cvetkovich, and Lyn Pykett have demonstrated the political, class, gender, and commercial anxieties which the sensation novel exacerbated, and which were often foregrounded in the arguments that swirled around it. What is interesting, however, is the way in which even the most sophisticated of such studies pay scant attention to theorizing questions of genre and genre formulation. Hughes comes the closest to an explicit recognition of such a process with her assertion that "[e]ven in the mid-Victorian period, formal realism never existed in a vacuum but developed according to a 'constant dialectic' with conflicting notions of art" (70), and it is this idea which needs to be pursued further. What most critics appear to accept is that realism was an established genre against which sensationalism came into conflict, but it is just this assumption that is problematic. My argument is that the sensation fiction controversy served not to oppose a new genre to a preexisting one, but rather that the formulation of "the sensational" was an essential, constitutive strategy which reified "the realistic" in ways which had been unachievable before.

As Bakhtin has argued, "individual examples of the novel are historically active, not a generic canon as such,"[4] and this state of heteroglossia was profoundly disturbing to many literary/social critics of the time. Justin MacCarthy, writing for the *Westminster Review* in 1864, declares that "[t]he novelist ought to be the happiest of all authors. He enjoys the most perfect freedom known to literature. . . . He is allowed an almost complete immunity from the trammels, and prescriptions, and pedantries of criticism. . . . Perhaps this happy freedom was greatly owing in the first instance to the fact that criticism deliberately ignored the novelist altogether, and regarded him as a creature outside the pale of art. . . . It is only of recent days that critics have begun seriously to occupy themselves in the consideration of prose fiction."[5] Despite his apparent celebration of the "happy freedom" available to Victorian novelists, MacCarthy's essay is manifestly engaging in the activity he states those novelists should be pleased to have avoided—an evaluative criticism which is meant to begin controlling writers who are no longer "creature[s] outside the pale of art." Unsurprisingly, therefore, in an article which spends over half its length discussing George Meredith, the reader is informed "[i]n our own literature Mr. Wilkie Collins is undoubtedly an admirable story-teller. He is not to be compared for a moment with Mr. Meredith in intellect, and fancy, and true perception of human feeling; but he is a good story-teller, and his books are read everywhere, while Mr. Meredith's novels only extort the half-reluctant admiration of some rare groups of intellectual readers" (38–39). The purpose behind this evocation of Collins, here clearly standing in for sensation fiction, is obvious, as the critic begins to establish "prescriptions" for his audience. The advent of a newly defined, reprobated form of fiction became an opportunity to remedy the situation of Bakhtinian "carnival" that seemed to hold sway with the novel. Victorian reviewers, using their entrenched power to define both "successful" and "failed" literature, proceeded to address the perceived lack of unified reader response in their middle-class audience by creating an improper genre against which to define an acceptable realist standard. And one way to understand how this process worked can be found in modern reception theory.

Hans Robert Jauss, in *Toward an Aesthetic of Reception,* states that

> [j]ust as there is no act of verbal communication that is not related to a general, socially or situationally conditioned norm or convention, it is also unimaginable that a literary work set itself into an information vacuum, without indicating a specific situation of understanding. To this extent, every work belongs to a genre—whereby I mean neither more nor less than that for each work a preconstituted horizon of expectation must be ready at hand . . . to orient the reader's (public's) understanding and to enable a qualifying reception.[6]

Jauss's conception of a "horizon of expectation" is useful in several ways. First of all, the term itself emphasizes the way in which a work or works can only be known against a "background" of perception which "silhouettes" it/them. If such a background does not exist, distinctions are difficult to make, and in order to achieve them it must be created. The early stages of the sensation fiction debate demonstrate just such a process. In purely formalist terms the three "seminal" texts of the genre are more disparate than similar. The first-person, multinarrative mosaic of detection in *The Woman in White* has relatively little in common with the third-person, linear domestic melodrama of *East Lynne,* while *Lady Audley's Secret*'s combination of the two creates a hybrid effect which is itself unique. Ann Cvetkovich is therefore right to assert that, "[a]s defined by the Victorian critics, the term 'sensation novel' refers more to the genre's status as mass culture than to its particular narrative style or content."[7] Sensation fiction is constructed not as a unified form, but as an alterity against which opposed literary/cultural expectations may be recognized.

Jauss's formulation also emphasizes the essentially double-sided nature of genre. He declares that "literature and art only obtain a history . . . when the succession of works is mediated not only through the producing subject but also through the consuming subject—through the interaction of author and public" (15). Paul de Mann reiterates this succinctly when he observes that "Jauss can legitimately claim that the 'horizon of expectation' mediates between the private inception and the public reception of the work."[8] This concept is crucial in resolving the apparent paradox of a writer such as Eliot generating realist texts in the absence of the formalized generic "existence" of realism. That is, a genre cannot be created solely by authorial innovation, but must be ratified by the "consuming subject" of an audience whose textual experience both incorporates and generates genre expectations. As already suggested, however, this process can only occur in some form of dialectic. "Where do genres come from?" Tzvetan Todorov rhetorically asks. And he answers himself, "Quite simply from other genres. . . . There has never been a literature without genres; it is a system in constant transformation, and historically speaking the question of origins cannot be separated from the terrain of the genres themselves."[9] By learning what sensation fiction was, Victorian readers learned what realist fiction was (and vice versa), and could thus partake in constructing the horizon of expectation required.

"Required for what?" might be the next question, and although Jauss is not explicit about the specific results of this process I think his implications are clear. He argues,

> it must also be possible to take a synchronic cross-section of a moment in the development [of genres], to arrange the heterogeneous multiplicity of contemporaneous works in equivalent, opposing, and hierarchical structures, and thereby to discover an overarching system of relationships in the literature of a historical moment. (36)

The invocation of "hierarchical structures" is particularly important for this synchronic moment, because the manifest purpose of the 1860s genre debate was to generate a canon of legitimate fiction. The point was not just to define realism and sensationalism in relationship to each other, but to generate a clear set of expectations that the first was *superior* to the second. Since sales figures demonstrated that audiences were not at all convinced of this, it became necessary to ensure that the formulated horizon of expectation contained an evaluative function, and Victorian reviewers were more than happy to provide the criteria. Thus Thomas O. Beebee, in his study *The Ideology of Genre,* designates canonization as "one of the potential use-values associated with certain genres,"[10] and it is not an exaggeration to say that it was *the* use-value of sensation fiction. The quotations from MacCarthy's *Westminster* essay have already hinted at the manner in which this process works, but a specific example of how Victorian reviewer discourse functioned is helpful in understanding more precisely just what is at stake in the entire controversy.

For some reviewers sensation fiction was straightforwardly immoral, and these writers had a difficult time holding back their intense disgust at what they saw as a perversion of English fiction. Oliphant is one such author, and she often constructed herself as a stalwart opponent of the ethical contagion being spread by improper types of novels. Perhaps the most fervent of such responses, however, was Henry L. Mansel's article "Sensation Novels," which appeared in the April 1863 *Quarterly Review.* Although Mansel does provide something like a critical evaluation of what he claims are the formal characteristics of sensationalism, comments such as "[t]here is something unspeakably disgusting in this ravenous appetite for carrion, this vulture-like instinct which smells out the newest mass of social corruption, and hurries to devour the loathsome dainty before the scent has evaporated"[11] suggest a less-than-objective engagement with his topic. Nonetheless, when he is able to (partially) control his visceral distaste for what he is discussing, he does make some revealing statements, such as the following comment early in the essay:

> The sensation novel is the counterpart of the spasmodic poem. They represent "the selfsame interest with a different leaning." The one leans outward, the other leans inward; the one aims at convulsing the soul of the reader, the other professes to owe its birth to convulsive throes in the soul of the writer. (483)

This connection to a form of ridiculed and discredited late Romanticism is not coincidental. Sensation fiction's roots in romance and Romanticism, and its antagonism to more realistic forms, were obvious. One of the reasons Mansel's language is so fraught is because he can only perceive the sensation novel as a relapse and a regression back toward less acceptable kinds of writing, and he is worried not only about what this implies about his audience, but also what it implies about the status of novels in general. Later in the piece he does something very similar, but with a somewhat different target:

> From vice to crime, from the divorce-court to the police-court, is but a single step. When fashionable immorality becomes insipid, the materials for sensation may still be found hot and strong in the "Newgate Calendar" . . . and there emerges the criminal variety of the Newspaper Novel, a class of fiction having about the same relation to the genuine historical novel that the police reports of the "Times" have to the pages of Thucydides or Clarendon. (501)

Here Mansel manages to denigrate the Newgate novel, which applied romance to crime and the lives of criminals, while at the same time rebutting claims of verifiability by authors like Charles Reade, who delighted in demonstrating that his sensational plots came straight from newspaper stories. Once again the reviewer connects sensation fiction to an earlier type of Romantic writing that is constructed as inferior to its Victorian, realist successors, and in this case he also provides the model against which the bastardized form is found wanting. Historical novels trace their lineage back to Thucydides, while Reade's trace theirs back to scandal sheets and hack journalism. Having fulfilled "the duty of the preacher" (514), Mansel can with good conscience leave his topic, since he has demonstrated the unworthy nature of sensation novels in terms of both content and predecessors.

But of course it is possible that Mansel's readers might not appreciate being "preached" at. The extreme vehemence of his attack, ending as it does with a straight insult to his audience in the declaration that "when the reading public wakes up from its present delusion, it will discover . . . that its affections have been bestowed upon an object not very different in kind from the animal of which Titania was enamoured" (514), at least partly undercuts its effectiveness. What is required is a more measured approach, and it is this shift in tone and focus which makes W. Fraser Rae's "Sensation Novelists: Miss Braddon," published in the September 1865 issue of the *North British Review*, as interesting as Mansel's more well-known piece. This article, positioned as it is two years later in the sensation fiction dispute, demonstrates the attitudes that had developed and become more entrenched as that debate advanced. It also, however, purportedly attempts to move away from the ethical arguments which added so much heat to reviewer exchanges, so that issues of genre hinted at by Mansel are much more explicit in Rae.

Braddon, by this point established as the "queen" of the sensationalists, is used by Rae to embody all the weaknesses of the genre. Yet he begins by declaring "[w]e shall purposely avoid applying a moral test to these productions."[12] Taking on the persona of what he calls "the impartial critic" (203), Rae replaces the standard ethical attacks on sensation fiction with the promise that the work will be "judged by a purely literary standard" (181), but the distinction between morality and technique becomes impossible to maintain, and the "standard" is far from "impartial." The article is an omnibus review, and provides short plot descriptions of, and commentary on, seven of Braddon's early novels: *Lady Audley's Secret, Aurora Floyd* (1863), *Eleanor's Victory* (1863), *John Marchmont's Legacy* (1863), *Henry Dunbar* (1864), *The Doctor's Wife* (1864), and *Only a Clod* (1865). Unsurprisingly, the largest amount of space is given to Lady Audley, and Rae quickly establishes one of his central theses when he declares "[t]he short extracts we have given serve to show that the personages are not like living beings. They prove also how thoroughly ignorant Miss Braddon is of the ways of the world and the motive springs of the heart. With the exception of Phœbe Marks, the lady's-maid, not a single personage has any resemblance to the people we meet with in the flesh" (186). This being the case, the "artistic faults of this novel are as grave as the ethical ones" (Rae 187), a neatly turned statement which attempts to demonstrate that while the reviewer is well aware of the novel's ethical faults he is not going to allow that awareness to cloud his aesthetic judgment.

Over and over Rae uses as the touchstone of his critique the idea that the characters, emotions, and events presented in Braddon's texts, and by extension all sensation novels, are "unnatural" (Rae 187) Focusing on the author's gender, he argues that "[f]rom a lady novelist we naturally expect to have portraits of women which shall not be wholly untrue to nature" (Rae 189), but he dismisses her by suggesting that her female characters are "wanting in the traits which constitute a true woman." The unexamined assumption that what is "natural" to the essayist is equally 'natural' to his audience is the main rhetorical strategy here, as is the idea that a preexisting paradigm for literary evaluation is clearly in place. This becomes most obvious in his dismissal of a main character in *John Marchmont's Legacy.*

> Paul Marchmont, the villain, is hardly so overpowering as his accomplice. . . . Had he been drawn after the life, he would have been endowed with some redeeming qualities. When a man acts as a villain, he does not, as Miss Braddon seems to think, cease to be a man. Even had Paul Marchmont been what we are told he was, he would not have committed suicide; but have sneaked away with whatever property he could steal. This authoress adds another to the many proofs she furnishes us with of her entire ignorance of human nature and mental processes, by making Paul Marchmont commit suicide after the manner of Sardanapalus. (195)

Rae's apparent ability to know how a fictional villain would "really" behave "outside" of the text that constructs him reveals the ideological underpinnings of his analysis, insisting as it does that the novel not disrupt acceptable norms of response as determined by a securely materialist, middle-class, reading subject. And this quotation's concluding allusion drives home the point. Byron's play *Sardanapalus, A Tragedy* was published in 1821, in a single volume which also contained *The Two Foscari, a Tragedy* and *Cain, a Mystery.* The poet's story of a debauched ruler forced into heroic action before finally choosing self-inflicted death over defeat is quintessentially Byronic, and even the hint of such Romantic motivations has no place in the worldview of a Victorian reviewer establishing the parameters of proper fiction. As with Mansel's piece, this review suggests that sensationalism's evocation of earlier romance forms and their vision of individual behavior driven by passion and desire shows an "entire ignorance of human nature and mental processes" which disqualifies it as legitimate art. Rae is both appealing to, and attempting to compose, a type of verisimilitude based on a limited set of mimetic representations, an effort which culminates in the review's central statement: "A novel is a picture of life, and as such ought to be faithful" (203). A more overt declaration supporting the conventions of realism would be difficult to imagine, without using the word itself, and the horizon of expectation being generated is obvious.

Given this aesthetic, Rae's comments on *The Doctor's Wife* are interesting. As is now well known, this novel is "Braddon's Anglicization of Flaubert's *Madame Bovary.*"[13] There is no evidence in the review that Rae recognizes this connection, so Braddon's attempt to imitate Continental naturalism might be expected to earn his approval, but the best he can manage is a somewhat less categorical rejection:

> In the case of *The Doctor's Wife,* Miss Braddon very nearly wrote what was literally true. Had the plot been very slightly altered, and certain passages omitted, this novel would not have contained any one burning for revenge, or thirsting for blood. There are fewer artistic faults in it than in any of the works we have discussed. It proves how very nearly Miss Braddon has missed being a novelist whom we might respect and praise without reserve. But it also proves how she is a slave, as it were, to the style which she created. "Sensation" is her Frankenstein. (Rae 197)

Tabitha Sparks has noted that Braddon's text is indeed a mixture of the naturalistic, the sensational, and the sentimental (202–4), and Rae therefore deserves at least to be credited with consistency in his aesthetic response. Leaving aside yet another allusion to a Romantic text, what is significant here is the *rigidity* of generic convention being established. Even the smallest element of the sensational is enough to contaminate a text to the extent that it fails, so that Braddon's inability to "slightly" alter her plot and omit only "certain passages" means that she falls right back into the category of second-rate novelist. This desire for complete generic purity tellingly reveals what lies at the core of the sensation fiction debate, for the critically imposed uniformity of novelistic method legitimizes prose fiction by discerning, in absolute terms, what is to be taken seriously and what is not.

Rae's difficulty, however, was that the popularity of sensation novels suggested that his criteria were far from widely accepted. This being the case, he cannot rely solely on theoretical literary distinctions, but must also try to generate an appropriate audience response both to sensation fiction and to his evaluation of it. Sprinkled throughout the review, therefore, are references to the "discriminating reader" (187) he assumes will be in full agreement with his evaluations. Opposed to this ideal reader are those "lowest . . . in mental capacity" (204) who are not. And Rae does not hesitate to use what might be called aesthetic/moral blackmail in his efforts to correctly align subscribers to the *North British Review* with his position. Once again Braddon and her writing are used as the debased "other" against which the norm may be established, but in evaluating *Henry Dunbar* the reviewer's supposed detachment from ethical concerns disappears.

> In her preface Miss Braddon tells us that "the story of *Henry Dunbar* pretends to be nothing more than a story, the revealment [*sic*] of which is calculated to waken the interest of the general reader, for whose amusement the tale is written." The most astonishing thing about this is, that Miss Braddon should seriously consider a tale of crime as fitted for the "amusement" of anybody. Her notion of what "the general reader" is may be the correct one. We earnestly trust, however, that he does not possess the morbid tastes of Miss Braddon, and is a less contemptible personage than she considers him to be. (196)

The lines are drawn very clearly here. Any reader who does not wish to be accused of possessing "morbid tastes" or of being a "contemptible personage" knows precisely how they should respond to sensationalism and the author who embodies its failures.

Thus the distinction is not just between "true" and "false" literature, but also between a segmented audience, some of whom are capable, and others incapable, of distinguishing the difference. Rae is, in effect, addressing both sides of Jauss's equation, as he encourages one type of "producing subject" while at the same time carefully delineating a particular "consuming subject" to go with it. It is in pieces such as this that generic formulations are solidified, and become retroactively "obvious" to subsequent readers. As well, having created a hierarchy of both genre and audience, it is now possible to canonize the acceptable set of works, and to dismiss any others.

To approach this from a somewhat different, though related, angle, I would like to return to Thomas Beebee. His text also employs ideas adopted from contemporary communication theory as delineated by Ross Chambers in his book *Room for Maneuver: Reading (the) Oppositional (in) Narrative*. Specifically, Beebee utilizes the concept of "noise to signal," and he makes the following observations:

> The concept of "noise" . . . tells us that categories and entities can only be developed against a background of non-entities and non-categories; systems, in other words, can function only by means of the non-systemic they necessarily produce. . . . [T]his concept of "noise" [can be applied] directly to sites of literary conflict such as canonicity. . . . Now, beside the fact that they are both acts of sorting, canonicity and genre are also related in the sense that the recognition of an artifact as belonging to a certain genre can automatically exclude it from even potential canonizing. . . . [G]enre is . . . a site of such noise, the cusp between different use-values of texts and between discursive entity and non-entity. (17)

Sensation fiction becomes the background "noise" against which the "signal" of the now precisely defined and categorized realist novel can be heard, and of course the purpose of any good stereo "tuner" (or educated reader) is to eradicate the noise, leaving only the signal. In the 1870s the sensationalism debate subsides, not because sensation fiction is no longer written, but because the purpose of that debate has been achieved, as canonized, mimetic realism becomes the only serious kind of literature worth "tuning in." The impact of this process on the reputations of authors such as Collins and Braddon is obvious, but to illustrate its effects in a more complex way it is revealing to turn to an author increasingly discussed as sensationalist—Thomas Hardy.

Hardy's original attempt at fiction, *The Poor Man and the Lady*, was turned down for publication by both the Macmillan and the Chapman & Hall publishing houses, with Hardy later discovering that the Chapman reader was none other than George Meredith. In a subsequent meeting Meredith suggested that the author's next effort should have "a more complicated 'plot,'"[14] and the result was Hardy's first published novel, *Desperate Remedies* (1870), an unabashed piece of sensation fiction. Or at least it was unabashed at the time, for subsequently Hardy did all he could to distance himself from the text and its questionable generic lineage. After all, the novice writer attempting to break into the world of nineteenth-century letters could hardly suspect that he would become the "historian of Wessex," let alone the Grand Old Man of British literature. Yet the attempt to construct *Desperate Remedies* as an anomaly in Hardy's fiction is not supported by contemporary reviews of his work. Thus, for example, the *Westminster Review* responded to his first great success by noting that "the fault of *Far From the Madding Crowd* is undoubtedly its sensationalism . . . if we analyse the story we shall find that it is nothing else but sensationalism, which, in the hands of a less skilful writer than Mr. Hardy, would simply sink the story to the level of one of Miss Braddon's earlier performances."[15] Since *Far From the Madding Crowd* was published in 1874, and this review in 1875, such observations demonstrate that the issues of sensationalism (let alone disparaging comments on Braddon) had definitely not ended just because the 1860s had passed. And if further proof of this is required, there is the January 4, 1879 *Saturday Review*, which says of *The Return of the Native* that the "harmony of ill-tutored minds so highly pitched could hardly fail in a sensational novel to end in discord and tragedy."[16] From these earlier works to the events in his last two novels, such as the overtly melodramatic villainy of Alec d'Urberville in *Tess of the d'Urbervilles* and the adultery, bigamy, and murder/suicide in *Jude the Obscure,* it is obvious that Hardy employs sensationalism from the beginning to the end of his career as a novelist.

When that career was over, however, and he had achieved both prestige and success, his response was an attempt to "contain" such elements in his work, and one way to do this was to establish parameters for his own *oeuvre*. Therefore, in the general preface to the 1912 Wessex edition of his collected works, Hardy carefully divides his fiction into three categories. The first, "Novels of Character and Environment," are described as those "which approach most nearly to uninfluenced works; also one or two which, whatever their quality in some few of their episodes, may claim a verisimilitude in general treatment and detail."[17] In this grouping are placed the six novels now generally accepted as "major," along with *Under the Greenwood,* and in using the word "verisimilitude," a term crucial to realist theory, Hardy attempts to override those aspects of the sensational which might prevent these texts from achieving the status he feels they deserve. The argument that sensation fiction could not produce believable characters and situations has already been shown to be the central "literary" criticism of the form, and Hardy's insistence that these texts accurately present "character and environment" establishes clearly the values against which they are meant to be measured.

The title of his second grouping, "Romances and Fantasies," is calculated to suggest a lowering of expectations. By 1912 to designate a novel a romance or a fantasy was to clearly signal it need not be taken very seriously, and this "sufficiently descriptive definition" (Hardy 44) for *A Pair of Blue Eyes, The Trumpet-Major, Two on a Tower,* and *The Well-Beloved* ensures they are given less weight than the first group. And the final category takes this process even further. The "Novels of Ingenuity" are said to

> show a not infrequent disregard of the probable in the chain of events, and depend for their interest mainly on the incidents themselves. They might also be characterized as "Experiments," and were written for the nonce simply; though despite the artificiality of their fable some of their scenes are not without fidelity to life. (Hardy 45)

In this way *Desperate Remedies, The Hand of Ethelberta,* and *A Laodicean,* Hardy's three most obviously sensational novels, are dismissed as improbable, incidental, and ephemeral "experiments" which reside well to the rear of his "true" writings. Identifying them as the "third class" (Hardy 44) of his fiction, with all the hierarchical implications that term connotes, signals the readers of the Wessex edition that they are not representative, and should not be held against him. The general preface is very specifically a "conscious gesture of canon-formation,"[18] as Hardy attempts to influence the public reception of his novels in a way which will match his now elevated reputation. In private, however, his attitude was very different, as the following entry in his literary notebooks demonstrates.

> The division of novels into sensational & anti-sen[sational] <or realistic,> a mistake—wh. arises from the inability of the imperfect artist to be at the same time realistic & sens[ational]. A good novel should be *both,* and both in the highest degree. . . . No novel is anything, for comedy or tragedy, unless the reader can *sympathize* with the characters. If the author can thus touch his reader's heart, & draw his tears, he cannot be too sens[ational].[19]

What this brief exploration of Hardy's retrospective attitude toward his fiction demonstrates is the "success" of the sensation fiction debate. Although quite clearly aware that his style depends on mixing the realistic and the sensational, by the end of the nineteenth and the beginning of the twentieth century "pure" realism is so firmly identified as the genre of serious writing that Hardy must attempt to fit his novels into the horizon of expectation which has been created even at the cost of denigrating some of his own books. And on a very basic level this strategy worked, since Hardy's canonical status was built on a critical response which accepted that both his intention and his achievement were essentially realist. Henry Mansel and W. Fraser Rae would have approved of the standard of judgment (although whether they approved of the actual novels is another question).

I began with what I described as a provocative statement, but I'd like to conclude by modifying it somewhat. After all, it is possible to argue that the English novel is *always* in a state of epistemological crisis. From the early conflict between Richardson and Fielding, through disputes over the gothic novel, the Newgate novel, the silver fork novel, the High Church novel, sensationalism, realism, naturalism, modernism, postmodernism, and now neorealism, prose fiction's genre contortions are, to return to Bakhtin, possibly its single constant characteristic. I would still maintain, however, that the sensation novel debate, in its duration and extensive effects, was a watershed event. Far from being an ephemeral controversy over a soon-to-be-defunct genre, it was crucial in constructing a horizon of expectation that shaped not only the rest of the nineteenth century, but the twentieth as well. The split between "popular" and "high" fiction that it codified has never really been bridged, and the development of the high modernist reaction against realism could not have been constructed without the establishment of a countersensationalist conception of the realistic. Historicizing generic sensationalism thus helps us understand the criteria for "literariness" which has dominated English studies until very recently, and contributes to our understanding not only of genre formulation, but to the canonizations which have profoundly shaped the discipline.

NOTES

1. Margaret Oliphant, "Sensation Novels," *Blackwood's*, 574.
2. Winifred Hughes, *The Maniac in the Cellar*, 6. Further references to this work are cited by page in the text.
3. Deborah Wynne, *The Sensation Novel and the Victorian Family Magazine*, 5.
4. Mikhail Bakhtin, *The Dialogic Imagination*, 3.
5. Justin MacCarthy, "Novels with a Purpose," *Westminster Review*, 24–25. Further references to this work are cited by page in the text.
6. Hans Robert Jauss, *Towards an Aesthetic of Reception*, 79. Further references to this work are cited by page in the text.
7. Ann Cvetkovich, *Mixed Feelings*, 15.
8. Paul de Mann, introduction, xiii.
9. Tzvetan Todorov, "The Origin of Genres," 15.
10. Thomas Beebee, *The Ideology of Genre*, 17. Further references to this work are cited by page in the text.
11. Henry Mansel, "Sensation Novels," *Quarterly Review*, 502. Further references to this work are cited by page in the text.
12. W. Fraser Rae, "Sensation Novelists: Miss Braddon," *North British Review*, 181. Further

references to this work are cited by page in the text.

13. Tabitha Sparks, "Fiction Becomes Her," 197. Further references to this work are cited by page in the text.

14. Michael Millgate, ed., *Life and Work,* 64.

15. Unsigned review, quoted in Cox, 32–33.

16. Unsigned review, quoted in Cox, 53.

17. Thomas Hardy, general preface, quoted in Orel, 44. Further references to this work are cited by page in the text.

18. Michael Millgate, *Testamentary Acts,* 119.

19. Quoted in Lennart Björk, ed., *Literary Notebooks,* 163–64.

- 3 -

CENSORING HER SENSATIONALISM

Mary Elizabeth Braddon and The Doctor's Wife

CATHERINE J. GOLDEN

IN THE 1860s, Mary Elizabeth Braddon established her reputation with the success of *Lady Audley's Secret* (1862), becoming the undisputed queen of Victorian sensation fiction and the circulating library.[1] As Kate Flint notes in *The Woman Reader,* sensation fiction was a literary phenomenon "devoured by women" and characterized by "the presence of sexual desire and sexual energy."[2] Criticized for being plot driven, sensation fiction stunned readers with its luridness: poisoning, drug abuse, adultery, sexual scandal, violent crime, and kidnapping. In *Lady Audley's Secret,* Braddon delivers—along with a dead body—child desertion, bigamy, attempted poisoning, and madness through her golden-haired heroine, Lucy Graham Audley. Braddon, whom Margaret Oliphant labeled "the inventor of the fair-haired demon of modern fiction,"[3] won many admirers among leading London literati—William Makepeace Thackeray, Charles Dickens, and Edward Bulwer-Lytton, to name a few. More vocal were critics who violently attacked Braddon for making sensationalism attractive. Braddon admittedly flouted Victorian social convention, allegedly corrupting impressionable minds in the two or three novels she penned a year and the shocking fiction she published anonymously and pseudonymously in penny dreadfuls. Some of the most savage personal attacks were unsigned reviews, such as Oliphant's tirade in a piece called "Novels" published in *Blackwood's Magazine* (1867). Oliphant, also a prolific novelist, hid her harsh criticism of Braddon beneath a veil of anonymity that Braddon's biographer Robert Lee Wolff believes she "probably never penetrated."[4] Oliphant also linked Lady Audley's bigamy with Braddon's decision to live with the married John Maxwell, who had an insane wife (the two married in 1874 when Maxwell's wife died). Braddon—who, like Charles Reade, first earned a living on the stage—raised five out-of-wedlock children with Maxwell plus her five stepchildren from his first marriage, braving harsh censure from those "in the know" who believed her fiction echoed these sordid aspects of her personal life.[5] Other leading sensationalists, such as Wilkie Collins and Reade, similarly defied conventional morality both in their personal lives and by writing within a genre considered the "bastard child of classic Victorian realism, something to be read as a curiosity but certainly not to be taken too seriously," as Richard Fantina and Kimberly Harrison note in their introduction to this collection (x). Oliphant's harsh critique characterizes beliefs of the guardians of British morality, who found it fitting that the mother of five "bastards" excelled in writing works considered fictional "bastards."

If, as Wolff laments in *Sensational Victorian*, "Her success and reputation bade fair to trap her in the genre she had invented" (8), in her eighth novel, *The Doctor's Wife* (1864), Braddon consciously attempted what we might call today a literary "makeover." Frustrated that her public failed to notice her versatility as a writer following the success of *Lady Audley's Secret*, she longed to create a work of art that critics would not simply dismiss as "sensational." In *The Doctor's Wife*, Braddon bowdlerized Gustave Flaubert's *Madame Bovary* (1857) and, in effect, censored her own sensational writing style to be conventional enough to appease her harshest critics. However, *The Doctor's Wife* falls below her top level of fiction: Wolff considers her mature fiction, such as *Joshua Haggard's Daughter* (1876) and *Ishmael* (1884), the finest of her eighty novels. *The Doctor's Wife* also pales in comparison to *Lady Audley's Secret* and *Madame Bovary*, but it offers a window into Victorian social history—specifically the heated transatlantic debate over what was called women's novel-reading habit and the rigid morality of antifiction critics, many of whom attacked Braddon. In presenting a heroine who prospers despite her addiction to sensation fiction, Braddon ultimately delivers a critique of Victorian culture, posing a threat to Victorian establishment critics by disarming her opponents in the heated debate over women's novel reading.

Critics have long considered *Madame Bovary* the novel that best speaks to the immorality and dire results of novel consumption and addiction through its characterization of Emma Bovary. Flaubert's imaginative wife of a dull, provincial country doctor takes her life by arsenic poisoning because her existence can never match the romantic conceptions of her lurid novel reading. The tedious reality of Charles Bovary as well as Emma's adulterous liaisons with first Rodolphe Boulanger and then Léon Dupuis pale against the heightened romance of her fictional worlds, leaving Emma to search in life for "the most beautiful things she had read"[6] in books. In an 1864 letter to Bulwer-Lytton, Braddon confides that *Madame Bovary* also served as a model for *The Doctor's Wife:* "The idea of the Doctor's Wife *is* founded on 'Madame Bovary,' the style of which struck me immensely in spite of its hideous immorality."[7] Laundering the sensationalism of Flaubert's work, which has an exquisite style and a compelling heroine, Braddon nonetheless illuminates fears surrounding sensation fiction in an era noted for its strict morality and near idolization of the domestic sphere and the quintessential angel in the house.

Sarah Stickney Ellis, Catharine Beecher, and Harriet Beecher Stowe represent a view prominent in advice books by nineteenth-century British and American writers who worried that access to sexual knowledge promoted a false view of life and immoral ways, leading women to discontent or, worse, to ruination. In *The Mothers of England* (1843) and *The American Woman's Home* (1869), respectively, these well-regarded authors speak against overindulgence in novel reading, which Braddon ultimately rewards.[8] To many antifiction critics and leading medical authorities, such as Dr. Edward H. Clarke, author of *Sex in Education* (1873), novel consumption led to addiction and, naturally, to moral decline. As cultural critic Lee F. Heller cautions, "[I]f books could provide guidance, they could also lead readers astray."[9] Most objectionable were racy French novels, inexpensive "blue books" or "shilling shockers" also called "horror Gothic" (tales of supernatural horrors and violent crimes), Newgate novels (which sentimentalized vice and crime), romances, and sensation fiction. Fierce opponents of women's novel reading targeted these kinds of fiction for their ability to corrupt and their addictiveness, inducing a druglike dependence much like an opiate. "Trashy" works were thought particularly dangerous to susceptible readers—namely, middle-class schoolboys, newly literate laborers, and young women. Advice books of the period overflow with stories about girls ruined by novels consumed too freely. Indiscriminate reading was said to taint a woman's morals and weaken her mind. Girls who consumed too much fiction—it was believed—did not think enough. If she must read novels, commentators argued, then she should read edifying works by moral, upstanding authors to uplift her, such as the high church novels by Charlotte Mary Yonge. One advice writer, R. C. Waterston, recommended history and religious biography as the safest reading choices for women.[10]

Warnings against excessive consumption of novels—akin to slogans promoting responsible and safe drinking (e.g., MADD), drug use (DARE), and eating (e.g., Weight Watchers)—peppered nineteenth-century advice books and periodicals and reached a wide audience. While to some Victorians reading was a mark of gentility necessary for a woman's education, fervent opponents of women's novel reading feared the moral and medical ramifications of consumption and addiction. The trope of consumption is so steeped in antifiction criticism that Lady Laura Ridding admits in her 1896 article "What Should Women Read?" that "It is a trite comparison to liken literature to mental food; but the analogy is useful for our present purpose."[11] Drawing on medical and culinary metaphors, Ridding equates works that educate, cheer, enliven, or morally improve to "a wholesome variety of food—well cooked, well digested, nourishing" (29). Romance and sensation fiction do not appear on her menu for a well-balanced reading diet: "The strawberry ices of literature glow on every railway bookstall in the shape of the lighter magazines, the society and comic papers, fashion journals, sensational stories. These are harmless occasional reading, but a mind glutted with them needs medicine as much as a greedy child after a surfeit of sugar-plums" (29). Ridding allows special indulgence in "sugar-plums" but wonders if readers possess adequate willpower to consume them only now and then.

In *Maternal Counsels to a Daughter* (1855), Matilda Pullan similarly equates a craving for light fiction to "that of a child for cakes" and cautions that such reading "must be restrained within due bounds, or it will be injurious. No pastry will ever be a proper substitute for a solid joint."[12] Braddon compares an addiction to thrillers to an appetite for tobacco and pudding: Sigismund Smith, her fictional sensation writer in *The Doctor's Wife* (whom Wolff claims is based on Braddon herself), "was the author of about half a dozen highly-spiced fictions, which enjoyed an immense popularity amongst the classes who like their literature as they like their tobacco—very strong"; he wrote in weekly numbers for "a public that bought its literature in the same manner as its pudding—in penny slices."[13] Even Braddon concedes that her romance consumer's reading is "intellectual opium-eating" (29), drawing her character into the arguments that condemned sensation fiction (including her own) for its addictiveness and immorality. Nonetheless, Braddon ultimately challenges these arguments: she insists that tempting fiction, despite its addictiveness, need not have permanent effects, and she grants her heroine a fairy-tale fortune rather than condemn her.

Like Emma Bovary, Braddon's Isabel Sleaford Gilbert is a romanticist, a dreamer, and an equally bored doctor's wife, who does not perceive fiction as a Romantic artifice, but a model to emulate in life. Lacking the luxuriance and exquisite style of Flaubert's novel that inspired it, *The Doctor's Wife* regurgitates the basic plot of *Madame Bovary:* fanciful Isabel Gilbert grows disillusioned with her provincial married life since it never can match her romance reading; she then enters into a relationship with an aristocratic "lover." We first meet eighteen-year-old Isabel alone in a setting out of a painting. Isabel is "lolling in a low basket-chair, with a book on her lap, and her chin resting on the palm of her hand, so absorbed by the interest of the page before her that she did not even lift her eyes when the two young men went close up to her" (23). The garden setting, her languid pose, and absorption in her book anticipate Winslow Homer's depiction of a woman consuming the latest fiction in *The New Novel* (1877). However, Isabel is reading in Camberwell in an overrun garden near Albany Road, an area of London where Braddon lived when she was approximately Isabel's age. Braddon equates the "neglected" setting to her reader's unsupervised education: "it was in this neglected garden that Isabel Sleaford spent the best part of her idle, useless life" (23). Although Isabel closes her book to greet Sigismund Smith and his companion, George Gilbert, "she kept her thumb between the pages, and evidently meant to go on with the volume at the first convenient opportunity" (23–24). As soon as tea is over, Isabel escapes to resume reading under her favorite pear tree. She continues this pattern of reading out of doors during her marriage to George Gilbert and her subsequent relationship with Roland Lansdell.

Braddon dwells on Isabel's early education, which she describes as "a smattering of every thing at a day-school in the Albany road" (27). Obsessive novel reading since the age of sixteen largely accounts for Isabel's education. Like the heroines in tracts chastising women's unsupervised reading such as "What is the Harm of Novel-Reading?" published in the *Wesleyan-Methodist Magazine* (1855), Isabel ransacks the shelves of the circulating library. She knows by heart long, sentimental passages from her "pet authors" (28) and "just so much of modern history as enabled her to pick out all the sugarplums in the historian's pages,—the Mary Stuarts and Joan of Arcs and Anne Boleyns, . . . the Marie Antoinettes and Charlotte Cordays" (27). Like Emma Bovary, Isabel ferrets out the lives of remarkable ill-fated women who die at the stake or the guillotine, although their fates do not augur her own. Her obsessive reading even invites attack from her friend Smith, who comments, "she's dreadfully romantic. She reads too many novels" (30). Famous authors and those whose lives exist solely between the pages of a book seem real to Isabel. In fact, Braddon tells us that Isabel finds the drowning of her beloved Percy Bysshe Shelley "nearer to her than all that common business of breakfast and dinner and supper which made up her daily life" (158–59).

Isabel most poignantly resembles Emma Bovary in the way she reads novels with an uncritical acceptance. Not a complex character, Isabel perceives novels as models to imitate in life. Her marriage to a boring country doctor does not match her fictional expectations of romance. On first meeting Isabel, even the unimaginative George Gilbert recognizes that she "was fitted to be the heroine of a romance" (30). Isabel "wanted her life to be like her books; she wanted to be a heroine,—unhappy perhaps, and dying early" (28). Braddon repeats in the very next chapter, "Izzie had sat through the hot hours of drowsy summer days, reading her favourite novels and dreaming of a life that was to be like the plot of a novel" (41). Isabel is not sensual like Emma Bovary, but grossly naive and sexually innocent. When Isabel misunderstands the intentions of her aristocratic lover, Braddon concludes, "Isabel Gilbert was not a woman of the world. She had read novels while other people perused the Sunday papers; and of the world out of a three-volume romance she had no more idea than a baby" (253).

During her brief stint as governess to the nieces of Mr. Raymond, Isabel longs just for that: "She lived alone with her books and the dreams which were born of them, and waited for the prince, the Ernest Maltravers, the Henry Esmond, the Steerforth—it was Steerforth's proud image, and not simple-hearted David's gentle shadow, which lingered in the girl's mind when she shut the book" (72). The references to her novelistic daydreams go on ad nauseam: "She sighed to sit at the feet of a Byron, grand and gloomy and discontented" (72). Isabel glamorizes dishonorable, lawless characters—not only the robber Bill Sykes of *Oliver Twist* (1838), who brutally clubs good-hearted Nancy to death as she prays to her Maker, but proud Steerforth of *David Copperfield* (1850), who ruins and abandons Little Em'ly. Braddon even conjectures that Isabel "would have worshipped an aristocratic Bill Sykes, and would have been content to die under his cruel hand, only in the ruined chamber of some Gothic castle, by moonlight, with the distant Alps shimmering whitely before her glazing eyes, instead of in poor Nancy's unromantic garret" (72–73). She also romanticizes Florence Dombey's being turned out of doors by her father and Jane Eyre's starving on the moors. Those familiar with Isabel's favorite authors and characters likely have grave misgivings about her ability to analyze fiction. Isabel approaches her impending marriage like a romance novel: "Were there not three volumes of courtship to be gone through first?" (99) Still, Braddon insists that "Perhaps during all that engagement the girl never once saw her lover really as he was" (102). During her brief courtship, Isabel transforms plain and sensible George into countless fictional characters: "She dressed him up in her own fancies, and deluded herself by imaginary resemblances between him and the heroes in her books" (102). He becomes Charlotte Brontë's Edward Fairfax Rochester of *Jane Eyre* (1847) when he is "abrupt and disagreeable in his manner to her"; Dickens's Mr. Paul Dombey of *Dombey and Son* (1848) when he is "cold"; and Thackeray's Rawdon Crawley of *Vanity Fair* (1848) when he is "clumsy and stupid" (102).

In turn, she casts herself in matching roles and plays submissive Jane to the dominant Rochester, or domineering Becky to the bumbling Rawdon. An informed reader again might question her choices. Rochester bears the guilt of Bluebeard in hiding his mad wife in the attic of Thornfield Hall. Dombey's coldness is so entrenched that his final kindness to Florence after losing his fortune seems unconvincing. Rawdon at least loves the conniving Becky and becomes a good father to little Rawdy. But none of these protagonists approximates an ideal mate, even if each ultimately reforms. Isabel romanticizes the obvious flaws of these "heroes," recasts George Gilbert in their images, and fails to recognize her incompatibility with practical George. Braddon even calls upon book illustration to demonstrate Isabel's and George Gilbert's incompatibility. Isabel longs to look like Florence Dombey as Phiz depicts her in an elegant dress on her wedding day in *Dombey and Son,* but George chooses a practical "sombre brown-silk dress" (105) for her marriage.

Immediately after the wedding, Isabel realizes she has little in common with the country surgeon. During a dreary winter honeymoon, Isabel "began to think that she had made a mistake" (109) because "No prince would ever come now; no accidental duke would fall in love with her black eyes, and lift her all at once to the bright regions she pined to inhabit" (110). Isabel escapes the drudgery of being a governess through marriage, so financial gain is a motivator for matrimony (as in many sensation novels). Her excessive romance reading makes her dissatisfied with domesticity. Here Braddon nods to the moral argument against women's novel reading, perhaps pandering to her moral audience. Nonetheless, Braddon, like Flaubert, shows us the failings of the inadequate though kind and loving doctor. George Gilbert is devoted to his wife, much as Charles Bovary is to Emma, but Braddon makes him practical to the extreme, devoid of romance, and essentially a nonreader (109), a fault he shares with Bovary. Isabel's attempts to delight George with novels and poetry fail, as do Emma's with Charles. For example, when Isabel talks to George about the star-crossed lovers in Sir Walter Scott's *Bride of Lammermoor* (1819) "with her face all lighted up with emotion, the young surgeon could only stare wonderingly at his betrothed" (102). Braddon concludes that, like Esau in the book of Genesis, Isabel "had sold her birthright for a vulgar mess of pottage" (110).

Braddon's lavish literary references lend a heightened self-consciousness to *The Doctor's Wife*. Lyn Pykett similarly observes, "Although she does not rise to the heights of Flaubertian style in *The Doctor's Wife*, and she does not even attempt the studied impersonality of Flaubert's narrator, Braddon constantly strives for an effect of 'literariness,' not least through her extensive allusions to novels, plays, poems, and paintings."[14] Different from Isabel Archer of Henry James's *The Portrait of a Lady* (1881) and Emma Bovary, Isabel Gilbert does not possess even a private sense of superiority connected to reading. Rather, Braddon seems to use her character to show off her own knowledge to a reading public that dismissed her as a sensation fiction writer. By referring to works by her mentor, Bulwer-Lytton, as well as Dickens, Scott, Thackeray, Lord Byron, and Shelley, Braddon seemingly projects her fervent desire that *The Doctor's Wife* be associated with works by these respected authors. She even interjects "This is not a sensation novel" (358) in the third volume of the book. Braddon at best achieves an "effect" of literariness; much of her quotes come from stage adaptations of works she encountered as an actress (Pykett ix). That she arguably "offered up" these allusions "for the reader's self-congratulatory consumption" (xvi), as Pykett notes, speaks to the insecurities of a writer stung by harsh criticism. However, in providing exact titles, Braddon invites judgment about Isabel's reading. Braddon encourages readers actively to use specific texts to assess the ways Isabel reads, misreads, and romanticizes works that her life does not parallel.

Isabel's novelistic daydreams center on two Dickensian heroines, Edith Dombey and Florence Dombey of *Dombey and Son*. In fact, Braddon refers to *Dombey and Son* nearly two dozen times.[15] Neither Dickensian heroine is a likely role model.[16] Isabel focuses her imagination on the trappings of an unhappy marriage between the beautiful, proud, and bitter Edith Granger Dombey and the cold, proud, wealthy Paul Dombey. Isabel would like to marry a duke and "wear ruby velvet and a diamond coronet ever after, like Edith Dombey in Mr. Hablot

Browne's grand picture" (31). She seems to have eyes only for Edith's coronet and velvet, whereas Dickens, in the scenes before Edith's wedding, emphasizes Edith's despair that Dombey, in Edith's own words, "has bought me."[17] Edith Dombey expresses rage at a woman's powerless position in her gendered society: "There is no slave in a market: there is no horse in a fair: so shown and offered and examined and paraded, Mother, as I have been, for ten shameful years" (333). This cruel reality seemingly escapes the attention of Isabel and Braddon.

Isabel examines her face in the looking glass and "tried to look like Edith Dombey in the grand Carker scene" (155). In this scene, Edith Dombey rebuffs the advances of her husband's manager, Carker, who has enticed her to run away with him to France. Braddon, likewise, comments superficially about this scene: "Are you [Isabel] never to wear ruby velvet, and diamonds in your hair, and to lure some recreant Carker to a foreign hostelry, and there denounce and scorn him?" (78). Both references focus on beauty and artifice—the power of a woman to allure and renounce a male. They overlook the misery that the Victorian marriage market brings Edith Dombey as well as the moral overtones of Edith's compromised virtue. Rather, Isabel reads Edith's character in terms of her unsated desire for a grand romance akin to a novel, even one with a depressing plot.

Isabel also trivializes the dire fate of Florence Dombey. A motherless Dickensian angel, Florence yearns for the love of her father, who denies her very existence and bestows all his love on his dying male heir, little Paul Dombey. Florence's father punishes all who love her and evicts her from her home. Nonetheless, Isabel glamorizes Florence's fate: "[I]f she [Isabel] had only a father to strike her and turn her out of doors, the story of her life might be very tolerable, after all" (88). In her frequent references to *Dombey and Son,* Isabel romanticizes, in turn, Edith's grand wealth and Florence's privation. She reads *Dombey and Son* more astutely later in the novel when she realizes that in meeting secretly with Lansdell, she has been falsely suspected of infidelity: she had "become the thing that Mr. Dombey believed his wife [Edith] to be when he struck his daughter [Florence] on the stairs" (280).

Isabel miscasts her aristocratic "lover" as one of two polarized types from romance, hero and villain. Braddon consolidates Emma Bovary's dual temptations—Rodolphe Boulanger and Léon Dupuis—into Roland Lansdell, a mediocre poet who possesses the wealth of the viscount of Emma Bovary's daydreams. Braddon makes clear that "Roland Lansdell was not a hero; he was only a very imperfect, vacillating young man, with noble impulses for ever warring against the baser attributes of his mind; a spoiled child of fortune, who had almost always had his own way until just now" (333). Before they meet, Isabel falls in love with Roland through his poetry, derivative of Tennyson by his own admission. She carries a slim book of poems he wrote called *An Alien's Dreams* to the waterfall at Thurston's Crag where she reads alone and constructs an idealized conception of its author. When Isabel first meets the dashing though worldweary Lansdell, Braddon tells us, "The dream had come true at last. *This* was romance—*this* was life" (138). In fact, "He was the incarnation of all the dreams of her life" (139). Isabel initially feels a restless passion when she meets Lansdell—"The slow fever that had been burning so long in her veins was now a rapid and consuming fire" (135)—but their relationship remains entirely platonic. They meet by the waterfall to discuss literature. She reads in the vast library of his grand home, Mordred Priory, after he flees to the continent because he cannot bear to live without her touch. In fact, Roland's sexual attraction to Isabel dashes her romantic conceptions of him. Isabel's often-noted avoidance of sensuality dramatically divorces Braddon's novel from Flaubert's original. Even the shortlived, disappointing intimacy Emma experiences in her marriage to Charles Bovary is altogether absent in Isabel's marriage to George Gilbert. Braddon tells us, "She [Isabel] was fond of him [George], as she would have been fond of a big elder brother, who let her have a good deal of her own way" (118). Critics have speculated about the sexless honeymoon and childless marriage of Isabel and George Gilbert, which might also explain how she remains sexually innocent in her affair with Lansdell.[18]

Isabel naively believes Roland's love for her is as pure as Dante's for the married Beatrice Portinari or as self-sacrificing as Zanoni's for his beloved Viola in Bulwer-Lytton's *Zanoni* (1842). Isabel does not desire Roland; rather, she "had thought of him as a remotely-grand and star-like creature to be worshipped for ever by kneeling devotees offering perpetual incense, and entirely happy in the radiance of his countenance" (279). After Roland declares his passionate love, Isabel rejects him and concludes that he was not a Dante, and "[h]e was not the true and faithful knight who could sit for ever at the entrance of his hermitage gazing fondly at the distant convent-casement, which might or might not belong to his lost love's chamber" (277).

Isabel proceeds to miscast the disenchanted, lonely, yet ultimately worthy Lansdell into a false knight. He becomes Robert the Devil, a heartless Faust who seduces trusting Gretchen, and "Steerforth, handsome, heartless, irresistible Steerforth, with no pity for simple Em'ly or noble Peggotty's broken heart" (278). While Isabel reads Steerforth's character perceptively here, this allusion to *David Copperfield*'s bad angel offers another example of how Isabel miscasts Lansdell. Roland wishes to marry Isabel (had she been free) and loves her in a way that Steerforth, at best, merely fancies Little Em'ly. Braddon aligns our sympathy with Lansdell, a critical interpreter of Isabel's romantic imagination, who aptly recognizes: "I have only been the hero of a story-book; and all this folly has been nothing more than a page out of a novel set in action. . . . I must go away; and she will go back to her three-volume novels, and fall in love with a fair-haired hero, and forget me" (214). Proving himself a man capable of rare self-reflection, Roland begs forgiveness for his unconsummated desires in a manner unthinkable of Steerforth, who never shows remorse for sullying Emily's purity, destroying Ham Peggotty's happiness, or disrupting Daniel Peggotty's happy home. On his deathbed, Roland conceals the guilt of Isabel's criminal father (who caused his injury) in true martyr fashion to spare his beloved further pain. He repents in a manner akin to Eugene Wrayburn, when he believes he is dying in *Our Mutual Friend* (1865).

The dual death scenes of Isabel's husband and lover in the third volume arguably function as Braddon's concession to the conventions of sensation fiction. Roland's brief but brutal beating by Isabel Sleaford's father—a forger just released from prison, who had earlier sworn to kill Lansdell for incriminating him—has all the makings of sensationalism: Braddon particularly describes how "Mr. Sleaford's bludgeon went whirling up into the air, and descended with a dull thud, once, twice, three times upon Roland Lansdell's bare head" (353); only then does Isabel's father, nicknamed "Jack the Scribe," release his tight grasp around the throat of Roland, the "languid swell" (as Sleaford calls him) who helped the police hunt Jack "for the mere amusement of the chase" (353). Jack the Scribe's revenge, taking the form of bludgeoning and strangulation, leaves Roland nearly dead: we see him "crashing down among the fern and wild-flowers, with a shower of opal-tinted rose-petals fluttering about him as he fell" (353). In contrast, Braddon delivers the body of the good provincial doctor undramatically: George Gilbert dies a slow death from a fever he contracts from his poor patients whose lives he tries to improve. Gilbert never once believes his wife has compromised her love for him, despite the villagers' and his devoted servants' gossip. Lansdell, however, becomes a model for Christian mankind during his final hours. Braddon creates an "imperfect conversion" (389) as Roland recites lines from the Gospel according to John and Tennyson's *In Memoriam*.[19] In his pious death, Lansdell transforms into "something infinitely better and brighter than you ever knew him here. I never saw such a smile upon a human face as I saw just now on his" (395). Roland leaves Isabel his fortune, urging her toward greater things: "If ever you should find yourself with the means of doing great good, of being very useful to your fellow-creatures, I should like you to remember my wasted life, Isabel" (391). Dying, Roland nearly attains the stature of David Copperfield's good angel, Agnes Wickfield, who ever points David "upward."

Braddon does not kill off her addicted romance reader even though Isabel enjoys imagining her suicide: "death by poison was only a matter-of-fact business as compared to the still water and the rushes, and would have had a very inferior effect in the newspapers" (226). Isabel never considers infidelity: "the possibility of deliberately leaving her husband to follow the footsteps of this other man [Roland], was as far beyond her power of comprehension as the possibility that she might steal a handful of arsenic out of one of the earthenware jars in the surgery, and mix it with the sugar that sweetened George Gilbert's matutinal coffee" (276). These pointed references dismiss Emma's adultery and suicide by poisoning—choices Emma Bovary makes when driven by sensuality, a desire for material splendor, and ultimately despair. Rather than punish Isabel, Braddon reforms and then rewards her heroine, who was once addicted to "beautiful sweet-meats [books], with opium inside the sugar" (24). Isabel adds biography, philosophy, and history to her literary diet. Reading improving works in the library of Mordred Priory during Roland's travels, she "expands" her mind and worldview:

> Her mind expanded amongst all the beautiful things around her, and the graver thoughts engendered out of grave books pushed away many of her most childish fancies, her simple sentimental yearnings. Until now she had lived too entirely amongst the poets and romancers; but now grave volumes of biography opened to her a new picture of life. She read the stories of real men and women, who had lived and suffered real sorrows, prosaic anguish, hard commonplace trial and misery. (235)

Braddon's repetition of "grave" and "real" quickly establishes Isabel's sober, responsible frame of mind as a reader and future philanthropist. With Lansdell's fortune, Isabel—anticipating deeds George Eliot's Dorothea Brooke of *Middlemarch* (1872) only contemplates—builds model villages with good schools, properly ventilated homes, large ovens, big gardens, and state-of-the-art farming equipment.

Braddon admitted to Bulwer-Lytton that she was not satisfied with the ending. Although Bulwer-Lytton liked the first two volumes, he would have preferred that Braddon leave George Gilbert alive; Braddon agreed that was her original plan: "I always meant Sleaford [Isabel's father] to kill Roland, but to the last I was uncertain what to do with George. My original intention was to have left him alive, & Isabel reconciled to a commonplace life doing her duty bravely, and suppressing all outward evidence of her deep grief for Roland. Thus the love story would have been an episode in a woman's life, succeeded by an after-existence of quiet work and duty."[20] Even in this staid alternative ending, Braddon never contemplated killing off her heroine. Isabel's temporary indulgence in the "strawberry ices of literature" does not lead to dire consequences that commonly befall reading addicts. Tempting literature, despite its addictiveness, need not have dangerous side effects or permanent consequences. Isabel prospers and improves. Obsessive reading leads not to immorality, decline, and death—the fate of Emma Bovary—but to personal progress and a "fairy-tale" fortune in *The Doctor's Wife*. The third volume of *The Doctor's Wife* debunks the pervasive nineteenth-century tropes of consumption and addiction that fueled the fears of antifiction critics who opposed women's novel-reading habit on moral grounds. Even if Braddon set out to censor her sensationalism and softened some of the elements that define sensation fiction as a genre, her final volume flouts Victorian convention, retaining a spark of subversion. Braddon redeems her novel with a splash of sensationalism, ultimately disarming her opponents in the heated debate over what, where, when, why, and if a woman should read.

NOTES

1. This essay extends my work from chapter 4 in *Images of the Woman Reader in Victorian British and American Fiction*.
2. Kate Flint, *The Woman Reader*, 274. In her discussion of "compulsive forms of consumption," such as sensation fiction, she qualifies that "especially, although not exclusively, the reviewers presented [sensation fiction] as being devoured by women."
3. See Margaret Oliphant, "Novels" published in *Blackwood's Magazine* (1867).
4. Robert Lee Wolff, *Sensational Victorian*, 200.
5. For more information on Braddon's life and Oliphant's attack, see Wolff, 200–207.
6. Gustave Flaubert, *Madame Bovary*, 251.
7. Mary Elizabeth Braddon, quoted in Wolff, *Sensational Victorian*, 162.
8. See Catherine Golden, *Images of the Woman Reader in Victorian British and American Fiction*, 17–47.
9. Lee Heller, *Frankenstein*, 327.
10. R. C. Waterston, quoted in Golden, *Images of the Woman Reader*, 39.
11. Laura Ridding, "What Should Women Read?" 29.
12. Matilda Pullan, quoted in Flint, *The Woman Reader*, 51.
13. Braddon, *The Doctor's Wife*, 11, 12.
14. Lyn Pykett, introduction to *The Doctor's Wife*, ix.
15. Not surprisingly, Dickens preferred *The Doctor's Wife* above Braddon's other works. Wolff explains that Dickens's daughter Kate Perugini recalls her father favoring *The Doctor's Wife* while Thackeray, according to his daughter Anne Thackeray Ritchie, particularly liked *Lady Audley's Secret*.
16. As Pykett rightly notes, "[O]nly the most resistant readers of Dickens would be likely to regard Edith Dombey (one of Isabel's frequently invoked heroines) as a happy role model for the young wife of a provincial doctor" (introduction, xvi).
17. Charles Dickens, *Dombey and Son*, 332.
18. See Golden, *Images of the Woman Reader*, chapter 4 for further discussion of Emma Bovary's sensuality versus Isabel's naiveté and prudishness.
19. The final lines Roland speaks (392) come from Tennyson's *In Memoriam*, canto iv: "an infant crying in the night; an infant crying for the light; and with no language but a cry."
20. Undated 1864 letter from Braddon to Bulwer-Lytton, quoted in Wolff, *Sensational Victorian*, 165.

- 4 -

MARY ELIZABETH BRADDON AND THE "COMBINATION NOVEL"

The Subversion of Sensational Expectation in Vixen

ALBERT C. SEARS

IN HER 1867 review of sensation novels, Margaret Oliphant named Mary Elizabeth Braddon "the inventor of the fair-haired demon of modern fiction" and "the leader of her school."[1] Oliphant affirmed that to Braddon "the first honours ought naturally to be given, but her disciples are many" (265). In other words, Oliphant recognized in Braddon's sensation novels a defining pattern that other novelists merely copied. For better or worse, Braddon contended with such categorization. She was to many consumers of popular fiction "the Author of *Lady Audley's Secret*." The names "Braddon" and "the Author of *Lady Audley's Secret*" have largely become consonant with Victorian sensationalism. This correlation between name and genre is the legacy left to later readers of Braddon's numerous novels, those sensational and those antisensational like *Vixen* (1879), which complicates the conventions of the genre. Such sensational expectation, however, tends to conceal the ways in which Braddon manipulates and subverts readers' responses to sensational elements in her works.

Filled with references to other sensation novels, *Vixen* challenges readers to transgress their sensational reading patterns. One of the text's telling sensation novel citations is when the reader learns that Violet "Vixen" Tempest, the heroine, is a reader of the sensation novel *Foul Play* (1868) by Charles Reade and Dion Boucicault. *Foul Play* provides Violet moments of escape during an unsensational banishment to a spinster's home in Jersey. Most significant, her stay on the island is her fantasy of being *Foul Play's* heroine, Helen Rolleston, who becomes shipwrecked on a tropical island, alone with a man who desperately loves her.[2] Even though Helen is chaste and conventionally feminine, her improper circumstance, living unmarried with a man in an exotic locale, enables Violet to fantasize about her desire for Roderick Vawdrey, her love interest in *Vixen*.

When Violet first arrives in Jersey, she is disappointed that the island is not tropical as she had imagined; nonetheless, the experience to her is "as if I were cast on a desert island."³ She romanticizes: "[S]he thought of Helen Rolleston, the petted beauty in Charles Reade's *Foul Play*, cast with her faithful lover on an unknown island of the fair southern sea. But in this island of Jersey there was no faithful lover to give romance and interest to the situation. There was nothing but dull dreary reality" (251). That Violet would imagine being Helen, alone with a man on a tropical island, suggests impropriety. Such sensational reading fills Violet's mind with a fantasy that helps her escape from the dullness of living with an old woman in Jersey; however, Braddon carefully draws the discrepancy between Violet's sensational expectation and reality. After she has lived there for a year, "her lonely and monotonous existence" (299) does not match the sensation genre. Braddon represents what happens when generic expectation infiltrates the mind of the reader: narrative can only be received through generically conceived desires and expectations. Braddon invokes *Foul Play* to create sensational expectation, only to subvert readers' expectation of the genre.

Braddon contrasts Violet's reading behavior with that of Mabel Ashbourne, her contender for Roderick Vawdrey's hand in marriage. Mabel claims that Violet "can hardly read" (21), which is partly true, for Violet reads only novels. In addition to her pursuit of Latin and Greek, Mabel diligently crafts a book of poetry that is intended to rival Robert Browning. Although her book is criticized for being too abstruse and inaccessible, Mabel rebuts: "If I had wanted to be popular, I should have worked on a lower level. I would even have stooped to write a novel" (275). Through this statement and the allusion to *Foul Play*, Braddon distances herself from the confines of her earlier sensational productions and subverts her readers' sensational expectation. In speaking about such allusions in her discussion of *Joshua Haggard's Daughter*, Pamela K. Gilbert notes that "Braddon uses . . . references to popular literature . . . to critique attitudes toward popular literature and reading itself."⁴ Additionally, in the present volume, Catherine Golden's essay on *The Doctor's Wife*, "Censoring Her Sensationalism," argues that Braddon's references to other fiction ask readers to critique reading and misreading in the novel. Similarly, *Vixen* is reflexive of Victorian popular print culture and examines the production and consumption of texts while it complicates its own status as sensation fiction.

Even though Braddon worked to intervene in the nineteenth-century reception of her fiction, readers today have largely been interested in the sensational elements of her works. Elaine Showalter's groundbreaking discussions of Braddon during the 1970s returned to Oliphant's critical categories and reinterpreted them for a feminist audience. In *A Literature of Their Own*, Showalter claims that Braddon became not the author of dangerous books but the author of books that offered female readers "a carefully controlled female fantasy," especially in *Lady

Audley's Secret.⁵ For Showalter, Braddon's fiction "expressed female anger, frustration, and sexual energy more directly than had been done previously. Readers were introduced to a new kind of heroine, one who could put her hostility toward men into violent action" (160). While Oliphant and Showalter might seem oddly paired, they both corroborated the sensational expectation that Braddon's name arouses. In other words, both critics participated in what Michel Foucault has called the author function.

Foucault argues that an author's name partly controls a text, serving as a label for the kind of work that a writer typically wrote. He states that the author's name "performs a certain role with regard to narrative discourse, assuring a classificatory function. Such a name permits one to group together a certain number of texts, define them, differentiate them from and contrast them to others."⁶ The name "Braddon" and the attendant phrase "by the author of *Lady Audley's Secret*" exercise power over how her novels might be read, establishing an immediate context (sensation novel) that circumscribes their reception. Even though Braddon did write in other narrative modes, the functions of author and genre serve to regulate her fiction. In his biography of Braddon, Robert Lee Wolff reveals that she successfully experimented with other genres; however, her work is still, almost a hundred years after her death, organized by the brief phrase "by the author of *Lady's Audley's Secret*," homogenizing her prolific and experimental oeuvre. Wolff states: "Unfortunately for her reputation, Mary Elizabeth Braddon all her life remained 'the author of *Lady Audley's Secret*.' Even today, when she is remembered at all, she is still associated with her artless and somewhat trashy first great success."⁷ The expression "by the Author of *Lady Audley's Secret*" appears, even when her name does not, on the spines of her novels well after her first three-volume best seller was published in 1862. The title pages of most Braddon first editions also bear this phrase, even in novels like *Joshua Haggard's Daughter* (1876) and *Vixen* (1879), which break the sensation novel mold.⁸ For publishers, the label was unquestionably valuable, as Wolff notes of *Lady Audley's Secret*: "[It] was off at once to enormous sales, requiring eight three-volume editions between October and December 1862. The Tinsleys made so large a fortune that the elder brother, Edward, called his new house 'Audley Lodge' in appreciation" (Wolff, *Sensational Victorian*, 5). Thus, Braddon's name became synonymous with the sensation novel and its financial promise, and her name continues to serve as an index to her professional output, even in many recent discussions of her work.

Because of the categorization of her name, Braddon found herself in a creative bind. She was quite aware of her confines as a novelist, as her letters to Edward Bulwer-Lytton reveal: she claimed no strong commitment to writing sensation novels but wrote them because the reading public required them in their diet and expected sensationalism from her books. She expressed to Bulwer her efforts to negotiate marketplace demands and her desire to produce "serious" fiction. In

1862, as Braddon finished *Aurora Floyd*, she lamented: "I have written as conscientiously as I could; but more with a view to the interests of my publishers than with any great regard to my own reputation."[9] These tensions, which found their way into the texture of Braddon's fiction, run throughout her correspondence. However much she wanted to write in a less commercial mode, Braddon was dependent on the marketplace; she conceded, "I have learnt to look at everything in a mercantile sense, & to write solely for the circulating library reader, whose palette [*sic*] requires strong meat, & is not very particular as to the quality thereof" (Wolff, "Devoted Disciple," 14).

Braddon's answer to these dilemmas, as discussed by Wolff and Lyn Pykett, was to "elevate the sensational by art."[10] Braddon noted to Bulwer that in *The Doctor's Wife* (1864) she labored to produce a work of fiction that did approach "art" (Wolff, "Devoted Disciple," 22). In this novel, Braddon challenges her reader by proclaiming: "This is *not* a sensation novel."[11] It is, nonetheless, at times about the production and consumption of sensation novels, especially with the text's representation of a "sensation author," Sigismund Smith, who reveals to the reader the constraints of the sensationalist.[12] Smith on the one hand notes that "[w]hat the penny public want is plot, and plenty of it; surprises, and plenty of 'em; mystery, as thick as November fog," but he also states an alternative: "a good strong combination story" (Braddon, *The Doctor's Wife*, 45).

In *The Doctor's Wife*, the combination novel represents a blend of fictional modes. This form provides a writer a way to capture a different market of readers, especially when her reputation is already constricted. Within the fabric of Braddon's antisensation novels, she could adopt a narrative method that at once appealed to sensation readers and also interrupted generic categorization. The combination novel form would find its way into the structure of *Vixen* over a decade later.

Both Pamela K. Gilbert and Tabitha Sparks compellingly show that Braddon experimented outside the sensation mode. In her discussion of *Joshua Haggard's Daughter*, Gilbert recovers Braddon as an author of realist fiction, astutely arguing that even though Braddon wrote in the sensational and realist modes, she is remembered only as a practitioner of the former (184). Sparks argues correctly that *The Doctor's Wife* deploys competing narrative modes of sensationalism, realism, and sentimentalism "in order to trouble the generic conventions of each of these categories of fiction."[13] Gilbert and Sparks apply critical strategies that resist reading Braddon predominantly as a sensationalist; in the process, they recognize the complex narrative texture that results in Braddon's combination novel mode. *Vixen* represents another important case of Braddon's generic experimentation. In this work, Braddon deploys a narrative rhetoric to subvert her readers' sensational expectation.

Indeed, readers expecting a sensation novel from *Vixen* will not find a work bursting with incident. The novel charts the passage into womanhood of the central character, Violet Tempest, who suffers numerous challenges before she is finally united with her lover, Roderick Vawdrey. The plot pursues the realization of their love, especially as Roderick's forthcoming arranged marriage to Lady Mabel Ashbourne thwarts his affair with Violet. At the same time, Violet endures the loss of her father and rejects a marriage offer from Captain Conrad Carmichael.[14] In a bizarre twist, Violet's mother later marries Carmichael, who transforms from wounded lover to oppressive stepfather and banishes Violet to the island of Jersey to live with his spinster aunt. Because Violet cannot become financially independent until she reaches age twenty-five, she seems destined to lead a dreary and lonely life on the island, especially after Roderick is engaged to another. When Violet is abruptly called home to her dying mother, she reunites with Roderick to learn that he has not, after all, married Lady Mabel.

Even though there has been renewed attention to Braddon since the 1970s, critical interest in *Vixen* has been minimal. In its few interpretations, the work has been read both as a sensation novel and a departure from the genre. Wolff reads it apart from Braddon's sensation novels, suggesting that it is "a vehicle for vigorous radical social satire" (Wolff, *Sensational Victorian,* 278). Exploring the theme of sexual passion, Ellen Miller Casey interprets the novel as a "domestic romance" in which Braddon "abandoned the sensation mode" but "clearly exploit[ed] the convention she helped to establish" (75, 77). Fionn O'Toole, however, defines *Vixen* as a sensation novel, especially in the rebellious character of "Vixen."[15] Gillian Beer, too, reads the novel as sensational alongside the works of Wilkie Collins and Rhoda Broughton.[16] These various twentieth-century responses might be attributed to the way Braddon both evokes and undermines sensation fiction conventions in the combination novel form. Determining the exact genre of the novel merely cloaks the rhetorical strategies Braddon employs to subvert the sensational expectation resulting from her name. It is clear that Violet can be read as consonant with other sensation heroines, but if one defines the sensation novel as a work that depends upon suspense, *Vixen* falls short.

Nonetheless, *Vixen* is a fascinating novel for examining the "horizon of expectations" that Braddon combated. A novel titled *Vixen* feeds sensation readers' expectation, suggesting a narrative about a strong-willed, if not criminal, heroine. The character's true name, Violet Tempest, is also evocative of female villains in Collins's novels whose names provide indicators of their infamous, transgressive natures: Magdalen Vanstone (i.e., fallen woman) from *No Name* and Lydia Gwilt (i.e., guilty) from *Armadale.* Yet, while the heroine of *Vixen* certainly turns out to be "horsey" and occasionally "fast," she is not prone to the violence her name suggests. Throughout *Vixen,* Braddon writes against her reputation as a sensation novelist, evoking her most successful works in that genre as she disrupts readers' expectation for sensationalism. Even more complexly, Braddon writes against the sensation novel as critics and novelists (including herself) had defined it. While *Vixen* as a whole tends not to read as a Braddon sensation novel, it repeatedly creates and then subverts expectation for the various types of sensation novels that had been written. Indeed, *Vixen* operates as a combination novel when it evokes sensational plots: mysterious stories with gothic elements and stories about criminal and sexually daring women. The first chapter of *Vixen* brings together a number of these elements, suggesting that the text might fulfill sensational expectation.

Braddon opens with language suggestive of sensationalism, complete with gothic effects, as Roderick walks through the forest near Violet's home. The moon's "pale almost imperceptible crescent," the "ghostly look" of the forest, the oak logs that appear "like the naked corpse of a giant," and an "old man's house" that "had been an abbey before the Reformation" are all characteristic of a gothic landscape (Braddon, *Vixen,* 1). These effects suggest that Roderick will meet a ghost or a highwayman along his walk. Indeed, Braddon's description recalls Wilkie Collins's opening in *The Woman in White* when Walter Hartright encounters Anne Catherick on Hampstead Heath. The expectation that Braddon creates, however, soon dissipates, as Roderick encounters no mysterious personage, but the young heroine herself. While *Vixen* will not finally be a tale of gothic oppression or reveal any Tempest family secrets hidden in the abbey vaults, Braddon evokes sensational elements throughout the novel. The first pages are typical of Braddon's use of sensational elements elsewhere in the work: they are codes that establish sensational expectation but which do not yield such a narrative.

In the first chapter, "A Pretty Horsebreaker," the reader meets Violet, who is akin to Aurora Floyd, the author's earlier "horsey" heroine, who "spent half her time on horseback, scouring the shady lanes . . . attended only by her groom."[17] *Aurora Floyd* is very much concerned with the impropriety of the girl's behavior, especially the sexuality implied with her horse riding, as P. D. Edwards argues.[18] A reader of *Vixen* expects a similar plot, especially given the chapter title. The way in which Violet meets Roderick, jumping over a gate on her horse, implies a similar kind of "fast" and sexually sophisticated young heroine who has appeared in earlier sensation novels by Braddon and Rhoda Broughton. Such expectation seems confirmed when Roderick tells her: "I'm ashamed of you, Vixen . . . you'll come to a bad end some of these days" and she replies, "I don't care if I do, as long as I get my fling first" (2). The scene provides the same expectation that the heroine's name implies: a tale about how a young woman's passion and sexuality get her into dangerous scrapes. The heroine is hardly as violent or tempestuous as her name suggests, however, and Braddon soon complicates a reader's expectation for this kind of character.

Her father repeats to Roderick one of the family's treasured tales about how his daughter "flew at a great boy of fourteen and licked him" for mistreating a dog

(11). Braddon here uses her combination-novel method to reflect on her earlier sensation novels. The story invokes the famous scene in *Aurora Floyd* when the heroine passionately whips Steeve Hargraves for abusing her pet dog. What distinguishes the passage in *Vixen* from that in the earlier novel is the mediation of the narrative by Squire Tempest's retelling. Not only does he tell the tale frequently for his amusement, but Violet grows weary of hearing it. She becomes uncomfortable with how it has formed her identity in the minds of her family and friends. After the squire has told the story, for the thousandth time according to Violet, she asserts: "It's very horrid of you, papa, to tell such silly old stories. . . . That was nearly seven years ago. . . . I'm not the same Vixen that pushed the boy into the pond. There's not a bit of her left in me" (12). As sensation narrative, this thrashing story has gone through numerous editions without suffering in popularity among some of its audience. The retelling solidifies an expectation for her behavior, and she rebels against the pleasure that her father and Roderick take in the old story. Violet is a sensation heroine in the formula of *Aurora Floyd*, yet she proclaims that she has outgrown the old convention. Indeed, she wants to be perceived as more changeable, as a person ever in the process of becoming. By providing a narrative within a narrative, Braddon distances the reader from the sensational elements of *Vixen* and questions expectations for sensational material bearing her name. Merging modes of fiction, she appeals to a wider audience at the same time that she tries to challenge a limited perception of her work.

Still early in the novel, Braddon writes more explicitly in her combination strategy. When Squire and Mrs. Tempest discuss Roderick's twenty-first birthday party, the novelist interrupts her narrative mode: "Hush! what is this creeping softly down the old oak staircase? A slender white figure with cloudy hair. . . . Is it a ghost? No: ghosts are noiseless" (41). The ghostly figure, of course, is Violet. Although this disruption concludes as quickly as it begins, Violet appears to masquerade as Anne Catherick at the moment when Walter Hartright discovers her on Hampstead Heath in the *The Woman in White*. Violet stages the moment, conscious of the entertaining shock she delivers her father. Indeed, the squire's response, "I was just the least bit staggered. Your little white figure looked like something uncanny" (41), mimics Hartright's initial shock when Catherick's hand touches his shoulder. This narrative dislocation causes the reader once again to reflect on the construction of Braddon's central female character. If there is any secret in the novel, it is what type of Victorian heroine Violet will finally be. She plays the sensual sensational female, while other times she approaches criminality; however, Braddon's delineation of character in Violet declines to be fixed by the expectations of other characters.

Braddon also represents Violet's and Roderick's budding romance in a way that responds to the eroticism of many sensation novels, particularly those of Rhoda Broughton and Ouida. When the couple meets in the forest, Braddon yields to the sensuality between them, achieving the eroticism that had been so disparaged by critics. Braddon's use of exotic and gothic language to describe the setting intensifies this form of sensationalism: "One would expect to meet some ghostly Druid, or some witch of eld, among the shadowy track left by the forest wildlings.... The air was soft and cool and dewy, with a perfume of nameless wild flowers—a faint aromatic odour of herbs ..." (114). In this scene, Violet plays blindman's bluff with some children, becomes lost, and unexpectedly meets Roderick:

> She was on the point of taking off the handkerchief... when her outstretched arms clasped something—a substantial figure, distinctly human, clad in rough cloth.... [A] pair of strong arms clasped her; she was drawn to a broad chest; she felt a heart beating strong and fast against her shoulder, while lips that seemed too familiar to offend kissed hers with all the passion of a lover's kiss. (114–15)

Such a scene is precisely the kind that offended some critics of sensation novels. It is comparable to Broughton's *Not Wisely but Too Well* (1867) when Kate Chester and the secretly married Dare Stamer meet alone in the forest: "How supremely pleasant it was being borne swiftly along through the balmy summer evening; the breeze they met, gently kissing away the distressful redness out of cheeks that much crying had made burning hot! All alone with him! Not more than three inches distant from his great shoulder."[19] Braddon poses a reader almost voyeuristically, seeing, almost smelling the exotic world that Violet herself only half perceives because of her blindfold. Furthermore, the stranger whom Violet "captures" is not immediately visible to the reader either. The passionate man is not revealed until Roderick speaks, after he clasps and kisses her, taking advantage of her lack of sight. The passage is sensational for its eroticism and its engagement of the reader by concealing the mysterious man Violet encounters.

While Braddon represents sensuality rather like Broughton, she uses the combination-novel method to critique it in the voice of Violet's mother. The narrator relates another clandestine forest interlude between Violet and Roderick. When her mother gravely inquires about her lateness, Violet defends herself: "Is it a crime to be out riding a little longer than usual, that you should look so pale and the Captain so black when I come home?" (216). Mrs. Carmichael mimics book reviewers' frequent criticism of sensation fiction's transgression when she responds: "It is worse than a crime, Violet, it is an impropriety.... Had you been riding about the Forest all those hours alone, it would have been eccentric—unladylike—masculine even.... But you were not alone.... You were riding about with Roderick Vawdrey, Lady Mabel Ashbourne's future husband" (216). Through Mrs. Carmichael's voice, the narrative turns its thrust back on itself, questioning its own generic status. The novel begins to restrict Violet's behavior, because after Violet's discussion with her mother, the event occurs that triggers the young woman's banishment to Jersey.

Braddon once again evokes her former sensation heroine, Aurora Floyd, when Carmichael expresses displeasure over Violet's late night adventures. Violet, still clasping her whip "with a mischievous sparkle in her eyes," wonders "whether Captain Carmichael had ever been horsewhipped. . . . He would do things that deserved horsewhipping" (228). The suggestion of horsewhipping creates expectation that Violet will respond violently to Carmichael's confrontation and confirms that Violet has potential to be a "Vixen," a character formed out of Braddon's earlier strong-willed and transgressive heroines. The combination-novel structure, however, poses multiple plot options for multiple reading dispositions. First, the narrative entertains for the reader the possibility of high sensationalism in a young female horsewhipping a man. Then it absorbs the book reviewers' typical displeasure with strong-willed heroines by curbing Violet's impulse, as we shall see.

The scene escalates to a sexualized confrontation between Carmichael and Violet, as he attempts to oppress Violet. At the same time, he echoes the attitude of his wife, critical of Violet's behavior. He exclaims, "Your secret meetings, your clandestine love-making, shall be stopped. Such conduct as you have been carrying on of late is a shame and disgrace to your sex" (229). She responds to this restriction by falling back on the conventions that she has tried to outgrow. While she suppresses her compulsion to whip Carmichael, she does turn to violence suggestive of Violet's other important ancestor, Lady Audley. Violet attempts to fling a lamp at Carmichael, but instead sets the house on fire:

> She grasped the lamp with both her hands, as if she would have hurled it at her foe. . . . A great wave of blood surged up into the girl's brain. . . . [T]he heavy pedestal swayed in her hands, and then she saw the big moonlike globe roll on to the carpet, and after it, and darting beyond it, a stream of liquid fire that ran, and ran. . . . They two—Vixen and her foe—seemed to be standing in an atmosphere of fire. (229)

One of the few representations of female violence in the novel, Violet's conflagration intensifies the passion and anger she feels: after all, Carmichael might have been her husband.[20] At the same time, the scene is self-reflexive of Braddon's sensational origins with *Lady Audley's Secret* when Lady Audley coldly plots to murder Robert Audley by setting fire to the Castle Inn. Although Robert escapes Lady Audley's machinations, Braddon represents her behavior as malevolent and dangerous to Robert. In *Vixen*, one expects that Violet will similarly trap the oppressive Carmichael in the fire. Her exasperation appears as if it will bring her to the pinnacle in which she will act as the sensation heroines before her have done. Yet, in contrast to Braddon's early novel, the author subdues Violet's violence almost as quickly as it begins, when a servant extinguishes the fire: "In ten minutes the window stood blank, and black, and bare, with Vixen standing on the lawn outside, contemplating the damage she had done" (229). Within a few pages, Braddon twice evokes the sensationalism of her earlier fiction but subverts expectation that Violet will behave like Aurora Floyd or Lady Audley.

As the novel proceeds to its final volume, Braddon increasingly seeks to complicate the function of genre within the literary marketplace. Violet's banishment to Jersey, which follows the fire scene, permits Braddon to combine a number of sensation novel elements. At first, it seems that Violet will be "buried," hidden away much as Lady Audley and Collins's Anne Catherick are, especially when Violet inquires of her new home: "Is there a history hanging to it. . . . Has it been used as a prison, or a mad-house, or what? I never saw a house that filled me with such nameless horrors" (249). Yet, Carmichael corrects her perceptions, noting they are "fanciful." Indeed, her stay on the island turns out to be not what she or the reader expects: she is neither locked up for insanity, nor does she remain for her six years' duration. More significantly, Braddon dramatizes the narrative rhetoric in Violet's mind; the character approaches her banishment with sensational expectation, as if she has read Ann Radcliffe and Wilkie Collins, in addition to Charles Reade; however, there is little sensational incident of the kind Violet imagines. Reading her experience as if she were reading a sensation novel, Violet (mirroring *Vixen*'s reader) finds another genre with rather different contours.

While on the island of Jersey, Violet outgrows the patterns from which so many sensation heroines before her have been cut, to become an antisensation heroine. Braddon shows that her female characters and her work as a novelist have surpassed the mold that had formed readers' expectations for sensation fiction and for "Braddon" fiction. Throughout, *Vixen* is a novel that teases readers with sensational expectation, but in the end Braddon reveals that generic fashions have changed or at least should be questioned. The novel is very much about fashions, old and new, whether they are for fiction, home decorating, or dress. Tropical plants, orchids, and hothouses, for example, are some of the novel's preoccupations with new and passing fashions. Yet, Violet and Roderick prefer the native English plants and refuse to have hothouse flowers at their wedding. Braddon shows in the heroine's and hero's marriage a fantasy of traditional uncommercial England: "Rorie and Vixen live the life they love, in the Forest where they were born, dispensing happiness within a narrow circle . . . and the old men and women in the scattered villages round about the Abbey House rejoice in the good old times that have come again" (342). While the novel valorizes the couple's uncommercial life and subverts the expectation for commercial fiction, *Vixen* is a product on the fiction marketplace and must still negotiate marketplace forces.

It is clear that Victorian reviewers recognized that *Vixen* was not sensational.

What they largely did not notice was Braddon's subversion of sensationalism throughout the narrative. Only the *Academy's* notice endeavors to praise the novel, pleased that Braddon avoids her "popular," sensational mode of fiction.[21] The hardly praiseworthy reviewer from the *Athenaeum* notes that "[a] novel by the author of 'Lady Audley's Secret' is sure to find plenty of readers. Fortunately for the author's reputation they are not discriminating."[22] The reviewer acknowledges that the typical Braddon reader "expect[ing] exciting mysteries or surprising crimes [would] be sadly disappointed with 'Vixen'" (275). We can begin to see the critical contradiction in which Braddon found herself: reviewers were loath to praise her sensation novels but also were quick to disparage her departure from the "horizon of expectation" associated with her name. The unkind review in the *Saturday Review* recognizes the absence of crime in the novel by noting: "How, . . . the reader may with reasonable wonder ask, does the author manage to fill her book? Without criminals it might be expected that her volumes would stand as empty as the cells of the gaol of a county town where there is a Maiden assize."[23] In its conclusion, the review exclaimed: "But we are so lingering over Miss Braddon's *not unusual performances* that we are scarcely leaving ourselves space to describe the plot of the story" and proceeded to list the plot's few incidents (281; emphasis added). This final statement succeeded in making Braddon conform to critical expectation, claiming that Braddon was as "bad" as usual, despite her venture beyond sensationalism.

Book reviewers may have had difficulty understanding the combination-novel method in *Vixen,* especially when Braddon was still producing sensation fiction. Only two days after she finished writing *Vixen* in 1878 she began *The Cloven Foot,* a novel decidedly sensational, featuring a murder, bigamy, and double identity.[24] Because Braddon knew early in her career that her fiction appealed to the populace, she could not suspend sensational features in works such as *Vixen* that experimented with other fictional modes. By combining fictional discourses, absorbing responses from book reviewers, and manipulating readers' expectations, Braddon could venture beyond the authorial realm to which the name "Braddon" and "the author of *Lady Audley's Secret*" confined her. Twenty-first-century readers of Braddon are indebted to the renewed, largely feminist, "horizon of expectations" for Braddon's fiction: her works increasingly become more available to a wide readership. This new horizon, however, fraught with generic expectations for the sensation novel, can conceal the Mary Elizabeth Braddon who in her own day worked hard to surpass the function of genre at the same time she conformed to it. To understand her simultaneous engagement and resistance to the sensation fiction marketplace, we need a reading practice that is dialogic, one that reads for generic expectation, but also attends to the ways her narratives surpass generic boundaries.

NOTES

1. Margaret Oliphant, "Novels," 263, 265.
2. The passages alluding to Helen Rolleston, existing in the three-volume first edition published by Maxwell and many later reprints, have been excised from the recent Pocket Classics edition of *Vixen* (1993).
3. Mary Elizabeth Braddon, *Vixen: A Novel* (American Publishers, 1899), 251. Unless noted, all references are to this edition and cited by page in the text.
4. Pamela K. Gilbert, "Braddon and Victorian Realism: *Joshua Haggard's Daughter*," in *Beyond Sensation: Mary Elizabeth Braddon in Context*, 185. All further references are quoted by page number in the text.
5. Elaine Showalter, *A Literature of Their Own*, 163. For additional elaboration of Showalter's thesis, see also her article "Desperate Remedies."
6. Michel Foucault, "What Is an Author?" 107.
7. Robert Lee Wolff, *Sensational Victorian*, 4.
8. For photographic representations of numerous spines of Braddon first editions, see Robert Lee Wolff, *Nineteenth-Century Fiction*, xlii. Wolff's bibliographic entries for Braddon's fiction also reproduce the title-page text of her novels.
9. Wolff, "Devoted Disciple,"10. All references are to this edition and quoted by page in the text.
10. See Wolff, *Sensational Victorian*, 158–87, and Pykett, introduction to *The Doctor's Wife* (1998), vii–viii.
11. Braddon, *The Doctor's Wife*, 358. All references are to this edition and quoted by page in the text.
12. Wolff, *Sensational Victorian*, 126, reads Sigismund Smith as Braddon's "mouthpiece"; Pykett, ix, views Smith as Braddon's "fictional *alter ago*."
13. Tabitha Sparks, "Fiction Becomes Her: Representations of Female Character in Mary Braddon's *The Doctor's Wife*," 198.
14. According to Ellen Miller Casey, the name of Violet's stepfather was Captain Winstanley in the original serialized edition of *Vixen* in *All the Year Round*, "'Other People's Prudery,'" 82. The 1879 three-volume first edition published by Maxwell also follows this pattern. While most later editions are changed to Captain Carmichael, the Pocket Classics edition (1993) reverts back to Winstanley.
15. Fionn O'Toole, introduction to *Vixen* (1993), x–xi.
16. Gillian Beer, "Sensational Women," 26.
17. Mary Elizabeth Braddon, *Aurora Floyd*, 22.
18. P. D. Edwards, introduction to *Aurora Floyd*, xi–xiii. Margaret Oliphant also correlates female horsiness with immorality (272).
19. Rhoda Broughton, *Not Wisely but Too Well*, 59.
20. For additional discussion of the sexuality in this scene, see also Casey, "Other People's Prudery," 80–81.
21. Review of *Vixen*, *Academy*, 233.
22. Review of *Vixen*, *Athenaeum*, 275.
23. Review of *Vixen*, *Saturday Review*, 281.
24. Braddon finished the novel March 30, 1878, and began *The Cloven Foot* April 1, 1878 (Wolff, *Nineteenth-Century Fiction*, 122, 147).

- 5 -

"OF ALL THE HORRORS . . . THE FOULEST AND MOST CRUEL"

Sensation and Dickens's Oliver Twist

DIANA C. ARCHIBALD

IN "DICKENS as Sensation Novelist," Mirella Billi remarks, "Dickens has long been considered the father of sensation fiction and he undoubtedly created the genre" though she concedes "there are differences between him and his contemporary 'rivals,' whose work . . . he anticipated and decisively influenced."[1] As evidence for this claim, Billi begins with a brief analysis of the sensation elements present in *Oliver Twist*, published in 1838, well before the 1860s that most critics mark as the heyday of sensation fiction. According to Billi, the novel contains all the necessary elements: "intrigue, crime, mistaken or denied identities, the theft and hiding of papers, victims and persecutors," with "everything originat[ing] in the 'respectable' family, the middle-class home" (178–79). On the opposite extreme, Thomas Boyle pointedly remarks that *Oliver Twist* "cannot compete with Dickens's later work for sensationalism or serious social analysis. It is mere melodrama by comparison" and thus not an antecedent to the sensation novel. Clearly, there is a wide range of opinions about Dickens's relationship to sensation, though many see some sort of connection.[2]

Yet, if one assumes that Dickens, specifically in *Oliver Twist*, is writing sensation fiction, we may well ask what kind of sensation. Where did it come from? How did Dickens use sensation elements and why? What relationship does sensation have to realism in the novel? Isn't *Oliver Twist* supposed to be a Newgate novel? Are such generic distinctions even helpful? *Oliver Twist* defies categorization. It is and is not a Newgate novel. It is and is not sensation fiction. It is and is not realism. Ultimately, perhaps the most we can claim is that it is a hybrid of or a bridge between these genres.

Dickens himself resisted the labels attached to his fiction. In his preface to the 1841 edition of *Oliver Twist*, he attempts to counter recent attacks on his work. In a letter to R. H. Horne, he writes, "I am by some jolter-headed enemies most unjustly and untruly charged with having written a book after Mr. Ainsworth's fashion."[3] Harrison Ainsworth, perhaps the best-known Newgate novelist, first became famous with the publication in 1834 of *Rockwood,* a novel that glamorized the life of a highway robber. While the *Newgate Calendar* (1824–1828) included "Memoirs" of notorious criminals in Newgate Prison, surprisingly the treatment of the material in the four-volume collection tended to be "distinguished chiefly by its bland conventionality."[4] The narrators of various accounts sermonize against vice and uphold social stereotypes and mainstream Victorian morality. Newgate novelists like Ainsworth and Edward Bulwer-Lytton fictionalized these stories, romanticizing, critics said, the criminal life and thus promoting vice. Though wildly popular among some readers in their day, these novels were faulted by contemporary critics as not only immoral but also badly written—some of the same criticism later levied against sensation fiction. Indeed, these texts appear highly stylized and predictable to many modern readers as well.

It is understandable why Dickens's novel has, from the beginning up until the present, often been branded a Newgate novel. With the criminals of the London underworld featured so prominently in the book, with some of its characters apparently based on actual Newgate figures, and with some attempt made to show a relationship between social problems and criminals, the novel does follow some of the conventions of sensation. The novel was also serialized in a journal, *Bentley's Miscellany,* which would eventually become closely associated with the genre. In fact, four months before *Oliver Twist*'s last number was published, the journal introduced Ainsworth's blockbuster, *Jack Sheppard,* a novel about a "young 18th-century thief and Newgate escape-artist."[5] The two novels were naturally linked in the eyes of the reading public.

Clearly peeved by critics' attempts to brand him a Newgate novelist, however, Dickens distinguishes himself from such company:

> I had read of thieves by the scores; seductive fellows (amiable for the most part), faultless in dress, plump in pocket, choice in horse-flesh, bold in bearing. . . . But I had never met (except in Hogarth) with the miserable reality. It appeared to me that to draw a knot of such associates in crime as really did exist; to paint them in all their deformity, in all their wretchedness, in all the squalid misery of their lives; to show them as they really are, . . . would be to attempt something which was needed, and which would be a service to society.[6]

To Dickens, then, the fundamental approach of his novel is antithetical to the spirit of the Newgate novel. He seeks to paint an accurate picture of criminality to deter (as well as to entertain), not to produce a romanticized vision of the life of crime that may unwittingly (or purposefully) glorify vice. While his work shares some elements in common with the genre, its differences are far more significant, at least to the author. Most importantly, Dickens claims his realistic portrait of criminals (and, I might add, the psychological depth of these characters) will serve society by dimming "the false glitter surrounding something which really did exist, by showing it in its unattractive and repulsive truth" (viii). He may be showing how social ills contribute to criminality, but he is not therefore excusing the criminals from bearing responsibility for their actions. His criminals commit heinous crimes, and they deserve to be punished, the text seems to say, not held up as heroes.[7]

Perhaps the most horrific crime in the novel is Nancy's murder, a point of intersection between the three genres this novel hybridizes. The murder is, first, a tale of crime akin to but more sympathetic than those found in the *Newgate Calendar*, which did include some examples of domestic violence; second, it is a thrilling plot element that evokes an emotional, even physical, response in the reader, as with the sensation novel; and, third, it is carefully crafted psychological realism. These competing impulses result in a particularly powerful and complex subplot sometimes at odds with itself. For example, one might well argue that since Nancy is a prostitute and her lover a thief (Newgate conventions), the novel quarantines domestic violence within the lower orders. Nancy and Sikes are lower-class figures and thus differ significantly from later sensation fiction cases in which the abused and abusers are ladies and gentlemen. This class difference is significant; however, it need not prohibit us from seeing her murder as sensation. In fact, *Oliver Twist* uses sensation elements in other places in the novel as well.

The murder of a woman by her lover places violence at the heart of the home, linking criminality and the domestic space, a convention of sensation. While Nancy's is a lower-class home, the tale of that troubled domestic space is echoed in the actual and potential failings of the middle-class families elsewhere in the novel: the miserable marriage of the Leefords and Monks's willingness to betray his own half-brother demonstrate that all is not well in the family.[8] Such instances may be the closest precursors in the novel to the sensation conventions of the 1860s, for here we see that severe domestic disturbance can originate outside the lower class. The novel, in fact, contains other such examples. Oliver's very existence is evidence of his mother Agnes's fall, through seduction by a married gentleman. As a direct result of Agnes's fall, she dies; her family literally breaks apart; her sister, Rose, is tainted forever; and Oliver is doomed to a childhood of poverty, misery, and abuse. The violence of *Oliver Twist* does not begin in the lower class nor does it end with Nancy's murder; it is everywhere. Nancy becomes a focal point for the novel's violence because her death is so gruesome and shocking and because she is connected to all of the characters in the book regardless of class.

William Makepeace Thackeray, in "Going to See a Man Hanged," accused Dickens of painting a false picture of Nancy: "Boz, who knows life well, knows that his Miss Nancy is the most unreal fantastical personage possible; no more like a thief's mistress than one of Gessner's shepherdesses resembles a real country wench."[9] No doubt Thackeray expected Nancy to follow conventions established by the Newgate novelists, or perhaps the *Newgate Calendar* itself. But what Dickens responds to is how Thackeray (and perhaps others) see Nancy's "devotion to the brutal house-breaker" as "[un]natural." It is the girl's relationship with her abusive lover that warrants the most stringent defense:

> It is useless to discuss whether the conduct and character of the girl seems natural or unnatural, probable or improbable, right or wrong. IT IS TRUE. Every man who has watched these melancholy shades of life, must know it to be so. . . . From the first introduction of that poor wretch, to her laying her blood-stained head upon the robber's breast, there is not a word exaggerated or over-wrought. It is emphatically God's truth. (ix)

While one might quibble about the degree to which Nancy is sentimentalized or melodramatic, at bottom she *is* true. And the way in which she is true matters to our understanding of both Dickens's oeuvre and sensation fiction as a Victorian phenomenon.

At the height of the sensation fiction movement, Dickens gave public readings from his work on lucrative tours in both Britain and America. While developing new material in 1868 for these public readings, he chose to develop "Sikes and Nancy," a rendition of the murder so powerful that ladies in the audience fainted and Dickens himself purportedly suffered ill effects to his health. The version of the story read to audiences differs from the novel not in substance but in style. He heightens particular elements in the story in order to bring forward the sensation. Clearly Dickens saw the shock value of the gruesome scene in which Nancy is bludgeoned to death. Nancy's murder *is* shocking. What makes it so, specifically, is that the pair were lovers. Criminal underworld aside, Nancy and Bill shared a home and a bed, and his brutal murder of her is an extreme violation of the domestic space. Her murder still makes our skin crawl, our hearts pound, our eyes cry, just as it did for the Victorians. What keeps Nancy's murder from being mere melodrama—and the heart of what makes it so powerful—is its psychological realism. Many critics have claimed that sensation fiction favors an exciting plot over character development.[10] Significantly, the most sensational plot element of *Oliver Twist*—Nancy's murder—actually reveals much about her character, her pathological codependency. In Nancy's case, her actions and Dickens's details reveal more than the narrator does, yet the location of character revelations in plot rather than narration does not negate the text's ability to elucidate psychological truths.[11]

The character Nancy enters the stage as a mere prop but quickly becomes a more important member of the cast, considered by many readers to be the true hero of the novel. And though there is some disagreement about the meaning of

Nancy's saving Oliver and returning to Sikes, most critics agree that these final acts are key to understanding her character and her role in the novel. They usually label Nancy as a "fallen woman" or "whore with a heart of gold" whose death is a sacrifice for Oliver's sake. While examining Nancy in light of recent scholarship on fallen women has proven useful at times, such a framework also limits our understanding of her. For Nancy, by the end of the novel, would be much more accurately described as a "battered woman" who is unable to extricate herself from an unhealthy codependency than a "whore with a heart of gold." Most scholars persist, however, in reading her death without reference to her battering.[12] Billi claims that Nancy "is 'redeemed' by being murdered by Sikes" (181). George E. Kennedy proposes that Nancy is redeemed from the sins of her life as a prostitute through saving Oliver. "Redemption, Dickens believed, could be realized only through the imitation of Christ like endeavor," he claims, implying that Nancy's death is a kind of martyrdom, self-sacrifice of the stained for the safety of the innocent.[13] And Francoise Basch, who writes "[Nancy] refuses to flee, voluntarily sacrificing herself to expiate her sins," fails to see that Nancy's "loyalty" is determined more by her dysfunctional compulsions than any exercise of her will for her own redemption.[14]

Nancy does not die *in order* to save Oliver. He is saved already when she tells all on London Bridge. She dies because she goes *home.* Critics account for her return to Sikes in a number of ways. "Her downfall occurs because she is trapped by circumstances she cannot control and by her altruistic and decent conduct," says David Paroissien.[15] Whereas Robert R. Garnett claims that Nancy "is too firmly in the grip of the flesh" to leave Sikes and her old life"; she is "impelled by sexual feelings and desires. Though she responds to the glow of the spirit, the pull of the flesh prevails."[16] I argue simply that she dies because she can't break out of her codependent behavioral patterns and thus she returns to her abuser. Nancy fits the profile of a battered woman, and though such terminology is not Victorian, the concept was not foreign in the nineteenth century. Dickens himself was well aware of the behavior of women caught in such destructive relationships, and he knowingly draws an accurate and insightful picture of such pathology in Nancy. He wants his portrait to be "true"—unlike the Newgate novelists' characterizations.

In the Victorian period, a wave of information was published describing what modern psychologists later came to call "battered woman syndrome." Stemming from an attempt to gain sympathy for fallen women, a particularly large burst of writing appeared about the "Magdalen problem" in the 1830s and 1840s. Doctors, social workers, divines, and "more important, novelists and poets . . . were taking up the issue."[17] Dr. Alexandre Parent-Duchâtelet wrote in 1836 of how prostitutes often affixed themselves to an abusive man, and a Dr. Ryan also wrote, "With the lowest and coarsest classes [of prostitutes] reproaches, invectives, ill-treatment, blows, wounds and even broken limbs, are not capable of shaking their attachment to some men, for scarcely are they cured in hospital of their wound, than they return to them." Pierce Egan's *Life in London,* published in 1821, may also have provided background information for Dickens; Egan remarked about many of London's prostitutes that "these unfortunate women suffer themselves to be beaten by their protectors."[18] Dickens himself participated in this movement with his sketches of prostitutes (who were also battered by their pimps or lovers) in "The Pawnbroker's Shop" and "The Hospital Patient."[19]

Dickens had ample opportunity, then, to learn about battered women from reading and experience.[20] His choice to include such a character in *Oliver Twist* reveals his intense sympathy for such victims. We know that Dickens wrote the novel, in part, as a consciousness-raising work. The industrial revolution had played havoc with England's social systems. Factories displaced great numbers of people; slums spawned in the cities; poverty ravaged the populace, with women, children, and the aged as its most poignant victims. Prostitution and thievery meant survival for many of the poor; for others, these illegal pursuits were a better alternative than the extraordinarily harsh conditions of the industries open to them. Dickens's keen talent for observation, coupled with a concern for the plight of the poor, enabled him to fictionalize accurately the behavior of these "dregs of society" that so interested him. As a child working in a blacking factory and living on his own, Dickens had ample opportunity to observe the effects of living conditions on the poor. In his own words: "I know that I lounged about the streets, insufficiently and unsatisfactorily fed. I know that, but for the mercy of God, I might easily have been, for any care that was taken of me, a little robber or a little vagabond." Certainly Dickens's own childhood experiences must have sensitized him to the effect of environment on social behavior. Undoubtedly, he observed the destruction of lives that resulted from the unchecked laissez-faire capitalist expansion of the Industrial Revolution. As an adult Dickens became a journalist and social activist, working to improve the lives of the poor and, in particular, the plight of "fallen women." In 1846 Dickens, along with Miss Angela Couttes, opened Urania Cottage, a haven where a woman could "cease a way of life miserable to herself. Never mind society. . . . Society has used her ill."[21] Dickens's view of the "fallen woman" was intrinsically bound to her sociological and psychological state.

Dickens, then, had both the interest in and opportunity to observe the behavior of prostitutes and battered women. In spite of his sentimental editorializing of Nancy's final acts and his Victorian patriarchal value judgments about female sexual sin, Dickens's representation of Nancy's behavior moves beyond melodrama to psychological realism through a shocking event that forces us to rethink assumptions, particularly about gender. While it is important not to conflate modern and Victorian ways of understanding battered women, we can gain valuable insight by analyzing Nancy's character in light of what we now know about battered woman syndrome.[22] Our ways of speaking about domestic violence have changed, but the realities of life for the battered have changed little. Dickens was able to capture these realities surprisingly well; he seems to have put great care into developing Nancy. Dickens does not stop with merely showing that she is beaten or murdered. His picture reveals his intimate knowledge of the state of mind of the battered woman. He has painted a "true" portrait.

As Lisa Surridge notes, it is "well documented that middle-class Victorians preferred to believe that wife battery was largely restricted to the lower classes."[23] However, Surridge suggests that in Collins's *Man and Wife,* the "powerful subplot" of Hester's abuse inserts itself into the main plot of middle-class marriage and attempted murder through the "pairing of the middle-class heroine with a lower-class . . . character,"[24] thus revealing the pervasiveness of abuse across class boundaries. At first glance Nancy's portrait might seem to uphold the notion that domestic violence is contained within the "lower orders." But Nancy is linked so clearly to Rose Maylie that it is difficult to ignore the inference that all women are vulnerable to such abuse. Nancy herself draws attention to Rose's helplessness when she compares the two of them directly:

> "Thank Heaven upon your knees, dear lady," cried the girl [Nancy], "that you had friends to care for and keep you in your childhood, and that you were never in the midst of cold and hunger, and riot and drunkenness, and—and—something worse than all—as I have been from my cradle." (358)

In such passages, Dickens intends to show that the circumstances of Nancy's childhood have contributed to the misery of her present life. Most likely Nancy was either orphaned or abandoned by her parents at about age five.[25] Fagin is the only father figure Nancy knows, hardly the sort of "parent" to help her develop into a well-adjusted young adult. Rose was nearly abandoned as well and, the novel seems to say, has barely escaped a life like Nancy's. As Kenneth C. Frederick asserts, even the "picture of family life that the novel presents" (with its "good" and wealthy characters) "is . . . a vast emptiness where the center of affirmation might be expected to be."[26] In fact, the case can easily be made that the novel exhibits nothing but dysfunctional families.

Women are vulnerable. Through no fault of their own, they can be ruined, plummeting to the lower orders of society and into misery. It is not merely the specter of falling that Nancy raises in this scene. The middle-class woman is not safe even if she does not lose her class status; her danger is just more hidden from view. When Rose tries to convince Nancy not to return to her old life of prostitution and thievery, she asks, "What fascination is it that can take you back, and make you cling to wickedness and misery?" (362). Nancy clearly shows it is not her lifestyle that draws her back but a warped codependency, one to which any woman can fall prey: "'When ladies as young, and good, and beautiful as you are,' replied the girl steadily, 'give away your hearts, love will carry you all lengths—even such as you, who have home, friends, other admirers, everything, to fill them'" (362–63). Indeed, Rose does not yet know the story of her sister Agnes's fall, how she was ruined by the treachery of a man she loved. Yet, Nancy knows that women of all classes are vulnerable, that men of all classes can turn murderer—whether through overt brutality or selfish neglect.

Thackeray may have found Nancy's devotion to Sikes unrealistic, but Dickens knew better. Yes, Sikes is brutal: Bill "flings the girl from him" (152), gives Nancy "livid bruises on her neck" (190), "strikes her" when she tries to help him after his illness (343), and repeatedly gives "utterance . . . to curses and threats" (154). Other Victorian readers had trouble understanding how Nancy could stay with a man like Sikes, let alone love him. Yet Nancy's attraction to Sikes is understandable when one considers that abused women tend to be attracted to men as abusive as their parents. She perceives Sikes's abuse as a "heavy judgment" (363) for her "life of sin" (361). Having been raised by the likes of Fagin, she does not believe she is worthy to be loved, and Rose, along with the rest of society, does little to make her feel worthy of escape from this misery.

> When such as I, . . . set our rotten hearts on any man, and let him fill the place that has been a blank through all our wretched lives, who can hope to cure us? . . . pity us for having only one feeling of the woman left, and for having that turned, . . . into a new means of violence and suffering. (363)

Dickens's choice of words is especially important here. Note that although Rose talks about "saving" Nancy, Nancy herself uses the word "cure." This attachment to Sikes is like a disease. Nancy stresses that she "can't leave" Sikes and that she "must go back" (361). She is addicted to the relationship, to the suffering. And though she does not understand "what it is" that makes her stay, she understands that she cannot leave (361).

Despite the fact that the nature of Nancy's condition as a battered woman clearly influences most of her behavior in Dickens's novel, most critics have failed to take this element into account when interpreting Nancy's last acts. Rather, she is either dismissed as an overly wrought, sentimental figure—much the same way that sensation is sometimes downgraded—or she is lauded for her martyrdom and self-sacrifice. By labeling the murder as pure sensation, critics lose sight of the deeper psychological significance of Nancy's character. Marlene Tromp, one of the few critics to identify Nancy as a battered woman, contends that "Nancy's redemption depends not upon her ethics or a code external to her that overlays the tale, but upon her monetary worth to her social 'betters.'" Once she has served her purpose in helping Oliver to acquire his rightful wealth, she is killed off. While I agree with much of Tromp's argument, I disagree with her assertion that Dickens's novel suggests that "the threat of domestic violence is not a social problem" but a personal, individual, idiosyncratic problem.[27] Dickens has included far too many details linking individual circumstance to societal ills not to be showing that Nancy is one of many. Nancy loses her life because she cannot escape from the cycle of abuse in which she has been enmeshed from early childhood, abuse that is part of a system of violence against women. She believes that she must return to Sikes even if it means her death because he is the man she has chosen to punish her for being unlovable, and paradoxically, the man from whom she most needs to receive love.

Dickens intended to uncover the truth about the London underworld. He knew that here was a story that "needed to be told" (x). But for there to be hope for the "hundreds of others" (361) like Nancy and Bill—the street children, the castoffs, the hopeless—society must recognize the nature of this truth. They must accept that codependency relationships (relationships in which both participants—the abuser and the abused—are addicted to harmful behavior) are not romantic but destructive, and that women who stay with abusive men are not noble but diseased. Just as the criminals of Newgate novels ought not to be romanticized, so, too, battering ought not to be overlooked or endorsed. The sensational act of Nancy's murder draws us, heart and mind, into the life of an abused woman. Sensation persuades us of the truth like no argument can do.

Anthony Trollope placed novels in two groups: the sensational and the antisensational, called "realistic."[28] Ever since, this oppositional schema has remained in force. Yet, as Hughes puts it, sensation is "the violent yoking of romance and realism."[29] *Oliver Twist*, we might say, is the violent yoking of the underworld of Newgate, the shocking domestic violence and class awareness of sensation, and the accuracy and psychological truths of realism.[30] The fact that all can coexist might well make us question the parameters we set for these genres, however; for clearly sensation can be just as realistic as a domestic novel can be. Thus, it is surely inaccurate to claim that sensation fiction is only plot-driven and therefore does not provide any depth of characterization. Likewise, as this collection demonstrates, sensation fiction exists outside the confines of the 1860s; it was forming even in 1838 with *Oliver Twist*. Then again, maybe the Newgate novel and sensation fiction are neither of them accurate in describing a novel like *Oliver Twist*. Perhaps realism fits best of all. For the "real" includes the domestic, the sensational, the outrageous, the shocking, and the criminal.[31]

Indeed, we do not necessarily wish to think of domestic violence as real, but it is nonetheless. Lovers do batter their partners. All too often, in fact, such violence is "normal" in many homes. If we were to acknowledge how common such abuse is, however, we would be forced to investigate its cause. Nancy is one of the first sympathetically and realistically drawn battered women in British literature.[32] The fact that critics and readers have for years seen her merely as the "whore with a heart of gold" just demonstrates how tied we are to the labels that come before us. Dickens asserted in his 1841 preface that he was "glad to have" the truth of what he wrote "doubted, for in that circumstance [he] should find a sufficient assurance . . . that it needed to be told" (xviii). Perhaps this still holds true today.

NOTES

1. Mirella Billi, "Dickens as Sensation Novelist," 178. All further references are cited by page in the text.

2. See Thomas Boyle, *Black Swine in the Sewers of Hampstead*, 127. Marlene Tromp in *The Private Rod* claims that Dickens "was widely considered a forefather of sensation," but she classifies *Oliver Twist* as an "early pre-sensational account" since it "precedes the critical articulation of sensation as a genre" (3). Valerie Pedlar, on the other hand, in "The Woman in White: Sensationalism, Secrets and Spying," points to Wilkie Collins's *Woman in White* as "the first novel to have attracted the label" of sensation fiction (49), and she lists Collins, Braddon, Reade, and Wood as the "main sensation novelists," with Dickens merely a figure who joined this group "from time to time" (50), with such works as *Great Expectations* and *Our Mutual Friend*.

3. Paul Schlicke, *Oxford Reader's Companion to Dickens*, 405.

4. Boyle, 43.

5. Schlicke, 405.

6. Charles Dickens, *Oliver Twist; or, the Parish Boy's Progress* (Signet Classic, 1961), iv. All references are to this edition and are cited by page in the text. According to David Paroissien, "Sikes's persistent brutality to his dog may owe something to Hogarth's series of engravings, *The Four Stages of Cruelty* (1750). In them Hogarth traces the degeneration of a youthful animal-tormentor into a hardened murderer who is eventually hanged for killing his mistress," *The Companion to* Oliver Twist, 144. The fact that Dickens singles out Hogarth here as an exception may well also indicate his indebtedness.

7. Modern critics have discussed Dickens's London underworld elsewhere. See, in particular, Philip Collins, *Dickens and Crime*.

8. I am indebted to Lillian Nayder for these examples of sensation elements in the novel.

9. Quoted in Paroissien, *The Companion to Oliver Twist*, 23.

10. See, among others, Winifred Hughes, *The Maniac in the Cellar*.

11. Stephen Bernstein concurs: "In *Oliver Twist* . . . it is possible to . . . see Dickens, even this early in his career, addressing the problems of psychological complexity which would obsess him throughout his works." ("Oliver Twisted: Narrative and Doubling in Dickens's Second Novel," 27)

12. J. Hillis Miller, in *Charles Dickens: The World of His Novels*, does not see the pathological dimension to Nancy and Sikes's relationship but rather asserts that "[they] are inevitably destroyed by their guilty love, a love that is guilty because it is outside social sanctions" (33). Margaret Conrow, in "Wife-Abuse in Dickens's Fiction," claims that Nancy's actions are a more

or less positive assertion of her will in opposition to the "innate brutality and wickedness" of Sikes and Fagin (43). Deborah Nord Epstein, in *Walking the Victorian Streets: Women, Representation, and the City*, remarks, "It is the street prostitute Nancy . . . whose sacrifice purges the novel of danger and criminality" (81).

13. George E. Kennedy II, "Women Redeemed: Dickens's Fallen Women," 42.

14. Françoise Basch, "Dickens's Sinners," 213.

15. David Paroissien, *The Companion to* Oliver Twist, 260.

16. Robert R. Garnett, "*Oliver Twist*'s Nancy: The Angel in Chains," 506–7.

17. Eric Trudgill, *Madonnas and Magdalens: The Origins and Development of Victorian Sexual Attitudes*, 283.

18. Quoted in Paroissien, 239.

19. Found in Charles Dickens, *Sketches By Boz*, Vol. 19 of *The New Oxford Illustrated Dickens*.

20. As Dickens himself writes in the preface to *Oliver Twist*, Nancy's character was "[s]uggested to my mind long ago, by what I often saw and read of, in actual life around me" (ix).

21. Quoted in Edgar Johnson, *Charles Dickens: His Tragedy and Triumph*, 36, 315.

22. Modern psychology tells us in almost every way Nancy fits the battered woman profile. According to twentieth-century studies on intimate partner violence, such as Lenore Walker, *Battered Women,* and Robin Norwood, *Women Who Love Too Much,* battered women typically come from dysfunctional families and have low self-esteem, a background which leads them to become addicted to "needy" and "emotionally unavailable" men who inflict emotional pain and even physical violence upon them. Other signs of this personality profile include a predisposition to becoming addicted to alcohol or drugs and a frequent contemplation of suicide.

23. Lisa Surridge, "Unspeakable Histories: Hester Dethridge and the Narration of Domestic Violence in *Man and Wife*," 113.

24. Ibid., 103, 105.

25. In "A Visit to Newgate," most often noted for its early version of Fagin in the prison cell, Dickens had also described a prostitute visiting her imprisoned mother: "Barely past her childhood, it required but a glance to discover that she was one of those children, born and bred in neglect and vice, who have [sic] never known what childhood is . . ." (Dickens, *Oliver Twist,* quoted in Paroissien, 238).

26. Kenneth C. Frederick, "The Cold, Cold Hearth: Domestic Strife in *Oliver Twist*," 466.

27. Tromp, 16, 58.

28. Quoted in Tromp, 10.

29. Winifred Hughes, *The Maniac in the Cellar*, 16.

30. For example, much as the Newgate novel drew upon true reports of criminals in the *Newgate Calendar,* Sensation novels often used newspaper articles as source material. See Thomas Boyle for more information on Victorian newspaper accounts of crime. It was common enough for sensation writers like Collins and Reade, for example, to claim their work had a basis in fact.

31. "For Dickens, sensationalism has a place in fiction because it has a place in life." Valerie Pedlar, "The Woman in White: Sensationalism, Secrets and Spying," 64. Dickens even remarked once, "I am always deeply sensible of the wonderful exercise I have of life and its highest sensations," quoted by John Forster, *The Life of Charles Dickens*, 640–41.

32. She is followed by many more, including those created by Dickens in later works, most notably, Mercy in *Martin Chuzzlewit,* and Florence in *Dombey and Son,* and by characters in other Victorian novels like Wilkie Collins's *Woman in White* and *Man and Wife,* and Margaret Oliphant's *Salem Chapel,* and as Tromp argues even George Eliot's *Daniel Deronda.*

- 6 -

NATURALISM IN
CHARLES READE'S EXPERIMENTAL
NOVEL, *GRIFFITH GAUNT*

DIANNA VITANZA

GRIFFITH GAUNT, or Jealousy[1] (1866), the sensation novel Charles Reade called "a tale of the heart," is arguably his best work. While *The Cloister and the Hearth* (1861) is considered by most critics to be Reade's masterpiece, Reade himself preferred *Griffith Gaunt* to the more famous novel,[2] and others have singled it out for special praise.[3] Henry James, for example, observed that Reade's novels, "(the much abused 'Griffith Gaunt' included), make him, to our mind, the most readable of living English novelists, and prove him a distant kinsman of Shakespeare."[4] More recently, Wayne Burns claims that *Griffith Gaunt* "will bear comparison with George Eliot at her mature best,"[5] and Arthur Pollard, referring to *Griffith Gaunt*, asserts that "Charles Reade is overdue for a revival."[6]

What do these critics see in this neglected sensation novel that led them to praise it? I believe they realized that in *Griffith Gaunt* Charles Reade was experimenting with a new way of presenting character and human action that was shaped by the scientific revolution of the nineteenth century and the theories of Charles Darwin. In 1880 Émile Zola would explain this approach to the novel in two essays from *Le Roman experimental*, and he would use the terms "naturalism" and "naturalist" to define it. In "Naturalism in the Theatre," Zola compares the naturalistic novelist's task to that of the scientist:

> Naturalism is the return to nature; it is that operation which the scientists made the day they decided to start with the study of bodies and phenomena, to base their work on experiment, and to proceed by means of analysis. Naturalism, in letters, is equally a return to nature and to man; it is direct observation, exact anatomy, the acceptance and depiction of what is. The writer and the scientist have had the same task.[7]

Similarly in "The Experimental Novel" Zola argues that just as for the scientist "the experimental method leads to knowledge of physical life," for the novelist "it may also lead to knowledge of passional and intellectual life."[8] According to Zola "naturalist novelists" were, "in short, experimental moralists showing by experiment in what fashion a passion behaves in a social milieu."[9] Furthermore, Zola stresses the importance of both heredity and environment in determining "the intellectual and passional behavior of man."[10]

It has often been noted that Reade shared with Zola a commitment to the documentary method. W. C. Frierson notes that Reade was the "forerunner of Zola in the matter of documentation"[11] and R. M. Lovett and H. S. Hughes observe that Reade's method of documentation "reminds us that he belonged to a period influenced by the methods of science," and they, too, compare Reade and Zola in their common interest in social reform.[12] However, most critics deny that Reade's novels share any similarity of content or theme with those of Zola. Lewis F. Haines believes that the method of documentation is a superficial similarity and does "not signify any sympathy for or alignment with the so-called scientific methodology of contemporary naturalistic novelists as typified by Emile Zola."[13] Similarly, Winifred Hughes describes Reade's "passion for documentation" as "almost a parody version of the methods of Zola."[14] Although Hughes acknowledges that the "pioneering forays of Collins, Reade, and Braddon into forbidden territory served to open the way for the later development of naturalism,"[15] she does not explore in any detail this aspect of Reade's work.

However, a close reading of *Griffith Gaunt* demonstrates that, in fact, Reade moved much further toward naturalism than has been generally acknowledged and that he employed methods strikingly similar to those championed by Zola. Though Reade's novel by no means presents a fully developed deterministic cosmology, it does portray human beings as part of the natural order, subject to the same biological needs and animal instincts as the rest of the natural world, and it presents their actions as determined by their inherited personality traits and their particular circumstances. To reinforce this view, Reade, like most naturalistic writers, uses animal imagery extensively to describe his characters. Emerson Grant Sutcliffe notes that Reade "was prone to visualize and depict beings in terms of animal resemblances. Though the tendency was increased by *The Origin of Species,* instances occur in his stories before 1859."[16] Reade comments in one of his notebooks, "So many doubt whether man and beast have not a common origin. Read Darwin and the rest as well as the annals of animals."[17] Sutcliffe recognizes that Reade's characters "faintly foreshadow the denizens of the naturalistic fiction soon to be the vogue, in their likeness to animals and their obedience to instinct,"[18] but he does not see such imagery as central in Reade's work.

The instincts that drive Reade's characters in *Griffith Gaunt* are sexual passion and jealousy. Wayne Burns, however, argues that *Jealousy* is an inappropriate subtitle for *Griffith Gaunt*, contending that "jealousy does not, accurately speaking, constitute the theme or even the subject of the novel; at most it provides the titular hero with a 'humour' convenient for organizing the disparate elements of the action into a loose melodramatic plot."[19] On the contrary, in *Griffith Gaunt* Reade presents an extensive examination of the "passional" nature of men and women of quite different temperaments, each of whom experiences passionate jealousy in a distinctive way. In other words, Reade's novel reflects precisely the purpose of the naturalistic novel as Zola described it: *Griffith Gaunt* is Reade's "experiment in what fashion a passion behaves in a social milieu."

In *Griffith Gaunt*, Reade examines sexual passion and its kindred emotion, jealousy, through a series of triangular sexual relationships. Reade uses these sexual rivalries to demonstrate how easily people can succumb to their most basic animal instincts and to show how his characters are "the sport of circumstances," caught in what he calls "a chain of acts that look like crimes, but are, strictly speaking, consequences" (373). Furthermore, he emphasizes the importance of inherited personality traits, or what Zola would call "temperament," in determining the different ways in which individual characters respond to similar circumstances. For example, Reade contrasts the personalities of Griffith Gaunt and George Neville and the ways they express their jealous rivalry for the hand of Catharine Peyton; the personalities of Griffith Gaunt and Father Leonard and the ways they express their rivalry for the affection of Catharine Gaunt; and the personalities of Catherine and Mercy Vint and the ways they respond to their rivalry for Griffith's affection. In this treatment of human action as motivated by instinctual human drives, individual temperament, and particular circumstances, Reade clearly anticipates the methods of Zola and the American naturalistic novelists who were influenced by Zola, such as Frank Norris and Theodore Dreiser.

The three chief traits which inevitably determine Catharine Peyton's actions are her pride, her romanticized religious idealism, and her compassion. Because she is proud, Reade notes, she "carried herself a little too imperiously; yet she would sometimes relax and all but dissolve that haughty figure, and hang sweetly drooping over her favorites; then the contrast was delicious, and the woman fascinating" (231). When she looks at an admirer, she gives the impression that she is "thoughtfully overlooking him instead of looking at him." The result of such a gaze is that "a man feels small—and bitter" (231). Catharine, Reade says, had a "sweet, celestial, superior gaze, and for this and other imperial charms was more admired than liked" (231).

Reade makes clear that Catharine's pride finds its primary outlet in her zealous but romanticized religious idealism; she is "more enthusiastic in religion than in any earthly thing" (270). Though her idealism is sincere, her pride encourages her to be self-righteous and to seek martyrdom in self-sacrifice. In refusing Griffith's offer of marriage, she tells him that her "heart it bleeds for the Church. I think of her ancient glory in this kingdom, and, when I see her present condition, I long to devote myself to her service. I am very fit to be an abbess or a nun; most unfit to be a wife" (235).

Both pride and her romanticized view of religion lead Catharine to exaggerate her sinfulness, confessing that she is guilty of all the seven deadly sins. When her spiritual counselor and confessor, Father Francis, counters that her acts are only small sins, she declares proudly that "they are none of them small." Reade comments, "I really think she was jealous of her reputation as a sinner of high degree" (272). After her first confession to Father Leonard, he cuts through both her religious romanticism and her pride by saying, "My daughter, excuse me; but confession is one thing, gossip about ourselves is another." Father Leonard's "fine, but fatal" distinction has its effect, and when Catharine leaves the confessional, "her pride was mortified to the core" (299).

Though Catharine has a romanticized idea of religion, the compassion that underlies her religious zeal is authentic. Reade notes that she "was rather kind to the poor; would give them money out of her slender purse, and would even make clothes for the women" (231). She demonstrates her compassion in her unconventional approach to fox hunting. She loves the "gallant chase," "flying behind the foremost riders" and then "clear[ing] the ditch and its muddy contents" (232) that unseat the other riders. But when the dogs and hunters trap the fox in a grove, she watches as "the harassed fox stole out close to her, with lolling tongue and eye askant," and seeing "all the signs of his distress," she decides not to alert the other hunters and allows the fox to escape. She explains that she "pitied him; he was one, and we are many; he was so little, and we are so big; he had given us a good gallop; and so I made up my mind he should live to run another day" (233). The other hunters, who obviously have more conventional expectations of hunting, are understandably frustrated by Catharine's overly compassionate act.

Reade just as carefully paints the dominant character traits of Griffith Gaunt, making clear from the beginning that though Griffith is basically a good man, he has "a certain foible in his own character," the foible being that "he was instinctively disposed to run away from mental pain the moment he lost hope of driving it away from him" (235). Reade explains, "If Catharine had been ill and her life in danger, he would have ridden day and night to save her; but if she had died he would either have killed himself, or else fled the country" (235). Rather than condemn Griffith for this flaw in his character, Reade observes, "The mind, as well as the body, has its self-protecting instincts" (235).

Griffith's second character trait that Reade sees as the most significant influence on later actions is his violent jealousy. Though most of the other major characters of the novel also experience jealousy, they either sublimate it or use devious means to express it, but Griffith invariably explodes into rage. When Griffith encounters his rival, George Neville, Catharine "witness[es] the livid passion of jealousy writhing in every lineament" of Griffith's face, transforming it into "a face older, and discolored, and convulsed, and almost demoniacal" (237). Griffith tells Catharine that at the thought of her marrying George Neville, "my heart turns to ice, and then to fire; my head seems ready to burst, and my hands to do mad and bloody acts. Ay, I feel I should kill him, or you, or both, at the church porch" (237). Catharine, having seen this jealous rage, refuses for a time to marry him, saying, "I have often read of men with a passion for jealousy—I mean men whose jealousy feeds upon air, and defies reason. I know you now for such a man" (238).

George Neville is as passionate as Griffith in his pursuit of Catharine, with Reade noting that "the inflammable George made hot love" to Catharine, with "passion in every tone," that "he threw himself on his knees (custom of the day), and wooed her with . . . a burst of passionate and tearful eloquence . . ." (241). But George's temperament and experiences are quite different from Griffith's and lead him to respond to rejection without violence. For example, he has had a number of romantic experiences that "had given him fresh insight into the ways of woman," and so when he realizes he has a rival, he acts with restraint.

Catharine is at first unwilling to choose either Griffith or George, but Reade demonstrates that a change in circumstances can bring about a change in behavior. Thus when Catharine unexpectedly inherits estates that Griffith believed would come to him, she does the very thing she has determined not to do. Catharine admits over and over again that she does not really love Griffith enough to marry him, but she says, "if I don't quite love you, I like you too well to let you be unhappy. Besides I cannot bear to rob you of these unlucky farms" (288). Catharine's traits of character, along with the stroke of fortune that leaves her an heiress and Griffith almost destitute, lead her to marry Griffith against her better judgment.

As one might expect, Catharine is not happy in her marriage to Griffith because, though she has married in an act of self-sacrifice, the relationship does not satisfy her religious idealism. Thus, the new priest, Father Leonard, immediately threatens their covertly unstable relationship because for Catharine, he embodies that "something" absent in her husband. Catharine is drawn to him because he was, Reade says, "one of those ethereal priests the Roman Catholic Church produces every now and then. . . . This Brother Leonard looked and moved like a being who had come down from some higher sphere to pay the world a very little visit, and be very kind and patient with it all the time" (298). Leonard gives impetus to Catharine's pride, her self-righteousness, and her condescension toward her husband. In particular, Catharine sees an exaggerated difference between what she interprets as the spirituality of Father Leonard and the earthiness of her husband. Leonard also draws out her compassion. Because he seems "solitary and sad," she feels she "must take him under her wing" (305). The actions she undertakes in his behalf, though begun in admiration and pity, develop into sexual feelings that she does not foresee: "She had put her foot on a sunny slope clad with innocent looking flowers; but more and more precipitous at every step, and perdition at the bottom" (329).

Leonard has his own particular traits of character that make him susceptible to this sexual entanglement as well. Though he is "pious, pure, and noble-minded," he is "one of those high-strung men who pay for their periods of religious rapture by hours of melancholy" (305) and he also, "like many holy men, was vain" (317). Most importantly, Father Leonard has denied his sexuality by entering the priesthood. As Reade notes, Leonard "had undertaken to defy nature, with religion's aid" though "nature never intended him to live all his days alone" (327–28). Thus lonely and emotionally vulnerable, he is susceptible to Catharine's beauty, charm, and adoration.

Catharine and Leonard often meet in "the soft seducing twilight" (328) of a grove of trees called "The Dame's Haunt." Here Catharine's romanticism has free rein and, as Reade notes, it "was also a place well suited to the imaginative and religious mind" of Father Leonard (307). The grove allows Catharine's and Leonard's basic natural instincts to emerge. Here in the "calm solitude and umbrageous twilight," Catharine's "mind crept out of its cave, like wild and timid things at dusk," to acknowledge "that Leonard perhaps admired her more than was safe or prudent" (311). Indeed, Leonard falls in love with her before he realizes it. Reade explains that if Leonard could "have foreseen this, it would never have happened; he would have steeled himself, or left the country that contained this sweet temptation. But love stole on him, masked with religious zeal, and robed in a garment of light that seemed celestial" (328). Catharine is also sexually attracted to Leonard. Although she never acts on her passion, Reade uses a simple external physical gesture to reveal her inner psychological state: "Mrs. Gaunt, in the warmth of discourse, laid her hand lightly for a moment on the priest's elbow: . . . that delicate hand seemed to speak: it did not leave Leonard's elbow all at once, it glided slowly away—first the palm, then the fingers, and so parted lingerlingly" (316).

Because both Catharine and Leonard experience the warmth of sexual passion, they are also both vulnerable to the kindred emotion, jealousy. On one of several secret visits to Father Leonard's cottage Catharine discovers a woman's glove, and, not realizing the glove is her own, feels jealous of the unknown rival she assumes has left it. Reade describes this "strange feeling" that "traversed her heart for the first time in her life" as "a little chill, . . . a little ache, . . . a little sense of sickness" (308). Leonard, too, because he is jealous of Griffith, uses his position as Catharine's religious advisor and confessor to pry into her marital relationship. Distressed by a temporary reconciliation between Catharine and Griffith, he confesses his passion in "a cry of jealous agony, and then, in a torrent of burning, melting words, appealed to her pity" (329).

Unable to prevent Catharine from seeing Leonard, Griffith gradually begins to believe in his wife's infidelity, and when he finds her with Leonard alone in the grove, in a burst of jealous rage he throws Leonard to the ground and "literally trample[s]" him. Then yielding to his tendency to run away from pain, he cries, "I must go or kill" (337) and leaves the estate enraged.

This scene in the grove is a particularly good example of Reade's use of animal imagery to describe his characters. Griffith sets out to find his wife in the grove "like some beast of prey" (336); Catharine is "elastic as a young greyhound" (336) as she moves along talking softly to Leonard. When Griffith attacks Catharine and Leonard, he "uttered a yell like a tiger, and rushed between them with savage violence" (336) clutching Leonard's throat. After the attack Catharine attempts to return to the house "as naturally as a scared animal for its lair" (349), but before she can reach the house, she faints, and Caroline Ryder, Catharine's unfaithful maid who is secretly in love with Griffith, "watched her mistress like a lynx," and now bends over her "very like the hawk perched over and clawing the ring-dove she has struck down" (349).

From this point of the novel to the end, Reade's plot includes an increasing number of sensational elements, but those elements reinforce rather than undermine the novel as an example of naturalistic fiction. Donald Pizer draws this connection between naturalism and sensationalism:

> Naturalistic fiction . . . attracts many readers (while repelling others) because of its sensationalism. "Terrible things must happen to the characters of the naturalistic tale," Frank Norris wrote in 1896, and so it has been ever since. The sensationalism of naturalistic fiction, however—its violence and sexuality, for example—has an appeal which strikes deeper than the popular taste for the prurient and titillating. The extraordinariness of character and event in the naturalistic novel creates a potential for symbolism and allegory, since the combination of the concrete and the exceptional immediately implies meanings beyond the surface.[20]

Indeed, Reade uses extraordinary events throughout *Griffith Gaunt*, and in the final part of the novel he continues to examine various ways human beings experience jealousy, but at this point he focuses on the female rivals Catharine Gaunt and Mercy Vint.

After Griffith abandons Catharine and assumes the name of his gamekeeper, Thomas Leicester, he falls ill, to be nursed back to health by Mercy, the daughter of the innkeeper, and her suitor, Paul Carrick, "a young farrier." Almost immediately Griffith's jealousy shifts from Father Leonard to Paul Carrick and, though still married to Catharine, he soon finds himself in another triangular sexual relationship. Reade observes, "He was not in love with Mercy, but he esteemed her and liked her and saw her value, and, above all, could not bear another man should have her" (346). To defeat his new rival, Griffith marries Mercy, even though he commits bigamy in doing so.

This new set of circumstances allows Reade to demonstrate how Catharine and Mercy express jealousy in dramatically different ways. The women each learn of Griffith's bigamy through the real Thomas Leicester, who has become a traveling peddler. And by this time, the two women have even more reason to feel jealous and betrayed. Mercy has borne Griffith's child; and Catharine, temporarily reconciled with Griffith when he returns home on business matters, also has become pregnant by him. However, Mercy is a woman of "depth and strength of character" (347), "a soft-eyed Puritan, all unpretending dignity, grace, propriety, and sagacity" (395). Though she is deeply hurt by Griffith's duplicity, she, like George, does not react violently but "with a sort of deadly calm." She accepts the fact that though she loves Griffith, Catharine is his legal wife, and, "pale and trembling," she assures him, "I would not harm thy body, nor thy soul" (379).

On the other hand, Catharine, though she, as Griffith's legal wife, faces less humiliating circumstances than does Mercy, responds in a violent burst of jealousy and threatens Griffith's life. She becomes a "raging woman" who "in her fury, poured out a torrent of reproaches and threats that made [Griffith's] blood run cold" (385). Griffith secretly runs back to Mercy, but when a badly decomposed body is discovered in the pond on the Gaunts' estate, the authorities assume it is Griffith, arrest Catharine, and put her on trial for his murder.

Although Mercy intervenes to save her rival, Catharine, rather than feeling gratitude, hates Mercy, and because, as she says, "Human nature is human nature," believes Mercy hates her, too. But Mercy is not susceptible to violent emotions and in words echoing George's letter to Catharine declares, "I hate you not; and I thank God for it. To hate is to be miserable" (419). She testifies that Griffith Gaunt is alive and that the recovered body must be the peddlar, thus saving her rival from execution.

By contrasting Mercy and Catharine's behavior, Reade illustrates his belief that individual differences in personality or temperament rather than individual morality determine the ways in which a person responds to circumstances. Furthermore, because Griffith, George, Leonard, Mercy, and Catharine each act out of their own nature, Reade does not judge them. Indeed, Reade refuses to condemn even Griffith's bigamous marriage to Mercy, noting that the union is "one of those gentle, clinging attachments that outlast grand passions, and survive till death; a tender, pure affection, though built upon a crime" (356). Though Victorian society would have judged Mercy as a fallen woman, Reade asserts that Griffith's "unlawful wife had hitherto done nothing but improve his character" (373). And though Griffith may have committed acts that Victorian society would see as crimes, Reade makes clear that Griffith remains morally innocent: "This man, blinded at first by his own foible, and after that the sport of circumstances, was single-hearted by nature; and his conscience was not hardened. He desired earnestly to free himself and both his wives from the cruel situation; but to do this, one of them, he saw, must be abandoned entirely; and his heart bled for her" (373).

Indeed, Reade does not mete out punishment to any of the characters as a consequence of their errors. Throughout the novel all the characters respond to the circumstances in which they find themselves by acting in ways consistent with the traits of character that Reade has delineated. No matter what errors his characters commit, Reade sees them as morally guiltless and thus resolves the plot to the benefit of all the characters. Ultimately Griffith reunites with Catharine and, because he saves her life through a miraculous blood transfusion, rekindles her love for him. Reade comments, "She only wanted a good excuse for loving him as frankly as before, and now he had given her one" (432). At the same time George Neville marries Mercy Vint, whom he has come to admire and love. Even Father Leonard, though he "fell in love with his neighbor's wife," is excused for his mistake since he was "but a boy . . . fresh from his seminary, . . . without a grain of common sense" (366). Thus, even the fallen priest does not merit punishment and simply leaves England to pursue his priestly vocation far away from Catharine.

Reade's interest in writing about "sensational" events that he documented from real life and his belief that characters who are the "sport of circumstances" can still maintain their human nobility and act heroically foreshadow fundamental ideas of naturalism. Pizer points out these tensions in the naturalists' view of the world and of the characters who inhabit it. Like Reade, the naturalist, Pizer says, focuses realistically on the everyday world, but at the same time finds the unusual in the everyday. The naturalist

> discovers in this world those qualities of man usually associated with the heroic or adventurous, such as acts of violence and passion, involving sexual adventure or bodily strength, which culminate in desperate moments and violent death. . . . But he also suggests a compensating humanistic value in his characters or their fates which affirms the significance of the individual and of his life.[21]

Griffith Gaunt succeeds as a serious artistic effort because it is both a sensation novel and a naturalistic novel. The events which take place may be "colorful" and the characters may behave in ways that violate conventional Victorian social norms, but neither the events nor the characters are unrealistic. In his notebooks, Reade documented many "sensational" incidents that really happened and recorded details about many real men and women who acted in unconventional ways. The sensational incidents that have been the focus of most criticism of the novel are not present simply to titillate the reader. On the contrary, they illustrate the importance of human nature, individual temperament, and circumstances in determining human action and reveal Reade's faith in man's ability to act heroically anyway. *Griffith Gaunt* thus represents Reade's own experimental novel that reflects the emerging literary movement of the last decades of the nineteenth century and prepares the way for a more fully developed naturalism.

NOTES

1. Charles Reade, *Griffith Gaunt,* in vol. 7 of *The Works of Charles Reade, A New Edition in Nine Volumes, Illustrated with One Hundred and Twelve Full-Page Wood Engravings* (Peter Fenelon Collier, [1895?]). All references to the novel will be from this edition, and page numbers will be indicated in the text.

2. Charles L. Reade and Compton Reade, in *Charles Reade . . . : A Memoir,* 297, report that when Reade was complimented on *The Cloister and the Hearth* as being his best novel, "the author's eye flooded indignation, and he told his eulogist, then and there, that if that was his opinion, he was only fit for a lunatic asylum."

3. Although Charles Dickens objected strongly to the sexual content in *Griffith Gaunt* that he considered "extremely coarse and disagreeable," he nevertheless described it as "a work of a highly accomplished writer . . . ; a writer with a brilliant fancy and a graceful and tender imagination." Quoted in Malcom Elwin, *Charles Reade: A Biography,* 188–89.

4. Henry James, *Notes and Reviews* (1921), 207.
5. Wayne Burns, *Charles Reade: A Study in Victorian Authorship,* 13.
6. Arthur Pollard, "*Griffith Gaunt:* Paradox of Victorian Melodrama," 221.
7. Émile Zola, "Naturalism in the Theatre," 200–1.
8. Émile Zola, "The Experimental Novel," 162–63.
9. Ibid., 179, 177.
10. Ibid., 173. Zola declares, "Without risking the formulation of laws, I believe that the question of heredity has a great influence in the intellectual and passional behavior of man. I also accord a considerable importance to environment. Here it would be necessary first to consider Darwin's theories; but this is only a general study of the experimental method as applied to the novel, and I would be lost if I tried to go into detail."
11. William Coleman Frierson, *The English Novel in Transition, 1885–1940,* 9.
12. R. M. Lovett and H. S. Hughes, *The History of the Novel in England,* 245–46.
13. Lewis F. Haines, "Reade, Mill, and Zola: A Study of the Character and Intention of Charles Reade's Realistic Method," 480.
14. Winifrid Hughes, *The Maniac in the Cellar: Sensation Novels of the 1860s,* 75.
15. Ibid., 190.
16. Emerson Grant Sutcliffe, "Psychological Presentation in Reade's Novels," 537.
17. Quoted in Sutcliffe, 537.
18. Ibid., 542.
19. Burns, 264.
20. Donald Pizer, *Twentieth-Century American Naturalism: An Interpretation,* x–xi.
21. Pizer, 3.

- 7 -

SWEDENBORG AND THE DISINTEGRATION OF LANGUAGE IN SHERIDAN LE FANU'S SENSATION FICTION

DEVIN P. ZUBER

WHILE NOT as successful or famous as Wilkie Collins or Mary Elizabeth Braddon, the Anglo-Irish author Joseph Sheridan Le Fanu (1814–1873) made invaluable contributions to the sensation novel. Both David Puntner and Neil Cornwell have argued that Le Fanu instigated a new way of writing about psychological terror which moved the sensation form toward the symbolist novel and the later work of Henry James.[1] Le Fanu himself seemed to feel that something set his work apart from his peers. In his most famous novel, *Uncle Silas: A Tale of Bartram-Haugh* (1864), Le Fanu attempted to shirk the label of sensation altogether, pleading in the preface for critics to "limit that degrading term" and rather consider *Uncle Silas* as "part of the legitimate school of English romance" in line with Walter Scott's canonical work.[2] And yet with its secret murders, sexually charged undertones of incest, and *doppelgänger* doubles, *Uncle Silas* contained the classic ingredients of what made sensation so popular. Some modern critics have tried to argue that these elements warrant Le Fanu's categorization as an extension of the Gothic historical tradition, but the major authorities on sensation—such as Patrick Brantlinger—concur that Le Fanu indeed participated in the genre, whether he liked it or not.[3] It was certainly as a "sensationalist" that Le Fanu was read and received—his reviewers frequently hailed him as "the Irish Wilkie Collins," and Geraldine Jewsbury tantalizingly promised *Athenaeum* subscribers how "the reader will be frightened at his own shadow when he goes to bed" after finishing *Uncle Silas*.[4] As Nicholas Rance has further shown, Le Fanu's London publisher, Richard Bentley, pressured Le Fanu to make *Uncle Silas* recognizably "English" (rather than Irish) and set exclusively in "modern" times so it would be more like the contemporaneous themes in Collins and Braddon, and thus explicitly marketable as sensation fiction to British readers.[5]

Twentieth-century criticism has amplified how this suppressed Irish past came to haunt Le Fanu's work. Le Fanu stands today as a fascinating cultural hybrid in the sensation canon, writing from the margins of Anglo-Irish Dublin, and his ambivalence toward the sensation label, with the roots of that term affixed to metropolitan London, are partially explained by his conflicted political and cultural identity. Commentators both past and present have also noted something else marking Le Fanu as different and other, distinguishing him from the English sensationalists: a repetitive reference to the works of the Scandinavian mystic Emanuel Swedenborg (1688–1772). While unfamiliar to most readers today, by the 1860s Swedenborg's eighteenth-century works on symbolic correspondence and spiritual worlds had influenced authors as diverse as Coleridge, Balzac, and Barrett Browning. Swedenborg's name accordingly surfaces in sensation fiction in wider contexts of Rosicrucianism, Masonic orders, and other esoteric circles, but nowhere to the same degree and extent that his ideas appear in Le Fanu. Rather than simply allude to the Swedish mystic to hint at the occult, as Collins or Dickens had done, Swedenborg is intimately part of Le Fanu's creation of complex characters whose identities are bound to the slippages and failures of language. These failures, in turn, relate to the crises of identity that Le Fanu's Anglo-Irish class increasingly faced in the latter half of the nineteenth century. Without Swedenborg's theory of correspondence or his notion of influx from a spiritual world, Le Fanu could not have uncannily anticipated post-structural work on linguistics and hybrid identity, nor would Le Fanu's oeuvre be theorized as critically important for moving the gothic mode away from clanking chains and clichéd ghosts toward a subjectivity of the self, where the true terrors of the night are the uncertainties of one's own mind.

Although Le Fanu began incorporating Swedenborgian ideas in his short stories as early as 1851, it is the later sensation novellas that make up the collection *In a Glass Darkly* (1872) and *Uncle Silas* that most clearly demonstrate Le Fanu's genius for adapting Swedenborg. *Uncle Silas* is narrated by a young heiress named Maud Ruthyn and the plot hinges on unsolved murders and the dispossession of her large inheritance. The action claustrophobically unfolds in two mansion estates, one owned by Maud's father and the other by her mysterious Uncle Silas, a religious visionary addicted to opium. A limited number of characters cross into the closed worlds of these mansions, further distinguishing Le Fanu's novel from the broader scope of sensationalists whose plots freely rove the extent of the British Empire. Maud in *Uncle Silas* is permitted no egress like the characters in Collins's *The Moonstone* (who crisscross between India and England), and her entrapment on the estates is mirrored on a hermeneutic level of the text by its circular use of Swedenborgian ideas. Not a single character is untouched by a dizzying reduplication of allusions to the mystic. Maud reads Swedenborg's *Heaven and Hell* (published in 1758) at several points, as does her absentminded father.

An unnamed acquaintance of Maud's father's relates to her a parable of Swedenborg's spiritual world that terrifies her when her mother dies. Maud's diabolical governess, Madam Rougierre, is another Swedenborg reader, and her scheming wicked uncle Silas hypocritically pontificates to Maud that the "affections are eternal; and being so, celestial, divine, and consequently happy, deriving happiness, bestowing it" (396). Here Silas parrots a section from *Heaven and Hell* titled "Heavenly Joy and Happiness" in which Swedenborg writes of eternal joy as a celestial "affection of innumerable delights."[6]

Furthermore, all the major male characters of *Uncle Silas* dress like Swedenborg, as if his personal identity had been fractured and dispersed through the text. When the novel opens, the reader joins Maud watching her father in "a loose, black velvet coat" pace the floor of his remote mansion, appearing and disappearing into shadows (13). The gentle-but-ugly Dr. Bryerly, in turn, is "a lean figure sheathed in shining black cloth" (32), and when Maud finally meets Uncle Silas in the second volume, "he rose, tall and slight, a little stooped, all in black, with an ample black velvet tunic, which was rather a gown than a coat" (200). In a novel that is sparse on the details of clothing, this recurrence of black velvet is more than coincidence or a comment on Victorian fashion. Swedenborg's prodigal life had evoked much curiosity and interest by midcentury, and well before the composition of *Uncle Silas* numerous biographies and sketches of Swedenborg's unusual life had been circulating through Europe. Typically featured were accounts of how Swedenborg, whenever invited out, wore some sort of black velvet jacket—which became one of the only graphic details of Swedenborg's attire that nineteenth-century biographers had at their disposal.[7] While it cannot be ascertained if Le Fanu actually read any of this biographical material, his broad references to different parts of the twelve-volume *Arcana Caelestia* (1749–56) demonstrate the scope and time he devoted to Swedenborg. Besides the *Arcana* and *Heaven and Hell*, Le Fanu seems to have also been familiar with Swedenborg's scientific work *Regnum Animale* (1744–45), published in English as *The Animal Kingdom* (1843–44). The medical-like prologues from *In a Glass Darkly* that clinically discuss "openings of the internal sense" are particularly reminiscent of this work.

As if the velvet jacket echoes were not enough, the Swedenborgian doctor in *Uncle Silas* has a highly indicative name: Emmanuel Bryerly. By changing Swedenborg's Emanuel to Bryerly's Emmanuel (with two *m*'s), Le Fanu misspells language while suggesting the past, a characteristic trope that runs through most of his fiction. Sir Wynston Berkeley in the short story "The Evil Guest," for example, brings to mind the Irish philosopher George Berkely (no *e*), and the Wycherly in *A Lost Name* (1868) clearly evokes the dramatist William Wycherley (an *e* added). According to W. J. McCormack, this serial repetition of language and history creates a "prison house of names" that breaks down identity itself—language becomes "not the purpose designed playground of an integral Self, but an autonomous, arbitrary and necessarily ambiguous medium in which self itself is repeatedly translated, rewritten, silenced, disengendered and disinterred."[8] Emmanuel's "Bryerly" thus unearths echoes of "Beyer," the surname of an early Swedenborgian who achieved notoriety in 1769 when he was tried for heresy by the Swedish Lutheran Church in Gothenburg.[9] Like the actual Dr. Gabriel Beyer, Le Fanu's Swedenborgian doctor is suspected of heretical belief by the orthodox Anglicans of Maud's household.

Contemporary critics of *Uncle Silas* did not miss these unsubtle gestures toward the Swedish mystic. Jewsbury wrote in her *Athenaeum* review that "the use which the author makes of Swedenborgian tenets is very clever" and the scenes which invoke Swedenborg "serve to shadow forth the struggle between [Maud's] guardian angel and her evil genius, which is, in fact, the key-note underlying and pervading the whole story."[10] Jewsbury's comment reflects the way that Le Fanu uses Swedenborg's statements that each person is continually accompanied by spirits, invisible to the natural eye, who open and close associations to communities in heaven and hell. While the idea of angels or spirits who "keep watch" over individuals is nothing new, Swedenborg radically suggested that the ubiquitous presence of such spirits was deeply interwoven into human identity, into the functions of memory and language. The first quote below comes from *Heaven and Hell*, the second, from the *Arcana*; both works are referred to throughout Le Fanu's later fiction:

> When spirits come into us, they come into our whole memory and from there into all our thinking—evil spirits into the matters of memory and thought that are evil, and good spirits into the matters of memory and thought that are good. These spirits are totally unaware that they are with us. Rather, as long as they are, they believe that all these matters of our memory and thought are actually theirs. (292)

Swedenborg roots this connection between spirits and man—this unsettling mutual space of shared memories—into systems of language:

> Another spirit too imagined that he was myself. He was so sure of it that he believed, when he talked to me in my native tongue, that he was using his own; for he said that that language was his. But he was shown that the language proper to spirits is entirely different and that it is the universal language of all languages. He was shown that ideas flow from that language into my own native tongue, so that *spirits do not speak independently but within me.*[11]

Thus, if all memory and language were open to other beings in a way that their identities were blurred—that such spirits would believe our memories were actually theirs—Swedenborg's spiritual world could present a challenge to the notion of a coherent, autonomous self. This destabilization resonates with postmodern ideas about identity, particularly those of Jacques Derrida. In his landmark essay, "Freud and the Scene of Writing," Derrida conceives of the mind as a text constantly visited by a doubling of language that represses memory: an inscription from stimuli of infinite traces—a "perpetually available innocence"—and a simultaneous repetitive writing of these traces to create the *différance* necessary for signification. "Writing," thus, for the mind-as-text, "is unthinkable without repression."[12]

In his most famous short story, "Green Tea" (1869), Le Fanu uses Swedenborg to explore the role of language in forming the self, and the dangerous consequences if Swedenborg's boundary between spirits and the individual were effaced. Its plot revolves around the Reverend Jennings, a reclusive Anglican scholar who has become plagued by visions of a demonic monkey that no one else can see. Jennings turns to the story's narrator for help, a German doctor of metaphysical tendencies named Martin Hesselius. While exploring Jennings's library, Hesselius discovers that the reverend has marked out numerous passages from Swedenborg's *Arcana Caelestia*, including one that states "if evil spirits could perceive that they were associated with man, and yet that they were spirits separated from him . . . they would attempt by a thousand means to destroy him; for they hate man with a deadly hatred."[13] Jennings's tormenting monkey operates as either a psychic hallucination or as one of Swedenborg's evil spirits made manifest; the narrative remains open to both interpretations. At the end of the story, Dr. Hesselius fails to exorcize the monkey from Jennings who resolves his despair by committing suicide. Jennings's last presence in the text takes the form of a wild note written which curiously suggests a dissolution of the self, an unraveling of character in language as his identity becomes subsumed to the presence of the ominous monkey—an anonymous "it" that also expresses the return of Derrida's repressed:

> DEAR DR. HESSELIUS: It is here. You had not been an hour gone when it returned. It is speaking. It knows all that has happened. . . . It reviles. I send you this. It knows every word I have written—I write. This I promised, and I therefore write, but I fear very confused, very incoherently. I am so interrupted, disturbed. (29)

Maud's father in *Uncle Silas* is also a reclusive reader of Swedenborg, and while Austin Ruthyn does not hallucinate or commit suicide, he is often depicted as being on the borders between shadows and light, reappearing and disappearing from Maud's view as if he hovered between a natural and spiritual world. The chapter titles also use ghostly sounding language, from "Dr. Bryerly Emerges" and "Dr. Bryerly Reappears" to Madame Rougierre's return in "An Apparition." But Madame Rougierre is no ghost, and Dr. Bryerly and Maud's father cannot vanish into spiritual worlds. The only uncanny aspect about these characters and their comings and goings is the suggestive words that frame them. Like the Reverend Jennings's letter in "Green Tea" that betrays a loss of self-coherence and an otherworldly presence intruding into a personal text, Swedenborg's spiritual world in *Uncle Silas* makes itself most present within the effects of language, rather than as concrete supernatural visions. The novel is replete with voices that speak from elsewhere, particularly from the fringes of Maud's mind when it is besieged by terror. After Maud has been removed to her uncle's estate, she is torn with anxiety over whether her uncle is plotting against her (as she increasingly dreads) or whether he is truly innocent and rather wrongly maligned by society (as her father had firmly believed). After gazing at pictures of ferocious wolves and an engraving of Van Dyke's picture of Belisarius, Maud hears a stern whisper in her ear—"Fly the fangs of Belisarius!" Maud nervously tries to attribute this to her imagination, especially as no one else in the room hears the voice, "yet to this hour," she writes, "I could recognize that stern voice among a thousand, were it to speak again" (355). This disembodied voice that speaks against imminent danger strikes an immediate resonance with a moment in "Carmilla," Le Fanu's later vampire tale from *In a Glass Darkly*. There, the young narrator, Laura, is also in grave danger, and hears an unknown voice "sweet and tender, and at the same time terrible, which said, 'Your mother warns you to beware of the assassin'" (268). The theme of lonely, isolated characters who are startled by unfamiliar voices that well up within themselves likely reflects Le Fanu's reading of a particular passage from Swedenborg's *Heaven and Hell* where "people who lead solitary lives sometimes hear spirits talking with them . . . people who are constantly thinking about religious matters, so wrapped up in them that they practically see them within themselves, also begin to hear spirits talking with them" (249). After the death of Maud's mother, we are told how Austin Ruthyn closeted himself from society to exclusively study Swedenborg's theology. While the narrative never delves into Austin's mind, Maud informs the reader that he has a habit acquired from his "solitude and silence" of assuming that the context of his invisible thoughts was "legible" to others, as if they were a text, and unexpectedly commenting on them out loud. He also disturbs Maud in a conversation when "he looked round, but we were alone. The garden was nearly always solitary . . ." (112). The novel may not directly evince Austin Ruthyn hearing voices from the spiritual world, but after his death he seems to become such a disembodied voice. When Maud decides to disobey her father's will by staying away from Uncle Silas, she imagines her dead father's face "hanging in cadaverous folds, always with the same expression of diabolical fury." Maud is torn by guilt over her disobedience, and after falling into a worn-out sleep she "distinctly heard papa's voice" commanding her to go to her uncle's estate (179).

The closing words of *Uncle Silas* sound like a prayer from Maud to better comprehend these otherworldly voices. She writes:

This world is a parable—the habitation of symbols—the phantoms of spiritual things immortal shown in material shape. May the blessed second-sight be mine—to recognize under these beautiful forms of earth the angels who wear them; for I am sure we may walk with them if we will, and hear them speak. (444)

These words are a direct evocation of passages in Swedenborg's *Heaven and Hell* that concern language and correspondence, and the duality between the spiritual and natural that Maud refers to permeates her entire experience in the novel. Very often the architecture or landscape she beholds symbolically reflects her state of mind, whether it be a "sympathy" she feels toward gloomy storms, or a ravaged and wild landscape streaked with beautiful silver trees that evokes for the reader descriptions of her Uncle Silas's ruined mind, crowned with silver hair, shot through with moments of brilliance. This standard deployment of literary symbols is made more specifically Swedenborgian when the novel applies the "correspondence" of Maud's interior state onto other characters around her. One of Swedenborg's distinctions within Neoplatonism and theories of typology was his rendering not only of landscape spiritually symbolic, but every quotidian aspect of nature as reflective of a higher human state. "In a word," says *Heaven and Hell*, "absolutely everything in nature, from the smallest to the greatest, is a correspondence" (106). This is seen in Swedenborg's particular exegesis of Genesis and Revelation that reads persons and places as both symbolic "churches" and states of individual mentalities; its frequent invocation by Le Fanu reinforces the curious refraction of Maud's identity out onto her cousin, Milly, and the wild girl who lives on her uncle's estate, Meg. Here again, Le Fanu is playing with language and identity in the proliferation of "m" names that links these characters into a sort of orthographic triptych. Shortly after Maud arrives at Bartram-Haugh, her cousin comes to visit her and closely inspects her physical appearance. Milly and Maud look strikingly alike: both have the same color hair, the same shade of eyes, only Milly appears as a sort of comical, grotesque inversion of the more refined narrator, with dresses that are far too short for her plump legs. Both have grown up secluded from society on remote estates, with eccentric fathers who dabble in Swedenborgianism, and both have suffered from an absence of mothers. Milly is much more the country bumpkin than Maud due to her lack of formal education, and one of Maud's chief projects becomes to make her cousin a better person, teaching her etiquette and language skills. If Milly corresponds to an aspect of Maud's psyche, it would seem to be as a representation of what Maud's will and self-determination can accomplish. While Maud fails to establish full agency for herself, often lapsing into the stereotypical Gothic heroine who swoons and becomes paralyzed with horror, she does take a dynamic role in improving Milly's character.

A more serious representation of Maud is found in Meg, the daughter of Pegtop Dickon, one of Silas's wicked servants. While Meg looks nothing like Maud or Milly—she has "sooty black hair" and a face "swarthy as a gypsy's"—she shares the experience of growing up in seclusion without a mother (209). Meg more particularly functions as a metonym for the violence that threatens Maud. Uncle Silas ultimately plans to drive an iron spike through Maud's head after drugging her to sleep, an intention to which Maud remains oblivious until the denouement of the novel. As Maud begins to become slightly suspicious that something is not right with Silas, she witnesses Meg being viciously beaten by a drunken Pegtop Dickon in the forest, hit so hard in the head with his cudgel that she drops to the ground, unconscious. Immediately thereafter, when Maud sees her Uncle Silas, he says honeyed words of paternal reassurance, bends over Maud and kisses her forehead. This is one of the only scenes where Silas physically touches his niece. The particular placement of his cloying kiss on Maud's body links both backward to Meg's smashed and bloodied forehead, and forward toward Silas's plan to violently penetrate Maud's skull with a stake.

To read Meg and Milly as split aspects of Maud's character is to also acknowledge the classic double that haunts sensation fiction. Winifred Hughes writes that sensation novels "reveal a recurrent preoccupation with the loss or duplication of identity . . . everywhere in the lesser sensation novels the unwitting protagonists experience their strange encounters with the empty form of the *doppelganger*."[14] The most famous example of such doublings is perhaps the climactic moment in Wilkie Collins's *The Woman in White* (1860), where Laura discovers her own name on a tombstone that has been falsely erected for her. For Le Fanu, the symmetrical nature of Swedenborg's correspondences would seem to strengthen this genre tendency, and perhaps push it further. As Swedenborg's correspondence imparts the possibility of a double meaning latent behind everything, Maud's *doppelgängers* are not "empty forms," as Hughes terms it, but full of significance for much to which she remains oblivious. What is most strange about *Uncle Silas* is Maud's inability to correctly read such symbols and correspondences, especially in light of her closing prayer to let "the blessed second sight be mine." She consistently fails to accurately perceive the dangers to her life, to see herself represented in Meg, just as she fails to recognize the goodness of Dr. Bryerly, despite his unattractive appearance. The claustrophobic network of allusions to Swedenborg attune the reader to the symbolic nature of the text—that we are, as Maud acknowledges, in a world that is like a parable—but the signs and signified remain detached within her mind, and left up to the reader to thread together.

While Maud may pray to hear the language of angels as Swedenborg once did, earlier in the novel his *Heaven and Hell* profoundly unsettles her. In a rare moment of present-tense narration, Maud informs the reader that she tried to read the text but "grew after a day or two so nervous" that she had to lay it aside (24). The Reverend Jennings expresses similar anxiety in "Green Tea," stammering to Hesselius that he thinks Swedenborg "is rather likely to make a solitary man nervous" (12).

Thus while Swedenborg's correspondence consistently provides Le Fanu's characters with a symbolic framework to map out their interiority, these characters' nervous failures also disturbingly indicate a collapse of identity, a reduction of the self to the bare rudiments of language. Jennings's dissolvement into the chaos of a fragmented note, the floating disembodied voices of *Uncle Silas* that Maud fails to heed, the proliferation of spelling games that Le Fanu layers atop his characters' names—with all these aspects, it is as if history and the social space have been emptied into the shells of grammar and syntax, where only the surface of language remains to make order out of senseless situations. In particular, Le Fanu's serial repetition of historically allusive names—Bryerly echoing the Swedenborgian Gabriel Beyer, for example—anxiously bears out Michel Foucault's proposition that the nineteenth century witnessed a widespread disintegration of language as a stable system of representation. Foucault writes, using words that aptly capture Le Fanu's oeuvre, that in this paradigm shift,

> Language as the spontaneous tabula, the primary grid of things as an indispensable link between representations and things, is eclipsed in turn; a profound historicity penetrates into the heart of things . . . and, above all, language loses its privileged position and becomes, in its turn, a historical form coherent with the density of its own past.[15]

Ultimately, Le Fanu's unstable language seems best contextualized within Ireland's national and cultural crises of identity, especially the fierce Gaelic and English debates that later fueled the energies of the Irish Renaissance. Furthermore, while works like "Green Tea" and *Uncle Silas* may be set in England, their topoi of destructive isolation and rural violence directly reflect Le Fanu's own harsh experiences growing up in western Ireland. Le Fanu had watched his father (an Anglican rector) become disenfranchised by Catholic nationalists, and more than once the stones thrown by angry peasant mobs near the family house in County Limerick had endangered the lives of Le Fanu's siblings and cousins.[16] On a certain level, Swedenborg's uncanny placement of a spiritual world inside the natural world mirrored the Le Fanu family's own dual existence in two conflicting realms, the Anglo and the Irish, and the devastating effects of having these worlds irrupt into each other in his fiction could reflect Le Fanu's own difficulty in negotiating his hybrid identity. The symbolic fixity of Swedenborg's correspondence may have further answered nostalgia for political and spiritual order, for a time when cultural signification was not so quickly shifting and changing.

With all its complexity, Le Fanu's work anticipates later developments in fiction that grew out of the sensation and gothic tradition. Elizabeth Bowen was one of the first to argue that "*Uncle Silas* was in advance of its time . . . it is not the last, belated Gothic romance but the first (or among the first) of the psychological thrillers."[17] As symbols of characters' psychological interiors, the layers of correspondence that flow around Maud or manifest themselves in the monkey of "Green Tea" looks toward Jung and Freud's work on dreams and the subconscious. Le Fanu's incorporation of Swedenborg's otherworldly epistemology also creates characters who are so intertwined with the physical surfaces of language that they are ripe objects of study for post-structuralist theories on linguistics and identity. Le Fanu's characters are embedded in the sort of world depicted by Ferdinand de Saussure, who posited that language always functions in a self-referential manner that has no intrinsically natural relation to an external reality outside the text. Joseph Sheridan Le Fanu is thus not only important for understanding the permutation of the gothic from the *Mysteries of Udolpho* (1794) to the sophisticated ambiguities of *Turn of the Screw* (1898), but his work continues to strike many readers as peculiarly modern. This resonance depends on the ways in which Le Fanu was able to adapt Swedenborg's ideas to the framework of sensation fiction and beyond.

NOTES

1. David Punter, *The Literature of Terror*, 236, and Neil Cornwell, *The Literary Fantastic*, 94.
2. Joseph Sheridan Le Fanu, *Uncle Silas: A Tale of Bartram-Haugh*, (Penguin, 2000), 3–4. All future references are to this edition and cited by page in the text.
3. Patrick Brantlinger uses Le Fanu to illustrate that "sensation" and "gothic" can occasionally be indistinguishable terms; however, his statement that Le Fanu allows the "supernatural" to dominate over the realistic is misleading, and ignores the secular tone that permeates *Uncle Silas*. Patrick Brantlinger, "What Is 'Sensational' about the Sensation Novel?" 8.
4. Geraldine Jewsbury, "New Novels," 16–17.
5. Nicholas Rance, *Wilkie Collins and Other Sensation Novelists*, 157.
6. Emanuel Swedenborg, *Heaven and Hell*, 413. All future references are cited by paragraph number in the text; the numbers follow the tradition of Swedenborg scholarship whereby all references are to Swedenborg's paragraphs, and not page numbers.
7. For a complete list of nineteenth-century biographies on Swedenborg, see the appendix in James Hyde, *A Bibliography of the Works of Emanuel Swedenborg*. For an account of Swedenborg's velvet attire, see Sigstedt, *The Swedenborg Epic*, 363–65.
8. W. J. McCormack, *Dissolute Characters*, 156.
9. Cyriel Sigstedt, *The Swedenborg Epic*, 387–409.
10. Jewsbury, "New Novels," 16.
11. My emphasis added; Swedenborg, *Arcana Caelestia*, 6199.
12. Jacques Derrida, *Writing and Difference*, 225.

13. Le Fanu, *In a Glass Darkly* (Wordsworth Limited Editions, 1995), 10. All future references are to this edition and cited by page in the text.

14. Winifred Hughes, *The Maniac in the Cellar*, 21.

15. Michel Foucault, "The Order of Things," 383.

16. See the memoirs by Le Fanu's brother, William R. Le Fanu, *Seventy Years of Irish Life*, 63–65.

17. Elizabeth Bowen, *Collected Impressions*, 6.

- PART TWO -
Sensational Representations of Corporeality, Gender, and Sexuality

The following essays focus on portrayals of gender and sexuality. Tamar Heller discusses Rhoda Broughton's decision to resist contemporary standards of female beauty and decorum in *Not Wisely but Too Well*, arguing for the novel's place among canonical feminist novels. Galia Ofek, focusing on the many references to women's hair in sensation fiction and in contemporary critical responses to it, identifies and contextualizes this fetishization in the novels of Braddon and Collins, as well as in lesser-known works. Looking also to nineteenth-century discourses for new insight into sensation fiction, Andrew Mangham uses medical treatises to identify dangerous masculine impulses in *The Woman in White*. Richard Fantina explores a wide range of Charles Reade's work to highlight transgressive sexuality, specifically cross-dressing characters and homoerotic desire. Both Nancy Welter and Lindsay Faber examine relationships between women with Welter finding an incongruous complementarity in Le Fanu's vampire tale "Carmilla," and Rossetti's "Goblin Market" and Faber focusing on sisterly rivalry in Broughton's *Cometh Up as a Flower*. Jennifer Swartz discusses the issue of women's property and Collins's reading of the law of coverture in *The Moonstone*.

- 8 -

"THAT MUDDY, POLLUTED FLOOD OF EARTHLY LOVE"

Ambivalence about the Body in Rhoda Broughton's Not Wisely but Too Well

TAMAR HELLER

THE UNMARRIED, twenty-six-year-old daughter of a clergyman, Rhoda Broughton burst upon the literary scene in 1867 with the publication of her first two novels, *Cometh Up as a Flower* and *Not Wisely but Too Well*. Portraying unconventional young women whose passion drives them to the brink of adultery, both works were classified as sensation fiction. So risqué was Broughton's work considered that when her uncle Joseph Sheridan Le Fanu, who had serialized *Not Wisely but Too Well* in the *Dublin University Magazine,* sent the manuscript to the London publishing firm Bentley's, their reader, Geraldine Jewsbury, indignantly rejected it. Despite being written and serialized before *Cometh Up as a Flower,* then, *Not Wisely but Too Well* was published in volume form only after the *succès de scandale* of the second novel. (Substituted for the rejected manuscript as supposedly more decorous, *Cometh Up* still provoked shocked—and sales-boosting—outcry.)[1] Although not all reviews of Broughton's sensation fiction were negative, she was nonetheless associated with the aspect of sensationalism its critics found especially disturbing, an increased candor about female desire on the part of women writers. In a famous diatribe in 1867, Margaret Oliphant singled out the recently published *Cometh Up* as an example of female sensationalism at its most pernicious: "It is a shame to women so to write; and it is a shame to the women who read and accept as a true representation of themselves and their ways the equivocal talk and fleshly inclinations herein attributed to them."[2]

My focus in this essay will be the erotic sensationalism[3] of *Not Wisely but Too Well,* called by Jewsbury in her scathing reader's report "the most thoroughly sensual tale I have read in English for a long time."[4] As Broughton's first novel, *Not Wisely* deserves attention for defining the most innovative feature of Broughton's sensation fiction: a detailed, ideologically complex depiction of the female body and its desires. Dwelling on heroine Kate Chester's luscious, Titian-like form, Broughton challenges Victorian discourses that deny female appetite. At the same time, however, the narrative is ideologically double-voiced, celebrating Kate's exuberant fleshiness on one hand but, on the other, making her do penance for her transgressive desire. Madly in love with the dangerous aristocrat Dare Stamer, Kate is ready to elope with him before she finds out he is already married. After vainly trying to forget him by doing charitable work under the aegis of a young clergyman, she nearly runs off with Dare again, but, rescued from the verge of fallenness by her new sponsor, eventually decides to become a Protestant Sister of Mercy. In the original serialization, the rejected lover shoots to death first her and then himself the night before she enters the convent, while, in the less sensational triple-decker version, Kate joins the sisterhood after Dare is killed in a carriage accident.

Replacing images of robust embodiment with a thematics of self-starvation, *Not Wisely but Too Well* constructs an anorexic narrative that ultimately chastens its heroine's unruly flesh. Espousing a dualism that rejects the "muddy, polluted flood of earthly love"[5] in favor of the spirit, by the novel's end Kate Chester contains her wayward erotic urges. Yet this containment of sexual appetite does not merely acquiesce to Victorian strictures against female passion. Beset with ambivalence about what Oliphant calls the "fleshly inclinations" of women, *Not Wisely* also expresses considerable anxiety about those of men. In addition to signifying self-punishment, Kate's flight from desire may be read as a means of escaping disturbing aspects of male sexuality associated not only with illicit passion but—more radically—with marriage itself. Broughton thus constructs a narrative split between radical and conservative elements, at once critiquing women's lack of autonomy within Victorian culture and serving as a cautionary tale about the dangers of female appetite.

Kate's Body

It is appropriate that Broughton's sensation fiction addresses the problem of female appetite given that the genre itself was distrusted for appealing to voracious female readers. Frequently characterized by its critics as a type of unwholesome food, sensation fiction, as Henry Mansel put it, satisfied "the cravings of a diseased appetite."[6] Pamela Gilbert has shown how detractors of Victorian popular fiction used images of food poisoning to claim that the novels spread disease and moral contamination.[7] Such social adulteration was considered particularly problematic in the case of the *female* consumer since a woman has, according to Oliphant, "one duty of invaluable importance to her country and her race which cannot be over-estimated—and that is the duty of being pure" (275). Oliphant and other critics of sensationalism worried that, by devouring immoral fictions, female readers would incorporate their impurity and spread it throughout society, thus undermining the chastity that is "of such vital consequence to a nation" (275). Significantly, Oliphant places the trend toward sexual explicitness in fiction in the context of contemporary discussions of "Women's rights" (275), and hence women's growing dissatisfaction with domestic ideology.

Broughton's depiction of female appetite in *Not Wisely but Too Well* would seem to bear out Oliphant's concerns about an incipient rebellion against domesticity. Indeed, in a sympathetic review of both *Not Wisely* and *Cometh Up* in the *Spectator*, a critic noted the correlation between the full-figured bodies of Broughton's sensation heroines and their hunger for a life outside conventional restraints:

> In each story the central figure is the same—a girl of a full and noble nature, round as to her lines mental and bodily, with full bust and an exuberant mental life, despising conventionality and contemning the usual cut-and-dried formulas for living, ensnared, but not stained, by a burning passion for a man who cannot, or does not, become her husband [.] [8]

Quoting Kate's cry over the impossibility of her love for Dare—"O why will not God let us have what we like?"(56)—this critic characterizes Broughton as a "novelist of revolt" who, like Charlotte Brontë and George Eliot, expresses discontent with traditional gender roles.[9] Like Jane Eyre, Caroline Helstone, and Maggie Tulliver, heroines whom feminist critics have analyzed as figures for transgressive appetite,[10] Broughton's full-bodied heroines are female Oliver Twists, asking for more of everything they are not allowed—sexual, intellectual, and emotional fulfillment.

Unabashedly big, the bodies of Broughton's sensation heroines defy conventional definition. Whereas Nell of *Cometh Up* is distinguished by her height and flaming red hair, Kate Chester (whose hair is also "ruddy" [220]) is remarkable for the "round" body and "full bust" referred to by the *Spectator* reviewer. The narrator, an unnamed male figure who claims to have been unrequitedly in love with Kate, describes her buxom form in terms reminiscent of a wet T-shirt contest: "Her thick white-muslin frock was as common and plain as a frock could be . . . but, for all that, how close it sat, without a crease, to that well-sculptured form, how clearly it defined the outline of that fairy bust!" (104). While the association of the narrator with voyeurism is disturbing in ways I will return to later, Broughton uses the male voice to contest her culture's emphasis on female disembodiment. Indeed, by contrasting Kate's figure with Victorian ideals of female slenderness, the narrator suggests that it is not female appetite but its absence that is unhealthy:

> Now for Kate's figure. I do not think it was exactly of the cut of the Venus de Medici, but, for all that, it always seemed to me rather ensnaring to the fancy, in its partridge-like plumpness, soft undulating contours, and pretty roundnesses; so removed from scragginess, and free from angles. Many *women* affirmed that it was too full, too developed for a girl of twenty . . . but no *man* was ever yet heard to give in his adhesion to this feminine fiat. Anyhow the light did seem to fall lovingly . . . on the "bounteous wave of such a breast as never pencil drew," and on the waist— no marvel of waspish tenuity, but naturally healthily firm and shapely. (11)

Recalling Walter Hartright's delighted realization in *The Woman in White* that Marian Halcombe is not wearing a corset,[11] the narrator's reference to Kate's waist as "naturally healthily firm and shapely" implies that corsets are unnaturally constraining, thus echoing criticism of tight lacing common in the late Victorian period.

The Victorian campaign against tight lacing reflected both radical and conservative ideological agendas.[12] Some doctors, indeed, inveighed against corsets because they might damage the female reproductive system and hence women's fitness as mothers. The narrator's appreciation of Kate's form suggests as well the erotic appeal of female plumpness for men. Yet feminists also mounted critiques against the rigid containment of the female body and its desires represented by the corset. Reflecting this perspective, Broughton links unnatural slenderness to a docile adherence to feminine propriety, as in her description of the "17-inch wasp waist" of Kate's conventional sister, Margaret, whose form "displayed very unmistakably that want of development which is so grievous and common a fault among English girls" (15). The narrator states: "I have heard people say that Margaret's figure was more refined than Kate's. If that be the case, a skeleton's was more refined still" (16). Anna Krugovoy Silver has read the Victorian ideal of the corseted "slender-waisted" woman as an example of "the discipline of the body" that "links Victorian beauty culture to the intense self-control of anorexia nervosa."[13] Escaping such discipline and its associations with skeletal starvation, Kate presumably is free to indulge appetites that are healthy, natural, and life-giving.

This association of Kate's lush embodiment with vibrant nature and sexuality is pronounced in a scene where, before she discovers he is married, Dare takes her to a conservatory filled with vivid tropical blooms. Contrasting Kate's body, which displays the "ripe womanly development of one of Titian's Venuses," with the "emaciated prettiness of modern young ladies" (107), the narrator records her orgasmic reponse to the flowers: "Kate was in ecstasies. She ran hither and thither, smelling first one, and then another" as she cries, "Delicious!" (107). Kate's fervent appreciation of the "intoxicating" (107) hothouse flowers suggests a correspondingly intense capacity for sexual arousal. As if to mimic the contours of her full-figured body, her desire for Dare overflows all boundaries: "a bottomless depth, a wild, mad, reckless fervour of passion" (30); "[f]rantic passion, utterly uncurbed" (56).

With such references to lack of restraint, however, the narrator oscillates from approval of Kate's body to moral disapprobation, calling her love for Dare "that muddy, polluted flood of earthly love" (30) that prevents her from aspiring to "higher, better love, which might have refreshed and watered her soul for the garden of God" (30). Discarding his earlier celebration of the flesh, the narrator echoes the language of moral contagion deployed by critics of sensationalism. Kate has apparently contracted her feverish desire from Dare, whose "mad wild-beast passion" for her is like a "stinking stagnant pond" (296). The fecal overtones of this language of pollution also surface in the image of Kate escaping for clandestine trysts with Dare through the "back door" (79) of the house she shares with her guardian. As Leonore Davidoff has argued, in the symbolic geography of Victorian culture the "back passages" of the house, the realm of servants, were associated with the abject—dirt and the lower classes, aligned both with the excrement-producing lower regions of the body and its shameful sexual urges.[14] Heedless of the maidenly modesty that prohibits unchaperoned meetings with a man, Kate identifies herself with these taboo nether regions and their threat of social contamination.

In one of the few analyses of *Not Wisely but Too Well,* Pamela Gilbert usefully identifies images of contagion that cluster around Kate, particularly in the latter part of the novel when, after suffering brain fever as a result of thwarted passion, she becomes a charity worker in the London slums and eventually a nurse during an epidemic. Such proximity to the dirt and disease of the lower classes figures Kate's own ambiguous position between the respectable and the abject: "Kate hovers on the border between proper, sexually chaste middle-class womanhood and unrestrained passionate transgression, between health and disease, between good and evil."[15]

To Gilbert's list of liminal states, however, should be added the novel's own generic hybridity. Shifting from a humorous female *bildungsroman,* whose refreshingly irreverent protagonist recalls Jane Austen's and Louisa May Alcott's heroines, to a fallen woman melodrama awash in morality, Broughton's narrative draws attention to its own inability to create an original plot that positively depicts female desire. To account for the transformation of her rosy, funny protagonist into a lugubrious penitent, we must not underestimate the enormous challenges Broughton faced in depicting a sexually desirous heroine in an era which censured even repentant fallen women. Of Isabel Vane, the hyperbolically remorseful adulterous wife of *East Lynne,* the ever-redoubtable Oliphant declared, "Nothing could be more wrong and fatal than to represent the flames of vice as a purifying, fiery ordeal, through which the penitent is to come elevated and sublime."[16] Indeed, the *Athenaeum* reviewer was similarly unimpressed by

Kate's rejections of Dare and her subsequent religious fervor, growling that "[w]orse than even the immorality of the whole novel are the stupid, misplaced attempts at sermonizing throughout."[17]

The generic instability of Broughton's narrative thus owes much to the collision of her unconventional representation of female desire with contemporary mores. I would like to offer, however, another perspective on the novel's apparently confusing shifts in tone and generic convention. In its patchwork of plot conventions and obsessive literary allusions, *Not Wisely* is in dialogue with predecessor texts that similarly attempt to portray female desire, including its most obvious source in the male canon, Shakespeare's *Othello*, from which Broughton derives her title and—in her original version of the novel—the ending in which the male lover kills the woman.[18] Yet descriptions of the English Dare as racial Other—a "great ugly black fellow" (46)—recall not only Shakespeare's Moor but Charlotte Brontë's Byronic Edward Rochester, who like Dare seductively combines an unconventionally dark, "ugly" face with a lithe, muscular body. Borrowing liberally from *Jane Eyre*, in fact, the plot of *Not Wisely* owes more to a female literary tradition than to the male canon represented by *Othello*.

A significant precursor for Broughton in its innovative portrayal of female desire by a woman writer, *Jane Eyre* also anticipates *Not Wisely*'s depiction of male desire, especially as it poses a threat to female autonomy. Taking into account the intertextual dialogue between Broughton and Brontë, and its links to a tradition of Wollstonecraftian feminism, I will now examine how the increasingly negative images of corporeality in *Not Wisely* reflect anxieties about women's sexual subjection.

Seraglios, Sex, and Somatophobia

Not Wisely but Too Well recycles a number of elements from *Jane Eyre:* the would-be bigamist, trapped in marriage with a woman he despises; his attempts, once the respectable girl discovers he is married, to persuade her to become his mistress; the girl's rejection of this sexual temptation; and her subsequent relationship with an ascetic young clergyman (the St. John Rivers figure, here recast as the heroic missionary to the slums, James Stanley). At the same time, Broughton's novel differs significantly from Brontë's in several ways, notably in its ending—or endings, because neither the original serialization nor the triple-decker conclude with the death of the inconvenient first wife and the lovers' marriage. Like Rochester, whose transgressive sexuality is tamed by the accident that leaves him symbolically castrated, Dare is also punished for his attempted bigamy, becoming, in the triple-decker version, the victim of a carriage accident. Unlike his predecessor, however, he is not humbled and redeemed but dies unrepentant and apparently damned.

Admittedly, some of Broughton's revisions of *Jane Eyre* sacrifice the aesthetic richness of Brontë's text, especially her complex portrayal of Rochester, who is both a sympathetic and unsympathetic figure. On the less sympathetic side, Rochester is associated with the female Gothic of his first wife's imprisonment, a plot a number of feminist critics (and Jean Rhys) have read as a symbolic manifestation of his fear of her sexuality and Otherness. Moreover, in his relationship with Jane, Rochester is overbearing and capricious, toying with her while pretending to be engaged to another woman. Yet—more sympathetically—he also genuinely suffers from his hasty, arranged marriage, in which he was the pawn of his father's greed, and despite his faults he loves Jane tenderly. Dare, in contrast, is more the one-dimensional cad of melodrama, a seducer who considers women "fair game" (32) and flashes satanic "lurid" (111) gleams from his eyes. His confession to Kate of how he became entangled in marriage with a working-class woman (Broughton's version of Otherness, as opposed to Bertha's colonial antecedents) provokes considerably less sympathy than Rochester's account of the horrors of marriage with Bertha; Dare's wife is not insane and continues to love the husband who neglects her.

By making Dare a flatter, less compelling figure than Rochester, though, Broughton also provides a more negative reading of the version of masculinity Brontë's hero embodies. By de-emphasizing Rochester's sympathetic characteristics, Broughton underscores the power struggle between the male and female leads we see in Brontë's novel, particularly in the period between Jane's engagement to Rochester and her discovery of his preexisting marriage. Significantly, the images that Broughton imports from this section of *Jane Eyre* are those of harems and sexual enslavement, images with which Brontë suggests Rochester's disturbing tendency to possess and objectify Jane.

In *Jane Eyre,* the harem motif conveys the economic inequality between Rochester and Jane which makes her fear that in being "kept" by him[19]—a formulation that likens a wife to a courtesan—she will lose her cherished autonomy. When Jane objects to his showering her "like a second Danaë" with jewels and fine clothes, Rochester exclaims that he "would not exchange this one little English girl for the grand Turk's whole seraglio," an "Eastern allusion" that Jane finds as degrading as his largesse (229). Likening him to a "sultan" who condescendingly views "the slave his gold and gems had enriched," Jane retorts, "I'll be preparing myself to go out as a missionary to preach liberty to them that are enslaved—your harem inmates among them" (229, 230). Recalling Mary Wollstonecraft with this vision of Jane preaching liberty to female slaves, Brontë echoes the rhetoric with which *A Vindication of the Rights of Woman,* and the feminist tradition it influenced, condemns women's economic and sexual domination. Claiming that male control of money makes marriage a form of "legal prostitution," in the *Vindication* Wollstonecraft likens the wife who adorns herself to please her husband to the inhabitant of a harem: "In a seraglio, I grant, that all these arts are necessary; the epicure must have his palate tickled . . . but have women so little ambition to be satisfied with such a condition?"[20]

Broughton recasts Brontë's images of female sexual enslavement—which thus have a feminist literary genealogy—in a scene in *Not Wisely* in which Dare inspects Kate's beauty as she stands "as good and docile a little creature as could be seen, with her hands folded, and her eyelashes caressing her cheek—on approval, like a Circassian slave at the market of Constantinople" (105). Significantly, this scene occurs immediately before the one I discussed earlier in which Kate visits the conservatory of tropical flowers with Dare. Invoking slave markets and tropical blooms, Broughton emphasizes Kate's vulnerability to male subjection. Even though she is likened to a Circassian, or white slave, Kate is placed in the role of racial Other whose master colonizes her body. This identification of Kate with racial Otherness becomes even more explicit when, before they start for the conservatory, Dare orders her to wear a hat:

"But before we go you'll be kind enough to put on your hat, won't you? Or you'll be burnt all manner of colours," he added. . . .

"I shall do nothing of the kind!" said Kate rebelliously. "I don't care if I'm burnt as black as a coal!"

"I should like to see you then," said Dare; and his lips curved into one of his gleaming laughs. "What a dear little negro you should make!" (106)

While in this scene Kate, like Jane Eyre, rebels against Dare's sexual mastery, she is still so enthralled that she is unable to perceive the disturbing implications of his attempts to control her body. Broughton does not emphasize women's economic inequality to the same degree as Brontë; Kate does not murmur against Dare's economic power as does Jane, although significantly Broughton repeats the plot of a woman of lesser status attracting an overbearing upper-class man. What Broughton concentrates on, however, is the Brontëan association between the possessive male and sexual bondage. Dare's embraces evoke the female Gothic plot of the "feminine carceral"[21] as he holds Kate in "iron bondage, as if he never intended to loose her out of that strong prison again" (112). Even more ominously, he threatens to "cut your dear little soft throat here, this very minute, if I thought any other man would ever kiss you again as I have done to-day" (113)— a comment that prefigures the violent ending of the novel's original version.

The negative aspects of Dare's sexuality could be ascribed to his role as seducer. But, like Wollstonecraft and Brontë, Broughton does not limit her critique of male domination solely to its illicit manifestations. Ashley Smith has pointed to the similarities between Dare and a man who would seem his mirror opposite, Kate's staid guardian, the Reverend Josiah Piggott, an "anxious patriarchal hypochondriac."[22] In thrall to "Daddy Piggot," his mousy wife parodies the dutiful helpmeet:

> She always said "Yes, love." I believe if he had said, "And now, my dear love, I think, if you please, that we will cut off your head," she would have said "Yes, love," as glibly as possible. (47)

Both Dare's threat to cut Kate's throat and Mrs. Piggott's willingness to have her head cut off underscore, as Smith notes, the danger men pose to female voice and identity.[23]

As Reverend Piggott's name suggests, his version of male domination is associated with negative images of the body. Nicknamed "Piggy" by Kate and her siblings, the clergyman is so corpulent that "two or three very handsome men might have been made out of him, for there was fleshy material enough in the vast acreage of his mild pendulous cheeks" (16). Piggott's flabby girth is an example of the text's somatophobia, a term coined by feminist critics for discourses that express a fear of embodiment. At one point, indeed, Kate wishes Hamlet-like that her too-solid flesh would melt, apostrophizing her plump arm as an "[u]gly great fat thing" (57). While this image early in the novel humorously underscores Kate's difference from the stereotype of the slender, lovelorn woman, it prefigures an increasing anxiety about embodiment in the novel which is linked to anxieties about marriage. The conventional, formerly wasp-waisted Margaret grows "*embonpoint*" (321) once she is engaged to an equally boring man and settles dully into domesticity; a brace of marriageable, fashionable young cousins of Kate's are distinguished by their girth, together constituting a "so many tons' weight of womanhood" (228). Such somatophobic images are in tension with the strand of somatophilia, or love of the body, that presents Kate's fleshiness positively. The very implication of somatophilia, however, with male sexuality renders it problematic; in this light, Broughton's choice of a male narrator who salivates over Kate's body links the celebration of female embodiment with the threat to female autonomy posed by male fantasy and voyeurism.

It is again useful to compare Broughton with Wollstonecraft, whose work displays an extreme ambivalence to the body and sexuality. Likening romantic passion to the doctrine "Let us eat, drink, and love, for tomorrow we die," Wollstonecraft dismisses such hedonistic appetites in favor of reason: "Why must the female mind be tainted by coquettish arts to gratify the sensualist?"[24] In this Wollstonecraftian tradition, *Jane Eyre* suggests a similar tension between female embodiment and male appetite. In love with Rochester, the formerly thin and love-starved Jane puts on "flesh and strength" (125). Yet the seraglio images imply that desirable female flesh is also controlled flesh, an association borne out by the corpulent Bertha who, once a "fine woman" (i.e., a buxom one), is now an imprisoned "bulk" despised by Rochester (260, 251). In her desperate effort to escape Rochester's overbearing demands to be his mistress, Jane flees Thornfield, nearly starving to death on her journey.

Similarly, Broughton suggests that if women indulge their sexual appetites, they will become prey for men; in the scene where Dare inspects Kate's voluptuous body as if she were a Circassian slave, we hear that his eyes "feasted now royally" (105) on her in a kind of erotic cannibalism. In order to evade male control, then, Kate must avoid being reduced to a "great coarse mass of flesh and blood" (269), as Dare calls his first wife. And, although she had earlier declared, "I like a manly man . . . I'm not ethereal enough to have much sympathy with people who are all soul and no body" (173), Kate replaces the "substantially bodily flesh and blood" presence of Dare (59) with the dualistic philosophy of the clergyman James Stanley, who represents an alternative to sexual appetite.

Anorexic Strategies

In *Jane Eyre* Jane's clergyman cousin St. John Rivers embodies freezing asceticism. Likened to both ice and "white stone" (334), he suppresses his desire for a rich man's beautiful daughter and proposes instead to Jane, whom he deems a more durable assistant for his projected labors in India. Figuring an excess of rectitude in contrast to Rochester's excess of transgressive sexuality, St. John, like Rochester, is a kind of seducer. Jane almost gives in when he threatens her with damnation if she turns him down, but, just as she had rejected Rochester's urgings to become his mistress, she says no to St. John, whom she claims is "killing her" with his loveless domination (351). Returning to a chastened, diminished—and now marriageable—Rochester, Jane chooses tamed passion over St. John's inhuman discipline.

In *Not Wisely but Too Well*, however, Kate's clergyman friend James Stanley is a kinder and gentler version of his Brontëan prototype. Just as she had portrayed the Rochester figure less sympathetically than Brontë, Broughton portrays the figure associated with religious discipline more sympathetically. Heroically laboring not in India but in the London slums, "Jemmy" cherishes an unrequited longing for Kate herself but refuses to express it. Unlike Jane, who chooses Rochester instead of St. John, Kate rejects Dare in order to become James's missionary companion in the slums—though not his wife—serving as a nurse during a fever epidemic that ultimately claims the saintly clergyman's life.

Given the somatophobic link between fleshliness and marriage elsewhere in the novel, it is notable that James is described as a kind of hunger artist. Surveying his "poor fragile body" (160), Kate even exclaims that "You might, if all trades failed, make an honest livelihood as 'living skeleton'" (153). "[C]rucifying the flesh with the affections and lusts" (307) as he struggles with his desire for Kate, James plans to "eat less, starve out this earthly demon" (206) in order to subdue his sexual urges. Just as Dare's "stinking wild-beast passion" had been catching, so Kate contracts James's addiction to "inflicting divers mortifications and macerations" (232) on desire. While she does not become literally anorexic, Kate's adoption of James's anorexic ethos is signaled by her intense pallor. Previously described as pale but subject to intense blushing (a Victorian signifier for sexual arousal), Kate, as the narrator claimed, used to look "more like a dog-rose than any lily" (72). By the time she assists James in the slums, however, she is "hardly less fair than the lilies" (341) in her paleness. This pallor contrasts with the rosy health of her now-married sister, who in becoming a "fat and comfortable" wife had also "got a colour like a dairymaid" (321).

While Kate escapes Dare's sexual subjugation, however, in her new-found self-abnegation she does not escape all versions of male control. In fact, by imitating James's asceticism, in many ways Kate exchanges one form of male domination for another. Freed from Dare's overbearing passions, Kate is now subject to James's commands, as in the scene where, intercepting her planned elopement with Dare, he "subdued and vanquished her utterly" (301). Moreover, one could read Kate's suspiciously hectic religious fervor—her yearning to practice a "system of flagellation, and fasting five days a week" (306) similar to rituals in "such a convent as that of the Perpetual Adoration" (304)—as simply a more tortured, repressed form of her sexual passion for Dare. At the same time, though, Kate's sublimated sexuality dispenses with men, particularly in the triple-decker version, in which both Dare and James die.

Thus, although Broughton's ending for the triple-decker could be seen as a "bowdlerized" rewrite of the original gory conclusion,[25] Broughton's revision also gives Kate more autonomy after the deaths of Dare and James, placing her in a community of women who represent an alternative to marriage. In this light the exchange between Kate and Margaret when the former broaches her plan to join an Anglican sisterhood suggests that heterosexual love, far from being the "main plot of a woman's life" (49), as the narrator called it earlier, is simply one of multiple options:

"Kate, I always hated those sisterhoods; they have been a curse to numberless families, I am certain; a number of women huddled together, cut off from their lives, and their friends, and all their prospects in life. Why cannot women keep to their right functions of marrying and being happy?"

"Be happy if they can, by all means; people's ideas about happiness differ, you know." (359)

Although Margaret promises Kate that she can live with her and her husband and be "as independent as possible" (358), Kate decides instead to join the sisterhood, a plan she actually follows through on in the triple-decker version, when, following Dare's death, she claims she must find "some work in the world to do" (386): "She joined that band of holy devoted women whom Evangelical clergymen condemn as acolytes and handmaidens of the Scarlet Woman" (387).

Linking convents with women's efforts to find "work to do" outside marriage, Broughton underscores the subversive aspects of Victorian sisterhoods. The foundation of Anglican female religious orders in the mid–nineteenth century occasioned much controversy, not only because of the link of convents with the "Scarlet Woman" of Catholicism, but because, as Margaret notes, by entering convents women escaped immersion in domesticity. (Indeed, this evasion of marriage might have seemed more transgressive than the sins of any "scarlet" woman.) As Martha Vicinus says, "Anglican sisterhoods were one of the most important women's communities in the nineteenth century.... A religious community empowered women, validating women's work and values."[26] Emphasizing the incipient feminism of a religious vocation, and prefiguring later incarnations of the New Woman, Sister Kate devotes herself to a life whose telos is not marriage but the alleviation of social ills.

In this sense, the conclusion of the triple-decker version of *Not Wisely* is protofeminist in its evasion of the marriage plot, even if it might strike modern readers as disturbing that this protofeminism is entangled with somatophobic distrust of the body. Yet the association of feminist thought with somatophobia was pronounced during the Victorian period, as Lucy Bland argues in her provocatively entitled *Banishing the Beast: Sexuality and the Early Feminists*. In campaigns against the sexual double standard such as the attempt to repeal the Contagious Diseases Act, Victorian feminists, as Bland says, subscribed to a dualism that identified the "beast" of "selfish, egotistic, sexual lustfulness" with male desire and sought to tame it.[27] Not surprisingly, given women's vulnerability to sexual exploitation and unwanted pregnancy, Victorian feminists thus tended to agitate less for female sexual liberation than for the containment of male sexual appetite. Recalling the discourses of temperance and purity used by Victorian feminists, in *Not Wisely* Kate similarly banishes the "wild-beast passion" of Dare and, suppressing her own desire, chooses a celibacy that enables her to keep lustful men at bay and avoid marriage with its submission to men.

This protofeminist somatophobia is linked to the elements of the text I have described as "anorexic." Anorexia was itself a Victorian phenomenon, first mentioned in an address to physicians by William Gull in 1868, the year after *Not Wisely*'s publication, and defined in greater detail in a paper he wrote in 1873.[28] Moreover, anorexia has been associated with the discontent with domesticity we find in Victorian feminism. For instance, the famous anorexic hysteric Anna O., of Freud and Breuer's groundbreaking *Studies on Hysteria*, became a noted socialist feminist after her cure; intellectually starved by domesticity, she developed a revulsion at eating along with her other symptoms.[29] Hunger-striking suffragettes also enacted literally the figurative anorexia of hungry women in Victorian novels.[30] At the same time it would be inaccurate to see anorexia as a successful or empowering form of protest. Rather, the anorexic body is the site of ideological conflict, representing, as Susan Bordo reminds us, both "protest and retreat in the same gesture."[31] Hungry for more than traditional definitions of femininity can give her, the anorexic subjects her body to a brutal discipline in which protest doubles as self-punishment. Similarly, Kate Chester embodies discontent with domesticity and its restraints on female passion, yet can only rebel against domesticity by penitentially suppressing sexual desire.

However, at least in the triple-decker version of *Not Wisely* Kate survives to early middle age. In *Cometh Up as a Flower*, Broughton's second sensation novel, the heroine, Nell Lestrange, wastes away at twenty-two from consumption after almost eloping with her lover and fleeing the stifling marriage she had contracted for economic reasons. In this case separating the sexually attractive (and penniless) male lover from the sexually repulsive (and monied) husband, in *Cometh Up* Broughton again deploys Brontëan images of female slavery to critique marriage.[32]

In analyzing *Cometh Up* I have used the term "disembodied embodiment" to describe Broughton's paradoxical strategy for representing her sensation heroines' desires, at once evoking and evaporating female passion.[33] One could theorize that it was this impasse—her inability to imagine acceptable forms of female and male sexuality—that caused Broughton to cease writing sensation fiction. In a retreat from the daring experiments of her youth, during the remainder of her long career (the last of her more than twenty books was published posthumously after her death in 1920), Broughton wrote novels that, more straightforwardly than her first two, tended to be courtship narratives. Significantly, though, even if she was less obviously transgressive in her portrayal of sexuality, Broughton continued to question marriage and domesticity in novels such as *Good-bye Sweetheart* (1872), *Belinda* (1883), and *Dear Faustina* (1897)—the last of which ends with the heroine deferring marriage so she can do settlement work.

Speaking of Elizabeth Gaskell, Hilary Schor has pointed to the difficulties faced by the woman writer who attempted to "reshape the forms of Victorian fiction."[34] In her own courageous experimentation with fictional form, Broughton broke new ground, testing in her sensation fiction the limits of representing female desire. Never a self-identified feminist but nonetheless a "novelist of revolt," she deserves to be considered alongside Gaskell, Eliot, the Brontës, and other Victorian women writers whose work has invited feminist analysis. As criticism of Victorian sensationalism rediscovers her contribution to the development of the genre, it is finally possible that both the challenges Broughton faced as a woman writer, and her achievements, will be properly appreciated.

NOTES

1. For more on the publication history of *Not Wisely* and *Cometh Up*, see Marilyn Wood, *Rhoda Broughton: Profile of a Novelist 1840–1920*, 11–13.
2. Margaret Oliphant, "Novels," *Blackwood's Edinburgh Magazine*, 274. Subsequent references will be cited by page in the text.
3. The term "erotic sensationalism" is used to describe Broughton's version of sensation fiction in vol. 4 of the series *Varieties of Women's Sensation Fiction*, gen. ed. Andrew Maunder.
4. Geraldine Jewsbury, cited by Monica Correa Fryckstedt, *Geraldine Jewsbury's Athenaeum Reviews*, 87.
5. Rhoda Broughton, *Not Wisely but Too Well* (Tinsley Brothers, 1871), 30. All references to this novel will be to this edition and cited by page in the text.
6. [Henry Mansel], "Sensation Novels," *Quarterly Review* 113 (April 1863); excerpted in *Sensationalism and the Sensation Debate*, ed. Andrew Maunder, vol. 1 of *Varieties of Women's Sensation Fiction*, 33.
7. Pamela Gilbert, *Disease, Desire and the Body in Victorian Women's Popular Novels*, 17–23; see also her "Ingestion, Contagion, Seduction: Victorian Metaphors of Reading," 66–77.
8. Review of *Not Wisely but Too Well* and *Cometh Up as a Flower*, *Spectator*, 1173.
9. Ibid., 1172–73.
10. See, for example, Sandra Gilbert and Susan Gubar, *The Madwoman in the Attic*, 372–98; Diane Long Hoeveler, "*Jane Eyre* through the Body: Food, Sex, Discipline," 116–23; Nina Auerbach, "The Power of Hunger: Demonism and Maggie Tulliver," 230–49.
11. Wilkie Collins, *The Woman in White*, ed. John Sutherland (1996), 31.
12. For more on pro- and anti-tight-lacing perspectives, see Anna Krugovoy Silver, *Victorian Literature and the Anorexic Body*, 37–40.
13. Silver, *Victorian Literature and the Anorexic Body*, 34.
14. Leonore Davidoff, "Class and Gender in Victorian England," 19.
15. Gilbert, *Disease, Desire and the Body*, 121.
16. Margaret Oliphant, "Sensation Novels," *Blackwood's Edinburgh Magazine*, 567.
17. "Review of *Not Wisely but Too Well*," *Athenaeum*, 569.
18. For more on intertexuality in *Not Wisely but Too Well*, see Helen Debenham, "*Not Wisely but Too Well* and the Art of Sensation," 9–24. For comments on *Jane Eyre*, see 12–13.
19. Charlotte Brontë, *Jane Eyre*, ed. Richard J. Dunn, 3rd ed., 229. Subsequent references will be to this edition and are cited by page in the text.
20. Mary Wollstonecraft, *A Vindication of the Rights of Woman*, 148, 29.

21. D. A. Miller, "*Cage aux Folles:* Gender and Sensation in Wilkie Collins's *The Woman in White*," in *The Making of the Modern Body: Sexuality and Society in the Nineteenth Century,* 120.

22. Ashley Smith, "Dangerous Sexuality in *Not Wisely but Too Well,*" unpublished essay (University of Cincinnati, 2004), 2.

23. Smith, "Dangerous Sexuality," 2.

24. Wollstonecraft, *Vindication,* 31.

25. Debenham, "*Not Wisely but Too Well,*"10.

26. Martha Vicinus, *Independent Women: Work and Community for Single Women 1850–1920,* 83. For more on Anglican sisterhoods as an alternative to domesticity, see Susan Mumm, *Stolen Daughters, Virgin Mothers: Anglican Sisterhoods in Victorian Britain.*

27. Lucy Bland, *Banishing the Beast: Sexuality and the Early Feminists,* xiii.

28. Joan Jacobs Brumberg, *Fasting Girls: The Emergence of Anorexia Nervosa as a Modern Disease,* 115–19.

29. Josef Breuer and Sigmund Freud, *Studies on Hysteria,* trans. James Strachey, 23, 26–27.

30. See Linda Schlossberg, "Consuming Images: Women, Hunger, and the Vote," 87–106.

31. Susan Bordo, *Unbearable Weight: Feminism, Western Culture, and the Body,* 174.

32. For the economics of marriage in *Cometh Up,* see Tamar Heller, introduction to *Cometh Up as a Flower,* xxxvii–xxxviii.

33. Heller, intro., xiii.

34. Hilary Schor, *Scheherezade in the Marketplace: Elizabeth Gaskell and the Victorian Novel,* 84.

- 9 -

SENSATIONAL HAIR

*Gender, Genre, and Fetishism in the
Sensational Decade*

GALIA OFEK

THIS ESSAY discusses the deployment of women's hair in sensation fiction from the 1860s, and the contemporary critical response that it triggered. Victorian critics found the representation of hair in sensation novels excessive and exaggerated, and thought that it testified to the poor quality of both characterization and descriptive power in such fiction. I wish to reassess the validity of these claims, and suggest that in fact, hair was so central to both sensationalists and their critics because it shared many of the features which were conceptualized as the generic quiddities of sensation fiction. Thus, the deployment of hair constituted not only an element but also an embodiment of the sensational, in its preoccupation with contradictions of prevailing versions of femininity, its constant negotiation and redefinition of feminine identity, its distrust of misleading appearances, its fascination with materiality, its topicality, and its function as a wide common denominator with the marketplace and contemporary habits of consumption.

Part of the very foundation of the patriarchal Victorian culture consisted of an acceptance of traditional gender characteristics—both anatomical and behavioral—which differentiated male from female, and "fallen" from virtuous women. As Richard Altick observes, the most prominent Victorian authors gave detailed descriptions of their heroines' hair: Charles Dickens, George Eliot, and Anthony Trollope offered their readers "detailed identikit inventories of a woman's features . . . [and] above all, her hair."[1] These authors took part in the cultural discourse which perceived women's bodies in general, and their hair in particular, as texts or signs that could be readily interpreted or classified. In 1859, Dickens published *A Tale of Two Cities*, where the ideal and ethereal woman, Lucie Manette, was "[e]ver busily winding the golden thread . . . weaving the service of her happy influence through the tissues" of the lives of her father, husband, and child.[2] Lucie's golden hair was interwoven with gentleness and domesticity in this metaphor which, to a great extent, permeated the whole narrative of the novel, as indeed the title of the second book suggests ("The Golden Thread"). Her rival, the destructive antagonist Madame Defarge, was dark-haired, and indeed, dark hair signified fallen or dangerous female sexuality (for example, the dark Edith Dombey and her double, Alice Marwood, in *Dombey and Son* from 1848), whereas gold hair was deployed by Dickens as a symbol of feminine redemptive and healing powers (like Jenny Wren's hair in *Our Mutual Friend*, 1865).[3] George Eliot, too, depicted the sweet, gentle, and submissive Lucy in *The Mill on the Floss* (1860) as blonde, as opposed to the tempestuous, black-haired Maggie, and focused on the magical, redeeming powers of Eppie's golden hair in *Silas Marner* (1861).[4] This was the dominant and influential paradigm against which sensation novelists defined their heroines in the following decade. Their project was briefly described by Wilkie Collins, who remarked that "the generally accepted tall, black-haired . . . type of Lady Macbeth" was all a mistake. "You may depend upon it," said he, "that she was a rather small, fair-haired, blue-eyed woman."[5]

And indeed, sensation novelists started undermining the traditional system of codification by striking at the very root of Victorian faith in the equation of golden hair and angelic femininity. They proceeded to show that dark hair was not necessarily indicative of dangerous sexuality, and ended up suggesting that no external sign could possibly capture modern womanhood, which was unfathomable, resisting unconditional univocal definition or "reading." The representation of women's hair thus facilitated the authors' engagement in a debate which challenged traditional social and literary conventions, and explored new definitions of the feminine, the heroine, and the novel.

The Woman with the Yellow Hair

In 1867, Margaret Oliphant criticized what she viewed as Mary Elizabeth Braddon's excessive and pointless deployment of hair in her novels. Braddon, she said, was "the inventor of the fair-haired demon of modern fiction." Wicked women turned into "the daintiest, softest, prettiest of blonde creatures; and this change has been wrought by Lady Audley, and her influence on contemporary novels. . . . Hair, indeed, has become one of the leading properties in fiction. . . . What need has woman for a soul when she has upon her head a mass of wavy gold?"[6] This essay will trace several of Lady Audley's literary "mothers," and show that Braddon was by no means the "inventor" of the "fair-haired demon"; that Lady Audley's golden locks did not appear in a cultural, literary, or social lacuna; and that the "mass of wavy gold" in sensation novels was not just an arbitrary sign.

In the beginning of the 1860s, two pieces were published anonymously, both under the title *The Woman with the Yellow Hair*. Both employed the "golden-haired domestic goddess" trope to ridicule and criticize the traditional values of the Victorian bourgeoisie. The first *Woman with the Yellow Hair* was published in 1860 and was reprinted twice, once in the same year and then in 1861. Its author, Harry Hazleton, may have been wary of making his identity known at the time because his work defied Victorian respectability.[7] The preface to the novel announced its similarity to Dickens's novels, but in the same breath praised Hazleton's "fearlessness of language" and "utter defiance of all those powerful conventionalities which have cramped and fettered modern novelists." *The Woman with the Yellow Hair*, as opposed to the prudish literature of the day, promised to "revolutionise the world of novel writing," to "unmask VICE and HYPOCRISY" and to "depict life as it really is."[8] The preface clearly testifies to the novelist's intention to ridicule and challenge the literary conventions of Dickens rather than to follow him. And indeed, this is exactly what Hazleton did, first and foremost by the seemingly angelic, à la Lucie Manette heroine that he created.

The title heroine, Nelly Raymond, is a distinct prototype of Lady Audley, being at once "a glorious golden-haired goddess" and a "yellow-haired calculating machine" (26, 117). At the same time, she is a caricature of heroines like Lucie, since none of the values associated with Lucie's golden hair, namely, truth, loyalty, domesticity, and purity, can be found in her character. On the contrary, she is an illegitimate child, an inveterate liar, an ambitious actress, a woman who lives in sin with the hero, and, to add insult to injury, is unfaithful to him. She is a sexually licentious social climber who uses her beauty—and her golden hair—to ensnare rich lovers. Thus her golden hair becomes the site at which wealth and female sexuality are inevitably linked. I suggest that this literary vogue for wicked, greedy, golden-haired heroines may have originated in a revolt against the standard insipid model of womanhood in many domestic novels of the midcentury, a model which associated virtuous women with sexual passivity, lack of ambition, and unworldliness. Even poetic justice is turned on its head, with Nelly winning riches, living extravagantly and sinfully, and refusing to be married or restricted in any way at the end. "There really isn't," claims the author, "that triumph of virtue in real life which accompanies the Victorian melo-drama" (178). Yellow hair marks a conscious departure from the contemporary literary system of representation through the encoded physicality of women, which lacks credibility because it is too formulaic and does not correspond to different models of femininity in real life. Aiming to be more true-to-life than standard domestic novelists, Hazleton uses Nell's hair to shatter a social and literary myth of clear-cut classifications: "I regret to have to say it, because you know in novels, [the] wicked ones are always, as it were, stamped and labelled. You may tell them at a glance" (163).

The second work of the same title was written and published in November 1861 by Percy Fitzgerald.[9] It was published anonymously in the *Dublin University Magazine*, and in 1862 was reprinted in a collection of stories, *The Woman with the Yellow Hair and Other Modern Mysteries*. The story's emphasis on the ominous yellow hair is significant in the discourse of sexuality in sensation fiction. First, it follows the path that has been marked by the previous book of the same title, as the yellow-haired lady is, again, the very opposite of her angelic counterpart in a long literary tradition. Here, too, the golden-haired lady gains both lovers and riches, and remains unpunished and triumphant, in contrast to the prevailing moral judgment and the respectable literary production of the day. But, more surprisingly, it also heralds a later tale of a blonde social climber who nearly becomes a murderess in a rotting isolated mansion. In 1862, Lady Audley, following Fitzgerald's heroine Janet, uses her blonde hair to seduce a rich nobleman, and also tries to drown a man in her garden. Miss Janet Faithfull is a yellow-haired beauty who is to be married to the wealthy Henry St. John Smith. He and his younger brother travel together to the Faithfull mansion. On his first night there, the younger brother awakes late at night to follow the woman with the yellow hair, who has wandered into the wild gardens in her neglected mansion. There, he finds, she holds a meeting with a lover. Furious, he threatens her with the disclosure of her secret to his brother, to which she reacts by seducing him, making ample use of her hair: "The yellow hair . . . now at last got free, and came tumbling in a perfect gush to the ground. The younger brother was dazzled" (33). Bewitched by Janet's seductive hair, he agrees to keep her secret, and to meet her the night after, when she drowns him in the garden pond. Having disposed of the dangerous brother, she marries the elder brother, as planned, and the story concludes with a description of her happiness as a beautiful, rich, and respectable wife in the higher social circles in London, where "her yellow hair is famous" (52).

While Fitzgerald may have been influenced by Hazleton, I think that he was, in all probability, indebted to Augustus Sala for his choice of heroine. Both writers contributed to Dickens's magazines, and Fitzgerald acknowledged "a great regard for [Sala] personally, equalled only by [his] admiration for his really brilliant gifts."[10] Sala, who was appointed by Maxwell to be the editor of *Temple Bar* (1860–63), introduced the fair villainess to contemporary readers as early as 1860, with the first serial for his journal, *The Seven Sons of Mammon*, which featured Florence Armytage, a "she-demon with yellow ringlets" who had "twenty thousand little fiends nestling in her golden curls."[11] Ostensibly a respectable widow, she lives by fraud, blackmail, and, when necessary, forgery and murder, thus becoming a prototype of future demonic blondes such as Lady

Audley. Further, like Braddon after him, Sala insisted on the economic rather than sexual motives of the criminal behavior of Armytage, whose hair is the physical embodiment of a world ruled by mammon worship: "her golden ringlets seemed to belong, somehow, to Mammon" (1. 137). It is clear that Braddon read Sala's serial and admired it before she wrote her successful *Lady Audley's Secret* (September 1862): writing to Sala in the spring of 1861, Braddon thanked him for his praise of her work in his "most charming of letters," but deprecated any comparison between her apprentice work and *The Seven Sons of Mammon*.[12]

It is unlikely that, within two years, the golden-haired heroine would have turned into the obvious symbol of sexual and financial corruption, just by coincidence or even merely by literary example and counterexample. While agreeing with Elisabeth Gitter's observation that golden hair was linked, by association, both with gold and sexuality, and was therefore central to the ambivalent cultural preoccupation with both,[13] I contend that the contextualization of this symbol within sensation fiction is crucial to a better understanding of its meaning. In my view, the fascination of golden hair lay with specific contemporary controversies within the public debate on the "Woman Question." For golden hair was invested with its attributes of materiality, unwomanly ambition, licentiousness, and greed, all of which threatened the conjugal establishment, only after 1857, the year when both the Divorce Act and the Petition for Married Woman's Property Bill took place. Both motions developed into a decade of public debate over the economic empowerment of women and the threats which financial independence could pose for traditional social structures.

Golden hair, within the framework of sensation fiction, is the embodiment of these threats. Woman's right to gain financial independence destabilized traditional gender roles, and consequently called for new representations of gender in a new genre. As the very core of the potential change in women's status was financial, it was translated into the symbolic color of gold in an already existing discourse on woman's sexuality through the medium of her hair. At the same time, however, golden hair also represents the powerlessness of women in patriarchal society, as it stands for a high exchange value. If we take the commodification of women to its logical and metaphorical extreme, golden hair marks a woman as the ultimate commodity. Fitzgerald's Woman with the Yellow Hair justifies her behavior to the younger brother: "I dare not think or choose for myself—because I am dragged a fashionable slave to the market, set up and sold" (32). And indeed, in the competitive marriage market, where women tried to secure their economic status, golden hair seemed to be an important, nearly symbolic property, as exemplified by *The Woman with the Yellow Hair*, and by her successor Lady Audley: they both gained money, and exacted from their husbands what proved to be a very high price. Thus golden hair turns into a sign of victimized femininity which turns against its victimizer, patriarchy.[14]

Lady Audley's Marketable Hair

Braddon's questioning of the domestic feminine ideal and its representation through the yellow-hair trope was, therefore, an important contribution to the ongoing negotiation of the definition and representation of femaleness, rather than an unprecedented invention. Braddon's representation of golden hair, however, had more radical social implications than all those previous works. The authoress, who, like her predecessors, chose to undermine social stratification by allowing her golden-haired heroine social and financial mobility, went a step further by teaching "women readers how to pretend to be members of a class into which they were not born."[15] Indeed, the novel is more than one woman's story, and in some parts it reads like a manual for female readers. Helen's way to gold is, literally, her golden hair, and the latter is represented as vital to her success, and, more alarmingly, to the success of every ambitious woman. Braddon's deployment of the "most wonderful curls in the world" exposes an image-oriented society, where all that glitters is, if not genuine gold, a metaphorical gold mine where rich husbands and great wealth may be yielded.[16] For, as soon as Helen manages to lure Sir Audley into an imprudent marriage by displaying her beautiful "yellow curls," which flash "hither and thither like wandering gleams of sunshine" (121), she tells Phoebe (and the reader) while the maid arranges her hair for the night: "You *are* like me. . . . Why, with a bottle of hair-dye, such as you see advertised in the papers, and a pot of rouge, you'd be as good-looking as I, any day, Phoebe." (58) The power that attends such good looks has already been exemplified by the lady herself, and therefore the sentence is unsettling: any socially ambitious or greedy girl can emulate the heroine Lucy, provided that she dyes her hair yellow.

The novel's phenomenal success, and its subversive social messages, provoked contemporary critics to discuss Braddon's preoccupation with hair with a seriousness that was not given to the lesser novelists who preceded her. One of Braddon's contemporary critics, Fraser Rae, condemned her deployment of hair in *The Doctor's Wife* as a means to disseminate such dangerous social ideas, and protested against the prominence of hair in Braddon's materialist worldview and fiction: "Of course, the possession of such . . . hair is made the theme of many impassioned paragraphs . . . in perfect accordance with the peculiar philosophy of this authoress, she makes Roland Landsell give vent to the following novel remark: 'With red hair and freckles, Mrs. Gilbert might go to perdition, unwept and unhindered.'"[17] Whether Braddon truly believed that appearances mattered, or not, she was certainly wise enough to realize their growing economic value in a bourgeois, image-oriented society, and to exploit them accordingly. While ostensibly suggesting that, with the right hairstyle, any girl could become a lady, Braddon herself was involved in the broader marketing enterprise of selling illusions to her readers. Just like the countless contemporary advertisements which tried to sell hair dyes, concoctions, and wigs through promises of eternal youth and beauty, so did she promote the idea of social and pecuniary advancement through the usage of artificial hair, hair dyes, and a scrupulous beauty regime. As I have argued elsewhere, from the fifties, hair had become a sexual, sociocultural, and commodity fetish in England ("Tie Her Up," 185–86). Pykett claims that the recurrent descriptions of hair typified "Braddon's habitual fetishization of woman's hair,"[18] but I think they only typified her excellent understanding of, and contribution to, the already powerful process of hair fetishization in fashion, trade, painting, and the literary marketplace. Thus, Lady Audley's golden curls paved Braddon's own way to financial success at least as much as they served the heroine and the woman reader. On the one hand, she created the emerging sensational aesthetics which was fleshly and sexual, colorful and designed by women and for women, all of whom indulged in material passions. On the other hand, she took care to disseminate the new subversive aesthetics through the medium of hair as a metonymic circumlocution, which, though an obvious cipher to sexual issues that were forced into indirectness, could not be seriously censured or censored. At the same time, her presentation of Lady Audley's golden hair, which is invested with the Victorian erotic and commercial overvaluation of hair, serves both economic and sexual narratives to negotiate the issues of social and gender restrictions in a changing society.

Dark Hair Obscures the View

Henry James claimed that in *Aurora Floyd* (1862), "Aurora's hair, in particular, alternately blue-black, purple-black, and dead-black, [wa]s made to go a great way."[19] There is no doubt it did go a long way, being, once again, a medium for Braddon's reconsideration of traditional representations of femaleness. This time she chose to challenge the image of the dark and dangerous woman. Braddon takes great care to first evoke all the traditional hair codes of dangerous femininity, and then expose them as empty literary signs. Thus, for example, Aurora's "masses of ebon hair uncoiled and [fell] about her shoulders in serpentine tresses that looked like shining blue-black snakes released from poor Medusa's head to make their escape amid the folds of her garments" is a singularly ominous description.[20] All the more so, as it represents the view of her husband who knows she conceals some dark secrets from him. In a parallel narrative movement, Braddon produces in Aurora all the signs of evil female sexuality, just in order to prove that they are misleading, so that Aurora may emerge as an amiable and innocent, if somewhat imprudent, heroine. Continually surprising the readers and frustrating their expectations, Braddon seems to point out that such confusion is due to fixed, and often erroneous, sociocultural and literary constructions of femininity. Moreover, although James rightly suggested that Braddon described Aurora's hair using a plethora of shades—purple-black, blue-black, and dead-black—the varying shades of black were not necessarily pointless. Rather, Braddon seems to have deliberately obfuscated any precise classification of the heroine. On a symbolic level, this range of hues may be seen as a commentary on social and literary conventions which result from rigid and conservative categorization of women. Aurora's name could be completely blackened, and her character lost, with no consideration for the subtle shades of her misbehavior. Thus in Braddon's recurrent and varying descriptions of the hues of Aurora's black hair there may be an insinuation that even "fallen" women are not all black.

In *John Marchmont's Legacy* (1863), where Braddon was most seriously engaged in the efforts to construct a convincing heroine,[21] she seemed to express her concern that any literary representation of that much-contested mystery, a woman, was woefully limited: "Those masses of hair had not that purple lustre, nor yet that wandering glimmer of red gold, which gives peculiar beauty to some raven tresses. Olivia's hair was long and luxuriant; but it was of that dead, inky blackness, which is all shadow. It was dark, *fathomless, inscrutable, like herself* [emphasis added]."[22] By having the heroine and her hair conflated, Braddon invests the latter with iconographic significance, but at the same time qualifies and undercuts it by showing the sheer difficulty of describing or defining hair, and, by the same token, woman. At once conscientious and merciless, religious and fleshly, wise and passionate, Olivia's character is shifting, always misunderstood, or "misread," by her father, her husband, and Edward, defying any narrow construction of femininity as much as her hair defies categorization, codification, or easy "reading." Thus, Olivia's hair in this novel actually underscores the limitations of both literary representation of women and sociocultural configuration of the female gender.

Pre-Raphaelite Red Turns Real

It is likely that what Oliphant found truly upsetting in Braddon's vivid, excessive representation of hair in *Lady Audley's Secret* was not only the "intense appreciation of flesh and blood" and the "eagerness of physical sensation," but also, and perhaps mainly, the idea that such images could influence female readers, prompting them to be immodest, fleshly, and greedy, and predicating a real social change. And indeed, such semiotic, hermeneutic, and sociopolitical insecurities are ingrained in the novel itself, most distinctly in Lady Audley's portrait, which functions as a parable of artistic representation that interferes with, and eventually overwhelms, reality.

Lady Audley's physicality, and particularly her hair, corresponds to the Pre-Raphaelite model that became increasingly popular and influential in the 1860s. Lady Audley's portrait is a self-conscious, self-reflexive tribute to the Pre-Raphaelites, being "a faithful reproduction of . . . the Pre-Raphaelite Brotherhood" (69–71). As such, it also reproduces the same fetishized hair: "No one but a Pre-Raphaelite would have painted, hair by hair, those feathery masses of ringlets with every glimmer of gold, and every shadow of brown . . . the [same] brilliancy of color . . . the red-gold gleaming in the yellow hair" (69–71). Even while denying that anyone who did not belong to the Pre-Raphaelite brotherhood could produce such hair, Braddon was reproducing it herself, and turning it into one of the trademarks of the emerging sensation genre. At the same time, of course, she exploited the Pre-Raphaelite trope of the fiendish, beautiful woman to add dimension and character to her own heroine. Notably, in such Pre-Raphaelite moments, Lady Audley's hair is "red-gold" rather than just yellow, in accordance with the Pre-Raphaelite predilection for this specific hue in their rendition of women's hair.

The portrait has a central role in the ambiguous conclusion of the novel. While shutting Lady Audley herself out of society, and by the same token, out of the world of self-production and self-redefinition in which the lady excels, Braddon's last description of the deserted, defeated patriarchal mansion dwells on that portrait. Braddon seems to imply that, on a metaliterary level, even in the absence of the transgressive heroine, the author's redefinition of female representation has mobilized a new aesthetic and social discourse, which will not end with the punishment of Lady Audley, or with the book itself. The portrait is still there, albeit hidden by a curtain, waiting to be looked at and discussed. Moreover, it is a subversive and perpetual discussion, for the painting will outlive all other characters, and the baronet "is not informed of" the fact that "people admire my lady's rooms, and ask many questions about the pretty, fair-haired woman" (446).

The new aesthetic and social discourse that emerged with Lady Audley's sensational hair indeed posed "many questions about the pretty, fair-haired woman." It seems that Lady Audley's hair acquired a life of its own in reality. Whereas in the 1840s and 1850s dark hair was more desirable and fashionable than yellow hair, by 1865 the latter turned into a much-coveted and highly priced product; it was about 50 percent dearer than black or brown hair (1.5 guineas to less than 1 an ounce).[23] In May 1866, *Punch* showed that English women fell under the sway of the sensational trend of yellow hair. A dark-haired lady is seen talking to her hairdresser, the title "Authority." She pleads with him: "[A]nd so, Mr. Frizzelind, you think I ought to have my hair washed yellow! And pray, Why?" "Well, Ma'am," replies the hair-dresser with due authority, "Black hair is never admitted into really good society now, you know!"[24] As yellow hair became the rage in 1860s London, and more and more women chose to dye their hair in order to achieve Lady Audley's glamorous locks, the line between art and nature became, indeed, dangerously thin. Braddon's literary trope challenged the concept of fiction as a mimetic art that imitated—and therefore followed—life. Rather, the fictional yellow hair turned into an all-too-real force that influenced women's self-consciousness and shaped their self-image at a crucial stage in their quest for a new definition of female sexuality. But the red-gold hue that was closely associated with the Pre-Raphaelite portrait, with Lady Audley's setting on fire the public house where Robert Audley lodged in the chapter "Red Light in the Sky," and with the heroine's bloodiness became no less inspirational and influential in the following years.

In the late 1860s, red hair reigned supreme in London, although it had been considered unfashionable and unsightly for many years previously. This revolution in hair fashions was wrought by another sensational heroine. Moreover, through her it was closely associated with aggressive, bloody femininity; fleshly desires; and flaming sexuality. Like Braddon, Wilkie Collins unsettled traditional social and hermeneutic hierarchies, and ruffled critics' feathers. In *Armadale* (1866) he introduced Lydia Gwilt, who, like Lady Audley, was an impostor and a governess; but as opposed to Audley, whose babyish, fair locks seemed angelic at first, Lydia's red hair signified mature, dangerous, daring sexuality from the start. Lydia, too, is readily associated with the Pre-Raphaelite movement's representation of femme fatales through her hair: "This woman's hair, superbly luxuriant in its growth . . . was *red!*"[25] Collins, whose father was a painter and whose brother belonged to the Pre-Raphaelites, incorporated the red-haired beauty into his work. As Altick claims, until sensation, heroines with unequivocally red hair were rare. However, references to red hair from the early 1850s onward were rendered immediately topical by the acrimonious debate over Pre-Raphaelite painting, as "burning auburn" became a hallmark of the Pre-Raphaelite style. In 1856, red hair was not yet a legitimate aesthetic model, as can be seen in the *Athenaeum*'s criticism of Millais's painting that year: "Mr Millais must have been staying at the village which Goldsmith immortalizes as 'Sweet *Auburn,* loveliest village of the *Plain,*'[26] for plain people with red hair seem this year his idiosyncrasy. . . . About all his pictures there is a red-haired inflammatory atmosphere very eccentric and unpleasing."[27]

Therefore, Gwilt's flamboyant hair and character (a poisoner, a forger, and a bigamist) were both a statement of unconventionality that challenged prevalent models of femininity on aesthetic, literary, and social levels. Gwilt uses her flaming hair, which embodies her deviant sexuality, to ensnare and entrap all the male characters in the novel. As Lydia herself notes, her hair is the focus of male attention: "[O]ne meets such rude men . . . in the railway. . . . And though I dress quietly, my hair is so very remarkable" (463). But Lydia's hair is also closely associated with art (Pre-Raphaelite) and artfulness, or artifice, which is the etymological source of "fetish."[28] Lydia's hair is a consumer-oriented spectacle, emphasizing—and advertising—the value of impressive hair as a means to obtain money, success, and attention, shifting the focal point from the natural to the artificial, and advocating feminine self-construction through consumerist cosmetic artifacts and red hair dyes. During her career as an impostor and a men-and-fortune hunter, Lydia is assisted by Mother Oldershaw, whom Altick identifies as an allusion to "Madame" Rachel Leverson who opened a beauty parlor in London (1863), and extracted "large sums of money" from "gullible women whose beauty she claimed to be able to preserve, or enhance, by means of various cosmetic preparations" (541–45). In their correspondence, Oldershaw advises Lydia, from her "Ladies' Toilette Repository," to conceal her thirty-five years with makeup and cosmetic potions, and to go "money-grubbing in the golden Armadale diggings" (159). However, Lydia's hair has already been "adulterated" by Oldershaw's hands: as one character notes, "she went back [to Mrs. Oldershaw] in the interests of her own magnificent head of hair. The prison-scissors, I needn't tell you, had made short work of it with Miss Gwilt's love-locks, in every sense of the word—and Mrs Oldershaw . . . is the most eminent woman in England, as Recover-General of the dilapidated heads and faces of the female sex" (535–36).

As Lydia became the center of the narrative, and took an authorial and active part in it, the critics' reviews protested angrily that she could not possibly represent a "true" or "real" woman.[29] No doubt they were horrified at the thought that such a heroine could be living among them, and tried to consign her red hair and smoldering sexuality to the lurid realm of sensational fantasy: "When a very high effect is intended, red is the hue par excellence," said Oliphant derisively in 1867 (269). One could see why she wished to ridicule, and to oversimplify, the prominence of red hair in sensation fiction. Limited only to the world of fiction, red hair was less threatening, whereas in fact, it was already turning into a meaningful semiotic and social phenomenon that blurred the borderlines between reality and fiction. It also testified to the power that Lydia's hair, as an empowering sexual fantasy, had over women. As Altick notes, "where nature refused to assist" the new vogue for red hair, "artifice—unmitigated, unwomanly deceit—rushed in to supply the lack" (320–21). Justin McCarthy wrote in June 1876 that one could see in the drawing rooms of the moment women who looked as if they had just stepped out of the frames of the Pre-Raphaelite paintings, "bright red hair" and all. "How," McCarthy wondered, "did all these Pre-Raphaelite girls manage to come to life so suddenly? Were they all born with that red hair . . . ?"(Altick 321–22).

Conclusion

Two years after *Armadale,* in 1868, Eliza Lynn Linton wrote her conservative, antifeminist commentary about "The Girl of the Period" for the *Saturday Review*. Linton nostalgically evoked the traditional ideal of a natural, gentle, selfless womanhood, lamenting its loss and ridiculing the fashions that came to be associated with the modern woman. It is, therefore, significant that Linton herself chose to represent the "girl of the period" as "a creature who dyes her hair and paints her face," and that "this rampant modernization" of femininity was characteristically wearing "false red hair."[30] The emphasis on flaming red hair in reality, following art and fiction, shows to what extent sensation fiction was both influenced by, and influencing, both the marketplace and the debates of the day. It also shows that women's hair in sensation fiction was not only a response to, but also part of, the discourse on modern femininity.

Representations of hair in sensation fiction facilitated the deconstruction of an important mode of signification on which social, political, cultural, and literary structures were contingent. The new sensational aesthetics and the considerable effect it had on contemporary readers resulted in the rejection of absolute hierarchical distinctions between nature and artifice, "high" and "low" literature, ethereal and evil femininity, female victims and female victimizers, female readers and female heroines.

NOTES

1. Richard Altick, *The Presence of the Present: Topics of the Day in the Victorian Novel,* 330. All subsequent references are cited by page in the text.

2. Charles Dickens, *A Tale of Two Cities,* (Oxford University Press, 1998), 257.

3. For a more detailed discussion of Dickens's characterization of heroines through hair imagery, see Galia Ofek, "'Tie Her Up by the Hair': Dickens's Retelling of the Medusa and Rapunzel Myths," 184–99.

4. See Ofek, "Medusa's Head: The Representation of Maggie's Head of Hair in *The Mill on the Floss,*" 85–89.

5. Nathaniel Beard, "Some Recollections of Yesterday," *Temple Bar,* 325.

6. Margaret Oliphant, "Novels," *Blackwood's,* 263, 269. All further references are by page in the text.

7. Harry Hazleton, a journalist, wrote and published several other books, some anonymously.

8. [Hazleton], *The Woman with the Yellow Hair: A Romance of Good and Bad Society*, 343. All references are to this edition and are cited by page in the text.

9. Percy Fitzgerald, *The Woman with the Yellow Hair and Other Modern Mysteries*. Fitzgerald was a prolific journalist and writer. All references are to this edition and are cited by page in the text.

10. Fitzgerald, *Memoirs of an Author*, vol. 1, 104.

11. George Augustus Sala, *The Seven Sons of Mammon*, vol. 2, 59.

12. Peter David Edwards, *Dickens's 'Young Men': George Augustus Sala, Edmund Yates and the World of Victorian Journalism*, 75.

13. Elizabeth Gitter, "The Power of Women's Hair in the Victorian Imagination," 936–54.

14. It is interesting to compare the symbolic value of golden hair in sensation fiction of the early sixties with Christina Rossetti's contemporaneous representation of Laura's golden hair in "Goblin Market." As Nancy Welter claims in another essay in this book, Laura's golden curl turns into a figure of exchange that "commodifies her body" in the "patriarchal economy" of the goblin world, symbolizing her subjection to the male value system; her loss of virginity; and the failure of an alternative, ideal female economy. But whereas the sensational golden-haired heroine accepts that her hair is a figure of exchange in a male-dominated economy, she—unlike Laura—does not succumb to the patriarchal value system, but rather subverts and manipulates it to her own advantage. Men cannot tempt her to sell a golden lock for a piece of fruit, because she is determined to "sell" her hair to the highest bidder, and uses her symbolic gold to seduce and defeat men.

15. Katherine Montwieler, "Marketing Sensation: *Lady Audley's Secret* and Consumer Culture," 43.

16. Mary Elizabeth Braddon, *Lady Audley's Secret* (Oxford University Press, 1998), 8. All references are to this edition and are cited by page in the text.

17. William Fraser [Rae], "Sensation Novelists: Miss Braddon," 198.

18. Lyn Pykett, *The Improper Feminine*, 98.

19. Henry James, "Miss Braddon," *Notes and Reviews*, 113.

20. Braddon, *Aurora Floyd* (Oxford University Press, 1999), 271.

21. See Norman Page, introduction to *John Marchmont's Legacy*, xv.

22. Braddon, *John Marchmont's Legacy* (Oxford University Press, 1991), 71.

23. Hermann Beigel, *The Human Hair: Its Structure, Growth, Diseases and Their Treatment*, 14.

24. *Punch*, May 5, 1866, 183.

25. Wilkie Collins, *Armadale* (Penguin, 1995), 277. All references are to this edition and are cited by page in the text.

26. This is a reference to Goldsmith's "Dedication to Sir Joshua Reynolds," in *The Deserted Village*.

27. "Review of Millais's Paintings," *Athenaeum*, 590.

28. The etymological source of the word "fetish" is vital to the understanding of hair's function in Victorian culture: fetish meant "artificial, skillfully contrived, made by art"; "factitious" as opposed to "genuine." See William Pietz, "The Origin of the Fetish II," 24–25.

29. For example, see Chorley's reviews in the *Athenaeum*, Collins: *The Critical Heritage*, 41, 147. Cited in Norman Page, ed., *Wilkie Collins: The Critical Heritage*.

30. See Elizabeth Lynn Linton, "The Girl of the Period," 339–40.

- 10 -

"WHAT COULD I DO?"

Nineteenth-Century Psychology and the Horrors of Masculinity in The Woman in White

ANDREW MANGHAM

Hidden Dangers: Obscure Diseases of the Brain

IN 1862, the *Cornhill Magazine* claimed that science was playing a significant role in the developing sense that hidden energies lurked beneath false appearances. "By science," it remarked, "man . . . concedes that the world is not what it seems":

> The world becomes doubled to us: it is one world of things perceived; one unperceivable. . . . All nature grows like an enchanted garden; a fairy world in which unknown existences lurk under familiar shapes, and every object seems ready, at the shaking of a wand, to take on the strangest transformations.[1]

Few scientific disciplines, it seems, had the ability to convince their followers that "unknown existences lurk[ed] under familiar shapes" like the branches of psychology concerned with obscure cerebral disorders. In 1860, the same year that *The Woman in White* appeared, Forbes Winslow assembled his theories on insanity to form the lengthy and eccentric volume *On the Obscure Diseases of the Brain and Disorders of the Mind,* one of the psychological treatises in Collins's own library.[2] As its preface reveals, *Obscure Diseases* aimed to offer "the unitiated, as well as those who are medically educated," a guide for detecting the easily overlooked symptoms of an "obscure," "insidious," and dangerous mental condition.[3] He warned that no individual is exempt from the advance of insanity and irrational behavior. Utilizing imagery that seems familiar to a reader of popular Victorian fiction, he inquires:

> Who has not occasionally had a demon pursuing with remorseless impetuosity his every footstep, suggesting to his ever-active and often morbidly-disturbed and perverted imagination the commission of some dark deed of crime, from the conception of which he has at the time recoiled with horror? (142)

It was a question repeated often by the era's psychologists. In 1858, Daniel Tuke and John Bucknill claimed that "there is a latent devil in the heart of the best of men."[4] Nobody, they contested, is exempt from disturbed cognitive phenomena. "Is not every bosom," Winslow added, "polluted by a dark, leprous spot, corroding ulcer, or portion of moral gangrene?" (142). He answers his own elaborate rhetoric in the affirmative and, citing the words of fellow psychologist John Abercrombie, cautions the reader to watch himself and those closest to him with the strictest scrutiny: "Hence the supreme importance of cultivating in early life the habit of looking within, the practice of rigidly questioning ourselves as to what we are, and what we are doing" (142).

Many Victorian psychologists believed that such vigilance was especially needful in regard to women. Studies like Gilbert and Gubar's seminal *Madwoman in the Attic* (1979) have established how the appearance/reality dichotomy was particularly key to nineteenth-century conceptualizations of femininity. *Temple Bar*, for example, earnestly warned its male readers against female flirts in 1869. "Let all men beware," it ominously advised, of "the typical flirt—the vampire who lives upon the hearts of men. . . . This terrible woman . . . generally comes in the most innocent guise—generally that of a little, soft, big-eyed girl."[5] In the period's medical textbooks, such ideas on the demonic underside of femininity developed into a representation of female nature as deceptive and incendiary. French psychologist Jean Esquirol wrote, for example, that "physical causes [of insanity] act with more frequency upon [women] than men. . . . [They] practice during their disorder, more concealment . . . , they speak with more repugnance of their condition, and try to hide it from themselves and others."[6] A significant number of the period's medics perceived women's physical constitutions, as well as their "want of occupation,"[7] to be the main causes of explosive mental conditions. In 1848, for example, John Millingen wrote:

> In woman, the concentration of her feelings (a concentration that her social position renders indispensable) adds to their intensity; and like a smouldering fire that has at last got vent, her passions, when no longer trammelled by conventional propriety, burst forth in unquenchable violence.[8]

Uterine health, especially the flow and ebb of menstruation, was thought to be a timely indicator of such psychopathological eruptions. The period's treatises on insanity are flooded with case histories of women who went mad because of overabundant or underactive menstrual activity. In 1867, for example, in the *Journal of Mental Science,* Dr. Teilleux cited the case of a woman who had killed three of her babies. He noted how "menstruation had always been irregular and painful, and the murder was committed immediately prior to the recurrence of the menstrual discharge."[9] James Prichard's *Treatise on Insanity* (1837) also included the example of a woman who "at each period of the catamenia . . . menaced every person with her knife" despite being "perfectly natural" at all other times.[10] According to Esquirol, such examples suggested that "we must be ever watchful of these metastases and suppressions."[11]

Such surveillance of the female sexual organs reached disturbing and extraordinary lengths in the 1860s when obstetrician Isaac Baker Brown promoted clitoridectomy as a cure for mental instability in women. For Brown, masturbation and sexual promiscuity were pivotal causes of female mental maladies and excising the locus of carnal pleasure, the clitoris, would remove the desire (and the ability) to indulge the sexual appetite. Brown's "practices" eventually led to his expulsion from the newly formed Obstetrical Society. Its members claimed that he had performed the surgery too eagerly and too frequently. The *British Medical Journal* reported how, at a meeting of the society,

> it is urged against Mr. Brown, that he is so possessed with the idea of the universality of the habit of self-abuse and its power of producing innumerable evils, that he resorts to the operation with lamentable frequency. As a consequence of this, practitioners are constantly meeting with patients who are not only unrelieved by this treatment, but are even left worse, to say nothing of the stigma which has been cast upon their moral character.[12]

The suggestion that Brown is "possessed" by his ideas hints at the possibility that, according to the Obstetrical Society at least, his attempts to locate and cure female mental illness had provided the surgeon with the means to fulfill his own unhealthy obsessions. The disgrace of Brown, I argue, reveals a midcentury concern that the detection and treatment of psychological disorders in women were inseparable from the subjective preoccupations of male practitioners.

In this essay, I argue that Wilkie Collins's *The Woman in White* is a text that explores the era's unbalanced fascination with "looking within" female nature. With reference to this, Collins's most famous novel, I suggest that, like the clitoridectomy debates, the book explores how male anticipations of women's madness might uncover more about the unbalanced nature of masculinity and the psychological strategies used to anticipate and control those forces than they did about the alleged "dangers" of femininity.

Staining the *Tabula Rasa: The Woman in White*

Throughout *The Woman in White*, Walter Hartright's detective work has much in common with the perceived analytical skills of nineteenth-century psychiatrists. After his early encounters with Anne Catherick, he develops an obsession with tracking her down and deciphering the mysteries surrounding her identity. "The way to the Secret," he writes, "lay through the mystery, hitherto impenetrable to all of us, of the woman in white."[13] As a man searching for an elusive figure (who typifies lunacy for him), Hartright emulates the mid-Victorian psychologist's aim to "penetrate behind the curtain" of humanity (Winslow 127) in search of transient signs of insanity. Winslow writes: "To the unskilled, untutored and untrained eye the disease is, in its early stages, occasionally altogether invisible" (79). Like this "disease," Anne frequently evades the grasp of men searching for her: "like a Shadow she first came to me," Hartright admits, "like a Shadow she passes away, in the loneliness of the dead" (569).

During his pursuit of Anne, however, Walter appears to turn his diagnostic methods onto himself, a process that also links him to contemporaneous psychologists. After reading her letter to Laura, for example, he considers whether Anne is "deranged":

> Those words and the doubt which had just escaped me as to the sanity of the writer of the letter, acting together on my mind, suggested an idea, which I was literally afraid to express openly, or even to encourage secretly. I began to doubt whether my own faculties were not in danger of losing their balance. It seemed almost like a monomania to be tracing back every strange thing that happened, everything unexpected that was said, always to the same hidden source and the same sinister influence. (80)

Employing a term coined by Esquirol ("monomania"), Walter's consideration of Anne Catherick's madness questions how far the process of detection or diagnosis is itself an unbalanced mental fixation. Walter's thought process echoes the way nineteenth-century psychologists would often have *their* diagnostic methods and theories refracted upon them. We have already seen, for example, how Brown's theories on the excessive carnality of insane women were converted, by his critics, into suggestions that he himself harbored unhealthy obsessions. In 1864, moreover, Winslow was also accused of displaying symptoms of the mental diseases he proposed to treat. The *Glasgow Medical Journal* boldly wrote of Winslow, for example, that the disorders he "discovered" were symptomatic of his own mental imbalances:

With the fullest conviction of our sanity, we should dread ... an hour's interview with this great flaw-finder; for either in our moral or in our mental constitution he would discover some screw loose, and by gently moving it backwards and forwards, would naturally find it looser and looser.... It is scarcely our business to speculate as to the origin of these comprehensive theories of the mind of the distinguished physician in question; but it may not be irrelevant to go as far as to assume, that when a man is constantly examining cases of real or supposed insanity, a period arrives when his judgement is in a certain manner affected by the continual practice which he has to undergo.[14]

Hartright's fear that tracing everything back to the same "hidden source" is symptomatic of monomania thus fits in with concurrent suspicions that the process of detecting obscure mental disorders was itself a psychopathological obsession. For *The Woman in White,* Collins expands the idea to portray Hartright and Glyde's relationships with Anne Catherick. The search for the woman in white and the clues to her identity become an introspective investigation into the obscure recesses of these characters' own minds.

When Hartright first meets Anne Catherick, on the road to Hampstead, his fears appear unnecessary and exaggerated. Long before he discovers that she has escaped from an asylum, she has the ability to make his blood run cold:

In one moment, every drop of blood in my body was brought to a stop by the touch of a hand laid lightly and suddenly on my shoulder from behind me.... I was far too seriously startled by the suddenness with which this extraordinary apparition stood before me, in the dead of night and in that lonely place, to ask what she wanted. (20)

Despite his shock, Walter looks upon the woman in white as a figure that needs interpretation. He wonders, for example, "what sort of a woman she was, and how she came to be out alone in the high-road, an hour after midnight" (21). Like the period's psychologists, he looks for signs of irrationality and sexual promiscuity in his mysterious companion: "[T]here was," he admits, "nothing wild, nothing immodest in her manner: it was quiet and self-controlled" (20). Yet, throughout his early encounters with Anne, the novel creates a sense that Walter's expectations of irrational or licentious behavior from her are unfounded and self-generated. Even when he discovers that she is an escapee from an asylum, for example, his intensified fears are counterbalanced by an implication that they are unnecessary. "What had I done?" he asks, "assisted the victim of the most horrible of all false imprisonments to escape; or cast loose on the wide world of London an unfortunate creature ... ?" (28–29). Hartright's concern that he has released an irrational woman on the London populace is juxtaposed by suspicions that he may have aided a prostitute or the victim of false imprisonment. Even supposing that Anne Catherick *is* truly insane, there is still no objective reason for Hartright's agitated reception of her. Helen Small notes, for example, how the characterization of Anne draws on a nineteenth-century trope of female love-madness. The lovesick woman, she reveals, may be "crazy," but she posed a direct threat to no one other than herself.[15] Beyond the initial shock of having a hand laid unexpectedly upon his shoulder in the dead of night, therefore, there are few objective reasons for Hartright's lingering, irrational responses to Anne. Her "dangers" appear to be the illusionary fabrications of his own invention.

By accepting responsibility for an "unfortunate creature" unleashed on an unsuspecting public, Hartright appears to have much in common with Victor Frankenstein. Both characters, for example, seem to release (what are believed to be) unreasonable beings into the world and yet the "dangers" of these "beings" are the products of their own construction. Whereas Frankenstein deliberately sets about building a monster, Hartright's demonic creation is built with more subtle and complex psychological tools. For him, Anne Catherick is a figurative *tabula rasa* onto which he daubs the most disturbing aspects of his own character. His ruminations over Anne's identity, for example, constantly shift and become self-directed:

> We set our faces towards London . . . I, and this woman, whose name, whose character, whose story, whose objects in life, whose very presence by my side, at that moment, were fathomless mysteries to me. It was like a dream. Was I Walter Hartright? . . . I was too bewildered—too conscious also of a vague sense of something like self-reproach—to speak to my strange companion for some minutes. (23)

Like Franklin Blake's search into the unfathomable depths of the Shivering Sands in *The Moonstone* (1868), Hartright's contemplations of the "fathomless mysteries" of the woman in white bring forth a realization that there are improper, latent depths to his own identity. In this scene, for instance, both he and Anne become conscious of the latter's vulnerability, as a solitary woman, approaching a male stranger in the dark miles from anywhere. Her whiteness testifies to her openness to violation: "[P]romise not to interfere with me," she implores "will you promise?" (22–23). The two potential definitions of the word "interfere" (as obstructing her means of escape and molestation) create an apt innuendo and Hartright also recognizes Anne's defenselessness:

> What could I do? Here was a stranger utterly and helplessly at my mercy—and that stranger a forlorn woman. No house was near; no one was passing. . . . I trace these

lines, self-distrustfully, with the shadows of after-events darkening the very paper I write on; and I still say, what could I do? . . . She came close to me, and laid her hand, with a sudden gentle stealthiness, on my bosom—a thin hand; a cold hand (when I removed it with mine) even on that sultry night. Remember that I was young; remember that the hand which touched me was a woman's. . . . Oh me! and I tremble, now, when I write it. (22–23)

This passage suggests that the reason for Hartright's trembling self-reproach is linked to an awakening sense of the dangerous possibilities of his own heterosexual desire. The woman in white appears, for example, while he is wondering what the young ladies at Limmeridge House look like. One of these "young ladies"— Laura—and the sexual feelings she will later ignite, appear to materialize in the form of her look-alike half sister. His frenetic question "what could I do? . . . what could I do?" could be read not only as a justification of his helping a dubious woman, but as a consideration of what the situation could have enabled him to do *to* Anne. What could he have done, he seems to ask himself, when he had the opportunity? What were his capabilities? In coming face-to-face with a woman "utterly and helplessly at [his] mercy," he is struck by a sudden awareness that this was a meeting that could have resulted in his raping or violating his helpless companion. It is *this* that I see as causing his blood to run cold and the narrator's pen to tremble. I suggested above that Anne's white costume could indicate her openness to violation; it seems hardly coincidental, therefore, that when the narrator recounts the scene, his "self-distrust . . . darken[s] the very paper [he] write[s] on." Staining the page symbolically fulfills the young Hartright's fantasies of defilement.

Anne Catherick is also linked to the innermost fears of Sir Percival Glyde. Because he is killed in the vestry fire, and cannot narrate his own version of events, his motivations, desires, and fears are mainly discernible through other characters' accounts of them and the conversation, overheard by Marian, with Count Fosco. In this scene, Glyde reveals how he has searched for Anne, believing her to be a danger to his social standing: "I had done my best to find Anne Catherick, and failed. . . . I'm a lost man, if I *don't* find her" (336–37). Percival fears that Anne knows he is illegitimate and, therefore, that he is ineligible for the Blackwater property: "I can ruin you for life, if I choose to open my lips," she tells him (549). Whereas for Hartright, Anne's whiteness represents her susceptibility to his violation, for Glyde it becomes a mocking reminder of his own blank identity. Yet, like Hartright's disturbed responses to Anne Catherick, the text reveals how Glyde's fears are a fictive product of *his* haunted imagination. Although Anne tells him that she knows his secret, her mother reveals how she actually knows nothing:

> I told him that she had merely repeated, like a parrot, the words she had heard me say, and that she knew no particulars whatever, because I had mentioned none. I explained that she had affected, out of crazy spite against him, to know what she really did *not* know. (550)

Glyde nevertheless insists on "shutting her up" verbally and physically (550). The woman in white becomes, for Percival as she did for Hartright, a blank page onto which he projects the fears and suspicions connected to his own selfhood.

Glyde and Hartright's search for the marriage registers also reveals more about the detectives than it does about the detected. Glyde and Hartright's race to discover these documents takes place in scenes where Glyde and Hartright come closest to meeting and their motivations seem to become indistinguishable. The factor that unites the characters of Glyde and Hartright most forcibly is the way the registers provide, like Anne Catherick, an index to the most unseemly aspects of both men's identities. Glyde's desperate attempt to avail himself of the documents, for example, echoes his attempt to find the woman in white in order to keep his secret concealed. For Hartright, however, they not only become a site for his projected violent sexuality, like Anne, but also reveal how such carnal urges are linked to the drawing master's latent fantasies of social advancement. There are telling similarities, for example, between the following passage and his first meeting with Anne Catherick on the London high road. He has just discovered the marriage registers and the secrets they reveal:

> My heart gave a great bound, and throbbed as if it would stifle me. I looked again—I was afraid to believe the evidence of my own eyes. . . . My head turned giddy; I held by the desk to keep myself from falling. . . . This was the Secret, and it was mine! A word from me; and house, lands, baronetcy, were gone from him for ever. . . . The man's whole future hung on my lips—and he knew it by this time as certainly as I did! (521)

These are hardly the sensations of an objective observer. As in his earlier encounter with Anne, Hartright develops a sporadic heartbeat, spinning head, and distrusts his own senses. In both scenes he also feels a covert satisfaction at having another person completely under his control. Like his earlier recognition of Anne as "helplessly at [his] mercy," he becomes elated over the fact that Glyde's "whole future hung on [his] lips." In the fire that soon follows, his psychotic tensions reach the climax they have been working toward ever since the night he first met Anne Catherick. Immediately prior to the conflagration he admits that "my head [was] in a whirl, and my blood throbb[ed] through my veins at fever heat"

(522). Soon afterward, the charred corpse of Glyde lay at his feet: "[T]here . . . stark and grim and black . . . was his dead face" (532). The baron's death could be read as the result of Walter's tensions reaching a volcanic climax. The description of Glyde's body as blackened, for example, echoes the portrayal of Anne's as whitened. The erotic defilement of the woman in white seems to have been fulfilled in the ruining (and blackening) of Percival.

When Hartright appropriates the baron's secret, therefore, his social tensions, as well as his sexual ones, reach an explosive dénouement. As Glyde is burned alive, in what seems to metonymically represent the fire of his adversary's violent passions, Walter inherits Percival's avaricious schemes and aristocratic standing. Although the text aims to present Hartright's motives as noble, his rescuing of Laura's identity results in his appropriation of the wealthy Limmeridge estate.

For both Hartright and Glyde, Laura Fairlie emblematizes their desires as Anne symbolizes their fears. In the likeness between Laura and Anne, the text presents the reader with clues to how the Victorians' fears and desires overlapped and, additionally, how this provided society with a method of exploring the horrors inherent to the dominant group. Numerous critical studies of *The Woman in White* have noted the likeness between Laura and Anne, yet few have demonstrated a reluctance to accept this similarity at face value. Like most opinions in the novel, we only have the narrators' testimonies to the likeness and, when we acknowledge how the text aims to portray individual testimonials as untrustworthy, our reasons for questioning the parallel become all the more pressing.

With both Glyde and Hartright, the resemblances between Laura and Anne are expressed at times when their desires are exercising a powerful dominion over their minds. In the overheard dialogue between Glyde and Fosco, for example, the conversation apparently moves in seamless transition from issues of property and inheritance to the likeness between the two women. Fosco inquires into the likelihood of Lady Glyde's leaving children in the event of her death. Percival answers that this "is not in the least likely" and he stands to inherit £20,000. When Fosco asks how he might recognize Anne, whom he has never met, Glyde responds, "[S]he's a sickly likeness of my wife" (333, 339). The admission that Laura is unlikely to bear children implies that her marriage to Glyde remains unconsummated. Indeed, for Glyde, Laura seems to be, first and foremost, the locus of mercenary lust. In her resemblance to the woman whom he believes is capable of destroying his aristocratic station, therefore, Percival reveals how pecuniary ambition carries its own paranoia of loss; a good position in society is apparently freighted with its own demons of destruction.

Unlike Glyde, the relationship that Hartright covets with Laura *is* sexual. For him, in the early stages of the novel, she is, primarily, the object of carnal desire.

"Think of her," he implores the male reader, "as you thought of the first woman who quickened the pulses within you" (50). He notices an "impression, which, in a shadowy way, suggested to me the idea of something wanting" (50–51) and eventually discovers that this is a likeness between Miss Fairlie and the woman in white. The moment of revelation occurs when Laura is looking especially alluring:

> My eyes fixed upon the white gleam of her muslin gown and head-dress in the moonlight, and a sensation, for which I can find no name—a sensation that quickened my pulse, and raised a fluttering in my heart—began to steal over me. . . . A thrill of the same feeling which ran through me when the touch was laid upon my shoulder in the lonely high-road, chilled me again.
>
> There stood Miss Fairlie, a white figure, alone in the moonlight; in her attitude, in the turn of her head, in her complexion, in the shape of her face, the living image, at that distance and under those circumstances, of the woman in white! . . . That "something wanting" was my own recognition of the ominous likeness between the fugitive from the asylum and my pupil at Limmeridge House. (59–61)

Dressed in white garments (which, when worn by Anne Catherick on the high road, had signified her openness to violation) and steeped in moonlight, Laura appears the very epitome of sexualized femininity. At the instant Hartright's gaze (centered suggestively on her dress) is aroused sexually, the shadowy woman in white makes an imaginary appearance. Hartright's ominous psychosomatic symptoms (the quickened pulse, the fluttering heart, the same "thrill" he felt on the high road) return along with his recollections of Anne. The "return" of the woman in white in this sequence seems to follow the return of Hartright's violent sexual urges. "Call her in, out of the dreary moonlight," he urges Marian (61). As in his encounter with Anne Catherick, he unconsciously asks himself, "[W]hat could I do?" He is aware of the violent threat his sexual attraction bears Laura— what he later calls his "dangerous intimacy" (63). The fearful woman in white is thus not only linked to Hartright's most oppressive fears, but also (through her resemblance to Laura) his strongest desires. This suggests that women—as the objects of psychological observation—provided an index to both the fears and desires of the contemporary male imagination.

In conclusion, *The Woman in White* reveals how the allegedly insane woman became a figure through which patriarchal society negotiated the dangerous, obsessive nature of its own motivations. Collins's most canonical novel seems to confirm the fear, hinted at in concomitant medical discourses, that the search for incipient madness in women spoke more about the subjective preoccupations of the detective/diagnostic gaze than it did about the alleged dangers of womanhood. What emerges from the interdisciplinary exchange of ideas is a portrait of the professional, bourgeois male as overrun by his pecuniary and sexual passions.

NOTES

1. [J. Hinton], "The Fairy Land of Science," *Cornhill* (1862): 37–38.
2. Collins's edition of *Obscure Diseases* was inscribed "from the Author to Wilkie Collins." See William Baker, *Wilkie Collins's Library*, 160.
3. Forbes Winslow, *On the Obscure Diseases of the Brain*, xi. Subsequent references to this edition will appear in the body of the text.
4. John C. Bucknill and Daniel H. Tuke, *A Manual of Psychological Medicine*, 273. Further references will be noted by page in the text.
5. [W. Black], "Flirts and Flirtation," *Temple Bar* (July 1869): 64–65.
6. J. É. D. Esquirol, *Mental Maladies*, 37.
7. Ibid., 36.
8. John G. Millingen, *The Passions; or Mind and Matter* (1848), 169.
9. Dr. Teilleux, "Triple Infanticide," *Journal of Mental Science* (1867): 556.
10. James C. Prichard, *A Treatise on Insanity*, 275.
11. Esquirol, 89.
12. Unsigned, "Clitoridectomy," *British Medical Journal* (1866): 664.
13. Wilkie Collins, *The Woman in White* (Oxford University Press, 1998), 465. Subsequent references to this edition will appear in the body of the text.
14. Unsigned, "Dr. Forbes Winslow's Evidence in the Townley Case," quoted in the *Journal of Mental Science* (1864): 296–97.
15. Helen Small, *Love's Madness*, 6–7, 206.

- II -

"CHAFING AT THE SOCIAL COBWEBS"

Gender and Transgender in the Work of Charles Reade

RICHARD FANTINA

WHILE EVEN many eminent Victorianists have scant knowledge of the work of Charles Reade, in his own day he was recognized as an often-controversial author of the first rank who, in a career that spanned five decades, produced fourteen novels, twenty-six plays, and over two dozen stories. So singular were his achievements and so individual his voice that both his champions and his detractors found it convenient to compare him to George Eliot.[1] Many hostile critics—"canting dunces" as Reade called them in *Griffith Gaunt*[2]—labeled him with the epithet "sensation author" because many of his stories dealt with the ubiquitous themes of murder, madness, bigamy, and other outré elements. Reade, however, felt comfortable in the popular association of his name with that of his friends and colleagues Wilkie Collins and Mary Elizabeth Braddon. Although Henry James compared him to Shakespeare and Swinburne felt that his work should "live as long as the English language," the decline in Reade's critical standing was complete by the turn of the twentieth century.[3] As Mary Poovey notes, "It took thirty years for Reade's reputation to collapse," which she attributes to a complex series of factors, including the "imperatives of professional journalists [i.e., literary critics], periodical editors, and the titans of the circulating libraries," all of whom sought a stable definition of *literature* and who enforced "the exile of writers like Reade from the literary canon."[4] Elton E. Smith attributes this to the reliance on the "old melodramatic formulae of black-white delineation," but adds that Reade, while "a stylistic conformist was at the same time a topical rebel."[5] Early in life, like one of his characters in *Hard Cash* (1863), Reade had begun to "chafe at the social cobwebs,"[6] and even critics who praised *The Cloister and the Hearth* (1861) felt that many of his domestic novels, like those of Collins and Braddon, exceeded the bounds of decency and decorum. Reade's self-appointed role as a campaigner for social causes, including most famously the reform of conditions in prisons and lunatic asylums, as well as his advocacy of women's rights, earned him many enemies. His frank portrayals of sexuality, including obvious (at least to today's readers) homoerotic passages, outraged many critics. Reade consistently returns to fictional and dramatic explorations of the dynamics of human sexuality, often as it intersects with emerging institutions of punishment and madness. These same themes concerned Michel Foucault a century later and his theoretical framework provides a convenient starting point for an analysis of the portrayal of gender and sexuality in Reade's work.

Sexual Pathologies: Gender and Transgender

In *The History of Sexuality* (1978), Foucault rejects the conventional wisdom of what he calls "the repressive hypothesis"[7] that views the Victorian era as prudish and reluctant to acknowledge sex. Rather, it is precisely because of the Victorians' obsession with sex that its practice became so regulated because such ordering enforced the maintenance of the integrity of the nuclear family as the centerpiece of the bourgeois worldview. Victorian society felt compelled to discreetly study, categorize, pathologize, and criminalize sexuality except in its most respectable form—in marriage and as a means of reproduction (104–5). According to Foucault, "the legitimate couple, with its regular sexuality, had a right to more discretion" and "what came under scrutiny was the sexuality of children, mad men and women, and criminals; those who did not like the opposite sex" (38) among others. Foucault writes that: "The growth of perversions is not a moralizing theme that obsessed the scrupulous minds of the Victorians. It is the real product of the encroachment of a type of power on bodies and their pleasures" (48). This encroachment is part of what Reade and the other sensation novelists are, at times perhaps unconsciously, rebelling against. Reade did not, of course, theorize these concerns and held some views that by today's standards appear conservative. However, like other sensation authors, Reade's work cannot be reductively viewed by twenty-first-century ideas of liberal and conservative. As an artist, Reade presents intensely sexual characters and, despite his disclaimers, several of his works demonstrate a fascination with both transvestism and same-sex attraction, newly identified as chronic perversions in the nineteenth century.

As a new system of regulation was gradually imposed upon human sexuality, the means used to enforce this control were ultimately the prison, the hospital, or the madhouse, institutions that Reade critiques as a contemporary witness in *It Is Never Too Late to Mend* (1856), *Hard Cash*, and other texts. Foucault writes of "the psychiatrization of perverse pleasure" in Victorian discourse in which "anomalies" were sought out and a "corrective technology" employed to adjust them (105).

Such "peripheral sexualities" as homosexuality, sodomy, onanism, tribadism, and masochism, which had been previously condemned as "vices" or "sins" to which any person might be prone, now became medical perversions, diseases, and "frauds against procreation" (117) associated with distinct individuals who were liable to land in prison or an asylum. With the emergence of the new medical discourse, which would find fuller expression later in the nineteenth century with the "science" of sexology, the idea of sodomy, for example, was displaced by the identification of the homosexual as a species unto itself. In an often-cited passage, Foucault writes: "We must not forget that the psychological, psychiatric, medical category of homosexuality was constituted . . . less by a type of sexual relations than by a certain quality of sexual sensibility . . . a kind of interior androgyny, a hermaphrodism of the soul" (43). Sexual outlaws were forced to proclaim their "crimes," to make "obligatory confessions"[8] which were used to develop a new medical taxonomy of perversions. The process that Adrienne Rich has referred to as "compulsory heterosexuality" developed throughout the Victorian era as both gender and sexuality became increasingly codified. In the separate spheres of Victorian gender relations, fluidity was not an option. Yet Reade's work challenges such rigidity and often presents self-consciously androgynous characters.

Reade devotes an entire story to this theme in the posthumously published "Androgynism; or Woman Playing at Man" (1911) in which two women fall in love with each other although one thinks the other is a man. So great was Reade's research and interest in androgyny that in this story (a true one, he claims), he states: "Between the years 1858–62 . . . instances of androgynism occurred, or were brought to light, with unusual frequency, and I devoted a folio of 250 leaves to tabulating them."[9] Reade, who more than most authors based his fiction on contemporary news reports, emphasizes that the tale he relates in "Androgynism" was not uncommon in those years, suggesting, if not an organized transgender movement, at least a good number of unself-conscious sexual radicals roaming the streets of London and other English cities. Many of these were from the working class, which, as Foucault notes, "managed for a long time to escape the deployment of 'sexuality'" (121). Kate, the working-class heroine of this story, presents herself to her husband one day in full male dress. His reaction is: "Why, Kate, what the dash—?" and the text answers: "'Dry up!' was the rejoinder, 'I'm not Kate, I'm Fred. That's me and you've got to recollect it'" (17). The narrative continues: "She stands now before her appalled spouse no longer to outward view feminine, but androgynous, sartorially epicene . . . and by no means unbecoming" (17). Kate's initial motive for assuming masculine garb is economic—so she can find work as a painter's apprentice. As Lillian Faderman notes of many cross-dressing women of the past: "It can only be speculated whether the initial impulse of these transvestites was sexual or social."[10] Faderman suggests that for many, sexual interest in other women "developed as their male roles developed"

(54). Kate/Fred quickly assumes the male role more completely and pursues a woman as sexual object because "overpowering instincts" had "repelled her from the male sex" (21). Reade takes his reader further into the masquerade of Kate/Fred as her androgynous beauty captivates the innocent Miss Nelly and: "down went the poor little heart before this beautiful thing as the corn before the sickle" (20); and "Nelly not only loved Fred; Fred also loved Nelly" (20). Toward the end of the story, while Reade insists that Nelly was the victim of a "detestable deceit," and that Kate/Fred had behaved as a "naughty hussy" (21), he advises "the critic to spare rather than squander sarcasm" (25). Reade wrote this story before the emergence of the New Woman who often dressed in "masculine" clothing. Yet seldom in New Woman fiction do we find anything nearly as homoerotic as Kate/Fred's love for Nelly. Although early in the text Reade, as narrator, states that he "would blush to be suspected of advancing the faintest scintilla of apology for such monstrous perversity" (22), that is what he effectively does throughout the story.

Reade's 1872 novel, *The Wandering Heir* (dedicated to M. E. Braddon), takes place in eighteenth-century England, Ireland, and the American colonies, and presents a reversal of sorts of the theme of "Androgynism" though the gender play is significantly different but no less remarkable for its time. In this case a man, James, falls in love with someone he believes to be another man, Philip, but who is actually a woman, Philippa, in disguise. Earlier in the novel, Philippa tells her pastor, "'t is but the price of a coat and waistcoat and breeches . . . and then I *am* a boy. Oh! 't will be sweet to have my freedom and not be checked at every word, because I am a she."[11] Philippa's comments reflect Faderman's point that many females "became transvestites in the first place because they desired greater freedom than women were permitted" (54), but that once identified as male they often became attractive to other women, as Nelly becomes smitten with Kate/Fred in "Androgynism." In *The Wandering Heir,* however, the cross-dressing Philippa solicits and wins the affection of a man. At one point James says to Philip: "Oh, thou dear good, sweet, wicked boy . . . let me kiss thee" (100). Later, after he has lost track of Philip, James pines for him saying: "His head was all wit; his heart all tenderness, his face all sunshine . . . and now, when Fortune seems to shine, he has deserted me. Oh, Philip! Philip!" (144). Soon after this, James and Philippa are reunited, and when she reveals her true sex their love intensifies, but she remains stronger both emotionally and intellectually than he, and continues to dress in men's clothing when she wishes "to speak her mind more freely" (179), or to set an example whenever she needs to pluck up her lover's courage. Well after she has revealed her female identity, Philippa appears before James, once again dressed as a man, and puns to him: "'Your spirits want a *philip,* Sir,' said she, 'and I must give them one'" (180; original emphasis). Only when she assumes the role of a man can Philippa stir the lethargic James to action.

Men, too, cross-dress in Reade's work. In *The Cloister and the Hearth,* during his sojourn in Italy, Gerard becomes "a rake, a debauchee, and a drunkard, and one of the wildest, loosest, wickedest young men in Rome."[12] He takes on as a protégé "a lad called Andrea . . . a youth of rare beauty," and escorts his new pupil, arrayed in full drag, to a party, fooling for a time the other libertines in attendance (306–9). In *Hard Cash,* after the imprisoned Alfred gains his freedom from an asylum, the authorities try to retake him at the home of his fiancée, Julia. Alfred quickly dons one of her cloaks and a bonnet and, as Julia reacts "with glee" at the sight of him, makes his escape as "a handsome, brazen-looking trollop six-feet high" (354–55). Reade was certainly aware of the transgressive behavior he was depicting despite his disingenuous remarks to the contrary, for in *The Wandering Heir* Philippa, an indentured servant in Delaware, consciously breaks the law even though she knows that her master "might have her seized for wearing man's clothes, and throw her into prison for life, so severe was this colony in that matter" (124–25). Again, Faderman confirms this point as she devotes a chapter to the persecution of female transvestites in Europe and America from the sixteenth to the nineteenth centuries (47–61).

Reade comes even closer to depicting homoeroticism among men in the characters of the sailors, Samuel Cooper and Tom Welch, in *Foul Play* (1868), cowritten with playwright Dion Boucicault. In describing the camaraderie of the two seamen, the text uses the terms "antique friendship"[13] and "a friendship as of the ancient world" (82), which is likely an allusion to the classical Greek celebration of sex between men. It was at Oxford, where Reade held a position during this period, that Walter Pater and his circle were expounding a "neo-Hellenism," a term that Richard Dellamora refers to as "a euphemism for desire, including sexual desire, between men."[14] Though Reade was not associated with Pater and the group that was pioneering aestheticism, because of his proximity at Oxford and his voracious appetite for information he was undoubtedly familiar with its ideas.

In *Foul Play,* Cooper and Welch are inseparable, and the novel's hero remarks: "Their friendship, though often roughly expressed, is really a tender and touching sentiment" (37). In a dramatic scene in a lifeboat after a shipwreck, Cooper is mortally wounded while trying to prevent cannibalism among some of the crazed survivors. His dying words to Welch, who has "tears in his eyes" (81), are, "I love you, Tom" (82). After the death of his friend, Welch "covered the body decently with the spare canvas, and lay quietly down with his own head pillowed upon those loved remains" (82). Shortly after this, the other survivors decide to bury Cooper at sea but Welch protests, "No, no; I can't let Sam be buried in the sea. Ye see, sir, Sam and I, we are used to one another, and I can't abide to part with him, alive or dead" (83). This crisis is averted as land is sighted and the lifeboat pulls ashore on a deserted island where Sam Cooper is finally buried. Soon afterward

Welch dies, as if in empathy with his companion, and his body is found "with his arms hanging on each side of the grave, and his cheek laid gently on it . . . with a loving smile on his dead face" (94). Nowhere in *Foul Play* or any of his other work does Reade depict overt homoerotic acts, and as we have seen, he claims to consider homosexuality a "monstrous perversity." Yet the two sailors in this novel come closer to a direct expression of homoeroticism than most other Victorian novels dared. While Reade does not explicitly embrace or endorse such transgressions, that he portrays them, sometimes with such relish and humor and at other times with such pathos, points to his readiness to question Victorian gendered values.

In "The Bloomer" (1857), Reade advances an early elaboration of the social construction of gender as the heroine, heiress Caroline Courtney, champions the cause of Amelia Bloomer's famous alternative dress for women, both by wearing the outfit and by proselytizing it. Caroline promotes this idea at a party and, dressed for the occasion in the cap and gown of an Oxford don, addresses the assembled guests. Of Caroline's drag outfit, the narrator relates that "she was more beautiful in this than even in a Bloomer."[15] Caroline announces that she means to "attack" the "principal error[s] . . . that pantaloons are essentially masculine, and sweeping robes feminine" (311). Caroline, attired in the "masculine" robe of Oxford as she speaks these words, presents the reader with a layering of gendered images: a woman dressed as a man whose outfit would be considered "feminine" but for his socially sanctioned position which only a man can hold. Caroline advocates both tolerance and diversity as she tells her guests: "Dance in your own way, dress in your own way, and let your neighbors have their way; that is the best way!" (313). These remarks undoubtedly reflect the views of their author as Reade was always a self-conscious, and sometimes intrusive, narrator.

In *A Woman-Hater* (1877), Reade abandons the anonymous narrator's voice altogether to make another statement on gendered dress. In this case Reade renews his assault on "tight-lacing," which he had begun in *A Simpleton* (1873), and indulges in straight polemic, using the corset as a metaphor for the restricted choices for most women, ingrained in them from the time they are young girls:

> Their very mothers—for want of medical knowledge—clasp the fatal, idiotic corset on their growing bodies, . . . [and the girl] grows up crippled in the ribs and lungs by her own mother, and her life, too, is in stays—cabined, cribbed, confined; unless she can paint, or act, or write novels, every path of honourable ambition is closed to her.[16]

As in "The Bloomer," Reade here again critiques the values his society places on gendered fashions and sees them as emblematic of far wider restrictions on women.

CHAPTER 11

Women-Haters and Lovers

Although Reade held some conservative views and was bound by many of the premises of his own Victorian reality, his unprecedented depictions of an array of alternative gender positions, from fashion to performance, are far ahead of his time. Many reviewers from the nineteenth century and most of those few who have since studied his work remark on Reade's compelling portrayals of female characters. Conan Doyle writes of "the humanity and the lovability of his women"[17] (135–36). To William Dean Howells, Reade's novels "winningly impart the sense of womanhood."[18] More recently, Winifred Hughes writes that "Reade stands nearly alone among mid-Victorians . . . in his perceptive creation of women as full, intelligent, sexual beings."[19] While acknowledging Reade's sometimes conventional attitudes, Diana C. Archibald suggests that "he consistently sets up startling challenges to conservative notions of femininity and domestic ideology."[20] However, in a harshly critical essay, Nicola Thompson claims that Reade "successfully replicated conventional middle-class notions of Victorian womanhood."[21] Yet even a superficial reading of Reade's texts clearly refutes this.

Reade lived and worked in the era of the feminine ideal of the "angel in the house," but as Foucault and others have shown, along with this illusory construction came the new analysis of "the hysterization of women" and the "thorough medicalization of their bodies and their sex" (146). Victorian medical discourse held that the female body needed to be contained and protected from its own desires, and that it was "thoroughly saturated with sexuality" (104). While Reade's work may at times agree with the latter part of that diagnosis, rather than condemn this view, he celebrates it. As Laura Hanft Korobkin notes, Reade's *Griffith Gaunt* had the effect of "encouraging female readers toward a more assertive sexuality."[22] Reade opens "Androgynism" with these words: "Women waste all their treasures: bestowing their affections on men . . . yet one must not be over-cynical at the expense of a sex superior as regards the quality of passion, and far more lavish of heart to us than we to them" (10). Reade's emphasis on "passion" elevates women in a manner that runs directly counter to the Victorian ideal of the "angel." The women he admires are adventurous, independent, and carnal, and contrast sharply to Thompson's view of Reade's "gendered extremes" (211), just as his men often defy Victorian standards of manhood.

Smith comments on Reade's "laudatory judgment of women and pejorative judgment of men" (74) and finds his female characters "unspeakably superior in heart, brain, and strength to the heroes whom he commands them to love" (60). An unambiguous example presents itself in the narrator's descriptions of the title character of *Griffith Gaunt* and his wife that "Kate was a superior being to him" (62), and that "she was troubled at times with a sense of superiority to her husband" (73). Reade's novels hardly "echoed and exaggerated conventional Victorian gender stereotypes," as Thompson asserts (210). Sometimes his female characters exhibit superior physical prowess as, in *Christie Johnstone* and "The Bloomer," heroines rescue men from drowning. Reade depicts powerful sexual desire in many of his female characters such as Julia in *Hard Cash* who, after a meeting with the handsome Alfred, "fluttered up the stairs to her own room with hot cheeks, and panted there like some wild thing that has been grasped at and grazed" (26). In the same novel, the statuesque "female rake" (407) Mrs. Archibald, "an artful woman of thirty" (299) and an official at the asylum, yields to her passion for the imprisoned Alfred and wields her power in an attempt to seduce him. What's more, Mrs. Archibald has a rival in her physically capable Nurse Hannah for, as the narrator relates: "that muscular young virgin was beginning to sigh for him herself with a gentle timidity that contrasted prettily with her biceps muscles" (247). In this novel, Alfred becomes the passive sexual object of two women, both with "masculine" attributes and in positions of social power over him, in a reversal of contemporary views of sexual desire. Such depictions hardly support Thompson's contention that Reade sought to "valorize the gendered constructions" of his era (211). Discussing *Griffith Gaunt,* Lillian Nayder writes of Reade's "use of sex and illegitimacy to represent women's wrongs and challenge the double standard" and favorably compares Mercy's son in that novel, born out of lawful wedlock, to Dickens's characterization of Esther in *Bleak House:* "The illegitimate child in Reade's novel indicts a wayward father rather than a wayward mother."[23] Here and elsewhere, rather than valorizing them, Reade consistently questions contemporary "gendered constructions."

Reade's most feminist novel, *A Woman-Hater,* advocates the right of women to enter the medical profession, a theme he had raised as early as 1863 in *Hard Cash* (32). Some of the points in *A Woman-Hater* directly mirror Foucault's remarks on the insensitivity of the new "medicalization" of the female body which became open to medical discourse as a field of study and inspection. Rhoda Gale, the aspiring young doctor, in telling her story to a sympathetic listener, recalls that in Zurich where she previously studied, when the women medical students were kept out of the infirmary: "female patients wrote to the journals to beg that female students might be admitted to come between them and the brutal curiosity of the male students, to which they were subjected in so offensive a way" (125. In nearly all of Reade's novels there are examples of corrupt or incompetent male doctors, and he welcomed the advent of women into the profession to counter them.

In addition to such egalitarian sentiments, some recent critics have identified lesbianism in *A Woman-Hater* in the relationship of Rhoda to two other female characters, Zoe Vizard and Ina Klosking.[24] The character of Rhoda is based on the career of Sophia Jex-Blake, whose attempt to break the gender barrier at the University of Edinburgh's medical program precipitated a riot.[25] Jex-Blake is quoted as saying, "I believe I love women too much to ever love a man,"[26] and Reade, who interviewed her in 1876, puts similar remarks in the mouth of Rhoda. While many of Reade's contemporaries found his work "indecent," if they did not accuse him of depicting lesbianism in *A Woman-Hater* it may have been because that term had not entered common usage nor had the practice been pathologized. *Blackwood's Edinburgh Magazine,* which with some misgivings serialized the novel, while expressing some concern over Reade's "love of plain speaking and warm flesh tints,"[27] was more dismayed over *A Woman-Hater*'s support for women in the professions than by any suggestions of lesbianism which apparently was still so unthinkable as to go unnoticed. Indeed, when eight years after the appearance of the novel male homosexuality became a crime (and remained one until 1967) under the Labouchère clause of the Criminal Law Amendment Bill, sex between women was ignored by the statute. As Queen Victoria is said to have remarked at the time: "Women do not do such things." Yet the lesbian theme in *A Woman-Hater* is clear to modern readers.

In the novel, Rhoda warns the villain, Severne, to stay away from Zoe, whom he is attempting to court. Rhoda tells him: "Unless I see Zoe Vizard in danger, you have nothing to fear from me. But I *love* her, you understand" (207; original emphasis). Although he remains her rival, Rhoda agrees that Severne is both charming and something more than handsome: "He is beautiful," she says. "If he was dressed as a woman, the gentlemen would all run after him" (197). Later, after she has transferred her affections from Zoe to Ina, Rhoda declares, "I love her better than any man can love her" (236). Rhoda and Ina pass an idyllic time in a country town where, as the narrator relates:

> Rhoda got her to Hillstoke, cooked for her, nursed her, lighted fires, aired her bed, and these two friends slept together in each other's arms. . . . Then she [Ina] enveloped Rhoda in her arms, and rested a hot cheek against hers. . . . The two friends communed till two o'clock in the morning: but the limits of my tale forbid me to repeat what passed. (275, 282, 283)

Later, when Ina becomes engaged to be married, Rhoda complains, "This is nice! . . . There—I must give up loving women. Besides, they throw me over the moment a man comes, if it happens to be the right one" (294). In *Griffith Gaunt,* Kate and Mercy also exchange numerous kisses and share a bed (208). Certainly these passages demonstrate deep female friendships characterized by a powerful physical element and strongly suggest expressions of lesbian desire.

Recovering Reade

While critics have claimed both Braddon and Collins as protofeminists, Reade, with perhaps more feminist credentials, has not been so identified. In addition, scholars have also pointed to homoerotic elements in *Lady Audley's Secret*[28] and *The Woman in White*,[29] but few have identified such elements in Reade's work though a close reading readily reveals this. Contemporary critics in England, Canada, and the United States condemned Reade's work as "unclean" and "filthy." Trained as a lawyer and by nature combative, Reade countered such charges with threats of lawsuits and name-calling of his own. After a particularly negative appraisal of *A Terrible Temptation* (1871), Reade wrote an angry letter to the *Toronto Globe* suggesting that he could sue or indict the writer of the review. He defended himself against charges of indecency by writing: "Whenever in a newspaper you see the word 'filth' applied to adultery or other frailty, the writer is a lewd hypocrite and a prurient prude."[30] Some years earlier *Griffith Gaunt* had provoked international controversy. Dickens enjoyed the novel but found portions of it "extremely coarse and disagreeable" and declined to testify on Reade's behalf in a libel suit he had initiated against the *London Review*.[31] As Korobkin points out, in 1874 Reade's novel was introduced as evidence in a sensational adultery trial in New York, parts of which were carried out "largely through a literary analysis of *Griffith Gaunt*" (47). In her essay on novel's role in that trial, Korobkin echoes the sentiments of Conan Doyle, Howells, Hughes, and Nayder by noting that Reade's work presents "intelligent, realistically sexual heroines" (45).

If Charles Reade is known at all in literary circles today, it is primarily for his critiques of the conditions in prisons and lunatic asylums or for his medieval novel, *The Cloister and the Hearth*. But there is a good deal more in Reade's texts that argues for his recovery in English studies. In addition to the brief observations made here on his work as an oppositional stance to prevailing Victorian gender norms, Reade's fiction and dramas could be more richly explored from feminist perspectives as an alternative to the common portrayals of women in nineteenth-century literature. While Thompson feels that "we cannot repress our repulsion" for Reade (211), as scholars rediscover his work they will likely think otherwise. Reade's work offers opportunities for a variety of critical approaches. His complex characterizations can inform a psychoanalytical analysis. Reade himself provides a historicist context for his work as he published a critique of *Hard Cash*, which assailed his "offences against decency, good taste, and truth,"[32] along with his response to it in subsequent editions of that novel. Indeed, Reade often refers to contemporary documents which informed his own novelistic creations. Reade also makes extensive use of colonial locales in many of his works, including *Hard

Cash, It Is Never Too Late to Mend, Foul Play, and *A Simpleton*. And while his use of these settings is often unenlightened, it can nevertheless provide a basis for postcolonial focuses on fictional representations of the Victorian empire. With increasing interest in the role of women within the colonial project, Reade's work offers examples of female "pioneers" that can form the basis of scholarly inquiry. And aside from the intriguing theoretical questions these texts pose, novels such as *Griffith Gaunt* should be rediscovered simply for the pleasures they can afford the casual reader.

NOTES

1. See Swinburne's comment in "Charles Reade," 346.
2. Charles Reade, *Griffith Gaunt* (Fields, Osgood, & Co., 1869), 72. All references are to this edition and are cited by page in the text.
3. Henry James, cited in Wayne Burns, *Charles Reade: A Study in Victorian Authorship,* 11. Swinburne, 346.
4. Mary Poovey, "Forgotten Writers, Neglected Histories: Charles Reade and the Nineteenth-Century Transformation of the British Literary Field," 434–35.
5. Elton E. Smith, *Charles Reade,* 9. All references to this work are cited by page in the text.
6. *Hard Cash,* 44. All references to this work are cited by page in the text.
7. Michel Foucault, *History of Sexuality,* 15. All further references are by page in the text.
8. Foucault, *Abnormal* 169.
9. Reade, "Androgynism; or Woman Playing at Man," 11.
10. Lillian Faderman, *Surpassing the Love of Men,* 54. All references to this work are cited by page in the text.
11. Reade, *The Wandering Heir,* 60. All references to this work are cited by page in the text.
12. Reade, *The Cloister and the Hearth,* 306. All references to this work are cited by page in the text.
13. Reade, *Foul Play,* 37. All references to this work are cited by page in the text.
14. Richard Dellamora, *Masculine Desire: The Sexual Politics of Victorian Aestheticism,* 33.
15. Reade, "Propria Quae Maribus" ("The Bloomer"), 310. All references to this work are cited by page in the text.
16. Reade, *A Woman-Hater,* 307. All further references to this work are cited by page in the text.
17. Arthur Conan Doyle, *Through the Magic Door,* 135–36.
18. Quoted in Burns, *Charles Reade,* 113.
19. Winifred Hughes, *The Maniac in the Cellar,* 103.
20. Diana C. Archibald, *Domesticity, Imperialism, and Emigration in the Victorian Novel,* 149.
21. Nicola Thompson, "'Virile' Creation Versus 'Twaddlers Tame and Soft': Gender and the Reception of Charles Reade's *It Is Never Too Late to Mend,*" 204. All references to this work are cited by page in the text.
22. Laura Hanft Korobkin, "Silent Woman, Speaking Fiction: Charles Reade's *Griffith Gaunt*

(1866) at the Adultery Trial of Henry Ward Beecher," 51. All references to this work are quoted by page in the text.

23. Lillian Nayder, *Unequal Partners*, 138.

24. See David Finkelstein, "A Woman Hater and Women Healers: John Blackwood, Charles Reade, and the Victorian Women's Medical Movement"; see also Hill, "Examining Women: Charles Reade's *A Woman Hater*, Lesbian Contagion, and the Debate on Medical Education for Women."

25. Finkelstein, 342.

26. Quoted in Helena Wojtczak from *The Life of Sophia Jex-Blake*, by Margaret Todd (65).

27. Quoted in Finkelstein, 340.

28. See Natalie Schroeder 1988; Richard Nemesari 1995; Ellen Rosenman 2003; Jennifer Kushnier 2002.

29. See D. A. Miller 1986; Nemesvari 2002.

30. Reade, *Readiana*, 263.

31. Quoted in Wayne Burns, 262; Nayder, 137.

32. J. S. Bushnan, "Private Asylums," appendix to *Hard Cash*, 411.

- 12 -

WOMEN ALONE

Le Fanu's "Carmilla" and Rossetti's "Goblin Market"

NANCY WELTER

CHRISTINA ROSSETTI'S "Goblin Market" and J. Sheridan Le Fanu's "Carmilla" refer in a veiled fashion to homosexual relationships between women. The veil, sisterhood in "Goblin Market" and vampirism in "Carmilla," allows the reader to have another interpretation of the homoeroticism in each text. Rossetti's poem, frequently seen as the more radical of the two texts, ends with an apparent restoration of a patriarchal order through procreation. "Carmilla" on the other hand, presents intensely conservative views of Laura and Carmilla's relationship, while challenging itself with an ending that refuses to restore order among the characters. These texts engage in a dialogue with each other on the nature of homosexual relationships among women and their dynamic within the dominant patriarchal order. Luce Irigaray's "Commodities among Themselves" presents a theoretical framework for this analysis. Her interpretation of female homosexual relations, and the patriarchal response to them, helps to expose many of the underlying tensions within each text. In the end, Rossetti's poem challenged convention in order to restore it, while Le Fanu's novella upholds convention only to destroy it.

Irigaray's essay analyzes the commodification of sexuality and contests Freud's ideas regarding homosexuality. She asks, "[W]hy is masculine homosexuality considered exceptional ... when in fact the economy as a whole is based upon it?"[1] In her view, political economy is created through transactions between men alone and "the *very possibility of sociocultural order requires homosexuality* as its organizing principle" (192). Women are commodities within this system, objects to be transferred among men, and are denied agency and recreated as objects of barter within the patriarchal mode of exchange. Even homosexuality among women is commodified as a product to be consumed by men or as a system in which women become figurative men, for only a man could, according to patriarchy, desire a woman. Irigaray rejects this patriarchal economy, and questions what would happen if *"these 'commodities' refused to go to 'market'?* What if they maintained 'another' kind of commerce, among themselves?" (196). For Irigaray, this refusal would create a new society, one in which women are empowered and masculine systems of exchange discarded. This utopian vision manifests itself in both "Goblin Market" and "Carmilla."

"Carmilla" and "Goblin Market" are not traditionally included in analyses of sensation fiction. Even though Le Fanu was occasionally referred to as "an Irish Wilkie Collins,"[2] he is frequently considered a borderline writer within the sensation genre, one with stronger ties to Gothic fiction through his use of the supernatural. Contesting such views, Devin Zuber, in his essay in this volume, discusses Le Fanu's work as within, albeit extending, definitions of sensation fiction. Similarly, my reading of the female relationships in "Carmilla" juxtaposed with those in Rossetti's poem highlights themes within the works that are common with those in more "canonical" sensation fiction. As Winifred Hughes explains, sensation fiction was concerned with the "introduction into fiction of 'those most mysterious of mysteries, the mysteries which are at our own doors.'"[3] Another distinctive aspect of the genre was the affect upon its reader; as Cannon Schmitt notes, "'[s]ensation' itself—in this context, a term that names a physical response on the part of both characters and readers—was thought to result from the yoking together of" realist and Gothic narrative structures.[4] "Carmilla," in this sense, is sensational in its focus upon Laura's emotional and physical reactions throughout the story. "Goblin Market" cannot be called realist; it presents itself as allegory, the story of what happens when a domestic utopia is confronted by the mercantile public sphere of men. However, with their focus on invaded domesticity, gender roles, and physical sensation, the poem and "Carmilla" share similar concerns with sensation fiction.

"Goblin Market"

Rossetti's "Goblin Market" presents the story of the fall of Laura and her subsequent rescue by her sister, Lizzie. On one level, this poem is a didactic story of the importance of family; on another, it subverts patriarchal culture by illustrating a world without hostile men, where the women must rely on one another. Laura and Lizzie live in a domestic utopia and an entirely feminine society. As Sandra M. Gilbert and Susan Gubar claim, Rossetti seems to be "positing an effectively matrilineal and matriarchal world, perhaps even, considering the strikingly sexual redemptive scene between the sisters, a covertly (if ambivalently) lesbian world."[5] Each evening their utopia is disturbed when they hear the cry of the goblin men selling their wares. These men become the catalysts for Laura and Lizzie's transition into adulthood and sexuality.

Laura is wise enough to warn her sister about the goblin men, but she is not strong enough to resist their seductive fruits. Tempted by their song of "Come buy, come buy" and by the appearance of their exotic fruits—"Men sell not such in any town"—Laura succumbs (4, 101), exchanging a lock of her gold hair for the fruit. According to Irigaray, "[h]eterosexuality is nothing but the assignment of economic roles: there are producer subjects and agents of exchange (male) on the one hand, productive earth and commodities (female) on the other" (192). Laura, by using her hair as a monetary object, commodifies her body. She allows the goblin men to set the terms of purchase, situating herself within their patriarchal economy and leaving behind the matriarchal society she shared with her sister. Lizzie forcibly removes her sister from the economic order of the goblins and creates a new system, one that very much resembles Irigaray's utopia, one where women have full agency, and where "[e]xchanges occur without identifiable terms, without accounts, without end . . ." (Irigaray 197). Before such a system can exist, each sister must negotiate her position within the goblin men's economy. They cannot create a new system of power without knowledge of the current system.

To rescue her sister, Lizzie goes to the goblin market. She assumes a masculine position of an "agent of exchange," carrying her coin in her purse (Irigaray 192). The goblins reject her coin, refusing to recognize her position as a fellow agent of exchange. In a scene that closely resembles "sexual harassment and physical abuse,"[6] they try to force her to eat, rubbing the fruits into her skin, soaking her in their juices. Still holding her coin, Lizzie returns to Laura, triumphant, and tells her,

> Come and kiss me.
> Never mind my bruises,
> Hug me, kiss me, suck my juices
>   Squeezed from goblin fruits for you,
> Goblin pulp and goblin dew.
> Eat me, drink me, love me;
> Laura, make much of me. . . . (465–72)

She freely offers her body to heal Laura, asking for nothing in exchange. In a clearly homoerotic sequence, Laura is saved by consuming Lizzie's body, or rather merely sucking the juices on her skin. According to Janet Galligani Casey, "[w]hat Lizzie (and consequently, Laura) learns is that sexual love for its own sake leads only to empty desire, but that it acquires a healing and fulfilling element when it has a spiritual dimension."[7] Casey's explanation would like to glorify sexual love that is both physical and spiritual, but she does not address the fact that the only time such a transcendent love occurs in the poem is between two women. Using Irigaray's theories, this is easily accounted for precisely because they are women, and they have placed themselves outside of masculine systems of economy and power.

The salvation scene between Laura and Lizzie is quite similar to the utopia that Irigaray imagines, in which "[n]ature's resources would be expended without depletion, exchanged without labor, freely given, exempt from masculine transactions: enjoyment without a fee, well-being without pain, pleasure without possession" (197). The transaction between the two sisters exemplifies a transaction without masculine control, and Joseph Bristow suggests their "communion can occur once they have detached themselves from the commercial marketplace of sex regulated by 'fruit-merchant men.'"[8] Richard Menke explains that "sisterhood manages to shut down the shop."[9] Through their transactions with the goblin men, they have managed to take themselves out of the masculine economy. However, they have not "shut down the shop," as Menke claims, for good. Lizzie can save herself and her sister, but their children must fight for themselves.

The poem cannot end with Laura and Lizzie having created a new relationship to each other and to the economic system that would turn them into objects. Instead, the poem ends with a restoration of order. "Laura awoke as from a dream, / Laughed in the old innocent way" (537–38). They grow and become wives and mothers, even though men are absent in the text. Their children are androgynous and are told to honor sisterhood, "[f]or there is no friend like a sister" (562). This vision of sisterhood, while wonderful and supportive, is also a return to a patriarchal order. It does not challenge the reality that allows the goblin men to sell their fruit and encouraged Laura to commodify herself. Instead, it presents the idea that a woman can save her sister, but cannot change the very systems that endanger women as a whole. They have not changed the reality of the danger, and "[t]heir mother hearts [are] beset with fears" (546). They can only hope that the principles of sisterhood and a healthy warning will be enough to prevent their children from looking to the goblin men for refreshment.

The nature of the experience shared by Laura and Lizzie is frequently contested in criticism of the poem. Recent critics, such as Casey, Mary Wilson Carpenter, and Antony H. Harrison, have historicized "Goblin Market" within the Anglican High Church movement and its efforts to restore religious sisterhoods.[10] Rossetti was deeply involved in the High Church movement and with its project to reform fallen women. Harrison claims that Rossetti believed that the world was inherently corrupt and notes that "the most consistently positive relationships among characters in Rossetti's poems are between mothers and daughters or between sisters. These relationships reinforce a spirit of subcultural solidarity that, ultimately, can deal with 'the world' only by renouncing it."[11] In privileging the context of the sisterhoods in Rossetti's poetry, Harrison fails to account for the sexual nature of the encounter between Laura and Lizzie, and his focus on renunciation leads him to ignore the sexual contexts that were very clear to contemporary readers.[12] Harrison claims Lizzie renounces sexual pleasure when she saves her sister, but, while he does address love in Rossetti's poetry, he does not address love between women.[13] The sisterhood of "Goblin Market" is a sexual construction, one where a fallen woman can only be saved by another woman— one who sacrifices herself in the process. The fall and the salvation are sexual. Both Carpenter and Casey address the sexual nature of the relationship. Carpenter, in her reading of the poem, claims, "*Goblin Market* suggests that female erotic pleasure cannot be imagined without pain," and further suggests that the poem "not only affirms the female body and its appetites but constructs 'sisterhood' as a saving female homoerotic bond."[14] While Casey does acknowledge the erotic and spiritual nature of love in the poem, she tries to remove the poem from its "feminocentric"[15] context by claiming that Rossetti's sisterhood is an androgynous notion and that "Rossetti is careful not to suggest that a 'sisterhood' must consist only of females."[16]

The ending of "Goblin Market," in many ways, seems detached from the rest of the poem. In this final stanza, Laura and Lizzie are doting mothers, and the very language of the poem changes. The goblin fruits are initially described as "[s]weeter than honey from the rock. / Stronger than man-rejoicing wine, / Clearer than water flowed that juice" (129–31). Now, the fruits are "like honey to the throat / But poison in the blood" (554–55). The rich, sensual description of the early stanzas has been replaced by a blunt reality. The final stanza, with its restoration to order, is the strongest connection between "Goblin Market" and Rossetti's other poetry. The ending restores order because, even though Rossetti could imagine a subversive homosexual economy, she could not, as Gilbert and Gubar claim in reference to Charlotte Brontë, "envision viable solutions to the problem of patriarchal oppression."[17] Rossetti could imagine a world in which patriarchal oppression had been defeated by sisterhood, but she could not sustain that state. Instead, Laura must renounce the joy she learns from her sister. She must turn away from an all-female utopia and embrace domesticity and motherhood.

Sisterhood, in the context of "Goblin Market," becomes a way for women to save one another from the patriarchal power structures. In the poem, women can shut down the shop of the masculine economy—but only temporarily. While Laura and Lizzie do win a victory over the goblin men, they do not foster real change, such as that dreamt of by Irigaray. Instead, they are reincorporated into the masculine economy through their production of children.

"Carmilla"

J. Sheridan Le Fanu's novella "Carmilla" also has a character named Laura who struggles with desire and patriarchal power structures. While Le Fanu's Laura is the narrator of her story, her judgment of Carmilla remains unclear. She is acted upon by Carmilla, a female vampire, and the men in her life act for her. Le Fanu's novella is more ambiguous than Rossetti's poem, for within "Carmilla," he both challenges the patriarchal political economy and attempts to restore convention.

"Carmilla" is unusual among vampire fiction, partly because both vampire and victims are female. While "Goblin Market" sees relations between women as a potential means of feminine salvation, in "Carmilla," such relations pave the way to eternal damnation. Even as "Carmilla" predates *Dracula* and yet uses many of the vampire conventions that will occupy the later novel, so, too, does it predate Freud's analysis of female homosexuality and closely mirror the ideas that Freud would publish in later years in "The Pyschogenesis of a Case of Homosexuality in a Woman." However, something within the relationship between Laura and Carmilla defies Freud's classification.

Within patriarchal economy, according to Irigaray, "as soon as she desires (herself), as soon as she speaks (expresses herself, to herself), a woman is a man. As soon as she has any relationship with another woman, she is homosexual, and therefore masculine" (194). In Irigaray's reading of Freud, "*it is only as a man that the female homosexual can desire a woman who reminds her of a man*" (194). This gender fluidity was a great source of distress for Freud, who felt that there may have been a biological reason for homosexuality, what Irigaray refers to as an "anatomo-physiological cause" (195). When analyzing a female homosexual, Freud was unable to find an "obvious deviation from the feminine physical type,"[18] although he does speculate that she may have had "hermaphroditic ovaries,"[19] but he could not be certain without a physical examination of the woman. Clearly, Freud felt that the woman's female organs disguised an essential masculinity. Irigaray questions what would have happened had he performed the exam: "[W]hat might Freud have discovered as anatomical proof of homosexuality, the *masculine* homosexuality, of his 'patient'? What would his desire, his inadmissible desire, for *disguises* have led him to 'see'?" (195; emphasis in original). She continues to explain that

> The dominant sociocultural economy leaves female homosexuals only a choice between a sort of *animality* that Freud seems to overlook and *the imitation of male models*. In this economy any interplay of desire among women's bodies, women's organs, and women's language is inconceivable. (196)

Le Fanu addresses, in turn, each of these descriptions of female homosexuality—the "anatomo-physiological," the disguise, the animalistic, the male imitation, and finally the interpretation that Irigaray alludes to at the end—a desire among women that is free from all of these markers.

Carmilla's homosexuality, on one level, can clearly be blamed on an anatomo-physiological cause. She is a vampire, and this provides a clear excuse for her desire to transgress heterosexual boundaries. As Tammis Elise Thomas makes clear, "Le Fanu does not present Carmilla's vampirism as a form of homophobic punishment for her homosexuality."[20] Rather, Carmilla was attacked/seduced at her first ball, as she relates to Laura: "'I was all but assassinated in my bed, wounded *here*,' she touched her breast, 'and never was the same since.'"[21] The sexual identity of Carmilla's attacker is never made clear, leaving the question of whether she was a homosexual before she was a vampire both unanswered and unanswerable. Her comment that she was "never the same since" does not clarify what was not the same—her sexuality or her vampiric nature. Either way, she was changed permanently by the attack.

Irigaray claims that Freud's "desire, his inadmissible desire, for *disguises*" led to his misunderstanding of the female homosexual (195). If there is a Freudian disguise present in "Carmilla," one must also ask what it was designed to mask. The fact that Carmilla appears to be a young woman disguises her true nature. Everyone at the *Schloss* instinctively trusts Carmilla; in fact, only two people ever penetrate her disguise. The first to catch a glimpse of her true, vampiric self is a traveling peddler. On seeing Carmilla, he offers his services as a dentist for she "has the sharpest tooth,—long, thin, pointed, like an awl, like a needle" (Le Fanu 269). He can see that her teeth are inappropriate for a young lady and claims that she has "the tooth of a fish" (269). However, he cannot penetrate her disguise fully to see that her teeth are entirely appropriate for a vampire. Even so, he instinctively animalizes her.

The only one capable of seeing through Carmilla's disguise is General Spielsdorf, the uncle of a prior victim. Laura's father readily believes Carmilla is his daughter's attacker, but Laura never seems to reject her friend's "disguise." In what Irigaray refers to as Freud's "(cultural) imaginary," it makes perfect sense that Carmilla's homosexuality would be a disguise for her vampiric nature; however, Laura is unable to make that connection (Irigaray 195). As the general narrates his tale, she remarks, "You may suppose, also, how I felt as I heard him detail habits and mysterious peculiarities which were, in fact, those of our beautiful guest, Carmilla!" (305). While she tells her reader, "I saw all clearly a few days later," what she sees is left unclear (315). The reader never fully knows if Laura joins the men in the text in condemning Carmilla. For Laura, Carmilla can be her friend, a female homosexual, and a vampire.

In her pursuit of Laura, Carmilla clearly assumes both a masculine and an animalistic form. She has pursued her victim for many years, first visiting six-year-old Laura's bedside. Laura recounts their first encounter: the woman "caressed me with her hands, and lay down beside me on the bed, and me towards her, smiling; I felt immediately delightfully soothed, and fell asleep again. I was wakened by a sensation as if two needles ran into my breast very deep at the same moment" (246). In this early visit, Carmilla is clearly engaging in a sexual act with the girl, one that combines vampirism and homosexuality. Carmilla has chosen her victim/partner, a role that is reserved for the dominant partner in sexual relationships. As a vampire, Carmilla's sexual identity is obscured, for, as Christoper Craft writes, "[l]uring at first with an inviting orifice, a promise of red softness, but delivering instead a piercing bone, the vampire mouth fuses and confuses . . . the gender-based categories of the penetrating and receptive."[22] Carmilla's pursuit of Laura is also a hunt. As a predator, Carmilla stalks Laura as prey, haunting her dreams, and even appearing to her in the form of a "sooty-black animal that resembled a monstrous cat" (278).

The text never explains why Laura is not present at the violent attack upon Carmilla's tomb. Laura's father, the general, and two medical men attend the event. They satisfy the demands of the law and officially identify the marks of vampirism in Carmilla (315). With this official identification, they are free to destroy her body, so "in accordance with ancient practice, [the body] was raised, and a sharp stake driven through the heart of the vampire, who uttered a piercing shriek at the moment. [. . .] Then the head was struck off, and a torrent of blood flowed from the severed neck" (315–16). Thomas refers to the scene as one "in which a group of patriarchal authorities justify their destruction of Carmilla by declaring her to be a monster."[23] One must ask which monstrosity they were attempting to kill—the lesbian or the vampire. Both would have been monstrous in their eyes, and both challenged their authority. According to Tamar Heller, in their execution, "these authorities perform a rape-like surgery on Carmilla."[24] Her body is forcefully penetrated by the stake as a means of reestablishing patriarchal authority. The men move from a coldly official identification to a brutal staking in an attack very similar to the assault on Lucy's tomb in *Dracula*. In both texts, men violently penetrate the female vampire's tomb and destroy her, forcefully reestablishing patriarchal authority over her transgressive body.

After Carmilla's destruction, Laura learns more about vampires from the men around her. She learns that vampires will often stalk their victims, and their desire for the victim resembles "the passion of love" (317). The vampire's hunt mimics the "gradual approaches of an artful courtship" (317). Here, she finds a description of her own confused relationship with Carmilla. She and Carmilla had become close very quickly, in a manner that sometimes startled Laura. Carmilla frequently professed her love, saying, "You are mine, you *shall* be mine, you and I are one forever," and '"Darling, darling,' she murmured, 'I live in you; and you would die for me, I love you so'" (264, 273–74). Carmilla's vampiric embrace is both a form of passionate love and an act of sexual reproduction. The text is clear that those killed by vampires will eventually become a vampire, and this seems to be Carmilla's goal for Laura. However, Laura's fate after death is not addressed in the story.

Carmilla is defined by the sociocultural interpretation of female homosexuality. She is, as Freud would no doubt agree, in disguise. Her penetrating teeth are the sex organ that would betray her true identity, and her lusts are animalistic. This combination of the masculine and the monstrous animal are clearly the terrible representations of the stereotyped female homosexual to which Irigaray refers. However, the text does not rest with such stereotypes as Laura's feelings for her friend are never truly defined or clearly stated. Early in the text, after describing one of Carmilla's "foolish embraces," Laura states that

> In these mysterious moods I did not like her. I experienced a strange tumultuous excitement that was pleasurable, ever and anon, mingled with a vague sense of fear and disgust. I had no distinct thoughts about her while such scenes lasted, but I was conscious of a love growing into adoration, and also of abhorrence. This I know is a paradox, but I can make no other attempt to explain the feeling. (264)

However, the text ends with Laura explaining "to this hour the image of Carmilla returns to memory with ambiguous alterations—sometimes the playful, languid, beautiful girl; sometimes the writhing fiend I saw in the ruined church" (319). She never manages to clarify her feelings beyond the paradox of abhorrence and adoration, yet Laura appears to accept both halves of her friend—the lover and the fiend.

In Irigaray's utopian vision, women would have "[e]xchanges without identifiable terms, without accounts, without end. . . . Without sequence or number. Without standard or yardstick . . ." (197). While Carmilla's desire for Laura is one of predator for prey, Laura's feelings for her friend are entirely absent of the desire for possession. Laura, for all of her puzzlement at Carmilla's ambiguous nature, is willing to accept Carmilla without limiting her personality. She nearly loses her life to her friend's predatory nature, yet Laura still cannot or will not dismiss Carmilla.

Laura stays outside of the patriarchal power structure. She lives for at least eight years after Carmilla's visit, and she narrates her own story, illustrating her paradoxical relationship with the vampire. The men in this text may have reasserted their authority over Carmilla, but Laura remains both inside and outside of their authority, ultimately destroying patriarchal convention through her very existence. Only with Laura's death, conveniently occurring outside of the narrative, can masculine authority be restored.

Conclusion

Both "Goblin Market" and "Carmilla" present complex relationships between women. While complicating these same-sex relationships, the texts raise critical and cultural questions regarding women's sexuality, gender roles, and homoeroticism, common threads within other sensational texts. Also challenging the Victorian domestic sphere and its reliance on the economic roles of women, the texts show the inherent instability of patriarchy, an issue that would be explored more thoroughly in other sensational works. "Carmilla" is often called a misogynist text for its negative portrayal of Carmilla's homosexuality, but critics who make that claim rarely analyze the sexuality of the narrator/victim, Laura. She presents a much different view of the relationship, a view that is never fully given voice. The text never explains what was "made clear" to Laura. Does she finally accept the idea that Carmilla is a dangerous vampire, or does she realize that the men have destroyed Carmilla because she presented a threat to their power? This tension helps to complicate the text and bring it closer to the sort of relationships between women valorized by Irigaray. "Goblin Market," on the other hand, is often analyzed for its sexual undertones, but critics often fail to address the desire between women in the poem. Yet this text, for all of its redemptive power given over to women, presents a return to patriarchy. Laura and Lizzie's domestic utopia was that of children; as adults, they become wives and mothers, assuming their place within a patriarchal economy. At one point, they had bought their way out of such an economy, but the end of the poem restores them to it. Even though both texts present relationships without masculine control, neither can sustain the sort of utopia Irigaray imagines in "Commodities among Themselves." Eventually, in each text, masculine authority returns.

NOTES

1. Luce Irigaray, "Commodities among Themselves," *This Sex Which Is Not One*, 192. All references are to this edition and cited by page in the text.

2. David Punter, *The Gothic Tradition*, vol. 1 of *The Literature of Terror: A History of Gothic Fictions from 1765 to the Present Day*, 203.

3. Winifred Hughes, *The Maniac in the Cellar*, 7.

4. Cannon Schmitt, *Alien Nation: Nineteenth-Century Gothic Fictions and English Nationality*, 112.

5. Sandra M. Gilbert and Susan Gubar, *The Madwoman in the Attic: The Woman Writer and the Nineteenth-Century Literary Imagination*, 2nd ed., 567.

6. Ibid., 428.

7. Janet Galligani Casey, "The Potential of Sisterhood: Christina Rossetti's 'Goblin Market,'" 69.

8. Joseph Bristow, "'No Friend Like a Sister'? Christina Rossetti's Female Kin," 265.

9. Richard Menke, "The Political Economy of Fruit: Goblin Market," 128.

10. See Casey, 71; Mary Wilson Carpenter, "'Eat Me, Drink Me, Love Me': The Consumable Female Body in Christina Rossetti's *Goblet Market*," 417.

11. Antony H. Harrison, *Victorian Poets and the Politics of Culture: Discourse and Ideology*, 144.

12. See Bristow, 267.

13. Antony H. Harrison, *Christina Rossetti in Context*, 114.

14. Carpenter, 417.

15. Ibid., 417.

16. Casey, 71.

17. Gilbert and Guber, 369.

18. Sigmund Freud, "The Psychogenesis of a Case of Homosexuality in a Woman," 18:154.

19. Ibid., 172.

20. Tammis Elise Thomas, "Masquerade Liberties and Female Power in Le Fanu's *Carmilla*," 53.

21. Sheridan Le Fanu, "Carmilla," in *In a Glass Darkly* (Oxford University Press, 1993), 276. All references are to this edition and cited by page in the text.

22. Christopher Craft, *Another Kind of Love: Male Homosexual Desire in English Discourse, 1850–1920*, 74.

23. Thomas, 59.

24. Tamar Heller, "The Vampire in the House: Hysteria, Female Sexuality, and Female Knowledge in Le Fanu's 'Carmilla,'" 89.

- 13 -

ONE SISTER'S SURRENDER

Rivalry and Resistance in Rhoda Broughton's
Cometh Up as a Flower

LINDSEY FABER

HELENA MICHIE writes of *Middlemarch* that "the sister plot . . . delays, defers, challenges and ultimately defers *to* the romance plot" (emphasis in original).[1] For nineteenth-century novels going back to Austen, sister relationships are little more than a device to further the courtship plot. Even the Victorian novel, which delights in sisters as doubles—usually displayed as opposites of dark and fair, conventional and rebel, sinner and redeemer—must reconcile them and their difference in favor of family harmony and a conventional ending to the marriage plot. In Rhoda Broughton's 1867 sensation novel *Cometh Up as a Flower,* however, it is the sister plot that dominates the courtship plot, as two sisters play out their rivalry by orchestrating and sabotaging each other's marital plans. Through this pair of sisters whose extreme differences are not so easily reconciled, Broughton resists a clear-cut and conventional approach to her characters, her depiction of sister relations, and her ending.

This is not to say that Broughton rejects the conventions of the Victorian novel, which often included stories of sisters whose relations, as Michie notes, "are competitive, problematic, and theatrical" (21). Nell Lestrange's first-person account disguises itself as a conventional romance, with Nell narrating her story and that of her sister Dolly on their paths to marriage. Defined by their difference in a typically Victorian portrayal, the Lestrange sisters are contrasts in both look and manner. Dolly, the conventional beauty, is "a very fair woman to look upon; a small oval face, liquid brown eyes that had a way of looking up meekly and beseechingly . . . a little sharp-cut nose absolutely perfect, a sweet grave mouth, and an expression nun-like, dovelike, Madonna-like" while Nell is unusually tall with "red hair and a wide mouth" and more likely to wear an expression of "youthful enthusiasm."[2] Furthermore, Dolly is superficially conventional, womanly, worldly, and cunning in contrast to Nell's irreverence, artlessness, and naïveté. When Dolly chides Nell for having "nothing but rags" to wear in company, Nell replies that she "shall make a better foil than ever," and indeed she and her sister work at foiling each other throughout the novel (319). For when Nell falls for the poor soldier M'Gregor rather than Sir Hugh, the bumbling aristocrat who can save their family from financial ruin, Dolly sabotages Nell's relationship with M'Gregor by forging a letter that derails the courtship. "This is, by far, the worst picture of sisterly behavior in all Rhoda Broughton's novels," writes Marilyn Wood in her study of Broughton's life and work.[3] Certainly, Dolly and Nell's fanatical rivalry, which manifests itself in an incessant exchange of insults and duplicitous attempts to control each other's future, is atypical of most depictions of Victorian sisterhood.

Broughton's ambivalence about marriage and conventional women's roles is an ongoing exploration of her writing, which was known for its subversive approach to the rebellious heroine. The sister-as-rival focus of *Cometh Up as a Flower* allows Broughton the opportunity to critique conventional approaches to women's place in the courtship plot. Amy Levin notes that in novels of sister relationships "one sister is frequently designated as the conventional one, and the other as rebel," yet the way Broughton employs and exploits this method is startlingly different from other writers of the period.[4] In contrast to depictions of sisterly loyalty, as in Collins's *The Woman in White*, or tales of sisterly redemption like Collins's *No Name* and Christina Rossetti's "Goblin Market," *Cometh Up as a Flower*'s sisterly rivalry revises the idea of female difference as complementary, balancing, or redeeming, instead presenting two sisters whose opposing natures clash in extremes of competitiveness, imbalance, and manipulation. Part of this imbalance is the complexity of the characters. Dolly is Broughton's take on the conventional sister, less a product of that tradition than, as Tamar Heller explains, "a successor to the quintessential femme fatale of sensation fiction: Braddon's Lady Audley."[5] Like Lady Audley, Dolly is a practiced con artist, her beauty and manners concealing her capacity for dissipation and deceit. It is rebel Nell, disdainful of the formalities of polite society, who, rather than being saved by Dolly's goodness, dies in the unhappy marriage into which she is tricked. Leila Silvana May writes that "the ambivalence toward sisterly passion detected in other forms is exaggerated in sensation fiction,"[6] and *Cometh Up as a Flower* presents this ambivalence in the extreme, as the sisters' rivalry propels them through competition and one-upmanship, forgery and deceit, revenge and attempted adultery, all to bring them to a conventional end.

For many nineteenth-century novels, sister relationships were means to a conventional end. Discussing two of the best-known courtship novels, *Pride and Prejudice* and *Little Women*, Nina Auerbach demonstrates how families of sisters, with the mother at the head, are "school[s] for wives."[7] Women's worlds of this kind are a matriarchy, in which "the mother's power is seen as all-suffusing" (36). Courtship and marriage are the next step in the "enforced passage into womanhood," and the mother helps to bridge this passage by "forg[ing] the family's liaison with the outside world of marriage" (36). Sisters, of course, can also play a role in these romances, either to further them—making an advantageous marriage that will, as in *Pride and Prejudice*, "throw them [their sisters] in the way of other rich men"—or frustrate them by acting as rivals.[8] Sisterhood, however, is never an alternative to marriage. Just as the heroine of *Jane Eyre*, despite her quest for identity and family, ultimately abandons the sisterhood of Mary and Diana Rivers in favor of a relationship with Rochester, marriage is achieved at the expense of sisterhood. A woman must leave her home and family for the "official authority of masculine protection" (Auerbach 36).

In Broughton's novel, however, the Lestrange sisters do not fit neatly into this model of matriarchy or a women's community. With their mother long deceased, it is the sisters' interaction that will have the dominant influence on the romance plot of the novel. Five years senior to Nell, Dolly acts, or at least is perceived as, a mother figure to Nell: "'My dear child,' says [Dolly]—in that maternal, elder sister, guardian angel strain which makes casual old ladycallers remark that 'Miss Lestrange is like a mother to her younger sister'" (297). Dolly not only bears their mother's name—Dorothea—but she has long ago "appropriated all [her] mother's ornaments," just as she publicly appropriates the role of lady of the house, engaging in outside visits and formalities and taking some superficial responsibility for Nell's upbringing (250). For as much as she likes to reproach Nell's behavior in front of others with "pseudo-motherliness," Dolly actually shows little interest in guiding her sister's education or character (322). Just as Dolly declines to instruct Nell academically, she makes no attempt to school Nell in more conventional womanly accomplishments. In any case, Nell has little desire for her sister's guidance. She clearly values the permissive upbringing she has been allowed by Sir Adrian, her preoccupied father, guided only by "dear mother nature," who is "not too demonstrative, and such a good listener; lets us say what we please, never contradicts us, nor gives us bits of advice, or pieces of her mind" (293). As Nell spends her formative years only accountable to these lax standards, it is no surprise that she does not feel the loss of the mother. In fact, she resents even the implication of a mother's authority:

> I had often heard other motherless girls deploring their destitute condition . . . but such sentiments, such regrets, met no echo in my heart—inspired me rather with strongest surprise and amazement. . . . I hugged myself on my freedom; my father was more to me than ten mothers. . . . If I had had a mother, I should have had to mend my gloves, and keep my hair tidy, and practise on the piano, and be initiated into the mysteries of stitching. (239)

Nell's distaste for a woman's education is understandable given her permissive and paternalistic upbringing, but her perception of mothers as rivals is surprising. While this may be partially informed by her interaction with Dolly, who is both mother figure and rival, it is also symptomatic of the amorphous gender roles of the Lestranges.

Treated by her father as a son or intellectual companion and with Mother Nature as her only female guide, Nell received an unconventional education for a woman, learning little of sewing, music, or the other traditionally female accomplishments that her sister has apparently mastered. When her new-found love and her sister's return convince her of her own inferiority, she turns not to the "women's" education she is lacking but to the book learning she has already partially acquired, clearly unconscious of the difference between the two: "Dolly did well to despise me; I was but a poor creature, and despicable; foolishest, childishest, among women. I knew absolutely nothing; I had not the least idea what the Bill of Rights was about, nor who fought the battle of Fontenoy, or any other battle either" (280). Because Dolly claims knowledge of "history and biography," "Shakespeare and the musical glasses," Nell assumes that Dolly's confidence and social superiority come from a better textbook education than she has had, rather than from a different kind of education altogether (281). Nell's belief that "Knowledge is Power" will ultimately fail her, as much of the knowledge Nell needs in her developing womanhood cannot be found in her father's library.

Nell is sheltered from her new womanly responsiblities not only by the confusion of roles, but also by a confusion of spheres. While the public world was seen as man's sphere and the private, domestic circle of home was reserved for women, in Nell's upbringing, these spheres are more complexly intertwined. Her father keeps as much to his home and his library as possible, in what Auerbach describes as "adapting to himself the remote privacy of ideal Victorian womanhood" (36). Dolly, on the other hand, is largely absent from the home sphere, paying visits, making connections, and keeping up public appearances. *Cometh Up as a Flower* depicts very clearly the way in which a romance plot requires women to be a part of a social sphere. It is this sphere, the woman's public sphere, in which Nell feels most uncomfortable, while she is perfectly happy in the private domestic world of her life with her father. Nell has reigned as queen over the sheltered existence she shares with her father, but it is clear that she is ill-equipped to be a part of the public realm of women. She views women as "prying and censorious. All the time you are talking to them you feel sure that they are criticizing the sit of your tucker, and calculating how much a year your dress cost" (238). Her attitude stems not only from her economic impoverishment but also from her own feelings of inferiority among women and exclusion from their world: "With my return to the drawing-room returned my sense of loneliness, my consciousness of shabby clothes. . . . All the other ladies knew each other very well, lived in the same circle, had the same pursuits, objects, interests. I, alone, shivered chilly outside the magic ring" (235). Nell finds herself an outsider to her own sex, and it is this reason why she longs to avoid women and be only in the company of men. Yet Nell is not invulnerable to female competition even in her closely guarded home sphere. While she is generally in her element independently managing her father's estate, she is sufficiently humbled by the return of her more sophisticated sister: "[I]n her absence, I felt myself to be a lovable, admirable, rational woman; once again in her presence, I returned to my old station of *gauche,* charmless, witless, school-girl" (279). Just as Sir Adrian secludes himself in his library to avoid the reality of his debt and decline, Nell attempts to compensate for her own perceived inadequacy as a woman by both avoiding and resenting other women.

Nell's ambivalence toward women and their world is nowhere so present as in her relationship with her sister, Dolly. Just as Nell calls attention to women as foils, she will make an acute effort in the telling of her story to distance and differentiate herself from her sister. Nell portrays herself and her sister in a language of opposites, both in character: "Dolly being strong-minded and I being weak-minded, I being the earthenware vessel, and she the iron one"; and in looks: "Dolly was beautiful, and the Lestranges had always been beautiful, and it was right that she should go forth and be a credit to the old house, and I was ugly, and the Lestranges had never been ugly, and it was meet that I should keep in the obscurity, for which I alone was calculated" (227). Levin notes that "in the nineteenth century, the need to establish difference was particularly important in the marriage market, where two sisters might be indistinguishable, bearing equal dowries" (18). The stigma of sameness is evident in the depiction of the other set of sisters in *Cometh Up as a Flower,* the Coxes, who are all named for flowers and whom "Ill-natured friends have christened . . . 'Free and Easy,' 'Freer and Easier,' 'Freest and Easiest'" (385). Nell's rhetorical strategy of differentiation, however, is more than a concern about the marriage market; it is motivated by her limited worldview, in which she sees everything in terms of opposites: "My code of morals, my system of rewards and punishments was very simple, the story book code . . . the good boy gets cakes and ale; the naughty boy gets a whipping" (337). Nell's clear-cut, black-and-white perception necessarily creates her own story as a battle between good and evil, whereby she must clearly separate herself, the good, from her sister, the evil.

The battle between good and evil taking place between the sisters both reflects and directs the battle of courtship. Relationships between men and women throughout the novel are often depicted in war imagery. It is appropriate that the two suitors who will battle over Nell are a soldier and an avid hunter, creating the idea that she is a prize to be won: "to decide their rival claims to the possession of my person, by single combat, by lots, or by heads and tails, whichever they chose" (368). Nell accepts this distinction matter-of-factly, and, in describing her sister's methods, she is similarly unapologetic for the war strategies of her own sex:

> Few, indeed, were those of the families dwelling round Lestrange that had not contributed a combatant to the siege of Sir Hugh Lancaster. . . . [Dolly] had never fought in the foremost ranks, nor had she ever been amongst the leaders of the Crusades, being too wary for that; but for all that she had laid lines of circumvallation, had set up battering-rams, and pointed cannon as sedulously as the noisiest, vapouringest of her rivals. (316)

Courtship is therefore more than just a battle of the sexes or a clash between two rivals; it is an all-out war. A family's future and security may be won, but achieving victory means destroying rivals as well as conquering the object. Like the American Civil War, which Sir Adrian follows with interest, it pits families and neighbors against each other, and without distinct sides or clearly defined lines it is difficult to judge an ally from an enemy. M'Gregor, despite his profession, makes this crucial mistake in his underestimation of Dolly. He expects that, as sisters, Dolly and Nell are on the same side and that Dolly will be a valuable ally in his battle against Sir Adrian's disapproval. But Dolly is a double agent, whose guerrilla tactics sabotage Nell and M'Gregor's engagement so Nell can be drafted into the family crusade in which she must set out to make Sir Hugh "the captive of [her] bow and spear" (372). Nell is never a willing participant in this war, and her final acquiescence to Sir Hugh's proposal is her surrender. She actually likens her acceptance to an amputation, indicating that she is no longer fit for battle (390). Her comparisons to Iphigenia and Jeptha's daughter (389, 401), however, are the most accurate, as Nell becomes a casualty of a war in which she wants no part, a sacrifice for her father's victory. Just as Sir Adrian sides with the Confederates, he upholds a patriarchal system that allows him to all but sell his daughter to the highest bidder. The separation of Nell and M'Gregor and their corresponding deaths (M'Gregor's on his way to battle and Nell's following news of his) make them victims of a battle neither understood nor wanted to fight.

Dolly and Nell's own battles end up having a direct effect on the outcome of this war, which is also a battle between convention and the unconventional. According to Levin, use of the conventional and rebel sister often "permit[s] the author to satisfy and undermine conventions in the same text" (20). Though the sisters' marriages to gentlemen of property satisfies convention, the sensational methods that bring about this ending—manipulation, forgery, deceit, revenge—are highly unconventional. While Dolly (and her surprisingly unconventional methods) will finally drive the courtship plot to its conventional end, it is Nell who will continue the struggle to resist it. Despite Sir Hugh's kindness, Nell refuses to be happy in her marriage, continuing to pine for M'Gregor: "I found that I thought of Dick infinitely more; more regretfully, passionately, longingly, now that I was Lady Lancaster" (418). When M'Gregor returns, Nell even intends to abandon her husband, her vows, and her soul to go with him to India. Here the courtship plot will expose the domination of the sister plot, as Nell discovers the strategies Dolly used to separate her from M'Gregor. The courtship plot upholds its own conventionality, as M'Gregor honorably refuses Nell's offer to leave her marriage for him. If Nell, however, cannot escape her own conventional ending, she can at least attempt to thwart Dolly's. Nell devises a revenge plot to expose her sister's malicious interference and ruin her chances for marriage with Lord Stockport by exposing Dolly's forgery. Ultimately, however, even the sister plot does not resist the conventional ending. Nell relinquishes her dreams for revenge and allows Dolly her storybook marriage. Nell's own ending—her death of consumption—is more ambiguous. Whether she is punished for her attempted transgression against her marriage or instead escapes a dismal future (receiving her own wish to die young) is left for the reader to determine.

Just as Nell surrenders in the battle against courtship, the battle against her sister, and the battle against convention, she will finally surrender against the other ongoing battle of the novel: the battle against womanhood. For *Cometh Up as a Flower* is not only a resistant courtship novel, it is also a resistant *bildungsroman*, the story of Nell's resistance to and rejection of her blossoming womanhood. Auerbach, in her portrayal of courtship and marriage as a rite of passage into womanhood, notes the way in which this necessarily means leaving childhood behind. In *Pride and Prejudice,* Elizabeth Bennet easily navigates this transition by her ability to direct her attentions fully forward: she has neither childhood to look back on nor facility to remember. Nell, on the other hand, is still strongly attached to her past and her memories, most obviously evinced by the retrospective story she is telling. Moving forward for Nell becomes all the more difficult and painful because it forces her to distance herself from the childhood she loved, without Elizabeth Bennet's capacity for forgetfulness. Nell's home, her relationship with her father, her freedom, and even her girlish innocence must be sacrificed as she becomes a woman, a role that has set expectations for her future. It is for this reason that Nell demonstrates such antipathy toward her sister, as Dolly stands for everything Nell must become. The battles between the two sisters are not simply sister rivalry, they are representative of Nell's battle against the conventional womanhood epitomized by Dolly.

In fact, Nell's struggle against her developing womanhood is most clearly evident in her continual attempts to distance herself from her sister. Dolly, a fully developed woman and conventional lady, encompasses everything Nell must and will become. Despite her apparent dislike of her sister and portrayal of Dolly's cruelty, Nell's descriptions of Dolly evince the mixture of fascination and disgust in her attitudes toward womanhood. Though she has gone to great lengths to oppose herself to Dolly in every way, Nell's descriptions are "dashed with envy" (228). She never fails to note her sister's superior beauty, dress, and manners, and describes them always with jealous fascination. What is so captivating about Dolly, however, is not merely her conventional beauty and womanly manners, but the power she manages to derive from her womanhood. Nell, "half child and half woman," has many of the same womanly endowments as her sister, only she has not yet learned how to turn them to a woman's advantage (321). Nell's beauty, girlish modesty, and guilelessness earn her the affection of both M'Gregor and Sir Hugh, yet her allurements are a natural result of her inexperience rather than, as in Dolly's case, a calculated attempt to be the kind of woman men desire. Dolly, looking "very girlish and simple" when trying to distract M'Gregor from Nell at the picnic, lifts eyes "of innocent wondering inquiry" and speaks with "confusion" and "pretty incredulity" (329–30). While for Dolly these attributes are a deliberate ruse, Nell exhibits many of the same traits because of her childlike innocence, and has no notion of how to turn these charms on or off. At the croquet party, Nell does not comprehend that her confused and demure responses to Sir Hugh and her unawareness of his attempts to single her out are only making her more attractive. In the portrayal of the two sisters, Broughton reveals a fascinating paradox of womanhood, in which a naïve girl must grow to be a worldly woman only to act again like a naïve girl.

It is the figure of Dolly, however, who most clearly characterizes Broughton's ambivalence toward not only sisterhood, but also conventional womanhood. The *Times* reviewer of *Cometh Up as a Flower* wrote of Dolly: "[S]he is not merely the most provoking of womankind, she is one of the most officious creatures we have met in the pages of fiction; cold-blooded, mercenary, revengeful, hesitating at nothing which will further her ends," and certainly in Dolly, Broughton presents a pessimistic portrait of female hypocrisy.[9] Dolly is not merely a competitive and manipulative sister, she is also the antithesis of Victorian femininity: jaded about love; cynical about religion; indifferent to her family; and revering only power, status, and wealth. Even brash Nell, despite her own skepticism of conventional formalities, is appropriately shocked by many of her sister's scornful statements. It is not Dolly's scandalous attitudes, however, that Nell finds disgusting; it is Dolly's outward behavior, her disguise of conventional femininity. Behind this façade, Dolly's extreme pragmatism and cynicism are at least, if not more, unconventional than Nell's childish rebellions. Yet despite her disdainful nature and duplicitous behavior, Dolly is the most successful character of the novel. Michie's reading of *No Name* claims that "feminine passivity will reap the very rewards that female aggression seeks and fails to achieve" (28). Yet, in *Cometh Up as a Flower,* Dolly is rewarded for taking action. By manipulating Nell into an unwelcome marriage, Dolly saves the Lestrange family, achieves an enviable marriage for herself, and survives when Nell does not. Yet unlike conventional sisters such as Norah Vanstone in *No Name,* Dolly achieves this not because she is good but because she calculating. She casts herself in the part of the conventional sister, instinctively understanding that this is the superior role. While in *No Name* it is the irreverent sister who is the actress, Dolly is both con-artist and actress, allowing Broughton to demonstrate that conventionality is the biggest act of all.

As much as Nell disdains this depiction of womanhood, it is clear that, despite her resistance, she is gradually developing into a woman throughout her story. In her retrospective narrative the nineteen-year-old Nell is shown to be truly guileless, yet it is clear in the telling of the story that the narrator has become more self-aware. As Nell tries to resist her own womanhood by resenting Dolly's, her original attempts to exaggerate the difference between herself and her sister actually emphasize their later sameness. The language of opposites breaks down as Nell becomes more and more like her sister. In what is not meant to be a compliment, Nell describes Dolly as a "tigress or panther," clearly forgetting that only a few pages before she herself has acted "fierce as a young tigress" (346, 341). Though Nell originally claims to be ugly in contrast to her sister's beauty, she must later admit to her "prettiness now without airs of mock modesty," as she eventually achieves the same superficial beauty as her sister (313). For Nell is at her most beautiful on the day of her wedding, when she is actually miserable, and at the end of the novel, when she is dying of tuberculosis.

Nell presents her narrative not as a female *bildungsroman,* but as a confession. Knowing "that only very bad wicked women ever cared for anybody but their husbands after they were married," reading "about a married woman, who ran away from her husband and suffered the extremity of human ills in consequence," having nearly betrayed her husband and resisted the confession that would ruin her sister and herself, her story is ostensibly an admission of her sins against conventional morals (418, 436). Yet it is also a confession of her failure to resist becoming a woman, what she has been struggling against throughout the text. In her storybook code Nell has long associated womanhood with wickedness, but following her own advance she must acknowledge the shades of gray left out of her childish philosophy. By marrying, leaving home, and acquiring fine clothes and ladylike manners, Nell has become a woman very like her sister, Dolly. Manipulating her sister's fate would be the final step in becoming a replica of her sister, and it is for this reason that Nell relinquishes her claims to revenge. The scenes where Nell wonders out loud whether or not she is going to show the forged letter to Dolly's fiancé demonstrate the way the sisters' roles are reversing. Nell is now the calm and collected woman, who hides her true emotions, while Dolly's façade falters for the first time as her vulnerability is exposed. Their only previous instance of physical contact is paralleled in this scene. Dolly, in grateful affection, "jumps up and throws her arms around [Nell's] neck" just as Nell at one point offers her "small white face to be kissed" (443, 319). While Dolly formerly upheld "women's kissing one another as a misapplication of one of God's best gifts," now Nell rebuffs Dolly to "keep [her] blandishments for the lover [she] has saved" (319, 443).

For Nell, womanhood and marriage are similarly inevitable and out of her control. Despite all of her resistance, she ultimately becomes almost entirely what she despises: a woman like Dolly. The final inevitability she submits to—death—only rescues her from becoming a mother and an old woman, or, in other words, Lady Lancaster. Nell has longed for death as an escape from a miserable future, and it is in death that she finds acceptance and recovery. Her final thoughts are of redemption, and she appears to find peace in the expectation of the death she has long desired. Nell's narrative achieves a sense of continuity and perpetuity; for while it ends with her death, it opens with thoughts on her burial. Here Nell rejects both her "reserved seat in the family mausoleum" and the opportunity of lying "between a mouldering grandpapa and mouldering great-grandpapa" (217). Rather than be laid with her husband's family, return to the comfort of generations of male Lestranges, or even rest in the churchyard where she first met M'Gregor, Nell chooses to create a separate women's tradition by wishing to rest "under that big old ash tree over yonder—the one that Dolly and I cut our names on with my jagged old penknife nine, ten years ago now" (217). Nell not only surrenders to her womanhood, she embraces it. In her final planting, Nature will be her cemetery and gravestone, marked with only Nell—a representation of her childhood—and Dolly—a representation of her womanhood—and her sister will be her only mourner. Finally, like the Coxe sisters with their flowery names and Dolly, described as a "tall garden lily," Nell has cometh up as a flower and as a woman (376).

NOTES

1. Helena Michie, *Sororophobia: Differences among Women in Literature and Culture*, 50. All subsequent references are cited by page in the text.
2. Rhoda Broughton, *Cometh Up as a Flower* (Pickering and Chatto, 2004), 228. All references are to this edition and are cited by page in the text.
3. Marilyn Wood, *Rhoda Broughton (1840–1920): Profile of a Novelist*, 23.
4. Amy Levin, *The Suppressed Sister: A Relationship in Novels by Nineteenth- and Twentieth-Century British Women*, 20. All subsequent references are cited by page in the text.
5. Tamar Heller, introduction to *Cometh Up as a Flower*, lx.

6. Leila Silvana May, *Disorderly Sisters: Sibling Relations and Sororal Resistance in Nineteenth-Century British Literature,* 123.

7. Nina Auerbach, *Communities of Women: An Idea in Fiction,* 37. All subsequent references are cited by page in the text.

8. Jane Austen, *Pride and Prejudice,* 84.

9. Review of *Cometh Up as a Flower, The Times,* June 6, 1867, 9.

- 14 -

"PERSONAL PROPERTY AT HER DISPOSAL"

Inheritance Law, the Single Woman, and The Moonstone

JENNIFER A. SWARTZ

IN THE Victorian era, a woman's place in the social hierarchy was the object of intense legal scrutiny as well as the frequent subject of sensation fiction. As Lyn Pykett notes, its authors often were preoccupied with the improbable as the sensation novel revolved around long-missing heirs, newly discovered wills, babies switched at birth, adultery, and bigamy.[1] According to Marlene Tromp, the Victorians were especially shocked by the way in which these novels regularly depicted women stepping beyond established social limits and violating legal restrictions.[2] Through this disruptiveness, sensation novelists were able to test the rule of law by asking readers to confront and examine the boundaries confining the Victorian woman.

Wilkie Collins investigates this challenge to the socially accepted norm of the Domestic Angel when he considers the legal principle of coverture in *The Moonstone* (1868). In particular, he examines coverture's implications for the single woman in addition to the already established limits it placed on a married woman. Coverture prevented a wife's control of property by transferring it to the authority of her husband and decreeing that her future inheritances fell under his administration as well. Yet a form of coverture also bound single women since they lived in a society that believed all women—regardless of marital status—were incapable of operating outside the domestic sphere. By examining coverture's multiple applications, Collins explores how it simultaneously served to confine a married woman to her role as the Domestic Angel and to treat a single woman as if she had no greater legal rights than her married counterpart.

Historical and Social Forces

Coverture dated from early English law and became more generally known in the eighteenth century with the publication of William Blackstone's *Commentaries on the Laws of England* (1765–69).[3] As a prominent legal scholar who aimed to make English law more accessible to the general public, Blackstone defined "coverture" as a condition in which "the very being or legal existence of the woman is suspended" at the time of her marriage since she and her husband became "one person in law."[4] When *The Moonstone* first appeared, the concept of coverture had been relatively well known for approximately one hundred years, and the legal position of women was becoming a focus of numerous Victorian social commentators, including Barbara Leigh Smith Bodichon and Frances Power Cobbe. In 1854, Bodichon wrote "A Brief Summary, in Plain Language, of the Most Important Laws Concerning Women: Together with a Few Observations Thereon." In addition to Bodichon, Cobbe critiqued the laws affecting women in "Criminals, Idiots, Women, and Minors," which, like *The Moonstone,* was published in 1868. This was a seminal year, for, as Tim Dolin notes, Bodichon's pamphlet was reissued in 1868 and that "[w]hen *The Moonstone* was appearing in a serial in Dickens's *All the Year Round* between January and August 1868 . . . a second Married Women's Property Committee had begun a renewed campaign."[5] This increased public awareness, Mary Shanley contends, led Bodichon, Cobbe, and others to focus on specific elements of marriage law because "they [intended] to do away with the legal support that the rules of coverture gave to patriarchal authority in the home."[6] Collins enters this ongoing social debate as he applies the standards of coverture to the single character, Rachel Verinder.

As the law stood, a wife did not have her own separate legal identity, and any property, money, or other items she inherited during her coverture transferred to her husband. Coverture and, by extension, inheritance law, worked much the same as a marriage settlement, in which the woman was the means of transmission of money or property from the father or guardian to the husband. With inheritances, if goods were left to a woman, she once more conveyed capital to her spouse. No such laws applied to a single woman, however, who was legally entitled to administer legacies in any way she chose. Yet, in a society that valued coverture, a single woman's legal rights (granted to her by omission since the law never really mentions her) were frequently ignored by those who believed she was no more capable of managing inheritances than a married woman.

Through coverture and the existing legal definitions of women's roles, the Victorians were not simply eradicating a woman's legally recognized self, but engaging in the larger project of staking out an economically powerful social space by differentiating the upper and middle classes from those further down the social hierarchy. A married woman became the means of transferring property, yet because the law prevented her from keeping it, was protected from the taint of commercial activity. If women retained control over inheritances, the carefully constructed separation between home and marketplace would disintegrate. By using the law to eliminate a married woman's legally defined self and preventing her from dealing with financial matters, a clear dividing line was created between the classes; women who did not have to work or administer money were higher class than those who had to labor for their bread. Thus, economic and marital status, the legal definition of a woman's role, and a woman's behavior in the home became inextricably linked signifiers of class placement and authority. Single women who did not fit tidily into this role of "wife" jeopardized this differentiation and either were treated as if they had no greater legal freedoms than a married woman or, as Cynthia Eagle Russett contends, were denigrated by social theorists who claimed they were not fulfilling their biological destiny of marriage and motherhood.[7]

The Moonstone

It is against this legal background that Collins asks the reader to consider coverture's purposes and problems, particularly as they apply to a single woman contemplating matrimony. The novel begins as Rachel Verinder inherits the Moonstone from her Uncle Herncastle; as it unfolds, it focuses on the nature of her suitors, her potential marriage, the disposition of her inheritances, and the theft of the Moonstone. Legally known as a *feme sole,* Rachel is not affected by coverture, yet those closest to her—including the family steward, her intended fiancé, and even her mother—treat her as if she possesses no greater legal rights than a married woman.

As a *feme sole,* Rachel is entitled to form her own opinions, and the house steward Gabriel Betteredge finds this self-sufficiency troubling. He says, "She judged for herself, as few women of twice her age judge in general [and that] Miss Rachel always went on a way of her own."[8]

The family lawyer, Mr. Bruff, echoes Betteredge's concern about Rachel's self-reliance; while recognizing her independence, he believes it to be largely unfeminine:

> Rachel Verinder's first instinct, under similar circumstances, was to shut herself up in her own mind and to think it over by herself. This absolute self-dependence is a great virtue in a man. In a woman it has the serious drawback of morally separating her from the mass of her sex. (278)

Since Rachel has been raised for marriage, motherhood, and domesticity, no one tells her of the threat to her property. As a result, her right as a *feme sole* to "shut herself up in her own mind" is abrogated. If she is a wife, or a *feme covert,* the Moonstone's protection would be out of Rachel's control, and Betteredge, her future husband, Franklin Blake, and her mother, Lady Verinder, act as if the loss of her legally individual self has occurred already.

While prevailing attitudes about a woman's abilities make it understandable that the men want to shield Rachel, her mother's desire to treat her as a *feme covert* is unusual, especially since Lady Verinder has unprecedented control over the family estate. When Sir John died, he put the property in trust through the law of equity and named Lady Verinder the trustee, giving her the same property rights as her single daughter (273). Normally, wealthy fathers who wished to avoid coverture's strictures used the law of equity to place their daughters' dowries in trust, which protected the property but denied women control over it.[9] Sir John's highly unusual choice meets with the approval of Mr. Bruff, since Lady Verinder is "capable of properly administering a trust [even though] in my experience of the fair sex, not one in a thousand of them is competent" (273).

Despite her singular legal freedom, Lady Verinder denies the same benefits to her daughter. While she also sets up a trust, at Mr. Bruff's behest, she limits Rachel's access to it (276). Initially, Lady Verinder's decision seems odd—as an independent woman, why does she not confer the same freedoms on Rachel that she received, even though the family lawyer thinks she ought to do otherwise? Realistically, however, she has few choices: Rachel is young, wealthy, and the object of fortune hunters. The only way the mother can ensure the daughter's financial security is to hide the threat to the Moonstone and to limit her control over the property.

Rachel's cousin Godfrey Ablewhite mounts the first attack on Rachel's Moonstone when he proposes the night of the birthday dinner (75). Godfrey, as we learn by the end of the novel, is in deep financial difficulties and has been leading a double life. This champion of numerous charities and fundraiser extraordinaire is an embezzler who keeps a mistress with expensive tastes, and Rachel's Moonstone appears to be the answer to his financial woes. Under the usual laws of coverture, if Godfrey married Rachel, he would gain control of the Moonstone and Rachel would have no legal right to challenge his decisions. As Rachel chooses between her single status and her suitors, she is poised between two very different legal definitions of a woman's role: one in which she is bound by few laws and one in which she is bound by many.

Her situation is further complicated by Franklin, the man she hopes to marry, when he takes the Moonstone from Rachel's bedroom while sleepwalking. While ultimately absolved of a desire to steal the Moonstone for material gain, he sets up a situation whereby Rachel is forced to act like a married woman while she is still single. Because of her desire to save him from prosecution, she says nothing about his taking the gem (96). By assuming the guise of protector before he is legally entitled to do so, Franklin thrusts himself and Rachel into unnatural roles—he acts like a husband, and, in order to shield him, she must act like a wife in that she does not offer testimony. As Blackstone writes, "[I]n trials of any sort [husbands and wives] are not allowed to be witnesses for, or against, each other . . . partly because it is impossible their testimony should be indifferent, but principally because of the union of person" (443). Before the theft, Rachel and Franklin are on the brink of becoming engaged, and she illustrates the first half of Blackstone's injunction—she could not give "indifferent testimony." Because Franklin places her in the position of acting like a wife, the only way to protect him is to remain silent, despite her obligations to assist the law. However, love is not the only reason for her inability to give "indifferent testimony." When Franklin takes her Moonstone, she thinks he has stolen it to pay his debts, and his apparent betrayal infuriates her. The combination of her love and her anger prevent her from giving "indifferent testimony" and she remains silent even though she is entitled to offer evidence.

The tension between what her legal responsibility would be if she was married and the legal rights she is permitted as a single woman are evident in Rachel's most passionate rejection of the police, which is related in Betteredge's narrative:

> Miss Rachel walked swiftly through to her bedroom, wild and angry, with fierce eyes and flaming cheeks . . ."*I have not sent for you!*" she cried out, vehemently. "*I don't want you. My Diamond is lost. Neither you nor anybody else will ever find it!*" With those words she went in, and locked the doors in our faces. (97)

Locking herself in her bedroom marginalizes Rachel's presence in the text. Her bedroom is not simply her sanctuary but a powerful signifier of her status. The bedroom and sitting room were part of a woman's private domain, symbolic of her feminine role, particularly if she were married. Her clothing, toiletries, and dressing table, where she prepares herself and her appearance for the day and the bed where children are conceived and born are located in her room. In the sitting area, a wife would plan and review the daily household duties. These two rooms were distinctly feminine and connubial spaces; her boudoir encapsulates her responsibilities as a wife and mother, and Rachel, having sought solace in her chamber, has her identity as a single woman eradicated. The first step in obliterating her identity occurs when Franklin enters that bedroom and takes the Moonstone in his misguided effort to guard her. She is neither married, nor a mother, nor in charge of the household, yet she is forced to assume the Domestic Angel role when Franklin invades her room. By entering her bedroom, appropriating her inheritance, and imposing his will, Franklin creates a situation whereby Rachel essentially changes from a *feme sole* to a *feme covert*, and she must endure the silence of her chamber in order to fulfill the "wifely" responsibility of not testifying against her "husband."

Rachel's silence pervades the entire text, especially since her story is told by everyone *but* her, as with Laura Fairlie in *The Woman in White* (1860). In that earlier novel, Walter Hartright edits the narratives and excludes Laura from her own story. Lenora Ledwon writes of *The Woman in White* that "the particularity of the women's voices is lost, and Walter 'covers' their story by imposing a linear, logocentric speech over lived female experience."[10] While Ledwon writes about Laura and Marian, who, she contends, are "non-subjects, objects under the law, while the men are legal subjects" (8), a similar eradication of Rachel's voice occurs in *The Moonstone*. As Rachel endures the solitude of her bedroom, she loses all claims to her Moonstone, her identity, and her story. Her actions are interpreted by and for others who can never fully understand the significance of either her material or legal losses. Those telling Rachel's story are a servant, her future husband, a policeman, her lawyer, and an impoverished female relative who hates her. These predominantly masculine voices (and the lone spiteful female perspective) are hardly the sources for an impartial narrative designed to expose the truth.

If Rachel weds, coverture would continue to enforce her silence; she would, however, gain social currency by contributing to the larger class project of marrying and producing heirs. As Elizabeth Langland writes, "Ironically, the very signifiers of powerlessness in the gendered frame of reference became eloquent signifiers of power in a class frame."[11] How power was defined determined a woman's role and worth: if strictly a legal concern, *femes soles* would have the most power since they were entitled to the same rights as a man, yet when class standing is the means by which power is measured, the *feme covert* wields greater authority than her single sister. Because a woman could not have both legal rights *and* class power (except for the notable exception of Lady Verinder), no woman could possess an effectively recognized voice in the society in which she lived.

When examining the issue through Langland's "class frame," it becomes clear that *femes soles* were almost completely ignored by the law and by a society that did not value them. A single woman's lack of class power is particularly evident in the novel's first narrative. Taking up almost half of the text, the first narrator is the family steward, Betteredge. He is far removed from Rachel in the social hierarchy, but he has decided opinions on what choices should be made for her. While Betteredge's great devotion to Lady Verinder and Rachel are evident, he is a genial and kindly misogynist, firmly convinced of the general inferiority of women. He cannot understand Rachel's choices because of his deeply ingrained opinions of women's nature and intellect as well as his position in the social order. Yet, this is the character that relates the first half of the Moonstone's disappearance. Because the household steward has the most significant narrative,

Rachel's exclusion from her own story is reinforced. She might be a single woman of means, but even the family servant has a more recognized voice than the daughter of the house ever will.

Her wealth cannot protect her from inequities such as these, and she becomes, as Adela Wills writes, the "marginalised Other."[12] Even her name signifies Otherness since, as Jaya Mehta notes, Rachel's surname is a common first name in India, a country where England was a colonizing force.[13] Moreover, her dark complexion that Betteredge labels as "out of fashion latterly in the gay world" (64), emphasizes her status as "marginalized Other." The first steps in her marginalization are her love for Franklin as well as her sense of duty toward him. She cannot betray him to the law, for doing so would ensure his imprisonment, just as her imposed silence exposes her to possible legal action. However, after the truth is revealed and her tale can be told, she still does not get to speak. Even though she has endured public humiliation and personal trauma, her marriage ensures that her silence is final because the law places all decisions in the hands of the husband.

It is Franklin's idea to compile and edit the narratives and to tell Rachel's story in separate accounts. He again assumes the role of spouse, but this time he is entitled to it since he and Rachel have wed. Because they are now "one person in law," Rachel's silence is required, for upon her marriage she lost her legal identity and must accept her husband's decisions, whatever they might be. Franklin says to Betteredge that "There can be no doubt that this strange family story of ours ought to be told. And I think, Betteredge, Mr Bruff and I together have hit on the right way of telling it" (21). The legal representatives of Rachel's interests, her husband and her lawyer, decide how best to tell her story, which still leaves her essentially locked in the silence of her bedroom. Furthermore, Franklin appropriates Rachel's experiences by declaring them to be "this strange family story of ours," as he decides to have everyone but the principal character participate in the narrative. Through their marriage, Franklin absorbs Rachel's legal self, her story, and her power over that story into his own identity. Rachel is controlled by the law throughout the text: she is silenced early on by her love for Franklin, which forces her to behave like a wife before she becomes one, and her silence is enforced by both the incompetent Superintendent Seegrave and the celebrated Sergeant Cuff to whom she cannot speak because they represent yet another branch of the law. Her silence will be required a final time; after she becomes Franklin's wife, she will be bound by coverture and never again have the legal right to tell her own story.

While initially *The Moonstone* appears to critique coverture's strictures, Rachel's subsequent happy marriage highlights some of the tensions inherent in the law. Collins seems to suggest that, in some instances, coverture is acceptable but only when a woman is married to an honorable man. Ledwon makes a similar observation about *The Woman in White* when she writes, "The moral seems to be that coverture is bad with a bad husband but right and proper with a good husband" (19). If a woman wed a man with no integrity, her lack of legal recourse placed her in an impossible position. In Rachel's case, if she had married Godfrey, coverture would have been untenable since he was a criminal, an embezzler, and a philanderer. However, her marriage to Franklin is a different matter altogether: she is content with her new status since she has wed a good and law-abiding man. Theoretically, her rights should be more constrained than they were when she was a *feme sole* but, in some ways, she has greater freedom after her marriage, which, according to Blackstone, was coverture's intent: "even the disabilities which the wife lies under are for the most part intended for her protection and benefit" (444). In Rachel's case, this is true. Her marriage to Franklin gives her greater protection and, while others tell her story, her silence is broken and her reputation restored. What Collins appears to be criticizing, then, is the assumption that every man is honorable, a supposition that Caroline Norton condemned fourteen years earlier in her 1854 collection of writings, "English Laws for Women in the Nineteenth Century."[14] By presuming the best about every man rather than the worst, the law actually denied women the "protection and benefit" Blackstone claimed on their behalf. By crafting a happy marriage at the end, Collins uncovers the inequities in the law which dictate that a woman is subject to her husband's whims since her voice is eradicated whether the union is harmonious or not.

Conclusion

By making Rachel occupy both legal roles open to the Victorian woman while she is still single, Collins illuminates a woman's tenuous legal position. Juxtaposing the diverse scenarios surrounding Rachel—fiancée or wife, inheritor or benefactor—Collins explores how society treated every woman as if she had no legal rights, even though the laws governing them were vastly different based on marital status. While England's lawmakers effectively eliminated a married woman's legal selfhood, they did not clearly define the status of single women, and thus women like Rachel could pose unwelcome challenges to gendered spheres.

To illustrate the cultural danger of such a challenge, *The Moonstone* disposes of every *feme sole* that appeared in its pages. Rosanna Spearman, the housemaid who loved Franklin, lies dead at the bottom of the Shivering Sand (333). Limping Lucy Yolland, Rosanna's only friend, disappears after harshly criticizing Franklin (309). Miss Clack is "living, for economy's sake, in a little town in Brittany" (201). Penelope, Betteredge's daughter, vanishes after she castigates Miss Clack for claiming Lady Verinder died unsaved (270). All four women must be eradicated since each threatens the Victorian social order. Rosanna loves a man outside her class and dares to think she can win his affection. Limping Lucy hates men, has no desire to marry or produce offspring, and advocates anarchy (192). Penelope vanishes because she is too opinionated for both a woman and a servant and violates class boundaries when she rebukes Miss Clack. Miss Clack also must disappear, but her offense is one which, despite her many failings, she cannot help— she is impoverished. By leaving England, her poverty and spinster status can no longer be an affront to those who are more capable of fulfilling the class demands of marriage and children.

Rachel, supposedly the strongest *feme sole* of all, marries and is expecting a child (463). Of the *femes soles* in the novel, she is most able to fulfill the demands of her class. Her love for Franklin is class appropriate, unlike Rosanna's desire for him. She willingly embraces the notion of marriage and rank, which separates her from women like Lucy who despise men and long for class warfare. While she is opinionated like Penelope, her ability both to "lock herself up in her own mind" and to allow herself to be silenced because she loves Franklin illustrate she is prepared to assume a wife's duties. Finally, her wealth guarantees she will be successful in gaining a husband, unlike the poverty-stricken Miss Clack. Tellingly, the novel's "happy" ending comes about through the death, disappearance, banishment, and marriage of every single woman in the text. A single woman, as the text indicates, might have legal rights but she was ultimately dismissed by a culture that valued marriage, domesticity, and class, often finding herself relegated to the margins of the very social systems she had been raised to embrace.

NOTES

1. Lyn Pykett, *The "Improper" Feminine*.
2. Marlene Tromp, *The Private Rod*.
3. For an analysis of Blackstone's motives, see Stanley Katz's introduction to the reprinted facsimile edition of the *Commentaries*. For discussion of coverture's early Norman-French roots and its eventual disestablishment by the Law Reform Act of 1935, see Hazel Lord, "Husband and Wife."
4. William Blackstone, *Commentaries*, vol. 1, bk. 1, 441. All citations from the law, both in the title and paper, are from the same edition, volume, and book. Future references will be cited in the text.
5. Tim Dolin, *Mistress of the House*, 68.
6. Mary Shanley, *Feminism, Marriage, and the Law*, 15.
7. Cynthia Russett, *Sexual Science*, 120.

8. Wilkie Collins, *The Moonstone* (Penguin, 1998), 65. All citations are from this edition; future references will be cited in the text.
9. Mary Poovey, *Uneven Developments*, 71–72. See also Shanley, 15.
10. Lenora Ledwon, "Veiled Women," 9. Future references will be cited in the text.
11. Elizabeth Langland, *Nobody's Angels*, 37.
12. Adele Wills, "Witnesses to Truth," 91.
13. Jaya Mehta, "English Romance," 645.
14. Poovey's chapter on Caroline Norton and the Married Women's Property Acts is extremely helpful. See *Uneven Developments*, 51–88.

- PART THREE -
Class, Racial, and Cultural Contexts in the Sensation Novel and on the Stage

The essays in this section deal with the response of sensation fiction and drama to issues of class, race, and empire. Andrew Maunder examines a little-known stage adaptation of Ellen Wood's *East Lynne* that ran at the working-class Effingham Theatre and that reflected local, working-class concerns. Focusing on *Aurora Floyd*, Lillian Nayder shows that Braddon uses window imagery to explore and test social boundaries. Tamara Wagner also emphasizes the importance of material and geographical context as she analyzes Collins's *Basil* as a response to the new suburban environment of an emergent middle class. Kimberly Harrison discusses Braddon's *The Octoroon*, which, written for a working-class audience, engaged issues of race and upward mobility. Both Vicki C. Wiley and Monica Young-Zook explore Collins's use of characters who are racial hybrids. Willey engages in the debate that surrounds Collins's imperial purpose in *The Moonstone*, reading it as a tolerant response to British brutality in the aftermath of the Sepoy Rebellion, and Young-Zook describes racial ambivalence in *Armadale*, comparing the depictions of Midwinter and his mother to the villainess Lydia Gwilt.

- 15 -

"I WILL NOT LIVE IN POVERTY AND NEGLECT"

East Lynne *on the East End Stage*

ANDREW MAUNDER

Introduction

> I cannot help thinking that a portion of "East Lynne's" success is owing to its being so much represented on the stage. Go where I will, I mean into country places, I am sure to see the walls placarded with "East Lynne." People see the play and the next day send and buy the book.
> —Ellen Wood to George Bentley, February 20, 1875

In February 1866, five years after Ellen Wood's story of an adulterous middle-class wife had become an international best seller, London's New Surrey Theatre produced what was billed as the premiere of *East Lynne* the drama. The production with a script by John Oxenford and starring the American tragedienne Avonia Jones was critically successful and highly popular. Jones would make something of a career playing the adulterous but penitent heroine, Isabel Vane, taking the play into the West End the following year, and then to Australia. The significance of this production has long been acknowledged. Katharine Newey and Veronica Kelly note that a trend was established and "after these first performances *East Lynne* became a staple for managements and performers in London until the end of the century."[1] Its sentimental and homiletic paeans to wifely loyalty and motherhood; the tragic predicament of its heroine who achieved iconic status; and its mix of murder, disguise, and lingering death proved the stuff of powerful "weeping" melodrama, offering significant resonance for Victorian audiences. In 1866, many critics marveled that translation from page to London stage had taken so long, especially since stage versions of other sensational best sellers—*The Woman in White, Lady Audley's Secret, Aurora Floyd*—had followed swiftly on the appearance of their final chapters. "When it is remembered," a writer for the *Era* wrote, "that the popular novel of *East Lynne* furnished many striking situations capable of effective stage treatment, the lapse of five years between the date of publication and the period of its presentation on the London boards in a dramatic form would seem to involve a mystery quite as provocative of wild guesses at a solution as any which perplex the readers of Mrs. Henry Wood's highly interesting story."[2] Yet Wood's novel *had* been performed on the London stage before this in an adaptation titled *Marriage Bells*. This was at the Effingham Theatre, Whitechapel, in November 1864. Situated deep in the labyrinthine East End, the Effingham formed part of a flourishing theatrical culture but one which few of those who saw Avonia Jones's performances would ever dream of attending. Nor, as her comments above suggest, was this a direction in which Ellen Wood ever thought of traveling. Yet the staging of *East Lynne* at the Effingham Theatre was more noteworthy than has been assumed. As Wood recognized, stage adaptations boosted sales of her novel. It has been calculated that the total sales reached five hundred thousand by 1900. But East End stage adaptations also introduced Wood to a new audience. This audience of course attended their local theater for other familiar attractions, and so would have watched performances of *East Lynne* as part of a wider spectrum of entertainments and against the backdrop of local preoccupations. That is, most of the audience watched the play in a particular context.

This essay considers the way in which *East Lynne* was recast for working-class audiences. Although critics have noted the ties that bind *East Lynne* and other sensation novels to melodrama, the place of these adaptations in Victorian popular culture has received scant attention. This is surprising. Like *Lady Audley's Secret, Uncle Tom's Cabin,* and *Jack Sheppard,* which also became part of the standard repertoire of Victorian theater, *East Lynne* belongs to a tradition of adapting novels for the stage that can be traced back to the end of the eighteenth century and the novels of Samuel Richardson, Walter Scott, Mary Shelley, and Matthew "Monk" Lewis. The fashion flourished and by mid-nineteenth century the appetite for stage adaptations appeared voracious. In 1860, the *Times* observed how "once a tale becomes generally popular, a desire to see it as a dramatic form immediately spreads like an epidemic. . . ." "Whether a story be fitted for stage purposes or not people do not even inquire, nor even care. They only want to see the personages they have read about clothed in a visible form and turn from the book to the stage as a child turns from letter-press to pictures."[3] These constructs of gullible audiences of limited intelligence that were coming under increasing scrutiny in discussions of sensation novels in the early 1860s also played a key role in debates about stage adaptations, to the extent that many observers came to view adaptation as symptomatic of a widespread degeneration of theatrical taste which pandered to the lowest common denominator, a form of physical assault or burglary, as bad as any of the crimes described in the novels. However, sensation novels were also, as critics noted, viewed as public property, their adaptations conducted on "socialistic" and commercial lines,[4] with what the *London Review* described as "an appeal to that low taste for criminal horrors . . . catered for by the Old Bailey reports." The *Review* went on to complain that "unnatural behavior and . . . improbable incidents . . . do not become less glaringly offensive, when detached from the less salient passages of the book and placed in close sequence upon the stage."[5] Henry Morley likewise labeled sensation adaptations "garbage," fitted only for the "literary taste in the uneducated,"[6] while the *Times*'s reviewer (cited above) was insistent that any dramatization "must be unsatisfactory" because of the "iron necessity" to omit details that the original novelist had deemed vital to the story.[7] The version of the novel which playwright-adapters and theater managers offered would be limited and specific and what in the original text might be "nice shades or complicated details" and "nuances of character" would be replaced by "broader and more marked effects . . . judicious groupings and well-arranged masses of colour."[8] Although the sensation novel was increasingly identified by critics as a corrupt and lazy cultural form, theater managements and actors quickly realized that these stories were worth exploiting. *East Lynne* was rarely a favorite of twentieth-century theater critics, most of whom dismissed as outright melodramatic and obvious its tearful story of a runaway wife haunted by guilt in the form of her dying child.[9] In contrast, Victorian producers' adaptations of the novel formed part of a lucrative business in which profits seemed guaranteed and were there for the taking.[10]

This essay builds upon suggestions made by Kerry Powell and others that we continue to try to better understand the strategies at work when popular novels by women were "re-fitted" for the stage.[11] It also follows Edward O'Shea's calls for us to recognize the extent to which every adaptation of a literary text involves a "reinterpretation or a repositioning of that text in a new cultural formation."[12] Although the social character of much Victorian melodrama is now less in doubt, and while Michael Booth has noted the degree to which the "social and cultural implications of a play . . . cannot be completely comprehended unless one is aware of the audience for which it was performed . . . ,"[13] examination of *East Lynne* and other sensation novels before Victorian audiences still represents a neglected area of investigation. Yet as Darryl Wadsworth has shown in a recent examination of the City of London Theatre's adaptation of *Bleak House,* it can be a productive one. What can happen is that the "class composition" of a particular theater audience plays a part in determining the "tone" of individual adaptations.[14] In a recent discussion of East End theater, Jim Davis also reminds us that approaching the social character of individual Victorian melodramas in terms of local audiences enables us to read more clearly their cultural immediacy and the ways in which social issues were "mediated to certain sectors of the population, at least in a theatrical form at certain places and at certain times."[15]

I would like to follow the implications of these approaches in relation to the Effingham Theatre's adaptation of *East Lynne* in November 1864; first by considering the "character" of the Effingham Theatre and its program; second by looking at how this theater's adaptation of *East Lynne* can be understood in the context of issues of class and poverty as they affected local audiences; third by noting briefly some of the differences between the Effingham version of the novel and the more famous version performed at the Surrey Theatre and subsequently the West End. Even as sensation novels were being borrowed from Mudie's circulating library, neatly packaged in three volumes for reading in the drawing room, they were increasingly being used in different ways for different kinds of theater audiences.

The Effingham Theatre

The Effingham Theatre, a so-called minor theater, was located firmly in the East End, at 236 Whitechapel Road, Stepney, with Morris Abrahams as its lessee. It was a tradition among Victorian observers to describe East End theaters as profoundly different from those in the vicinity of the West End.[16] Bracebridge Hemyng's comments about the Effingham, made in the section on "Prostitution" (part of Henry Mayhew's *London Labour and the London Poor*), reveal how entrenched this distinction was.[17] Because, as Hemyng noted, "Whitechapel has always been looked upon as a suspicious, unhealthy locality, a strange amalgam of Jews, English, French, German and other antagonistic elements that must clash and jar," the theater had never provoked much interest among middle-class critics and audience. Yet this, he argued, was unfair:

> Whitechapel has its theatres, its music-halls, the cheap rates of admission to which serve to absorb numbers of the inhabitants, and by innocently amusing them soften their manners and keep them out of harm's way. . . . The Earl of Effingham, a theatre in Whitechapel Road, has lately been done up and restored, and holds three thousand people. It has no boxes; they would not be patronized if they were in existence. Whitechapel does not go to the theatre in kid gloves and white ties. The stage of the Effingham is roomy and excellent, the trap work very extensive, for Whitechapel rejoices very much in pyrotechnic displays, blue demons, red demons, and vanishing Satans that disappear in a cloud of smoke through an invisible hole in the floor.[18]

A poem by Linneas Banks, delivered from the stage of the Effingham in 1867, asserted the theater's social purpose and its intention to ensure that "weary labour

... may come and gather new strength for the morrow," "shake off care's cankering sorrow," and "leave both happier and better." Banks went on to pledge good value and assure the "brawny" tradesman, "pompous beadle," and "sailor Jack," together with the "multitude from "Labour's hives" and working girls like "Mary gay in ribbons," that the theater would provide exciting entertainment, offering "good change for every honest shilling," plus escape from grim routine.[19] Although there was some overlap in the repertoires of East and West End theaters, the version of the world at midcentury which the theater presented would be dictated by the sympathies of its local clientele, and what was shown or not shown represented a clearly defined artistic policy catering to particular and unmistakable social and political assumptions.[20] This had particular implications for the dramatists supplying the theater. The *Era* noted how writing for a theater like the Effingham required the author to put on a kind of "literary harness," a contraption that would be comfortable enough as long as he (or she) remembered "two exigencies." "[O]ne is the company, which must be 'brought in'; and the other is the audience, whose peculiar tastes have to be consulted."[21] The same paper noted how *Garibaldi,* performed in April 1864 to coincide with the Italian patriot's visit to Britain, was played with "a very great amount of energy and speeches delivered upon the subject of freedom being 'highly relished by the auditory.'"[22] Earlier, in 1861, a production of *Nicholas Nickleby* was billed as *The Life and Adventures of Poor Smike.* No one it seemed was much bothered about the gentlemanly hero. These constraints on those authors trying to turn popular novels into plays, based in part on class lines, need to be acknowledged when examining individual adaptations such as *Marriage Bells,* or versions of the same source text across different theaters.

When G. A. Sala, a man not averse to some of the less salubrious haunts of London, described the Effingham as "a gaff," "dreadfully dirty and with a much dirtier audience," its stage populated by "bad bandit[s] in buff boots" and "young ladies in pink calico with their back hair down . . . expressive of affliction,"[23] he was playing on the theater's doubtful reputation as a squalid place of crude entertainment catering to the "great unwashed" and in need of policing. Sala's comments also reflect the requirements of a theater designed to cater to working-class audiences, and where the absence of self-consciously respectable fare such as classical tragedy, Shakespeare, and opera (traditionally the domain of the West End theaters) worked to privilege melodrama. The strongly held belief that the East End audiences had what Blanchard Jerrold described as a "tough palate," which needed regular doses of "highly spiced" dramas, played a large part in determining the contents of the Effingham program to the extent that plays devoid of "incidents of the most thrilling sensation and powerful and affecting situations" would not be performed.[24] The Banks's poem (cited above) is insistent that the "eager scores" who "elbow . . . each other roughly at the door" come for villainy and escapism, that what they want is a "storm of 'pathos' and 'raillery.'" Although some plays had their origins in the more murderous reaches of the classical repertoire—notably 1862's *Richard III; or, The Battle of Bosworth*—there was no social or artistic "reclamation" of the kind sought by Samuel Phelps at Sadler's Wells or James Anderson at the New Surrey.[25]

Submitted to the Lord Chamberlain on November 15, 1864 and performed on the nineteenth, J. Archer's adaptation of *East Lynne—Marriage Bells; or, the Cottage on the Cliff*—appeared at a theater which followed a clearly defined commercial and artistic strategy. Its worldview was a melodramatic one in which virtue would triumph over evil; classical drama was avoided and a working-class audience was assumed.[26] The theater relied on work from a range of playwrights—both "names" like C. H. Hazelwood and Mrs. Henry Young, and unknowns —and, as the reviewer for the *Era* noted in February 1864, was particularly fond of seeing novels on stage, "dramatic adaptations from tales in popular publications being constantly produced."[27] The 1864 season included Archer's *Marriage Bells*, an adaptation by Mrs. Henry Young of E. D. E. N. Southworth's *Left Alone; or, The Footsteps of Crime*; C. H. Hazelwood's *Jeannie Deans*, and another Scott adaptation, *Rebecca the Jewess*; T. P. Taylor's temperance drama *The Bottle; or, The Drunken Doom*; and *The Wild Tribes of London; or, Life in the East and West*. The melodramas often have a contemporary (urban) setting, and depict a range of sensational incidents—murder, armed robbery, forgery, seduction, bigamy, and false imprisonment.[28] Although not always antiauthoritarian, they address an audience which might view itself as being on the margins of society—which might be supposed to sympathize with (or be susceptible to) the panic caused when a baby is kidnapped by the gentleman villain in *Left Alone*, the fear which results from being wrongly tainted with the suspicion of crime, the distress caused by loss of employment through drunkenness, or the misery of the slaves in *Uncle Tom's Cabin*. As Banks had explained, there is no sense of outright didacticism; instead, careful attention is paid to society's victims, and the tone is constructed to sympathize with the British workman. Plays are rarely condemnatory of the working classes (and then only mildly), and assumptions about the importance of family, community, and work are upheld.

East Lynne at the Effingham

The question of the political role of nineteenth-century melodramas has been the subject of a good deal of critical attention. David Mayer has argued that "People attended theater because as well as offering entertainment and relaxation (and melodrama offers both) the playhouse is a place to confront issues and mediate social values, where plays themselves intervene in and obliquely or directly critique matters of daily concern."[29] Michael Booth has likewise pointed out that "Because melodrama was always in touch with the social concerns and cultural tastes of its audience it quickly absorbed the new industrial proletariat onto its structure."[30] This role was famously represented by works such as John Buckstone's *Luke the Labourer* (1826), Douglas Jerrold's *Black Eye'd Susan* (1829), and the controversial adaptations of Harrison Ainsworth's *Jack Sheppard*. The city was also regarded as a site which embodied the tensions and turmoils of society at large, in which family life and spiritual values were consistently under siege. Christine Gledhill describes how: "Much nineteenth century melodrama cues into the visual and social oppositions made visible by the startling juxtapositions of fast expanding heteroglot cities—rich/poor, upper class/working class, luxury/squalor—as well as by social experience of the sudden rise and fall accompanying the boom and bust cycles of industrialisation."[31] London, in particular, features almost as a character in many melodramas, a powerful influence on its heroes and heroines; as much a psychological as it is a physical place, adding to the sense of isolation and fears of personal oblivion.

One of the main sites at which this occurred was in theaters catering to working-class audiences: "While representations of city life were popular in the more fashionable theaters . . . the audiences in the east apparently could not tire of seeing the problems of the London poor resolved on stage."[32] This is apparent in the Effingham Theatre in 1864. Examination of Archer's version of *East Lynne,* alongside plays by Mrs. Henry Young and articles appearing in the local press, can demonstrate how each takes part in the ongoing construction and redefinition of working-class identity. Plays and news reports help suggest how it was possible for audiences to see Wood's original novel in a new light.

The Lord Chamberlain's files indicate that *Marriage Bells* was submitted for licensing on November 15, 1864 and premiered on November 19. Within a week the decision had been taken to extend its run and the *East London Observer* wrote of "the great success of the new drama." In adverts announcing the program for the last week in November, the theater boasted that *Marriage Bells* "produces greatest sensations in crowded houses" and as a story of seduction and victimization it seemed an obvious crowd-pleaser.[33] Like the original novel, the play's plot centers around social constructions of gender and male-female relations. On the surface this play is still a cautionary tale of seduction, focused on the downfall of Lady Isabel (here rechristened Emily), the aristocratic wife of the wealthy solicitor Mordaunt (Carlyle), at the hands of an earlier admirer, the debauched aristocrat Captain Alfred (Francis Levison). Persuaded by the "serpent"-like Alfred's suggestions that her husband is in love with a neighbour, Barbara, Emily succumbs to temptation and elopes with her former lover. Once abroad, she is woefully neglected by Alfred (by whom she has an illegitimate child) and faces a life of exile, penury, and stigma when her husband divorces her. With uncharacteristic resolution and strength, Emily returns to London where she tries to get work. Longing for her children, she tries to return in disguise to her former home in order to serve as governess to the children she deserted. By this time, Emily has been replaced as Mrs. Mordaunt by Barbara. Emily's disguise is quickly discovered and she is turned out of the house where she succumbs to a wasting disease and dies of a broken heart.

The importance of this first *East Lynne* adaptation lies in the ways in which the story is rerouted to fit the repertory style of the Effingham Theatre. There is an onstage murder and also a duel (between the wronged husband and the stock-in-trade aristocratic seducer, Captain Alfred). In Wood's novel the first of these events has taken place before the story begins; the second does not occur at all. Middle-class society still finds Lady Emily emphatically guilty of crimes against her husband and children because of her sexual deviance, but there is no mention of the train crash which in the novel leaves the adulterous wife limping and hunched, her tortured and disfigured body both the site of punishment for her transgression and a marker of her wrongdoing. Most striking, however, is the way in which the story is persistently being detoured or derailed, only to be recast as an indictment (from an expressly working-class point of view) of the one-sided prosperity of mid-Victorian Britain post-1851, a country in which, as one of the play's working-class characters notes, there are indeed "plenty of fine things here . . . if you have only got the money." In *East Lynne,* Ellen Wood does touch upon the question of working-class hardship in the character of the displaced judge's son, Richard Hare. However, her treatment of this issue remains on the margins—as it does in West End stage treatments. In contrast, the Effingham's version is awash with references to working-class poverty—so much so that at times the adultery plot and the naming and shaming of the criminal wife almost stops being the main focus. So, for example, in an exchange that does not occur in the original novel, the solicitor's clerk, Mr. Dill, is pushed center stage to provide an account of the "true" story of his upbringing:

MORDAUNT: My grandfather found him a ragged little fellow running about the streets; without a character he placed him in the office.
DILL: Where I have remained ever since. Heaven rest the kind man's soul. Your grandfather, sir, thought it a shame a man should be able and willing to work and yet want the common necessary comforts of life.
BARBARA: And so he took you to his home to feed and clothe you.
MORDAUNT: To find him work that he might feed and clothe himself and he has now remained with me merely to suit himself.

This is not altogether a new tone in Wood's novel; it builds upon elements latent in the novel. It is also reminiscent of the bourgeois ethos of self-help that the text espouses. But it is also typical of the Effingham's practice of deliberately incorporating a view "from below" into events. Such exchanges are not breaches of fidelity but conscious and significant dramaturgical gestures—from a working-class stance. Mr. Dill understands his early suffering as a product of class and location, a suffering which can be alleviated by the class above—the middle class—though not by charity but by the creation of opportunity. This responsibility is voiced by Mordaunt, who becomes, as he does in the novel, a kind of pious spokesman for middle-class individualism. According to this viewpoint, men and woman shape their own destinies. Differences in wealth among individuals is the result of their different abilities to master their bodies and to use them to accumulate capital. The worker who rents his labor to earn a wage is merely disposing of his body as he chooses. Mr. Dill stays in Mordaunt's employ because he wants to. He is not a victimized wage slave; he has economic self-determination.

Mr. Dill, of course, is one of the lucky ones. One of the effects of nineteenth-century capitalism was, as Karl Marx and Friedrich Engels argued, the creation of an economic system which brought people together to live and work in close proximity but pitted them against one another.[34] The worker became simply a cog or "tool" for hire in a huge machine, subservient to a vast, impersonal, dehumanizing competitive system. Read in this context, and performed before patrons who knew only too well that London could be a dehumanizing environment full of hungry mouths, it is possible to see how the Effingham's *East Lynne* becomes a play which takes on new dimensions, emerging as a record of social crisis and social conflicts.

At the center of the adaptation remains the disgraced, pauperized wife, Lady Emily, "friendless and forsaken" as she describes herself. As we might expect, the charity extended by the Mordaunt family to Mr. Dill does not extend to her. Indeed, as part of his quest for "vengeance" Mordaunt takes unusual pleasure in personally tracking Emily to present her with the divorce papers. "I made with heaven a compact to place this divorce in your hands, this the recompense of English Justice, to those who trample out love and tenderness of the human soul." Abandoned by Captain Alfred and shunned by the middle classes and the legal system, for whom her sexual lapse is too great a crime to tolerate, Lady Emily, a powerless, unskilled woman with an illegitimate child, is pitched into the East End, walking in "anguish" through its streets searching for work. She realizes that it will now be her fate "to live in poverty and neglect" since she has forgone that support network of "husband, children and friends" who combine "to make each day a holiday." However, just as she contemplates suicide, Emily is drawn into a new web of affiliation through her acquaintanceship with a kindly working-class woman, Fanny Hillford. In stark contrast to Wood's novel, where as Affy Hallijohn she is a promiscuous working-class girl on the make, the Fanny of the Effingham version is an outspoken (and respectably married) spokesperson for the poor, of whom Emily is the play's most visible representative. In an exchange which does not appear in the book, Fanny questions her husband's idea that misery and hardship are providential:

> CHUCKERS: It has been the will of providence to let all these unpleasant things take place and as in the end providence always works for the best, providence when it thinks proper will put everything right again.
> FANNY: What you say is very right but it's very hard to bear while it lasts, there are many poor creatures lost for the want of some kind loving hearts to stretch out a hand to help them, so they rush into the streets or starve with their infants and abandon them to strangers.
> EMILY: Oh never, never. I already feel strange. Give me my child and let me go.

The use of "they" in Fanny's address suggests that Emily's predicament—the fact that she looks set to become progressively swallowed, sucked down by the city—is not an isolated one. In autumn 1864, local East End newspapers were particularly interested in highlighting the underside of mid-Victorian prosperity and the fate of the innocent victims of a society beset by capitalism. This correspondence between life in *Marriage Bells* and that of people living in the streets surrounding the theater is most obvious in an article in the *East London Observer* on November 27, 1864, in the third week of the play's run. Headed "Trade Murder or How to Expend Our Redundant Women," it was prompted by a local cause célèbre: the death from overwork and poisoning of a single woman employee, Elizabeth Wood, in a white lead factory. The paper lamented the "misery and absolute want compelling famishing girls and destitute women to see their lives at a few months purchase at rate of six farthings a day."[35] Three weeks earlier the same paper had reported the discovery of the body of a child in the doorway of the Black Horse Tavern on Kingsland Road.[36] Later in November another article, "Death from Starvation," detailed how Mary Ann Bloomfield, an elderly woman who got her living from retrieving bits of cloth and bone from waste heaps, had discovered a man, "shockingly emaciated," lying "dead on a dung heap from the moral effects of exposure and destitution." The man appeared to have no family or friends and the coroner noted as "melancholy" the fact that "no-one should even know or care enough about him to identify his body."[37] An editorial in the same paper lamented the sense of hopelessness that prompted human beings "in the extremity of wretchedness [to] have laid down to die almost on our very doorsteps, surrounded by the wealth of the first city in the world, or in some obscure garret, far away from human sympathy; nay even at the workhouse door." "We must all," announced the paper, "feel deep sorrow at the degradation of a country that permitted its inhabitants to starve in the streets."[38] In the weeks that followed, readers of the paper were sufficiently fired up to write in calling for something to be done about the "shameful treatment of the poor."[39] As Christmas approached, concern was expressed about those who fell through the net of local charities during the festive season or were too proud to seek help, "suffering, unseen and unregarded . . . sinking for want of life's commonest necessities . . . the retiring poor, whose self-respect is stronger than even . . . the pangs of starvation."[40]

These local discussions, both in the press and in the coroner's court, show that different fears and ideas were being aired. Yet these were not the only voices addressing this question at this time. The development of melodrama in the nineteenth century occurs at the same moment as the emergence of industrialization. On stage at the local theater, the Effingham, in *Marriage Bells,* Fanny is just one in a number of angry sailors, factory workers, and abandoned urban poor to decry the system that disenfranchises them, and to remind the audience of the tenuousness of existence. Other plays such as Mrs. Henry Young's *Left Alone; or the Footsteps of Crime,* which played alongside *Marriage Bells* in November 1864, *The Wild Tribes of the London; or Life in the East and West,* which also did, and *Desolation* all worked to highlight the plight of the disenfranchised. In Mrs. Young's *Jessy Ashton or the Adventures of a Barmaid,* performed at the Effingham in 1862, there is a similar lament by the heroine who has no resources for survival:

> JESSY: I am poor and friendless—I have suffered misery beyond my years. Pity me . . . drawn . . . from my house, my love, my friends—fool that I was to think I might find safety in flight and hide myself in the world of the London . . . I am lost. Oh take me from this den of living horrors.[41]

If, as Jim Davis has suggested, we accept the idea that melodrama "reflects a way of seeing specific to the age which fostered it" and that it "functions historically as a means of revealing ideological values common in particular communities in nineteenth century England,"[42] then attempting to understand the thinking behind the Effingham's version of *East Lynne* means paying some attention to the environment in which it was performed. One way of coming to terms with the play's moral and ideological stance is to try and understand it as its first audience—the working-class audience of the Effingham Theatre in November 1864—would have done. This audience, who would not necessarily have read the original novel, encountered the play and its outcast heroine ("alone, alone in the world for evermore") juxtaposed with other texts. Local news—whether reported by word of mouth or in print—together with other urban melodramas worked intertextually to provide a kind of running commentary on the on-stage events, with the audience able to fill in the gaps.

It is for this reason that back on stage at the Effingham, as we move from the familiar generic elements of the play—the victimized woman, the aristocratic seducer who carries her off over the headland on a black horse—other kinds of agendas become apparent. While the Effingham *East Lynne* continually places emphasis on individual virtue or villainy (like her counterpart in the New Surrey version, Emily laments her own weakness at the hands of an aristocratic seducer), this version of the novel also suggests that laissez-faire capitalism is the real villain, more destructive and cruel than any seducer. Like Marx and Engels, the Effingham version takes up an anti-industrialist position. Wood's heroine is not just cast as a terrible anomaly—a disgraced wife and mother. Rather, Emily's experiences and her desire to make use of "the labour of my own hands" become specifically those of a working-class woman in London in the 1860s. And one context for the emotionalism of *Marriage Bells* is thus the urgency with which mid-nineteenth-century writers debated the figure of the alienated worker in a capitalist, free-market economy. Similar scenes are to be found in some of the better-known Victorian stories of industrial misery—Elizabeth Gaskell's *Mary Barton* (1848) and Charles Dickens's *Hard Times* (1854) are the most famous, but there are other stories set specifically in London, notably Andrew Mearns's *A Bitter Cry of Outcast London* (1883) and George Gissing's *The Workers in the Dawn* (1881), written to show the "ghastly condition . . . of our poor class. . . ."[43] Like these novels, *Marriage Bells*, like other Effingham plays, draws attention to the discrepancies between the platitudes of "self-help" uttered by men like Emily's husband, Mordaunt, a representative of Britain's prosperity, and the counterfoils of "misery and persecution" and "anguish" felt by the urban poor.

The radical nature of the recasting of *East Lynne* becomes more apparent when we compare the Effingham version to the New Surrey's version of the novel, staged in 1866—the production which helped fix the tone for later West End adaptations, itself transferring to the Lyceum Theatre the following year. The New Surrey catered to a heterogeneous (rather than specifically working-class) audience, one in which as the *Times* noted, "a successful piece may be regarded as a standard of the dramatic taste with which the middling classes . . . are imbued. . . . Their most favourite productions are those laid among the domestic circles in which the majority of the audience move."[44] In this theater's version of *East Lynne*, its adaptor, John Oxenford, downplays the subversive protofeminist elements of the original novel, recasting the story to display in a fairly unequivocal fashion, what Laurie Langbauer has labeled the "consolations of gender."[45] Wood's novel is transformed into a polemical dramatic text which attempts to reinvest middle-class women with a sense of their duties as mothers of the race, implicitly aligning those who would criticize matrimonial responsibilities with the fallen Isabel. This does not necessarily mean that everyone in the audience bought into this message. Nonetheless, the Surrey's patrons are shown the social capital built up through pregnancy and childbirth which may be canceled out by adultery. The adaptation sent them away to ponder the fullness of their own lives, in comparison with the miserable lot of an erring woman whose lack of self-control means that she is on a downward trajectory towards a kind of "non existence."

Although there are of course similarities between the Surrey and Effingham versions, the striking thing about the latter is the way in which it makes the erring wife the representative of all who are penniless, dispossessed, and isolated. It also depends on a direct identification between the Effingham's working-class audience and Lady Emily. The sufferings of this genteel heroine are not simply those of middle-class women enslaved by their gender, but of all those who are on the margins, who lack connection. In Wood's original novel, the narrator encourages sympathy for Isabel despite the adultery that puts her beyond the pale of respectable society. Archer's homiletic play acknowledges but does not dwell on the heroine's fallenness. Instead, it offers Emily new possibilities of identity. In an echo of the kind of organic society envisaged by George Eliot in her depiction of Raveloe in *Silas Marner* (1860), the Effingham's *East Lynne* also counsels that true human values can be found within the local community. "I charge you all," one character announces to the world at large, "think where you are—are we not all human akin to one great family? . . ." The speaker's ambiguous use of the pronouns "you" and "we" is pitched at the audience of the Effingham; those who were there had either just finished or were at work. These positive social forces lie, as they do in Eliot's novel, with society's respectable poor. Fanny scoffs at Emily's fear that her child will die because she can no longer "nourish" it; she offers herself and her husband as foster parents. "Are we not poor but respectable people, what is there to prevent us from receiving this little fellow?" "Look at him—I'm blessed if he isn't trying to talk, as though he would say, take me, don't leave my poor mother to struggle for me who is all forsaken and alone." To Emily's comment that "I do not deserve your kindness," Fanny responds, "But you do through the very fact that you want it." The emphasis on the extended human family leaves very little room for Lady's Emily's sense of "sin and shame" in which West End stage versions luxuriate; indeed, her repeated lamentations "alone, alone, in the world for evermore" are loudly dismissed as "nonsense." Emily does not throw herself into the Thames but moves in with Fanny and her husband. To term this embellishment "oppositional" in Raymond Williams's sense of challenging dominant culture may be a slight overstatement. After all, Emily does try to go back to her other children. Nonetheless, it remains a pervasive image. The play acknowledges both the necessity and the possibility of a different, genuinely working-class alternative to middle-class morality, one which raises two fingers to the callous straightjacket of bourgeois propriety and its mechanistic spirit.

However speculative the conceptualization of the experiences of watching the Effingham's *East Lynne* in 1864 is, we can at least begin to see the extent to which these adaptations and their writers raise a number of important questions about the virtual disappearance from theater history of a particular body of work, and inevitably about the history of the Victorian theater and about the ways in which theatrical canons have been formed.[46] The 1860s increasingly saw a pattern of a freewheeling "tradaptation," to borrow Patrice Pavis's phrase,[47] which became the dominant mode for the popularization of sensation fiction on stage. It was a tradition in which adapters butchered novels but also produced slyly subversive adaptations for different kinds of audiences, audacious and blatant acts of appropriation that repositioned and re-presented characters and plots. It was the East End in particular that consistently staged this transmuted sensation fiction. The 1860s increasingly saw East End theaters adapting sensation novels in such a way that they had the maximum purchase for local audiences, reinterpreting them in ways that suited local opinion. Critics of sensation fiction have paid only limited attention to this issue—the question of the appeal of characters such as Lady Audley, Isabel Vane, and Count Fosco for working-class audiences—but it deserves to be an important part of discussions of the ways in which sensation fiction was disseminated and of how the requirements of theatrical adaptation challenge the social dimension of a literary form.

NOTES

1. Katharine Newey and Veronica Kelly, eds., *East Lynne*, dramatised by T. A. Palmer, xiv.
2. Unsigned review, "The Surrey," *Era*, 11.
3. Unsigned review, "Surrey Theatre," *The Times*, 6.
4. Ibid.
5. Unsigned Review, "'Lady Audley': On the Stage," *London Review*, 244–45.
6. Henry Morley, *Diary of a London Playgoer*, 243. Cited by Katherine Newey, "Women and the Theatre," 543.
7. Unsigned review, "Surrey Theatre," 6
8. Unsigned review, "Dramatised Versions of Novels: *East Lynne* at the Surrey," *Sunday Times*, 8.
9. See Nina Auerbach, "Before the Curtain," 10–12.
10. Unsigned review, "The Drama that Never Fails," *Bioscope*, 923.
11. Kerry Powell, *Women and Victorian Theatre*, 101.
12. Edward O'Shea, "Modernist Versions of *The Tempest*," 543.
13. Michael Booth, "East-End and West-End: Class and Audience in Victorian London," 101.
14. Darryl Wadsworth, "'A Low Born Labourer Like You': Audience and Victorian Working-Class Melodrama," 213.
15. Jim Davis, "The Gospel of Rags: Melodrama at the Britannia 1863–74," 369.

16. See Heidi J. Holder, "The East End Theatre," 158–59.
17. Michael Booth has noted, however, how the assumption (recorded by Hemyng) that the Effingham was filled to the brim "with a rough noisy set of thieves and prostitutes" persisted. This helped ensure that the theater remained "beyond the social and cultural pale for the middle-class Londoner from the West." Michael Booth, *Theatre in the Victorian Age,* 5.
18. Bracebridge Hemyng, "Prostitution," 227.
19. Linneas Banks, "The Effingham," *Era,* 14.
20. Jim Davis, "The East End," 202.
21. Unsigned article, "The Theatres," 10.
22. Unsigned review, "The Effingham," 10.
23. George A. Sala, *Gaslight and Daylight,* 268.
24. Playbill: *The Black Doctor,* (1861).
25. For Phelps, see: Jim Davis and Victor Emeljanow, "Victorian and Edwardian Audiences," 100.
26. No reviews of this production have been traced, but the play was successful enough for it still to be playing in 1865. One advertisement reports that it is "pronounced by all who witness it as the most exciting Drama of the day," and "produces the greatest sensation in crowded houses." *East London Observer,* November 26, 1864, 8.
27. Unsigned review, "Minor Theatres," *Era,* 10.
28. Holder, 263.
29. David Mayer, "Melodrama," 146.
30. Michael Booth, "Melodrama and the Working Class," 101. See also Michael Booth, "The Metropolis on Stage," 211–24.
31. Christine Gledhill, *Melodrama,* 16–17.
32. Holder, "The East-End," 263.
33. Advertisement, *East London Observer,* November 26, 1864, 8.
34. See Jessica Maynard, "'Snowed Up': Marxist Approaches," 130.
35. Unsigned article, "Trade Murder or How to Expend Our Redundant Women," *East London Observer,* 6. See also "Poisoning by Lead," *Shoreditch Observer,* 8.
36. *East London Observer,* 3.
37. Unsigned article, "Death from Starvation and Exposure," *East London Observer,* 2.
38. Ibid., 4.
39. "Iota," *East London Observer,* December 3, 1864.
40. Editorial, "The Season and Local Charities," *East London Observer,* 2.
41. Mrs. Henry Young, *Jessy Ashton; or the Adventures of a Barmaid; A Drama in Four Visions.*
42. Davis, "The Gospel of Rags," 369.
43. P. J. Keating, *Into Unknown England 1866–1913: Selections from the Social Explorers,* 546.
44. *The Times,* April 8, 1845, in Jim Davis and Victor Emeljanow, *Reflecting the Audience: London Theatregoing 1840–1880,* 29.
45. Laurie Langbauer, *Women and Romance: The Consolations of Gender in the English Novel,* 9.
46. See Newey, "Women and the Theatre," for a discussion of how taking note of stage adaptations of sensation novels changes the historiographical map of theater development.
47. Patrice Pavis, introduction to *The Intercultural Performance Reader,* 19.

- 16 -

"THE THRESHOLD OF AN OPEN WINDOW"

Transparency, Opacity, and Social Boundaries in Aurora Floyd

LILLIAN NAYDER

REFLECTING THE red flames of the setting sun in the opening chapter of *Aurora Floyd*, the "long rows of narrow windows" on the front of Archibald Floyd's brick mansion both obscure and reveal the sensational social dangers hidden within. Functioning like mirrors, the glass panes prevent the "honest villager" who passes by from seeing inside the seemingly respectable home of his social superiors while simultaneously revealing to him the fall that awaits the Floyds—the result of various social transgressions committed by family members.[1]

Both a bridge and a barrier between private and public, inside and out, the window represents—and enables Braddon to realize—one of the central aims of sensation novels: to expose to the stranger's gaze the illicit relationships and the dark domestic secrets of well-established English families. As Braddon explains, the "modern tragedies" that make up sensation fiction differ from the ancient variety in occurring indoors, "in places where we should least look for scenes of horror" (289): within the "holy circle" of affluent homes (534). "I think of a quiet Somersetshire household in which a dreadful deed was done," Braddon's narrator tells us, referring to the case known to Victorians as the "Road Murder": "what must have been suffered by each member of *that* family? What slow agonies, what ever-increasing tortures, while that cruel mystery was the 'sensation' topic of conversation in a thousand happy home-circles, in a thousand tavern-parlours and pleasant club-rooms!" (533).[2] Hoping to witness "scenes of horror" among their masters and mistresses, Braddon's working-class spies look and listen through the windows and doors of the rooms from which they are excluded, eager to gain the knowledge that will place their social superiors in their power.[3] "Your servants listen at your doors, and repeat your spiteful speeches in the kitchen, and watch you while they wait at table," Braddon's narrator warns. "Nothing that is done in the parlour is lost upon these quiet, well-behaved watchers from the kitchen" (238). Thus Mrs. Powell, the paid companion of Aurora Mellish, presses "her pale face . . . against the window-pane" of the north lodge at Mellish Park to watch the secret meeting between her mistress and the horse trainer James Conyers and, much to her terror, brushes up against a second spy, the dismissed stable hand Stephen Hargraves, as she peers inside (267–68). Both servants eventually discover the scandalous fact that Conyers is Aurora's husband and hence that her marriage to John Mellish is a bigamous one.

In *Aurora Floyd*, the window is a gathering place for resentful and curious servants eager to bring low their employers. But more generally, it is the site where opposed figures and realms converge and where oppositions and divisions are alternately defended and broken down. Sometimes opaque or veiled and sometimes transparent or open, the window serves as a crucial social threshold in the novel and Braddon uses it to represent and test the social boundaries that preoccupy Victorian sensation writers.[4] The imagery of the window links issues of perception with those of social identity, division and instability—when, for example, the genteel Lucy Floyd wishes "she could have been a scullery-maid at Bulstrode Castle, so that she might have seen the dark face she loved once or twice a day through the obscure panes of some kitchen window" (219).

Performing one of its most socially conservative functions, the window merges the cultured interiors of the English middle class and gentry with the beauties of nature and, by suggesting their harmony, implicitly justifies class privilege and the established social order. "Seated at the open window, looking admiringly through festoons of foliage, which clustered round the frame of the lattice," Mr. Floyd's junior clerk, for instance, perceives Felden Woods as a "sacred spot" and reveres the banker's authority (293). At Mellish Park, the family estate of her second husband, Aurora herself sits "in the pleasant window, the full-blown roses showering their scented petals upon her lap with every breath of the summer breeze, and the butterflies hovering about her" (401). Yet the resemblance between the heiress and her dead mother, a low-born actress who appears in a different type of "open window"—the provincial stage—as well as Aurora's first, degrading marriage to Conyers, her own groom, remind us that class identities and social hierarchies are neither natural nor stable and that the genteel paradise glorified by Mr. Floyd's clerk may be a sham.

Indeed, Braddon calls attention to the artfulness of the figure in the window, comparing that figure to a "kit-cat"—a painted portrait in a frame (309)—and we come to suspect that the idealized image of the genteel Aurora in a casement naturally "festooned" may be as much a forgery as the oil portraits of alleged ancestors that Mr. Floyd has "painted to order" in London to hang on the walls at Felden Woods (276). Immediately before Aurora learns that her first husband is alive and that her union with John Mellish is bigamous, Braddon represents her in the open window and foregrounds the interplay between nature and art in her character:

> Aurora had recovered her spirits, and looked the very picture of careless gladness as she leaned in one of those graceful and unstudied attitudes peculiar to her, supported by the framework of the window, and with the trailing jessamine waving round her in the soft summer breeze. She lifted her ungloved hand, and gathered the roses above her head as she talked to her husband. (231)

Framed by natural beauty, Aurora appears "unstudied" but assumes an "attitude" or pose, her artfulness suggested by the very "framework" in which she appears— "a *picture* of careless gladness" (italics mine). To be properly viewed, Aurora's "graceful gestures and the play of her sparkling eyes" should be seen through an "opera-glass," Talbot Bulstrode decides, recognizing her behavior as a performance.

Throughout her novel, Braddon associates windows and doors with the artful construction of social identity, as characters purposefully redefine themselves to better succeed in life, passing through thresholds that are both literal and metaphoric. The two Scottish nephews of Archibald Floyd, for example, anglicize themselves when they join the family banking firm in London, changing their name to conform with those on "the brass plates that adorned the swinging mahogany doors of the banking-house"—"Floyd, Floyd, and Floyd"—properly "cross[ing] the threshold of [the] house of business" as potential partners: "the young gentlemen signed their names McFloyd when they first entered their uncle's counting-house; but they very soon followed that wise relative's example, and dropped the formidable prefix. 'We've nae need to tell these sootherran bodies that we're Scotche,' Alick remarked to his brother, as he wrote his name for the first time A. Floyd, all short" (46). Protecting her respectability, Aurora's mother constructs a new identity for herself when she crosses the threshold of a different type of business—onto the "dirty boards" of the public stage—adopting the "alias" of "Miss Percival" rather than appearing as Miss Prodder (51–52). A place where identities can be remade, the threshold of an open window aptly serves as the backdrop for Aurora's transformation from Mrs. Mellish to Mrs. Conyers, as her second husband reads to her the letter revealing the survival of her first: "So terrible a transformation had come over her during the reading of that letter, that the shock could not have been greater had he looked up and seen another person in her place" (232).

Foregrounding and subverting the opposition between the natural and the artificial, the authentic and the artfully constructed, the windows and doors at the landed estates of Braddon's novel also convey class instabilities among the characters, dividing the members of different social classes while also suggesting their social mobility and marking the violation of class boundaries. At Mellish Park and Felden Woods, the view from any given window signals the status of the room's occupant; lodged in dark and uncomfortable corners, servants may "look . . . out upon a patch of kitchen-garden" but their superiors enjoy long vistas of woods from the bow-windows of their "pretty, cheerful chambers" (370, 123). The most socially deprived figures in *Aurora Floyd* are those with no windows at all—the Cornish miners "buried in the darkness of a black abyss of ignorance a hundred times deeper and darker than the material obscurities in which they laboured" and who seem irrevocably fixed in their place despite Bulstrode's parliamentary efforts to improve their lot. At the estates in Braddon's novel, certain entryways are reserved for use by privileged figures, and servants are expected to "go round to the back" (274). Aurora's lowly uncle, Captain Prodder, is turned away from the front of Mellish Park, the footman closing "the two half-glass doors" in his face (346). Although Mr. Floyd welcomes his seafaring brother-in-law to Felden Woods, he does so behind closed doors, carefully shutting them before he acknowledges the family connection (304). However, the threatening upstart Conyers, hired by Aurora's second husband as the new horse trainer at Mellish Park, "goes straight to the principal door" upon his arrival "and r[ings] the bell sacred to visitors and the family." "Asked . . . with considerable asperity, what he was pleased to want" by the servant who answers the door, Conyers is admitted nonetheless (243). Conversely, when Aurora violates the codes of ladylike behavior by beating Hargraves with the handle of her whip, her disapproving second husband brings her home through "the back entrance," marking her social descent and his sense of her "disgrace" (194). When she is locked out of her home after meeting with Conyers and knocks to be admitted, he mistakes her for a servant who shouldn't use the front doors (274).

Represented as they "lean . . . against" window frames or stand on thresholds, Braddon's characters often straddle social categories, "half in and half out" (231). As a "finishing governess and companion" (96), Mrs. Powell is both genteel and working class, and she positions herself on various thresholds at Mellish Park; poised on these boundary lines, she reveals herself as a socially hybrid figure as well as a domestic spy. "'Allow me to shut the door, Mrs. Powell, if you please,'" John Mellish tells her in a characteristic moment, when she "d[oes] not seem inclined to leave her post upon the threshold" (362). Aurora, too, is often positioned on thresholds that convey the ambiguities of her social standing as an heiress with lowly social origins, a lady whose gentility has been produced by her father's commercial success, and a woman who has married down and unwittingly committed bigamy. Her position on these thresholds suggests her own failure to uphold social codes and class boundaries, and her passage through them signals her potential fall: when, ushered into a room for questioning by Bulstrode, she recalls the figure of Marie Antoinette "cross[ing] the threshold . . . to face her plebeian accusers" (135). Unlike the French queen, however, Aurora willingly crosses class lines, identifying with her inferiors. As her cousin Lucy explains to Bulstrode, "[I]f [Aurora] has any fault at all . . . it is that she has not sufficient pride; I mean with regard to servants, and that sort of people. She would as soon talk to one of those gardeners as to you or me; and you would see no difference in her manner, except that perhaps it would be a little more cordial to them than to us" (90). Despite her wealth, Aurora, like a resentful servant, is "rather inclined to be discontented with [her] lot," since "it [is] a poor thing, after all, to be rich and happy in a world where so many must suffer" (188). Significantly, when Braddon imagines Aurora's social descent and allies her with the working class, she represents the heroine as a ragged crossing-sweeper, a figure who presides over points of transition and thresholds (72, 188).

In *Aurora Floyd*, the figure most persistently associated with class discontent and the blurring of social boundaries is the mercenary "imposter" Conyers, who fools Aurora into marrying him to "wring . . . money from [her] father," representing himself as "a prince in disguise" (432–33). With the window serving as a barrier between social classes but also as a conduit among them, Braddon aptly portrays Conyers as he assumes his favorite position in the lodge at Mellish Park, "seating himself . . . upon the window-sill, an attitude which, like everything about him, was a half-careless, half-defiant protest of his superiority to his position" (254). Rather than doing the work he is paid to perform, Conyers masquerades as a member of the idle class, "loll[ing] on the window-sill, with his lame leg upon a chair, and his back against the framework of the little casement, smoking, drinking, and reading his price-lists all through the sunny day" (308). Anyone passing the north lodge might "see Mr. Conyers lounging, dark and splendid, on the window-sill . . . his handsome person framed in the clustering foliage which hung about the cottage walls" (309).

Sites of class identity and struggle, windows are barriers that resentful and ambitious servants hope to surmount and that their superiors try to defend, in part through the use of bolts and blinds (413), bells and iron bars (271). Braddon repeatedly stages the intrusion of working-class figures into windows properly belonging to the upper classes, as they make connections that ladies and gentlemen wish to sever or deny. Challenging Aurora's status as a lady, Matthew Harrison, a shabby acquaintance of her first husband, spots the heiress in London through the open window of her carriage. Although "he was the very last person . . . who seemed likely to have anything to say to Miss Aurora Floyd," he plants his elbows on the sill and "put[s] his head in at the carriage window," whispering to her familiarly and extorting money from her (70–71). Snakelike, Hargraves "slid[es] himself in through the open window" of John Mellish's study, crossing "the threshold of that sacred chamber" and making himself at home in the gentleman's chair (325). Once Hargraves learns of Aurora's first marriage and the bigamous nature of her second, he reappears in the study window: "[A] face that she hated made itself visible at the angle of the window opposite to that against which she sat. It was the white face of the 'Softy'" (403). Holding the window so that she cannot shut it, Hargraves "put[s] his head into the room," seizing Aurora's arm through the opening and forcing his disclosure upon her, "secur[ing] his revenge" (404–5).

A second struggle for control of a window occurs at the climax of the novel, when Hargraves is identified as Conyers's murderer and captured through the joint efforts of Bulstrode and Captain Prodder. Compromising his status as a gentleman, Bulstrode assumes the role of detective and investigates Hargraves's covert activity in the north lodge. Signaling his social descent by replicating Hargraves's behavior, he follows the stable hand by "plung[ing] head foremost into the narrow aperture of the lattice window and entering the lodge, confronting Hargraves and blocking his path when the latter makes "a rush towards the window" in retreat. "'What are you doing here?' asked Mr. Bulstrode sternly; 'and why did you come in at the window?'" (542). Interrogating the stable hand, Bulstrode poses a question to which the answer seems clear—like Bulstrode, Hargraves "come[s] in at the window" because the door is locked. Nonetheless, his question effectively focuses our attention on their shared point of entry and its significance for Braddon. Yet another figure comes through the window when Bulstrode is overpowered by Hargraves and about to become his second victim: Captain Prodder. Saving Bulstrode and capturing Hargraves, Prodder then fetches the constable, climbing through the window once again to do so. Playing with class boundaries through these comings and goings, and bringing the gentleman and the lowly merchant captain into alliance, Braddon culminates the scene by dissolving class boundaries altogether, when John Mellish, along with "grooms, gardeners, stable-boys, hangers-on, and rabble," bursts through the door and, "heedless" of his working-class observers, "f[alls] on his friend's breast and we[eps] aloud" (542–47).

Treating the narrow window as a common thoroughfare, Braddon presents a comic vision of class leveling and social disorder. Elsewhere, however, the access it affords seems more threatening, with the recurring image of Hargraves's face in the window conveying class resentment and the threat it poses to the status quo. This image appears not only when Aurora is endangered by public disgrace after Conyers's inquest and the discovery of their marriage certificate, but earlier in the novel, where it is similarly linked to transgression on Aurora's part and hence to Hargraves's ability to bring her low. Shortly before he beats her mastiff and incurs Aurora's wrath, leading her to beat him in turn, she "recognize[s] the white face of Steeve Hargraves at one of the windows of the harness-room" at Mellish Park. The result of a disabling fall he suffered while serving the father of John Mellish, an incident that "gives him a claim" upon Aurora and her husband (189–90), the whiteness of Hargraves's face—his "unnatural" and "ghastly pallor"—serves as the mark of his class injury in the novel.

In what seems an uncanny repetition of the two scenes in which Aurora "recognizes" Hargraves, Bulstrode's pale face appears to her in a window in the Grand Stand at York as, angry and impassioned, she declares that the horse named for her by John Mellish could not have lost the race fairly:

> As she turned to say this, her cheeks flushed with passion, and her eyes flashing bright indignation on any one who might stand in the way to receive the angry electric light, she became aware of a pale face and a pair of gray eyes earnestly regarding her from the threshold of an open window two or three paces off; and in another moment both she and her father had recognized Talbot Bulstrode.
>
> The young man saw that he was recognized, and approached them, hat in hand,—very, very pale, as Lucy always remembered,—and, with a voice that trembled as he spoke, wished the banker and the two ladies "Good day." (203–4)

Unlike Hargraves, a resentful servant who hates Aurora and hopes to do her harm, Bulstrode is the wealthy son of a baronet and claims to love the heiress; although he breaks their engagement when she refuses to disclose her secret to him—her degrading marriage to Conyers, whom she believes dead—his interest in her remains unabated. Nonetheless, his gaze at Aurora through the window mirrors that of Hargraves, just as his pale face recalls Hargraves's white one, and this mirroring makes Bulstrode's preoccupation with Aurora seem sinister. While his paleness suggests suppressed anger over the injury he has presumably suffered at Aurora's hands, his gaze, like Hargraves's, suggests that the heiress is threatened by the resentful surveillance of *both* men, collapsing the apparent opposition between them. Despite his sense of honor—or, rather, because of it—Bulstrode is as eager as Hargraves to discover "infinitesmal stains upon the shining robe of [Aurora's] virginity" (74–75). Wrongly believing he knows the truth about Aurora once the very existence of her secret is revealed, Bulstrode sees the woman he loves as a "wicked enchantress" or "soulless siren" (209). His misogyny thus parallels and compounds Hargraves's class resentment of the "great lady" (269), with male gallantry a cover for aggression against and distrust of women.

Described as "chivalrous," Bulstrode seeks the ideal woman but denegrates real ones, inspiring fear among his female acquaintances (74–75). In fact, male admiration and service prove harmful to women in Braddon's novel, where they become inseparable from surveillance, exposure, incarceration, and death. Accordingly, John Pastern, "the Patriarch" of the racing world, claims to "be only too happy . . . to do anything to oblige Mrs. Mellish" (209–10)—and "serves" her by recommending her *first* husband as trainer to her *second,* exposing her bigamy. Similarly, John Mellish convinces Aurora of his love for her by assuring her that he couldn't part with her under any circumstances, even if violence on his part was required to prevent their separation: "I would rather take you in my arms and plunge with you into the pond in the wood; I would rather send a bullet into your heart, and see you lying murdered at my feet" (259).

In depicting Bulstrode as he watches Aurora at York, Braddon not only represents male surveillance but challenges it, identifying Bulstrode as the object of Aurora's gaze, not simply as the gazer. Talbot "earnestly regard[s]" Aurora from the open window—yet Aurora is aware of his doing so and gazes back: "the young man saw that he was recognized." Whether open or closed, the window is double sided and often allows for perception from the outside as well as from within; as such, it not only enables Braddon to stage the spying that is one sided but also to represent mutual perceptions or recognitions and to develop a counterpoint between them.

The mutual gaze that the window allows is especially important in *Aurora Floyd* because of the challenge it poses to the sexual double standard—specifically, to the virtue of transparency in women as opposed to men. The most outspoken advocate of female transparency, Bulstrode idealizes the woman "whose transparent soul" could be "freely unveiled to him" (154) and believes he has found such a woman in Aurora. "My mother ... will reverence my Aurora's transparent soul and candid nature," he assures her (128). When Bulstrode realizes that Aurora has a secret and that her "soul" is partly hidden or obscured, he breaks their engagement. In Braddon's novel, opacity can signify insuperable class differences—when Lucy imagines herself a scullery maid watching Bulstrode, the gentleman she loves, "through the obscure panes of some kitchen window" (219). But for Bulstrode, it signifies female impurity: a woman's failure to meet his standard of complete legibility. Compared alternately to a transparent window and a text without subtext, the ideal woman is one on whom "every feeling and every sentiment write[s] itself upon her lovely, expressive face in characters the veriest fool could read" (258). As Bulstrode tells Aurora, "[T]he past life of my wife must be a white unblemished page, which all the world may be free to read" (157). For Bulstrode, who strives to obscure his own "secret" feelings and remain unread (113), opacity is a male prerogative; if the innocence of wives and daughters is to be maintained and households to remain "pure" (430), husbands and fathers must remain at least partly inscrutable and keep knowledge to themselves.

In Aurora's cousin Lucy, whom he marries, Bulstrode believes he has found a woman who approximates his ideal of transparency, a trait ensured by her infantilization: "Purity and goodness had watched over her and hemmed her in from her cradle. She had never seen unseemly sights, or heard unseemly sounds. She was as ignorant as a baby of all the vices and horrors of this big world" (94). Lucy thus serves a foil to Aurora and her knowing opacity. Appearing to Bulstrode "on the threshold of [an] open window," Aurora "darken[s]" it, "standing between him and the sunshine" (86); by contrast, Bulstrode "contemplates Lucy's face, marvellously fair in the [moon]light . . . streaming in from an open window" (93).

But if Lucy is transparent, a woman easily seen through and illuminated, that sight must be carefully curtained from public view, Bulstrode argues. In theory, "all the world" should "be free to read" her—but not in practice. That kind of publicity is left to such women as Eliza Prodder, who "had walked nightly on to a stage to be the focus of every eye" (57), her self-display analogous to a prostitute's—or to female domestics who lack a sense of propriety and display themselves in windows whenever a handsome man is hired, hoping to catch his eye. Under such circumstances, John Mellish claims, "Susan and Sarah, and all the rest of 'em, take to cleaning the windows, and wearing new ribbons in their caps" (273). A proper lady, by contrast, is curtained to all but a select few, "excelling in all womanly graces and accomplishments, but only exhibiting them in the narrow circle of a home" (86). "The name of the woman he had chosen had never gone beyond the holy circle of her own home, to be the common talk among strangers," Bulstrode thinks of Lucy reassuringly (534). Yet the curtains that protect and sanctify women effectively confine them, Braddon notes, restricting their view and making the world outside appear opaque; thus the window blinds at Mellish Park "dr[a]w golden bars upon the matted floor" (417). Surrounded by iron fretwork in the ladies' gallery of the House of Commons, to "screen her from any wandering glances of distracted members," Lucy strains her eyes "in her vain efforts to see her husband in his place on the Government benches, and very rarely seeing more than the crown of Mr. Bulstrode's hat" (426).

Ironically, Bulstrode's desire to veil his wife from view has been anticipated by Lucy herself. Despite her conformity to ideals of womanly subordination and self-effacement, Lucy is far from transparent, though her opacity hides secrets of a different kind than her cousin Aurora's.[5] In fact, as a proper lady, Lucy has been *trained* to be opaque, hiding her feelings from view: "Mrs. Alexander's daughter had been far too well educated to betray one emotion of her heart, and she bore her girlish agonies, and concealed her hourly tortures, with the quiet patience common to these simple womanly martyrs" (102). Lucy's martyrdom thus sets her apart from Aurora, who hides the fact of her first, degrading marriage but otherwise proves transparent, exhibiting her passions with great clarity:

> Good heavens! how hard it is upon such women as these that they feel so much and yet display so little feeling! The dark-eyed, impetuous creatures, who speak out fearlessly, and tell you that they love or hate you—flinging their arms round your neck or throwing the carving-knife at you, as the case may be—get full value for all their emotion; but these gentle creatures love, and make no sign. They sit, like Patience on a monument, smiling at grief; and no one reads the mournful meaning

of that sad smile. Concealment, like the worm i' the bud, feeds on their damask cheeks; and compassionate relatives tell them that they are bilious, and recommend some homely remedy for their pallid complexions. (219–20)

Expected to be both transparent and pure, and opaque and proper, the gentlewoman is placed in a double bind that not only damages her complexion but threatens her very existence, a point Braddon makes by comparing Lucy to such tragic heroines as Tennyson's Elaine and Shakespeare's Ophelia as well as the comic, lovelorn Viola (who sits "like Patience . . . smiling at grief"). Informed by John Mellish of "a secret which had escaped the captain's penetration" (146)—that Lucy loves him—Bulstrode dreams of her in terms that suggest her complexity as well as her danger:

[W]hen he fell asleep in the late daybreak, it was to dream horrible dreams, and to see in a vision Aurora Floyd standing on the brink of a clear pool of water in a woody recess at Felden, and pointing down through its crystal surface to the corpse of Lucy, lying pale and still amidst lilies and clustering aquatic plants, whose long tendrils entwined themselves with the fair golden hair. (147)

As Aurora indicates to Bulstrode, there are depths that lie beneath Lucy's transparent, "crystal surface"; ungauged and unacknowledged, they threaten to destroy her.

Challenging an ideal that imperils women, demanding that they be simultaneously transparent and opaque, Braddon makes transparency a virtue in men, presenting John Mellish—"this transparent, boyish babyish good fellow" (144)—as an alternative hero to Talbot Bulstrode; and she subjects men to the female gaze. Although Eliza Prodder is "the focus of every eye," the actress returns the gaze of her audience members, both covertly and overtly. From the curtained stage, her colleagues call her attention to her admirer Archibald Floyd, putting *him* on display: "They pointed him out to her through a hole in the green curtain, sitting almost alone in the shabby boxes, waiting for the play to begin, and for her black eyes to shine upon him once more" (54). Similarly, her daughter Aurora returns the gaze of Bulstrode and Hargraves, attempting to penetrate their opacities and make legible the male faces that appear "as white as a sheet of writing-paper" (191)—a mirror image of the "white unblemished page" that an ideal woman's life should resemble. "Looking critically at Talbot Bulstrode," as he had looked at her, Aurora "wonder[s] how any one could have ever gone near to the gates of death for the love of him" (204). And while her eyes are often "downcast" (86), even Lucy sharpens her gaze, trying to see through the curtains that obscure her view of "unseemly sights" and struggling with her husband for access to the threshold dividing private from public. When Aurora, her bigamy discovered, flees to the Bulstrodes' home from Mellish Park, Lucy seeks to join her in the library but her husband blocks the drawing-room door:

> "No, Lucy; no," answered Mr. Bulstrode, laying his hand upon the door, and standing between it and his wife; "I had rather you didn't see your cousin until I have seen her. It will be better for me to see her first." His face was very grave, and his manner almost stern as he said this. Lucy shrank from him as if he had wounded her. She understood him, very vaguely, it is true; but she understood that he had some doubt or suspicion of her cousin, and for the first time in his life Mr. Bulstrode saw an angry light kindled in his wife's blue eyes.
> "Why should you prevent my seeing Aurora?" Lucy asked; "she is the best and dearest girl in the world. Why shouldn't I see her?"
> Talbot Bulstrode stared in blank amazement at his mutinous wife. (428)

First "lingering near the door after her husband had closed it upon her" and then crossing the threshold and "lurking somewhere about the outside," Lucy questions the privilege and primacy of her husband's vision, his right to "see [Aurora] first," and ultimately disobeys his injunction to remain behind closed doors (429, 435).

Dividing public from private and male from female as well as upper from working class, the window provides an image for artistic self-expression and self-containment in *Aurora Floyd,* allowing Braddon to consider her own problematic status as a woman novelist who both reveals and obscures her private self in addressing her public. As Mary Stodart warned in 1842, the female writer is in danger of "laying bare . . . the workings of the inward heart," "proclaiming to the public that which passes within her own breast": "it is placing a glass window in her bosom, that every passer-by may look in and see the workings of her heart."[6] Often berated by Victorian critics as a public performer and "market whore,"[7] Braddon uses the window to make transparent the contradictions of the feminine ideal, which equates female propriety with a well-curtained privacy while also stipulating that a woman's purity must be such that "all the world" may view it (157).

NOTES

1. Mary Elizabeth Braddon, *Aurora Floyd* (Broadview Press, 1998), 45. Subsequent references are cited parenthetically in the text.

2. When, in June 1862, a four-year-old boy was murdered in his home in Road, near Wiltshire, his nursemaid was originally arrested for the crime, with the boy's discovery of her

illicit relations with his father the alleged motive. In 1865, the boy's sixteen-year-old sister, Constance Kent, confessed to killing him.

3. For an insightful analysis of eavesdropping in the nineteenth-century novel, its relation to the genesis of narratives, the intersection of public and private, and the transgression of gender boundaries, see Ann Gaylin, *Eavesdropping in the Novel from Austen to Proust*.

4. Anthea Trodd focuses on social boundaries and their violation in sensation fiction in *Domestic Crime in the Victorian Novel*, particularly the invasion of the private realm by the public. As Trodd notes, novels by such writers as Braddon and Wilkie Collins include "threshold figures"—generally policemen and servants—"who transact negotiations between the home and the external world" and hence threaten the sanctity of the domestic sphere (6).

5. Jeni Curtis makes this point in her reading of *Aurora Floyd*, noting that "the apparently transparent, good woman, Lucy, is shown to be more opaque, less 'lucid' than she seems. She is a woman in possession of a secret life, her 'natural' desires and her sexuality silenced in a patriarchal society that will not allow her to exist, to find the voice of true subjectivity." See "The 'Espaliered' Girl: Pruning the Docile Body in *Aurora Floyd*," 90.

6. M. A. Stodart, *Female Writers: Thoughts on Their Proper Sphere, and on Their Powers of Usefulness*, 134–35.

7. Emily Allen, *Theater Figures: The Production of the Nineteenth-Century British Novel*, 158.

- 17 -

SENSATIONALIZING
VICTORIAN SUBURBIA

Wilkie Collins's Basil

TAMARA S. WAGNER

MUCH MORE than a subcategory of nineteenth-century urban fiction, suburban Gothic played a crucial part in the sensation novel's development. Wilkie Collins's first venture into the genre, *Basil: A Story of Modern Life,* is symptomatically set in motion when the upper-class hero, driven partly by boredom, partly by a fascination with the everyday, the mundane randomly boards an omnibus. But if his casual habit of embarking on such voyages of social tourism aligns him with the figure of the flâneur, it ultimately propels him across the permeable boundaries of voyeurism into nearly fatal entanglements. In that his attempt at a cross-class alliance fails utterly, and sensationally, the novel invests in a new interest in social strata generally, but suburbs, as a developing literary space, specifically invite a sensational treatment as unfamiliar wastelands and rapidly denigrated epitomes of a new sense of bourgeois respectability. In this double liability, they form a fecund platform for domestic terror to break into and out from. *Basil* importantly transforms suburbs into sensational topographies, as the dissection of "modern life" promised in the subtitle probes seemingly tranquil domesticity to engender some of sensation fiction's seminal features. Yet unfortunately, suburbia's literary significance has regularly been subsumed by discussions of urban or domestic Gothic—a valid conflation in its way that, however, obscures the distinct features of the genre's distinct suburban imaginary. Before examining the making of suburban Gothic, I shall set Collins's novel within midcentury representations of suburbs as a space open for speculation (in fiction as well as finances). There the flâneur comes to grief to be transformed into a social speculator and commuter, an unwilling participant in the fraudulent moral and fiscal economies that Victorian suburbia has come to stand for.

Published in 1852, *Basil* preceded *The Woman in White,* Collins's most influential sensation novel, by eight years. It introduced pivotal features of the genre; most significantly its exploration of the middle or middling classes. However, even as the novel propounds bourgeois moral economies while questioning their promotion of financial contracts between marriage, as between business, partners, the ideal of the aristocratic gentleman is kept in place. Basil's proud father is horrified at his son's peculiar contractual agreement with a shopkeeper; Basil's brother is a profligate eldest son who spurns bourgeois ideologies of industry in ways that confirm stereotypes, yet family pride is dignified, and the heir's profligacy treated as an expression of cheerful exuberance. More startlingly, perhaps, the aristocratic Great House is insistently domestic, while the confines of suburban homes exude a stifling claustrophobia in which vulgar emulation meets suppressed violence.

The classic plot of a younger son's social misalliance and his family's impending humiliation meets the intrinsic horrors of the bourgeois home that Lillian Nayder has diagnosed as sensation fiction's "domestic Gothic."[1] As *Basil* influentially revises Gothic tropes, it is intriguingly in suburbia that it accomplishes this relocation. Tracing the transformation of eighteenth-century "female Gothic" in Collins's novels, Tamar Heller has persuasively argued that in *Basil,* Gothicism deploys domesticity as a site of potential female revolt, yet in that the transgressive woman is finally written out of the story, and the cuckolded hero—a figure of the writer—is doubled in the "class subordinate" clerk Mannion, the novel is "not so much about the desire to transgress as it is about the desire to escape the taint of the transgressors."[2] No matter who triumphs, the concept of domestic stability stands exposed as a forged fiction.[3] In sensationalized suburbia, however, Gothic is cast as the essence, rather than the perversion, of the confined spaces favored by the middle classes. Claustrophobic and yet apart from the bustling life of the city, suburban Gothic combines the sense of confinement that is central to domestic Gothic in general with the dangers placed in remote, desolate open places or dingy mansions associated with eighteenth-century Gothic. In other words, suburbia generates a "horror of the searching brightness of daylight, a suspicion of the loneliness of the place . . . , a yearning to be among my fellow-creatures again, to live where there was life—the busy life of London—overcame me. I turned hastily, and walked back from the suburbs to the city."[4] Basil's closely delineated feelings of horror impel him to retrace his steps from the dangerously desolate suburb back to the bustling, ironically safer, spaces of inner-city London. His ventures into a seemingly exotic space explode the emerging concept of "suburbanism" as a fraudulent fiction of successful home life as a bourgeois privilege.

"A Suspicion of the Loneliness of the Place": Making Suburban Gothic

Coined in Mary Ward's *Robert Elsmere* (1888), "suburbanism" has become a key word of bourgeois self-confinement. In *The Suburbans* (1905), T. W. H. Crosland eagerly took it up to highlight the repercussions of the nineteenth-century expansion of suburbs (and suburbanism) on petit-bourgeois self-definition. Bourgeois in its outlook, if not always in its inhabitants, with working-class suburbs making problematic middle-class ideals of the home, suburbia became an inviting site for the proliferating middling classes: "[M]an was born a little lower than the angels and has been descending into suburbanism ever since."[5] As Robert Fishman puts it, "If you seek the monuments of the bourgeoisie, go to the suburbs. . . . Suburbia is more than a collection of residential buildings; it expresses values so deeply embedded in bourgeois culture that it might also be called the bourgeois utopia."[6] But if Victorian suburbia embodies the promotion of bourgeois domesticity, emerging suburban imaginaries are surely crucial to Victorian literature. Outgrowths of midcentury suburban speculations (and their abandonment) carefully lay the land for the suburban Gothic in *Basil*. Located in "the newest of the new houses" in a "suburb of new houses intermingled with wretched patches of waste land, half built over" (31–32), the suburbanism of a "partly-detached" household repulsive in its glaring newness is defined against city and country. Mr. Sherwin's North Villa in Hollyoake Square—"unfinished like everything else in the neighbourhood" (32)—to which Basil stalks the linen-draper's daughter is representative of petit-bourgeois suburbanism. It is strikingly different from absorbed suburban villages that have retained some of their country customs and from the upmarket suburbia in which Basil's elder brother Ralph sows aristocratic wild oats. Before Basil ever sets foot into Hollyoake Square, he and his sister, in fact, enjoy excursions along the northern roads of London, as social tourists playing at country manners on the city's outskirts:

> These excursions we keep a secret. . . . Besides, if my father knew that his daughter was drinking the landlady's fresh milk, and his son the landlord's old ale, in the parlour of a suburban roadside inn, he would, I believe, be apt to suspect that both his children had fairly taken leave of their senses. (26)

Similarly, Ralph's (temporary) descent into suburbanism may be a "dropping down to playing the fiddle, and paying rent and taxes in a suburban villa! How are the fast men fallen!" (276). Yet it is managed in a genteel fashion, with no ties attached. Setting aristocratic bohemia above bourgeois commitment to contracts—and I shall come back to the rather peculiar marriage contract Basil enters into—this juxtaposition of versions of suburbia externalizes divergent attitudes to domesticity, aristocratic license, bourgeois moral conventions, and codes of behavior. When Ralph hears—alas, too late—of his younger brother's entanglement with a shopkeeper's daughter, he significantly does not deplore class-crossing affairs, but the legal implications this descent of the second son of "an English gentleman of large fortune [whose family] dates back beyond the Conquest" (2) into middle-class moralities means to the family pride. Confident of his social superiority and therefore, it is implied, esteemed by the lower classes as "the pleasantest, liveliest gentleman" (335), Ralph has a freedom that the pseudo-bourgeois Basil, infected by middle-class self-consciousness, has forfeited:

> I understand that you took a fancy to some shopkeeper's daughter—so far, mind, I don't blame you: I've spent time very pleasantly among the ladies of the counter myself. But . . . you actually married the girl! I don't wish to be hard upon you, my good fellow, but there was an unparalleled insanity about that act, worthier of a patient in Bedlam. (259)

The distinction between Ralph's bohemian villadom and Basil's miserable stalking of suburban wastelands most forcefully exposes suburbia as an internally stratified space. As nineteenth-century novels show, suburbs as different as once genteel villages incorporated into what after 1875 came to be known for statistical purposes as Greater London, the half-finished wastelands left behind by building speculations, and working-class suburbs degenerating rapidly into slums all feature as a space for "those ghastly heart-tragedies . . . which are acted and re-acted, scene by scene, and year by year, in the secret theatre of home" (75–76), as it is put in *Basil*. In *The Woman in White*, the abduction and substitution of the titular Women in White takes place in St. Johns Wood, where seemingly respectable Count Fosco sets up house with a view of obscuring the ends and means of his schemes—international plots that work through domestic exchanges, through the literal swapping of Englishwomen. The comparative remoteness of this residential area makes it perfect as a crime site that shields itself through its outward quietude. Similarly, the eponymous Cash in Charles Reade's *Hard Cash* (1863) is preserved from storms and pirates at sea only to engage new perils in a suburban bank. The ghost story "Green Tea" in Sheridan Le Fanu's 1872 *In a Glass Darkly* compares with *Basil* specifically well, as it sets out with an initially idle venture into the instable, socially permeable, existence of a commuter. Like Basil, its main protagonist is not accustomed to the public spaces of the omnibus. It is a temptation that leads him into a strange, alien world: "[S]eeing no cab near, I was tempted to get into the omnibus which used to drive past this house. It was darker than this by the time the 'bus had reached an old house."[7] As he passes this relic of the former village's better times, a demon materializes that drives him to his death. Charlotte Riddell's "City-novels," including the suggestively titled *City and Suburb* (1861) and *The Race for Wealth* (1866), even more pointedly show suburbans being washed up in the city "on the tops of omnibuses, or hurrying from the various railway termini" in the commuter's new race.[8] Nevertheless, as genteel suburbia continues to harbor primarily the rich and (in)famous, their fracases easily detract from critiques of middle-class domesticity. It is instead newly constructed suburbs and their commuting population that really bear the brunt of new interest in suburban developments.

Commuting, whether on omnibuses or trains, establishes most decisively the City-man's suburbs as distinct from the shabby-genteel villadom that offers retreats for the bohemian or the bankrupt. A speculative venture into new transport systems and building speculations, railways symptomatically ride through representations of Victorian suburbia. From the ambiguous functions of suburban railway lines in Dickens's 1848 novel about commerce, transportation, and exportation, *Dombey and Son*, to the portentous whistling of passing trains that set the scene for the final climax of Collins's 1883 *Heart and Science*, they rivet through the landscape, eating up villages and disgorging a suburban environment that fascinated novelists as a site marked (and marred) by the evolution of urban and suburban modernities. Published in the wake of the mid-forties Railway Mania, *Dombey and Son* not only has railways symbolically kill the company's worst exponent by mowing down a villainous clerk, but it links together the world of the novel. Despite his entry through the more old-fashioned vehicle of an idle omnibus ride, railways likewise drive *Basil*'s sensationalized suburbia:

> It was a very lonely place—a colony of half-finished streets, and half-inhabited houses, which had grown up in the neighbourhood of a great railway station. I heard the fierce scream of the whistle, and the heaving, heavy throb of the engine starting on its journey, as I advanced along the gloomy Square in which I now found myself. (158–59)

This gloomy "colony" (158) is an alien space that is nonetheless horribly familiar.[9] No wonder Basil's father is repulsed by the location of his son's marriage contract: it is the shopkeeper's haunt, expressive of all the fraudulent commercial speculation the middling classes came to embody and, through this alignment, of the famous fear that Britain was becoming a nation of shopkeepers. Basil later haunts the "neglected, deserted, dreary-looking" suburban hotel in which his wife commits adultery with the confidential clerk Mannion. He stalks him to bash him up; the newly macadamized road acting out the revenge of building speculation on suburban monstrosities. J. R. Kellett has termed such moral and architectural wastelands a new "type of no-man's land created by speculative building in the areas between railway sidings and industrial users on the outer fringe of an urban central district."[10] Although he cautions that the creation of slums at railway termini was "too large and general a process to be ascribed to the railways alone," building speculations undoubtedly had a hand in the process.[11] As Robert Fishman has more recently pointed out, while the beginnings of suburban expansion in the latter half of the eighteenth century were largely improvised, what drove suburbia was speculation in building projects.[12] Given that Victorian suburbia is commonly associated with (increasingly mocked) respectability, the sparse analysis of its representation as a dangerous, even mysterious, as well as disconcertingly stifling, space forms an interesting omission. As experiments with this new imaginary in *Basil* show, the potential of the sprawling suburbs of the time to act as a sensational site projects the social and cultural tensions created by midcentury urban developments.

The Ends of the Suburban Flâneur

Wilkie Collins's suburban Gothic has its origins in suburbs that exhibit a tendency to become run-down before building-projects have even been completed. Petit-bourgeois drawing-rooms figure instead of haunted mansions and back alleys; clerks as dangerous madmen; suburban ladies as depraved schemers; omnibuses as ferrying not only this camouflaged corruption, but, as in "Green Tea," as demons arising from a commuter's projected phantasmagoria. This expansion of the suburban in the literary imagination is nowhere as emphatic as in the hero's nearly fatal transposition from the Great House to suburban spaces of sensational horror in *Basil*. The "colony of half-finished streets" (158) constitutes an incursion into the countryside that has singularly failed to civilize or cultivate it and is therefore neither here nor there. It is truly a wasted space, unleashing wasted madmen as its natural outgrowth. But Basil comes to London's sprawling suburbs as a social tourist and a misdirected flâneur. The younger son of an English gentleman of large fortune, a member of "one of the most ancient [families] in this country" (2), he takes an idle interest in exploring exotic sites across what turns out to be threateningly permeable class boundaries. Traversing the city in his ennui, he is a connoisseur of social panorama. He becomes a voyeur and then an obsessed stalker. While the mere exploration of the urban underbelly aligns him with the figure of the flâneur, his much sharper, insistent, and ultimately infectious penetration of suburban spaces throws him up as the lower exponent (younger son) of the upper reaches of society absorbed by the expanding middling classes. Basil has consequently been seen as a transgressor of class lines in more senses than in his infatuation with a seemingly exotic woman alone.[13] An ambitious would-be writer, he has been linked to bourgeois professionalism,[14] and as

I have noted elsewhere, his delicacy approximates effeminacy, in the process conflicting gender boundaries in the novel: he falls in love with a physically well-developed, but insipid woman whose deceit almost drives him insane.[15] What interests us most here, however, is his transformation from careless and carefree flâneur into a monomaniacal stalker and, with it, the novel's move from cross-class romance to an exploration of sensationalized space.

What sets the story in motion is, after all, Basil's impulse to board an omnibus that has randomly pulled up in front of him just after he has cashed in a check in the city. Within the novel's overarching focus on finances, it is vital to remember that this sheltered young man, cosseted by a younger sister and patronized by a stern, but sternly honorable father, has just picked up his "quarter's allowance of pocket-money" (27) at his father's banker. This childlike dependence on aristocratic estates contrasts significantly with Sherwin's social ambitions and, more dangerously, with Mannion's shabby-genteel clerkdom. Basil's excursion into their exotic terrain continues the adventures he casually embarks on with his sister, only this time his involvement extends beyond the consumption of milk or ale (26). This, the novel suggests with an ambiguously conservative twist, is where the danger lies. As long as contact is restricted to monetary contracts, return to "proper" social spheres remains open. This juxtaposition of different excursion routes prefigures the automatic, but wrong, assumption Basil's father makes when Sherwin inquires after Basil at his father's house: "'—who is Mr. Sherwin?' 'He lives—' 'I don't ask where he lives. Who is he? What is he?' 'Mr. Sherwin is a linendraper—' 'You owe him money?—you have borrowed money of him?'" (197) The only relation Basil's father can conceive of is of a purely financial nature, and presumably related to money lending. Marriage into this class is unthinkable to a man so proud of his social standing that he can patronize laborers, but has an intense aversion to social climbers. When he dismisses Sherwin as a cheat, he has no idea that the Sherwins' schemes "to make their market of [Basil] as easily as ever" (186) have collapsed the fiscal into the familial:

> This money-lending tradesman, your "*friend!*" If I had heard that the poorest labourer on my land called you "friend," I should have held you honoured by the attachment and gratitude of an honest man. When I hear that name given to you by a tradesman and money-lender, I hold you contaminated by connection with a cheat. (197)

This conversation between Basil and his father brings out the centrality of locations in the novel. Suburbia defines Sherwin. His identity is bound up with his desolate, yet opulent, suburban residence. To Basil's father, the habitat of such a man fails to mean anything; to Basil, it has become the pivot on which his life revolves. Sherwin secures his need to return to the same haunts as an investment:

Basil is put on "probation" for the duration of one year after the wedding ceremony. During that time he is to prepare his father to secure the financial advantages on which Sherwin speculates. It is indeed central to suburbia's fraudulent economies that such domestic speculations feed on and into financial arrangements. The way Sherwin manages his wife, the most abject victim of the "secret theatre of home; tragedies which are ever shadowed by the slow falling of the black curtain" (76), his commercial exploitation of Mannion's and Basil's emotions, Mannion's investment in Margaret's education, the collapse of familial and fiscal contracts—these exchanges expose economies that promote, exalt even, conflations of domestic and financial fraud as interconnected social threats.

But only when Basil retraces his steps after the exposure of his adulterous wife, he notices how the once-alien landscape has become inscribed by his personal interest, has become his haunt, a site of profane "pilgrimage": "Dishonoured and ruined, it was among such associations as these—too homely to have been recognised by me in former times—that I journeyed along the well-remembered way to North Villa" (209–10). This revisiting is far removed from the enticingly exotic space the omnibus first promises him as "a perambulatory exhibition-room of the eccentricities of human nature . . . of all classes and all temperaments," and which he boards out of an "idle impulse [and with] the idea of amusement in my thoughts" (27). As nineteenth-century class stratifications go, the omnibus is a carnivalesque space, and this attracts Basil on a dull afternoon. The suburban omnibus transports Basil into a different sphere of life. What he speculates about dreamily while the 'bus moves him further into the fields of urban speculation drives his transformation through transportation. Once Margaret Sherwin boards the 'bus, his study of physiognomy and social behavior becomes erotic fantasy; his sensations concentrated on a veiled stranger "thrilling through me—thrilling in every nerve, in every pulsation of my fast-throbbing heart" (29). The flâneur turns into a voyeur greedily imagining what he can barely make out beneath the veil, her wrapped body promising future expansion: "There was the little rim of delicate white lace, encircling the lovely, dusky throat; there was the figure visible, where the shawl had fallen open, slender, but already well developed" (31). He stalks her, "cautiously and at some distance. . . . Already, strangers though we were, I felt that I should know her, almost at any distance, only by her walk" (31). Obsessed with the details of her body, he fantasizes on its changes in a penetration of veils and shawls, projecting the ripeness "which love alone can develop, and which maternity perfects still further, . . . when she heard the first words, received the first kiss" (30–31). Such unveiling is ironically granted when Margaret's adulterous liaison with Mannion comes to light; the revelation of a hideous network of depravity veiling their "fiend-souls made visible in fiend-shapes": "each raised a veil which was one hideous net-work of twining worms. I saw through the ghastly corruption of their faces the look that told me who they were—the monstrous iniquities incarnate in monstrous forms" (174). This exposure has carefully been prepared for, yet after the first shock at the "suburb of new houses" in all its revolting "newness and desolation of appearance" (31–32), Basil has been blinding himself:

> [A]t the moment when I [Basil] addressed him [Mannion], a flash came, and seemed to pass right over his face. It gave such a hideously livid hue, such a spectral look of ghastliness and distortion to his features, that he absolutely seemed to be glaring and grinning on me like a fiend, in the one instant of its duration. (130)

In Mannion's suburban bachelor home, a reduced gentleman's refuge behind a façade of clerkdom, he likewise reveals more than he intends to, but Basil clings to theories of optical illusion. Priding himself on his knowledge that to "study the appearance of a man's dwelling-room, is very often nearly equivalent to studying his own character" (120), he fails to recognize his double, perfunctorily dismissing that Mannion "was most probably my equal in acquirements: he had the manners and tastes of a gentleman, and might have the birth too" (123). Sherwin's seemingly submissive confidential clerk, Mannion indeed repeatedly insists that he is Basil's equal. His letter to Basil, at once a revelation and a threat, echoes the opening of Basil's narrative as "the second son of an English gentleman of large fortune" (2). Both are overshadowed by a father's pride: "I am the son of a gentleman. My father . . . was a gentleman in anybody's sense of the word; he knew it, and that knowledge was his ruin" (226–27). In his fluid class status as one who has forfeited a higher social sphere, his commercial (in Basil's case, commercialized) contractual agreements with Sherwin, his familiar position in the household, his speculation on Sherwin's financial lust, and ultimately in embodying a conflation of domestic deception and financial fraud, Mannion brings out the novel's manifold speculations on suburbia as a site of fraudulent familial, fiscal, and sexual speculation. In their fathers' legacy, their parallel positions further converge, at the same time fascinatingly setting fraud into the foreground: Basil's father having failed to procure Mannion's father a government sinecure, the latter committed forgery by imitating the richer man's signature. As Heller pointedly puts it, he was hanged as a forger because he resorted to a fiction. While this forgery has paved Mannion's fate as a "hack-author," who, by translating other works, lives off the "offal of literature . . . plagiarising from dead authors, to supply the raw material for bookmongering" (231–32), and then as a clerk who adulterates the household with which business has put him on a familiar footing, he also revenges his father when he commits adultery with Basil's wife.[16] In addition, as Basil abides by the rules laid out in his probationary contract, he ironically fosters fraud, paving the way for Mannion to reassert his influence over Margaret precisely because Basil does not supply sexual consummation.

A forger's son, a plagiarist, and a ruthless speculator, the clerk acts as the dark double of the disinherited son, the aspiring writer, and the cross-class lover. He is in good (or rather, equally bad) company with other speculating clerks in Victorian literature including, most famously, Uriah Heep in Dickens's *David Copperfield* (1850). In a study of "white-collar crime," George Robb lists this well-known 'umble servant among numerous embezzling clerks that, to a large extent, make up the "economic demonology" of nineteenth-century fiction, along with the Carker brothers of *Dombey and Son,* and, ironically, the most promising clerk in Trollope's *The Three Clerks* (1858).[17] Philip O'Neill has similarly argued that Mannion is "a combination of figures drawn from literature," but a stock-figure that is redeployed to articulate "an ideological repertoire."[18] As Sherwin takes everything on its monetary terms, identifying morality with bookkeeping and business acumen, he is symptomatic of a system that equates civilization with capitalism.[19] In short, this breaking in of business is part and parcel of the tradesman's suburban home. As Steven Mintz puts it, "Victorians often regarded the family as a walled garden, yet the family walled in as much as it walled out."[20] Privacy is violated, yet the "confidential" clerk's familiarity is much more threatening than his anonymity. Sherwin's house is symptomatically "partly detached" (32), with its blinds "all drawn down over the front windows, to keep out the sun" in a square as "desolately silent, as only a suburban square can be" (34). In this, it contrasts sharply with the bustle of London:

> London was rousing everywhere into morning activity, as I passed through the streets . . . I saw the mighty vitality of the great city renewing itself in every direction; and I felt an unwonted interest in the sight. It was as if all things, on all sides, were reflecting before me the aspect of my own heart. But the quiet and torpor of the night still hung over Hollyoake Square. That dreary neighbourhood seemed to vindicate its dreariness by being the last to awaken even to a semblance of activity and life. (48–49)

The city offers the freedom of anonymity that suburban confinement prevents *and* a sociability that is likewise absent from torpid residential areas. Arrival at suburbia marks the very end of the flâneur; the drying up of shop windows "filled with the glittering trinkets" (209) cut out the movement from flaneury via obsessed stalking to mundane commuting—a profane pilgrimage. Impelled by habit to return to his haunts, the stalker, stalked by his double, finds his "steps turned, as of old, in the direction of North Villa" and his "fairy-land architecture of a dream" evaporating to disclose, after "the friendly, familiar shop-window" and "the noisy street corner" on the way, "a long, suburban road into Hollyoake Square—the lonely, dust-whitened place, around which my past happiness and my wasted hopes had flung their golden illusions" (209–10). Ultimately, disfigured

Mannion, bearing the signs of suburban building speculation imprinted on his face, hunts down Basil on the Cornish coast and, as his double, appropriately ends up killing himself by falling off a cliff. After the death of both Mannion and Margaret, Basil can be reunited with his family, and together with his sister, Margaret's self-effacing, nearly ephemeral double, he escapes into a country cottage.

Despite the brief appearance of the wilds of Cornwall at the end of the novel, suburbia prevails as a memorable new site at once mundane and alien, a fruitful ground for sensation fiction. It is then hardly surprising that in Collins's best-remembered novel, it is on a suburban road that the titular Woman in White appears for the first time, and in a suburb that she is divested of her identity. Similarly in *The Moonstone*, with its juxtaposition of imperialist and domestic plots, and the invaded domesticity located primarily in a rural Great House, the real thief of the eponymous Indian diamond is a hypocritically pious philanthropist who leads a double life in the suburbs, a "side kept hidden from the general notice" in "a villa in the suburbs which was not taken in his own name, and with a lady in the villa, who was not taken in his own name, either."[21] In Mary Elizabeth Braddon's 1864 defense of the sensation genre, *The Doctor's Wife*, a "neglected suburban garden upon the 21st of July 1852" (31) is already parodied as an established sensational site, underlining the centrality of suburbia in sensation fiction, and vice versa, of sensationalism in the reshaping of this new literary imaginary.

NOTES

1. Lillian Nayder, *Wilkie Collins*, 72.

2. Tamar Heller, *Dead Secrets: Wilkie Collins and the Female Gothic*, 59. Compare Lyn Pykett, *The Sensation Novel from "The Woman in White" to "The Moonstone,"* 41; and Ann Cvetkovich, *Mixed Feelings*, 15.

3. Focusing on nineteenth-century representations of insanity and its policing, Nicholas Rance has suggested that the best of them "derive their effects from subverting a diversity of early and mid-Victorian ideologies" (*Wilkie Collins and Other Sensation Novelists: Walking the Moral Hospital*, 1). Jenny Bourne Taylor has taken up a phrase from *Basil* to underscore the concealed family drama that takes place behind the faceless façades of the bourgeois home: "in the secret theatre of home" (*In the Secret Theatre of Home: Wilkie Collins, Sensation Narrative, and Nineteenth Century Psychology*).

4. Wilkie Collins, *Basil: A Story of Modern Life* (Oxford University Press, 1990), 253; hereafter cited parenthetically in the text.

5. T. W. H. Crosland, *The Suburbans*, 80.

6. Robert Fishman, *Bourgeois Utopias: The Rise and Fall of Suburbia*, 4.

7. J. Sheridan Le Fanu, *In A Glass Darkly*, 30.

8. Charlotte Riddell, *The Race for Wealth*, 194.

9. Roger Silverstone details suburbia's history as a series of attempts of ambitious commercial men to escape from "the physical and cultural pollution of indigenous populations and commercial activity in colonial cities [and from] the noise, dirt and pressures of rapidly and chaotically expanding eighteenth- and nineteenth-century British towns and cities" at home (*Visions of Suburbia*, 5). *Basil* collapses these categories as it renders the petit-bourgeois household a threatening space in which foreign trade, speculation, and the double corruption of commercial activity and urban expansion drive a hard bargain.

10. J. R. Kellett, "The Railway as an Agent of Internal Change in Victorian Cities," 192.

11. Ibid., 188.

12. Fishman, 9–10. H. J. Dyos speaks of the suburb's "history of bad workmanship and bad debts" (*Victorian Suburb: A Study of the Growth of Camberwell*, 85). In "Slums and Suburbs," Dyos and D. A. Reeder moreover point out that suburban villas were quickly turned into slums, which were then "leap-frogged" (362) by suburbs in a rapidly sprawling spiral of overspeculating (*The Victorian City: Images and Realities*, eds. H. J. Dyos and Michael Wolff Paul, 362, 371–72).

13. See Michael Hollington, "Dickens the Flâneur," 71–87.

14. Heller, 38.

15. Tamara S. Wagner, "Overpowering Vitality: Nostalgia and Men of Sensibility in the Fiction of Wilkie Collins," 482, 499, and *Longing: Narratives of Nostalgia in the British Novel, 1740–1890*, 210–15.

16. Heller, 75. Heller further argues that the charge of forgery "conflates literary authority with criminality, implying that the artist in the marketplace has lost the authentic presence of the paternal word and can attempt only to copy it, driven by economic necessity" (75).

17. George Robb, *White-Collar Crime in Modern England: Financial Fraud and Business Morality, 1845–1929*, 4. The Victorians' "criminal upperworld" has received growing attention since Philip Jenkins complained in 1987 that "no scholar should write the history of Victorian crime based on the portrayal of Bill Sikes" ("Into the Upperworld? Law, Crime and Punishment in English Society," 101).

18. Philip O'Neill, *Wilkie Collins: Women, Property and Propriety*, 89.

19. O'Neill, 89.

20. Steven Mintz, *A Prison of Expectations: The Family in Victorian Culture*, 10.

21. Wilkie Collins, *The Moonstone*, ed. Sandra Kemp (Penguin 1998), 452. This invasion of imperialism into the domestic plot has been at the center of reassessments since John Reed's 1973 article "English Imperialism and the Unacknowledged Crime of *The Moonstone*," 281–90.

- 18 -

POLITICAL PERSUASION IN
MARY BRADDON'S *THE OCTOROON;*
OR, THE LILY OF LOUISIANA

KIMBERLY HARRISON

MARY BRADDON'S *The Octoroon; or, The Lily of Louisiana* was serialized in John Maxwell's *Halfpenny Journal* from November 1861 to March 1862. The novel was one of the many that Braddon wrote anonymously for the penny press while at the same time working on novels such as *Lady Audley's Secret* for which she imagined middle- and even upper-class readers. The *Halfpenny Journal,* subtitled *A Magazine for All Who Can Read,* ran from 1861 to 1865 and was directed, as its name implies, toward a newly literate urban working-class audience. Robert Wolff describes it as the cheapest of all Maxwell's magazines, providing lurid fiction to the lower classes.[1] As Jennifer Carnell explains, the *Halfpenny Journal* was a direct competitor to the popular *Reynold's Miscellany,* and both journals were paternalist in scope and philosophy, offering advice columns as well as melodramatic literature.[2]

The Octoroon, while published in the early years of the American Civil War, is set when tensions were high between the North and South but before military conflict. Braddon tells two intertwining stories, the primary of which concerns Cora Leslie, the octoroon of the title and the daughter of a New Orleans slaveholder, Gerald Leslie, and his slave. Educated in England, Cora does not know the secret of her birth until she returns to Louisiana against the wishes of her father, who faces financial ruin. When his creditors seize his estate, Cora is sold as a slave to a lustful planter who desires her for his mistress. Before her virtue, or her life, is lost, she is rescued by her English fiancée, Gilbert Margrave. The secondary story is the romance between Camillia Moraquitos, also a planter's daughter, and her father's protégé, Paul Lisimon, who is revealed to be the son of a former slave.

The novel capitalized on the public's interest in abolition and in the American Civil War. As Audrey Fisch explains, "English desires to see and hear all about

American slavery were nearly insatiable."³ Most of Braddon's readers would likely have been in support of abolition and of the North.⁴ Drawing on such interest and sympathies, the *Halfpenny Journal* compared its serial to the wildly successful *Uncle Tom's Cabin* and began its serialization simultaneously with Dion Boucicault's play *The Octoroon; or, Life in Louisiana*, which opened in London on November 18, 1861, a few days after Braddon's serial began.⁵ As an abolitionist text, Braddon's novel lacks the consistency and immediacy of Stowe's antislavery message. Likewise, in comparison to Boucicault's play, Braddon's narrative is less forceful in its antislavery design. Boucicault's play, in the original version, ended with the death of Zoe, Boucicault's octoroon. While in the London production Boucicault revised the last act to allow Zoe's survival, he did so only after bowing reluctantly to audience demands for a positive ending. The playwright disliked the revision as he felt that a story expounding upon the evils of slavery "could not accommodate a happy ending" without undermining the abolitionist message.⁶ In Braddon's *Octoroon*, readers are readily provided with a storybook domestic ending. While Margrave goes to America with the goal of mitigating slavery, the novel ends without reference to a large-scale vision of abolition. Even the slaveholder Augustus Horton, who plotted to buy Cora for his mistress, is left unpunished, still master on his plantation.

With Braddon's newly literate readers in mind, however, we see that the novel's purpose was not only to promote an antislavery message, but also to address domestic issues of social reform. In the novel, the rhetorics of abolition and of Victorian liberalism work together to promote a domestic agenda that responds to midcentury concerns regarding class reform. Braddon presents a message of slow and steady social and political change that has implications for the novel's working-class readers. The 1832 Reform Act had expanded the franchise to the prosperous middle class, but the urban working-class readers of the *Halfpenny Journal* would not receive the vote until the Second Reform Act of 1867. At midcentury, reform was a topic of national concern and was heightened in the public mind by the American Civil War, a conflict that brought to the forefront for the British their own unease regarding expanding the franchise. Some of the privileged classes feared that such reform would create an unrestrained democracy. The American Civil War magnified this fear, for as Donald Bellows explains, "many Britons . . . thought the Civil War was largely the result of democracy," which in their view was "a defective form of government leading . . . to anarchy."⁷ Braddon addresses midcentury concerns regarding Britain's own working class's readiness for the franchise, using her novel to promote the value of education and individual work and appealing to her working-class readers by hinting at the potential for social equality as a result of self-improvement. While Braddon's antislavery message implies gradual reform, it is radical in its vision of eventual social equality.

The novel's political message gives insight into Braddon's view of the purposes of working-class literature as she infuses her melodramatic novel with a liberal social vision. As scholars such as Patrick Brantlinger have shown, the nineteenth-century was marked by fears related to mass literacy and uncensored novel reading. Brantlinger writes of a nineteenth-century "anti-novel discourse" that portrayed novel reading as "addictive or seductive" and "a frivolous waste of time."[8] To counter the supposed negative effects of reading, critics urged that literature for the working classes aim to educate and instruct, not only to entertain. Margaret Oliphant, writing in 1858 for *Blackwood's,* argued that storytelling could be an effective way of teaching the lower classes. She writes, "[T]here can be little question that the most practical mental agent upon the masses, in their present condition of superficial intelligence, is the art of story-telling. . . . A genuine story, rapid, clear, and intelligible, something in modern guise . . . would tell a hundred times better than the prettiest essay ever delivered."[9] After the publication of *Lady Audley,* critics, including Oliphant, would direct their censure toward Braddon and her fellow sensation novelists; however, in *The Octoroon,* Braddon seems aligned with Oliphant on the benefits of instructional working-class literature. While Oliphant might have resisted *The Octoroon*'s subversive vision of potential class and racial equality, it is likely that she would have at least sanctioned Braddon's attempt to impact "the masses" through fiction.

Braddon, giving her readers the sensation and melodrama they desired, threads references from national events into her story that, true to the purpose of the *Halfpenny Journal,* seek to entertain and also to influence her readers. Although scholars have largely dismissed her penny-press fiction as "hackwork," as writing that took her time away from her literary efforts, Braddon takes part in national discussions through *The Octoroon.* Eve Lynch, studying Braddon's ghost stories of the 1870s, finds that Braddon endorsed the importance of charity in Victorian culture and the upper classes' responsibilities to the poor,[10] yet in the *Octoroon* as Braddon writes directly to working-class readers, she does not emphasize a paternalism in which the responsibility for the lower classes' welfare lies with the benevolence of the upper classes and which offered little chance for movement beyond one's sphere.[11] Instead, true to Victorian liberalism, social advancement is shown through the novel as the product of gradual education and individual progress.

Braddon defines her heroes as ideally masculine not by their class but through their hard work and subsequent success. Armand Tremlay, for example, is an artist who, with "hatred for the conventionalities of rank," defies class hierarchy in his pursuit of Pauline Corsi, a duke's daughter. Through "genius, energy, and patience" he becomes a renowned portrait painter and "amasse[s] a considerable fortune."[12] Echoing popular Victorian self-help philosophy, genius itself is not enough but must be accompanied by individual effort. Armand realizes that only through hard work will he "attain such eminence" that will allow him to propose to Corsi (180). Not content with his first fortune, he makes another digging for gold, again through perseverance and this time through hard physical labor.

Similarly, Paul Lisimon, Camillia Moraquitos's mixed-race lover, is also described through his dedication to knowledge and success. When a ward of Juan Moraquitos, Camillia's father, he refuses to indulge in the life of luxury his patron offers him, dedicating himself instead through self-education to "the stern routine of toil and study," determined not to "lead a life of hopeless idleness" (64, 62). When apprenticed to the immoral lawyer Silas Craig, Lisimon learns the legal profession despite Craig's disinterest in advancing his pupil's professional knowledge. Braddon emphasizes that while Paul did not need to work, he did. In a representative passage, she explains,

> Thus, where another would have rejoiced in the idleness of Silas Craig's office; where another would have abandoned himself to the dissipated pleasures that abound in such a city as New Orleans; where another would have snatched the tempting chalice which youthful passion offered to his lips, Paul Lisimon, in very defiance of his employer, slowly but surely advanced in the knowledge of the profession whose ranks he was predestined to join. (63)

Braddon allows her readers to see Lisimon's struggles to distinguish himself, emphasizing his diligence and dedication. Lisimon achieves his knowledge and reputation, and the hand of his childhood love Camillia, through slow, steady perseverance.

Lisimon not only works to educate himself, but also the slaves in the Moraquitos household. Finding their "simple but noble natures, obscured by the dark veil of ignorance," he looks "forward to a day when, from the ranks of these despised people, great men should arise to elevate the African race" (37). Lisimon's abolitionism assumes a gradual end to slavery that comes through the education and cultivation of black leaders—of great men. Such a view of societal progress through individual achievement was promoted in the midcentury not only by working-class newspapers and by Braddon's novel, but also by a multitude of self-help lectures and books, such as the extremely popular *Self-Help* by Samuel Smiles. First published in 1859, Smiles' book sold twenty thousand copies in the first year and fifty-five thousand within five years.[13] As did similar self-help authors and lecturers, Smiles promotes "individual industry, energy, and uprightness," linking "progress in individuals [to] civilization in nations."[14] Pitting himself and his philosophy against vast social change, he places the impetus for working-class improvement on the workers themselves, arguing that the "healthy spirit of self-help created amongst working people would more than any other measure serve to raise them as a class, and this, not by pulling down others, but by leveling them up to a higher and still advancing standard of religion, intelligence, and virtue." "Progress . . . of the best kind," Smiles explains, "is comparatively slow."[15] Smiles, of course, is not referring to American slavery; he favored abolition in the British colonies, including antislavery activists such as Granville Sharp and Thomas Clarkson in his lists of great men. But, neither is Braddon's only political message about the plight of American slaves. In general, while promoting the potential for social equality, she cautions against abrupt change, especially at the hands of her working-class readers who had not yet been given the vote but whose potential for political power threatened the status quo.

Braddon was not alone in using the example of American slaves to address working-class concerns. However, her strategy differs from that of working-class reformers who frequently relied upon the comparison of "industrial slaves" to black slaves in the colonies and in America. Prominent activists such as William Roscoe compared the disenfranchised to slaves; similarly, Joseph Barker likened the middle and upper classes to slaveholders, and in Scotland, Patrick Brewster compared the Scottish worker's plight to that of black slaves.[16] Such rhetoric encouraged workers to see similarities in their positions and that of slaves and motivated them through anger and indignation to fight for improved conditions and rights. Braddon, however, uses the worker/slave association differently. In her portrayal of American slaves, she emphasizes that they are products of their circumstances, that while they have the potential to improve themselves, their contexts have not allowed this to happen. This view of one's fate not as determined by birth or blood, or solely by one's "nature" likely appealed to readers both as abolitionists and as workers who themselves faced limited opportunity. Ultimately, however, to promote its domestic agenda, the novel positions readers to associate themselves with the upwardly mobile, hardworking romantic heroes.[17] To this end, the readers of *The Octoroon* are positioned as the American slaves' liberators. Emphasizing the readers' own empowerment to bring about change, the *Halfpenny Journal* argued that by subscribing to the paper and by encouraging others to subscribe, the readers were actually behaving heroically to "turn the mitigation of Slavery, if not the total abolition of the hideous traffic in Human Beings that the exigencies of Slavery both foster and sustain."[18]

Gilbert Margrave particularly compels readers' identification, serving as an ideal model for masculine achievement. Although Margrave is from "a good Somersetshire family," he is self-made in that his money comes largely from his invention of a machine to aid in cotton spinning. He is associated with his labor; for example, when his name is mentioned in the text, it is often preceded with a list of his professional activities. He is an artist, poet, and engineer, and through his work and success he represents what Braddon calls "the very type of manly energy" (2). Serving to link the readers' and Margrave's interests, Braddon assures her readers that the machine he invented, while capable to "supersede slave

labour," will not "militat[e] against the employment of the many" (45).
Additionally, through the character of Margrave, Braddon cultivates British nationalism by building upon the anti-Americanism that was prevalent in Britain at the beginning of the Civil War, caused by events such as the passage of the Morrill tariff in February 1861 and, more explosively, by the *Trent* Affair, beginning November 8, 1861, only a few days before Braddon's first installment of *The Octoroon* appeared.[19] In Louisiana, Margrave faces hostility from southern men. In addition to being shot in a dual by the planter Augustus Horton, "the Englishman" is threatened with being thrown overboard when traveling across the Mississippi with Cora and after defending her honor (99). Similarly, when he expresses contempt for Horton's inhumane treatment of Cora, local men warn him that "our folks are not over fond of your countrymen just now, and they wouldn't make much work of taking out their bowie knives" (163). Assuming her readers' knowledge of such international events that fostered anti-American sentiment, Braddon furthers an association between her readers and her British hero.

The anti-Americanism in the novel works to advance the narrative's abolitionist and domestic political views. Braddon distances her readers from the elite planter culture in support of her abolitionist message. She also communicates her domestic vision by promoting England as a land of opportunity and individual freedom, in contrast to America. The text presents England, unlike America, as an established nation that had previously rejected slavery and that, valuing freedom, offered more opportunity to its citizens. In most installments, readers are reminded of their national identities, and England is seldom mentioned unless accompanied by the adjective "free." Readers are reminded that "to the Briton there is no such word as slavery . . . in a free country the lowest labourer in the fields has as full a right to law and justice as the proudest noble in the land" (61). Implied through such passages is England's success in outlawing slavery gradually through court rulings as opposed to civil war, thus further reinforcing British national superiority.

Similarly, in contrast to America, England is portrayed as a nation in which families can thrive. As in Stowe's *Uncle Tom's Cabin,* the most sustained critique of slavery in Braddon's novel comes through her descriptions of what bondage does to families. Yet Braddon links the success of the institution of the family to British nationalism. For example, Cora rebukes her father for his treatment of her mother, his slave, stating that in the "free country" of England, she was taught "that the honour of every man, the love of every mother, are alike sacred" (59). Cora's father sees only England as providing opportunity for domestic bliss and dreams of an "English home, where the tyranny of prejudice could never oppress his beloved and lovely child" (17).[20]

While Braddon's novel promotes the value of work and individual effort, the present is marked by social hierarchy. For example, the sympathetic Mortimer

Percy, describing slave field hands, concludes that such "poor simple creatures" would be made "easily" happy with a "good master" (111). Cora's mulatto waiting maid is described as incapable of sophisticated thought. However, her shortcomings are a result of her "ignorance," not of her nature, and she is contrasted to Cora, "the highly educated and refined woman" (172), the product of years of formal education. While such passages seem initially to contradict the message of social change, they in fact support the text's commitment to progress through self-improvement and education.

The value of hard work and family in *The Octoroon* echoes that in *Lady Audley's Secret*. Braddon had begun *Lady Audley* in July 1861, before she started *The Octoroon*. While she put it aside when the journal in which it appeared, *Robin Goodfellow*, folded, she took up the novel again to publish in monthly installments for the *Sixpenny Magazine,* and in October 1862, it was published in three volumes. Considering that Braddon worked on the novels at times in conjunction, it is not surprising that some of the politics expressed are similar, although packaged for different audiences. In *Lady Audley,* it is through Robert Audley that Braddon condones work, by showing Robert's development from an idle and somewhat effeminate barrister into the ideal of Victorian middle-class masculinity at the end of the novel. To win Clara Talboys—to become the ideal Victorian husband—he must commit to "a life of serious work and application, in which he should strive to be useful to his fellow-creatures, and win a reputation for himself." Echoing *The Octoroon's* descriptions of Paul Lisimon, Robert pledges to "read hard and think seriously of his profession, and begin life in real earnest." Due to his hard work, within two years, the narrator tells us, Robert is a successful barrister, "a rising man upon the home circuit."[21] As with Braddon's heroes in *The Octoroon,* Robert's success comes only through his own resolve. While *Lady Audley* reflects the politics and work ethic found in *The Octoroon,* the communicated effect differs when considering the intended audiences. As *Lady Audley* was written largely for middle-class readers, the valuing of work and success serve to cement the middle-class's rising status in the British social and political arena. As Jenny Bourne Taylor points out, "Robert replaces the declining aristocracy, relic of an earlier era, with the rising professional middle class."[22] While both *Lady Audley* and *The Octoroon* endorse middle-class values, the latter does so in order to instruct. The industrious heroes serve as exemplars to promote to the working-class reader that success comes through hard work and perseverance.

While Braddon's social vision is largely in line with nineteenth-century middle-class liberalism, her message is pushed to radical extremes in its echoes of earlier nineteenth-century abolitionist ideals of human equality as the narrative implies the potential for eventual social progress, regardless of one's "nature," race, or even, by extension, class. Though she often uses her black or mixed-race characters to illustrate this point, the vision of social reform based on hard work and individual achievement is likely intended to have relevance for her readers. Such a suggestion of movement between the classes is similarly made in *Lady Audley's Secret* as Lucy Graham can easily slip into the role of the noble lady. Also implied is that her lady's maid Phoebe could just as easily pass as of noble birth with only the proper clothes and makeup. In her three-decker novel, such questions of identity are subversive for middle-class readers as they destabilize class structure. In *The Octoroon*, the effect is different and serves similarly again for instruction and motivation. Unlike in *Lady Audley* in which Phoebe needed only to procure the latest fashions and makeup to resemble her mistress, in *The Octoroon*, education and hard work are presented as keys to equal social opportunity.

Lisimon gives voice to the social vision of the "equal rights of the great brotherhood of man" (37), a phrase that in the text is printed in all capital letters. In endorsing human equality, Braddon relies upon evangelical abolitionist rhetoric to suggest equal rights even as such Enlightenment values began to lose currency in the late 1850s. As Robert Young explains, such racial views at midcentury were being replaced by imperial views of social hierarchy and fears of racial difference, which arose in the wake of events such as the Indian Mutiny of 1857 and the American Civil War.[23] Yet Braddon problematizes popular Victorian "scientific" definitions of race and difference by emphasizing that her characters' personalities and choices are governed not primarily by blood, race, or caste but instead by their contexts.

For example, Gerald Leslie's slave Toby's passive service and "dog-like" devotion are explained not as "natural" but as a result of slavery. As Toby explains, "[T]he habit of suffering teaches resignation to the slave" (56). Likewise, the common stereotype of the "lazy" slave is also contextualized and problematized. Early in the novel, the southern planter Mortimer Percy excuses the violent punishment of slaves, arguing that "the planter finds himself between the horns of a terrible dilemma; he must either beat his slaves or suffer from their laziness" (11). Yet, he later realizes that slaves' failure to perform their tasks might not be the result of laziness at all; he imagines Cora being compelled to work in the fields, and as she would not physically be able to accomplish her task, Percy realizes she would likely be flogged for being "too weak (or too lazy, as it will most likely be called)" (26). Such contextual recasting of the lazy slave stereotype also complicates a subsequent passage in which the slave Pepita is described as "lazy like all negresses." The characterization is called into question when read in context as it follows a brief sketch of Pepita's history in which the reader learns that she was Camillia Moraquitos's mother's nurse as well as Camillia's. Thus, Pepita's desire for a nap, which leads to her being labeled lazy, seems only reasonable when it is clear that she is an old woman with a history of hard work and service to the Moraquitos family (32). While Percy realizes that Cora would wrongly be considered lazy, the reader is called to make the same realization regarding Pepita.

Tristan, Juan Moraquitos's rebellious slave, is also shown to act in response to his context, not his nature. Initially, Braddon's portrayal of Tristan seems to echo strict racial stereotypes: he is described as a "thick-lipped and woolly-haired African," physical traits that mark him in Victorian racial schema as "the lowest type of a despised and abhorred race" (82). Additionally, his primary job is to entertain his mistress, and former childhood friend, Camillia by dancing for her, engaging in "impish tricks," and singing "wild, half-demoniac songs" (32, 35), activities that position him in the familiar minstrel role with which Braddon's readers would have been familiar. Minstrel troops were by the 1860s one of the most popular forms of entertainment for the British working classes, with the performances marked by caricature of slaves, most often American slaves.[24] Yet, Braddon subverts the stereotype of the happy, dancing minstrel; Tristan, who harbors romantic feelings for Camilla, sings and dances but is not the picture of the simple-minded slave.

Braddon writes of Tristan that "his was one of those natures, burning as Africa's skies, created, sometimes, like the venomous serpents of those tropical climes, only to terrify and to destroy" (80). Yet, in her description, her choice of the qualifier "sometimes" is telling, indicating the contextual nature of human behavior. Also, this depiction of Tristan's "savage" and destructive nature is further problematized as it is positioned in the text immediately prior to the narrative of Tristan's heroism in saving Camillia's life after her dress caught fire when a reading lamp fell on her skirt. Even more importantly, Braddon provides the reader with insight into Tristan's history and thus his motivations for his revengeful actions as she writes his response to hearing that he is not a suitable companion for Camillia:

> "A slave!" he muttered, . . ."A slave!" Yes, I have been told that often enough. I must have heard it in my cradle, surely, when they sold my father as they sold their cattle, and put a brand on my arm as they mark their sheep. . . . He pushed up the sleeve of his coloured calico shirt, and looked at his arm. The two letters, J. M., had been branded on the flesh a little above the elbow. Tristan stood motionless for some moments, looking earnestly at those two initials; then bursting into a mocking laugh, he exclaimed—"How clever they are! How powerful—how great! They can set their names upon our tortured flesh and mark *that* as their own; but they cannot brand our souls. . . ." (34)

As he plots to destroy Lisimon's romantic chances with Camillia, he acts out of bitterness that is caused by his own experiences as a slave, not by his savage nature. As expressed by the French governess Pauline Corsi (who bears a striking resemblance to Lady Audley), "There are wrongs that can transform an angel to a fiend" (155). In comparison to the novel's villains, Tristan's actions can be more easily understood. The working-class reader could perhaps sympathize with Tristan's resentment for those whose dehumanizing treatment of slaves serve only their interests and those of their families and businesses. In contrast, villains Silas Craig and Augustus Horton act in response to lust and revenge, motivations that could certainly be seen as less reasoned and even more "savage" than those that motivate Tristan.

In a scene that parallels Lady Audley's confession of madness, Tristan, after failing to thwart Lisimon and Camillia's romance, defines himself as mad and pledges to drink poison. As does Lucy in *Lady Audley's Secret,* Tristan cites madness to excuse his actions and to cloud his motives. When confronted by Lisimon, Tristan admits his love for Camillia, and his rival responds by calling him mad. Agreeing, Tristan replies, "Yes, I am mad. What can that slave be but mad who dares to love his mistress?" (203). While in her subsequent novel, Braddon leaves the verdict regarding Lucy's madness subversively open-ended, in *The Octoroon,* she negates Tristan's self-diagnosis, explaining Tristan's acts as motivated by unrequited love and as natural, not the result of insanity, since "the heart within is of the same form, though the skin is of another colour" (118). As she shows Tristan's actions influenced by his tragic circumstances instead of by his African blood or by madness, Braddon subversively challenges Victorian assumptions of difference as she calls into question the increasingly popular midcentury pseudoscientific racial theories.

Most sensationally for Victorian readers, in its emphasis on the brotherhood of man, the novel endorses miscegenation, placing the novel in the center of Victorian concerns of racial degeneration. Scientists and pseudoscientists debated the effects of mixing races, hypothesizing the corruption of civilization that would come through human "hybrids." For example, persons of mixed race were thought to have limited reproductive capabilities. While Victorian science could not dispute the offspring of mixed-race unions, theorists posited that after a few short generations, the capability for reproduction would end. Young explains that the "dispute over hybridity thus put the question of inter-racial sex at the heart of Victorian race theory." As stated by Joseph Gobineau, "the degenerate man . . . and his civilization with him, will certainly die on the day when the primordial race-unit is so broken up and swamped by the influx of foreign elements." Such discourses, David Spurr points out, are "connected to the fear that the white race could lose itself in the darker ones."[25]

In the light of such theory and such fears, Braddon offers a social vision marked by happy and socially respected mixed-race unions. While Cora and her English hero Gilbert Margrave's marriage takes place after the novel ends, readers are assured that it will indeed occur once the couple reach England. Paul Lisimon and Camillia will also marry. In contrast to Braddon's acceptance of such marriages, Boucicault's original play does not realize the union of Zoe and the European-educated George Peyton. The octoroon kills herself, in part to remove herself as an obstacle to the union of Peyton and Dora Sunnyside, a planter's daughter. While Peyton proposes to Zoe, arguing that he "can overcome the obstacle" of her race, she replies that she cannot. Boucicault's revised ending does allow for the eventual marriage of Zoe and Peyton, but the lovers plan to settle in an unnamed and distant foreign land, not in Britain.[26]

Braddon, however, brings her controversial couple directly to England, and disputing fears of racial and national degeneration brought about by mixed-race unions, Cora and Margrave are offered as an ideal English couple. Margrave is "handsome and accomplished," and Cora is described as the ideal English woman—the Victorian angel. She has

> the innocence of an angel beaming in every smile; with the tenderness of a woman lying shadowed in the profound depths of her almond-shaped black eyes. Features, delicately moulded and exquisitely proportioned; a tiny rose-bud mouth; a Grecian nose; a complexion fairer than the ungathered lily hiding deep in an untrodden forest. (3)

She will be, the text assures the reader, a "happy English wife" (172). Braddon's characterization of Cora as a good English wife is sensational and subversive, especially as by establishing the couple in England, Braddon does not contain the threat of racial decline to America.

Admittedly, Braddon's portrayal of mixed-race relationships are not as radical as they might have been. For example, despite the passage quoted above, Tristan's union with Camillia is not seriously entertained. And although Cora does "not seek to deny [her] origin" and Margrave sees her as "the lovely representative of an oppressed people," Braddon, through Cora's appearance, effectively erases her heroine's race, describing her throughout the story as having "lily-white" skin and pointing out that she was "removed in the eighth degree from the African race" with only "[o]*ne drop* of the blood of a slave . . . in her veins" (71). Her exoticism is seen only through her "almond shaped" black eyes and through dark color in her fingernails. Even as the novel suggests a "brotherhood of man," it fails to fully reject contemporary racial views as the mixed-race characters, those with a small percentage of African blood, are the ones who are fully integrated into mainstream society. In contrast, while both Toby and Tristan are freed, Toby remains in the service of the Leslies, and Tristan, potentially dangerous because of his resentment and unrequited love, plans to depart for Africa.

Nonetheless, Braddon's penny-press novel presents a layered social message that offers a challenge to dominant ideologies of race and conceptions of difference, hinting at potential for racial equality at a historical moment when British views of race were increasingly tied to imperial unease and opinions regarding class where tinged with uncertainty regarding ongoing reform. Writing of Braddon's politics, Lyn Pykett suggests that "Braddon is both a radical and a conservative, and that she is neither," concluding that Braddon "is a more complex and shifting entity than these labels would allow."[27] Through *The Octoroon* we see further evidence of the commingling of political ideologies in Braddon's work. In this penny-press novel, the mix of relatively conservative and radical views neatly serves the novel's purposes of guiding and engaging its readers. When we consider Braddon's readers and the periodical in which the novel was published, it becomes evident that while the narrative endorsed a gradual approach to social change, the subversive notion of equality implies challenges not only to racial but also to class ideologies and thus likely appealed both to readers' desires for domestic reform as well as for American abolition.

NOTES

1. Robert Lee Wolff, *Sensational Victorian: The Life and Fiction of Mary Elizabeth Braddon,* 80.
2. Jennifer Carnell, introduction to *The Octoroon,* xi.
3. Audrey Fisch, *American Slaves in Victorian England,* 53.
4. The dominant consensus among historians is that British workers favored abolition and thus the cause of the Union. Some argue, however, that working-class views varied. See particularly Mary Ellison's *Support For Secession: Lancashire and the American Civil War.* For additional historiography, see Philip S. Foner's *British Labor and the American Civil War,* chap. 2.
5. Boucicault's play had been performed in New York in 1859. While Wolff in his seminal biography of Braddon states that Boucicault's play was the basis for Braddon's serialization, Carnell disagrees, despite similarities of the title (introd., xiii). Although Braddon's novel bears many similarities to Boucicault's play, it does indeed differ significantly in both content and purpose.
6. Peter Thomson, ed., *Plays by Dion Boucicault,* 9. Only after continual pressure from his London audiences did he rewrite the ending. As Thomson points out, Boucicault responded bitterly to this public pressure, sarcastically announcing in the playbill that the new fifth act was "composed by the Public, and edited by the Author" who "trusts the Audience will accept it as a very grateful tribute to their judgment and taste, which he should be the last to dispute" (quoted in Thomson, 11).
7. Donald Bellows, "A Study of British Conservative Reaction to the American Civil War," 506, 526.
8. Patrick Brantlinger, *The Reading Lesson,* 3. Catherine Golden's work has focused on fears surrounding women's "promiscuous" reading. In her essay in this collection, she argues that Braddon responded to such cultural discussion, illustrating in her novel *The Doctor's Wife* that women's reading of sensation fiction did not endanger their moral development.
9. Margaret Oliphant, "The Byways of Literature: Reading for the Million," 206.
10. Eve M. Lynch, "Spectral Politics: M. E. Braddon and the Spirits of Social Reform," 244.
11. As historian Patrick Joyce explains in *Work, Society, and Politics,* although liberalism

dominated the mid-Victorian economic and political scene, paternalism was still a prominent ideology within working-class and factory culture.

12. Mary Elizabeth Braddon, *The Octoroon; or, The Lily of Louisiana*, 179–80. Hereafter, references to this work will be cited in the text parenthetically by page number.

13. Sales figures are provided by Asa Briggs in his introduction to the 1958 edition of *Self-Help*.

14. Samuel Smiles, *Self-Help, the Art of Achievement Illustrated by Accounts of the Lives of Great Men*, 265.

15. Ibid., 285, 118.

16. For excerpts of such rhetoric, see Betty Fladeland, *Abolitionists and Working-Class Problems in the Age of Industrialization*, 46, 144, 115.

17. This positioning implies primarily concern with a male audience, whose suffrage and general political power were more likely.

18. *Halfpenny*, quoted in Carnell, introduction, xi–xii. Of course, this is also a ploy to sell copies of the journal, but it does indicate the role Braddon textually constructed for her readers. They were not to see themselves as oppressed but as acting against oppression. Braddon's rhetoric draws upon that used in discussions of abolition in the West Indies; the British working classes were taxed to support antislavery reform and recognized in the press for their sacrifice for freedom. Harriet Martineau, in the *History of Peace*, illustrates this point, explaining that the "British peasant [. . .] as a freeman and a tax-payer, had helped to release [West Indian slaves] from bondage" (349). Braddon builds upon this image of the worker as liberator, with the rhetorical effect of positioning her reader in a position of power.

19. The Morrill tariff, passed by the Union, was seen in Britain to endanger free trade. The *Trent* Affair led to suggestions of war with America after the arrest of two Confederate diplomats and their entourage traveling on board the British vessel *Trent*.

20. Braddon had most certainly read Stowe's book, an immensely popular best-seller in England, and Carnell surmises that Braddon appeared in a stage version of the play in the early 1850s (introduction, xiii).

21. Braddon, *Lady Audley's Secret*, ed. Jenny Bourne Taylor (Penguin 1998), 428, 435.

22. Taylor, introduction to *Lady Audley's Secret*, xxxiii.

23. Robert J. C. Young, *Colonial Desire: Hybridity in Theory, Culture, and Race*, 119. R. J. M. Blackett, in *Divided Hearts*, agrees that in England by the late 1850s, "views about Negro inferiority were widespread" (43).

24. Blackett, 43–45.

25. Young, 102; Gobineau, quoted in Young, 104; David Spurr, *The Rhetoric of Empire*, 82.

26. Dion Boucicault, "The Octoroon," 147. As Thomson explains in his introduction to Boucicault's plays, the rewritten conclusion of the play has been lost. The synopsis of the new ending comes from an *Illustrated London News* review of December 14, 1861 (225).

27. Lyn Pykett, "Afterword," 280.

- 19 -

WILKIE COLLINS'S "SECRET DICTATE"

The Moonstone *as a Response to Imperialist Panic*

VICKI CORKRAN WILLEY

AS GABRIEL Betteredge attempts to persuade Ezra Jennings, the biracial doctor's assistant of Wilkie Collins's *The Moonstone* (1868), to call off his "medical enterprise" by invoking the wisdom of *Robinson Crusoe,* Defoe's novel magically opens itself to the page where Crusoe explains "[t]hat whenever I found the secret Hints or Pressings of my mind . . . , I never failed to obey the secret Dictate."[1] Rebuking Jennings for "this hocus-pocus of yours, sir, with the laudanum and Mr. Franklin Blake" (478), Betteredge, trusted steward of the Verinders' country house, attributes his disapproval of Jennings's plan to a "secret Dictate" that had occurred to him the night before and which, had he obeyed, would have prevented the doctor's assistant from restaging the events surrounding the theft of the Moonstone from Rachel Verinder's bedroom one year earlier. Fortunately for Jennings—and for Blake—Betteredge overcomes his doubts and participates in the experiment, although not without misgivings. Wilkie Collins, on the other hand, does not resist his own "secret Dictate" which urges him to move forward with an experiment of his own—to add to *The Moonstone* a subtext which, through the hybrid character, Ezra Jennings, calls for a reconsideration of the intensified sense of racial hatred and imperialist superiority that pervaded the British popular imagination in the aftermath of the Sepoy Rebellion of 1857.

When discussing the colonial subtext in *The Moonstone,* scholars often look to the 1857 Indian Mutiny. As Patrick Brantlinger suggests, "No episode in British imperial history raised public excitement to a higher pitch than the Indian Mutiny."[2] While the press virtually ignored the mutiny at its outset, coverage gained momentum after alleged firsthand reports of atrocities inflicted upon the women and children taken prisoner at Cawnpore began to filter back to Britain. Although Jenny Sharpe observes that "long before the British army regained control over its Indian territories, the tales of terror were discredited as having little or no historical basis,"³ sensational stories of the physical violation of female prisoners were firmly entrenched in the British imagination. Christopher Hilbert, in his extensive study of narrative accounts of the Indian Mutiny, concurs with Sharpe that "most of the appalling crimes rumored to have happened, and reported as facts in letters to England, bore scant relation to the truth."⁴ Yet sensational accounts such as the one quoted below from Lt-Gen. Sir Colin Campbell in 1858 became reality as represented in the British press:

> Wives were stripped in the presence of their husbands' eyes, flogged naked through the city, violated in the public streets, and then murdered. To cut off the breasts of the women was a favorite mode of dismissing them to death; and most horrible, they were sometimes scalped—the skin being separated around the neck, and then drawn over the head of the poor creatures, who were then, blinded with blood, driven out into the blazing streets. (Sharpe 230)

Collins alludes to the staying power of such misinformation through Ezra Jennings's reference to unnamed slander that had dogged him throughout his time in England. "Evil report," he says, "with time and chance to help it, travels patiently and travels far" (447).

The public encountered these lurid stories at a time when it was not only unaccustomed to questioning the veracity of what appeared in the papers (especially when some of the sources were clergymen or "eyewitnesses"), but also when, according to Lyn Pykett, it was developing a taste for sensation fiction.⁵ Feeding an incensed public's hunger for revenge concomitantly with its craving for sensational details, virtually all of the fiction that emerged as a result of the rebellion was not only jingoistic in nature but also reductive, compressing "social and moral complexities to simplistic oppositions between good and evil, victims and villains" (Brantlinger 206). Into this highly charged atmosphere enters *The Moonstone,* Collins's thinly veiled effort to counteract what Ian Duncan calls "imperialist panic."⁶

When Collins wrote his enormously popular novel, few would have regarded it as a politically subversive text. After all, the "villains" were Indians working in tandem with two other imported troublemakers—Herncastle's stolen diamond and the drug, opium—to challenge values not only revered through Gabriel Betteredge's homage to that paean of British imperialism, *Robinson Crusoe,* but also deemed inviolate by English middle-class society. Moreover, as those same core values held by Collins's readers survive foreign disruption—theft, drug use, and murder appropriately dealt with; damaged reputations put right; and the Victorian family left undisrupted—the novel appears to assuage imperial anxiety by venerating English cultural superiority. Indeed, as Margery Sabin suggests, even the half-English Jennings, while instrumental in revealing the identity of the diamond's thief, aids Franklin Blake and Rachel Verinder in the capacity of a "loyal Colonial servant."[7] Contemporary audiences would have expected nothing less from Collins, a popular and prolific author well known not only for *The Woman in White* but also for his association with *Household Words*, edited by his colleague Charles Dickens, who, in 1857, famously (or infamously) commented about the Sepoy Rebellion:

> I wish I were the Commander in Chief in India. The first thing I would do to strike that Oriental race with amazement . . . should be to proclaim to them in their language, that I considered my holding that appointment by the leave of God, to mean that I should do my utmost to exterminate the Race upon whom the stain of the late cruelties rested; and that I was there for that purpose and no other, and was now proceeding, with all convenient dispatch and merciful swiftness of execution, to blot it out of mankind and raze it off the face of the Earth.[8]

Although Dickens's comments were made in a private letter to a friend, they affirm a publicly held attitude of extreme racial bigotry that was exacerbated by fallacious reports of the Indian Mutiny and then reflected in contemporary writings. "The Perils of Certain English Prisoners," coauthored by Dickens and Collins and published in *Household Words* in 1857, was meant to commemorate "some of the best qualities of the English character that have been shewn in India."[9] Brantlinger observes that Dickens's famous social conscience did not extend abroad, noting instead that it "translated into approval of imperial domination" (207). Collins, however, proves an interesting exception as he deviates from Dickens's extremism by writing the second chapter of "Perils" from a somewhat less biased point of view, "parodying British racism" as Jaya Mehta suggests, instead of promoting it.[10] In addition, Mehta argues that in "A Sermon for Sepoys" (1858), Collins's other mutiny-inspired piece produced for *Household Words*, the author casts the Indians not as demons but as rebels "capable of being rehabilitated"—undoubtedly an unpopular position in the aftermath of the rebellion—and suggests that the story "calls into question the legitimating imperial narrative that the English rescued India from the depredations, corruption, and oppressions of her despotic native rulers" (618). While the vast majority of mutiny fiction (and nonfiction) shares Dickens's attitude of intolerance and promotes, wholesale, the superiority of England as the "conquering race" (Brantlinger 218), Collins's work does not. Although Tamar Heller suggests that Dickens's pro-imperialist stance may have made it difficult for Collins to "voice any more explicit reservations about imperialism,"[11] his early published reactions to the Sepoy Rebellion engender the more fully realized attitude of tolerance that surfaces in *The Moonstone* a decade later.

Although Collins avoids mention of the Indian Mutiny per se, he situates the main action of the novel in 1848, another period distinguished by rebellions both of a personal and a political nature. Personally, the year marked Collins's first publication, a biography of his artist father, *Memoirs of the Life of William Collins,* which, as Heller points out, "celebrates the bond between father and son" on the one hand but defies it on the other, "suggest[ing] an oedipal narrative in which the son can produce only once he has acknowledged, through the publication of the *Memoirs,* the death of his . . . father" (38–39). Politically, 1848 resonated with insurrections both on the European continent and abroad. As Mehta reminds us, this was a period of "democratic revolutions, especially in the Austrian Empire, Italy, France, and Germany," a "resurgence of Chartism in England which was also crushed," and, in India, a final defeat of the Sikhs which allowed for annexation of the Punjab territory in the following year (621–22). By primarily setting *The Moonstone* during this unsettled time, Collins utilizes the historical moment to insinuate implications of change into his narrative, which, as Albert D. Poinke notes, "subtly encourages readers to stop seeing India through the English lens of the Mutiny and to start perceiving it by the Indian light of the Moonstone."[12]

Like the Moonstone itself, Collins's narration is multifaceted, and while it outwardly champions traditional English values, it does so with an expediency of paradoxes that may have surprised its original audiences: the diamond becomes plunder, opium becomes the instrument of knowledge, and a mysterious hybrid character, Ezra Jennings, saves the day. If contemporary audiences were looking for a smug reiteration of English superiority and of Dickens's genocidal ideology, then they would not find it here. In fact, the "implicit sympathy for the three Indians at the end of the novel,"[13] first noticed in Geraldine Jewsbury's 1868 review of *The Moonstone* in the *Athenaeum,* would not have been possible without Collins's careful handling of Jennings. Franklin Blake, who initially admits that Jennings "made some inscrutable appeal to my sympathies, which I found impossible to resist" (436), characterizes the other man as a gentleman of "*unsought self-possession,* which is a sure sign of good breeding, not in England only, but everywhere else in the civilized world" (438), a public acknowledgement that the class comprised of "gentlemen" may include both upper-class Englishmen as well as those of foreign extraction. Indeed, like Jennings, Collins's Indians also exhibit gentlemanly characteristics even though they must finally resort to extreme measures in order to accomplish the recovery of the diamond—a far cry, however, from the demonic representations of Indians usually found in mutiny fiction.

Observing that "the highly charged nature of [the atrocities] not only haunts Anglo-Indian novels as a terrifying memory but is also silently constitutive of their stories," Sharpe contends that as a result of the Sepoy uprising, the English stereotype of the Indian male changes from "licentious, but effeminate, cruel, yet physically weak; duplicitous rather than savage," to "blood-thirsty Musselman" (235). It is in this climate, during the decade following the rebellion, that Collins wrote *The Moonstone* for an audience not only willing to embrace this stereotype but also eager to support an English moral victory over fictional Indian characters whom they, like Franklin Blake, perceived to be "murderers and thieves" (131). Yet, while Collins alludes to such attitudes perhaps in order to satisfy readers with a smugly imperialistic bent, he ultimately deviates from culturally pervasive notions of xenophobia: although the Indians are regarded with suspicion and disdain, they are generally treated with respect. Significantly, Collins gives Murthwaite, the Anglo-Indian traveler, the last word on the matter in his difference of opinion with Blake, countering Blake's defamation of the Brahmins with his own praise of them as "a wonderful people" (131). In addition, the author allows the hybrid character, Ezra Jennings, to suggest and execute a clever plan that occurs to none of his purebred English superiors—a plan so integral to plot and theme that it not only vindicates Franklin Blake of the theft of the diamond but also sets up his reconciliation with Rachel Verinder, further removing the threat of foreign invaders by restoring social equilibrium and facilitating the return of the diamond to its rightful place.

This is no accident. Collins venerates the biracial Jennings in order to engender a favorable reaction not only in Franklin Blake but also in the novel's readers, who might well have been predisposed to devalue a character tainted with racial impurity and a hint of scandal. Castigated to the outskirts of society by such intolerance, Jennings, whose mother was a colonial native, not only represents the Other but also British hegemony itself through his father, an Englishman. Anticipating Homi K. Bhabha's notion of hybridity, defined as "what is new, neither the one nor the other,"[14] Collins privileges Jennings, whose show of honor, integrity, and intelligence transcends not only the limitations of his biological background but also of his "doubtful character" (391). Moreover, the contrast between the racially impure but principled Jennings and the handsome but immoral Godfrey Ablewhite, an English hypocrite whose own racial purity is subsumed by a complete lack of scruples, stands out in high relief. Despite suffering augmented not only by poverty and abject loneliness but also by drug addiction and impending death, Jennings, according to Jewsbury's review, remains a man with a "beautiful and noble nature."[15] His characterization bears comparison to Collins's earlier racial hybrid, Ozias Midwinter, in *Armadale*. As Monica Young Zook illustrates in her essay in this collection, Midwinter also serves to subvert dominant Victorian political and social assumptions. In both *Armadale* and *The Moonstone*, Collins relies upon mixed-race characters to complicate his readers' assumption of British national superiority. Jennings, who through a sharply defined sense of decency, clears Blake's name although not his own, protects the reputation of his employer, Dr. Candy, and finally helps Blake and Rachel reconstruct the events surrounding the theft of the diamond, is credibly recast as a reluctant hero who wins the respect of his former detractors.

Such, however, was not always the case in the narrative. When Jennings first appears, Blake is struck by his unique appearance, comprised of a complexion of "gipsy darkness," a distinctive nose "so often found among the ancient people of the East" and "piebald hair," characterized by an indiscriminate juxtaposition of black hair with white:

> Round the sides of his head—without the slightest gradation of grey to break the force of the extraordinary contrast—it had turned completely white. The line between the two colours preserved no sort of regularity. At one place, the white hair ran up into the black; at another, the black hair ran down into the white. (390)

The startling placement of black hair next to white as well as the total absence of gray can be read as a metaphorical concomitance of two cultures—one imperial, one colonial—which must learn to coexist before any successful mixing can occur. Because racial equality of any sort would meet with resistance from much of his English readership, Collins situates Jennings on the outskirts of respectability; however, he meticulously catches this character in a double bind that precludes harsh judgment and elicits sympathy. Unable to extirpate the damage done to his reputation by an ambiguous past and a mysterious slander, Jennings suffers a debilitating lack of "character" only partially erased by his selfless devotion to helping others, an irony Collins uses to effect a favorable response from charitable readers who believe in the probity of good works. Synecdochically, then, Jennings embodies the inevitable result of the British colonial project—his hair emblematic of the white minority invading and dividing the darker-skinned majority, and his skin the ineluctable consequence of miscegenation. Although Duncan calls him "the novel's garish but honorable personification of racial and sexual adulterations" (308), Jennings's perceived "lack of character" prevents his exoneration and speaks, instead, to the existence of a culture-wide xenophobia that actively promoted divisiveness between the conqueror and the conquered. Most important, however, may be the ability of this amorphous individual to connect to something deep within the nature of the English themselves. Indeed, while Betteredge and Mrs. Merridew condemn Jennings for his physical unorthodoxy and ruined reputation, Blake and Rachel quickly recognize his goodness and accept him gratefully as a peer, perhaps because he embodies an idealized sense of decency, or perhaps because he reflects an innate Otherness that they recognize in themselves: the foreign-educated Blake, after all, is under suspicion for theft, and the darkly beautiful Rachel, headstrong and independent, is anything but the model of female complaisance that readers might be expecting.

Often read as an inverted imperial narrative with the foreign diamond invading and creating havoc in an upper-class English home, the novel asks discerning readers to question the British colonial project. Toward this end, the author makes brilliant use of Jennings, whose hybridity underscores his importance to the text. While he is partially Other, he is not entirely so, a point not lost on at least some readers who might have emphasized Jennings's Englishness over the ignominy of his Otherness, especially in light of the assistance he provides Franklin Blake and Rachel Verinder. Ironically, however, Jennings's insight emerges from his Otherness as well as from his firsthand knowledge of the "Oriental" drug, opium, another by-product of imperialism that Collins, a user himself, may be critiquing. However, without the ingenuity of Jennings, whom Duncan considers "outcast" and "weird" (301), the controlled, drug-induced reenactment of Blake's removal of the diamond from Rachel's bedroom would not have occurred, and the mystery of the Moonstone's disappearance might have never been resolved to everyone's satisfaction. Collins therefore uses Jennings to suggest that a synthesis is stronger than either of the two halves separately, again anticipating Bhabha, who calls for the "solidarity of different groups and movements working in coalition to create a new, progressive hegemony" (2378). Indeed, a new partnership comprised of Blake, Rachel, and Jennings succeeds in solving the mystery where the "celebrated" but shortsighted Sergeant Cuff (155), Collins's prototype of the modern police detective, has failed. Collins is clearly calling for an ideology of inclusion.

In doing so, the significance of Jennings's hybridity cannot be underestimated, since as a hybrid, he embodies characteristics of both races. Although Frances M. Mannsaker argues that the majority of mutiny fiction portrays "half-castes" as "tak[ing] only the worst qualities of each parent race—the stubbornness and pride of the English, without their courage and principle; the deviousness of the Indians, without their cultivation and dignity,"[16] Collins constructs his Eurasian character positively and sympathetically, against type and against audience expectations. While Jennings's hair may symbolize separateness, his blood—his essence—does not; and while the character may be physically weakened (for reasons unclear: possibly as a result of his "tainted" mixed blood but certainly relative to his opium addiction), he is neither intellectually nor psychologically impaired. Of all the characters in *The Moonstone*, only this complex and mysterious outsider is imbued with unique and powerful resources that allow him to succeed where others have failed. He stands as a rebuke to English bigotry.

Collins's privileging of the fusion of disparate parts is also exemplified by the Moonstone itself, which the author significantly chooses to leave intact. Both of the English diamond thieves, John Herncastle and Godfrey Ablewhite, had considered compromising the Moonstone's integrity by having the huge, but flawed, diamond cut into several perfect stones. Collins, however, ultimately leaves his Moonstone, like its famous antecedent, the Koh-i-noor diamond, intact. Cut, the diamond could stand for the colonial dismantling of India, which, necessarily, would have divided and diluted an indigenous national identity. Uncut, it suggests that a nation is stronger when its unity is not compromised. Consequently, by returning the unsullied diamond to its country of origin and its rightful place in the statue, Collins is suggesting that the cultural and religious icons—and by implication, the territorial integrity—of a conquered country should not be tampered with. As a metaphorical representation of imperial India, moreover, this "jewel in the crown" is problematic: the defect at its "very heart" is most certainly the indelible and uneasy intrusion of Britain's own alien Western culture upon its largest and most valuable eastern colony.

While Sue Lonoff argues that "mid-Victorians did not examine fiction for its deeper significance," she concludes that "they expected and relished clear moral instruction."[17] Betteredge himself asserts that "most things . . . have a moral if you only look" (72). *The Moonstone*'s juxtaposition of sympathetic treatment of the Other against an exposé of homegrown English hypocrisy should have met those expectations. Contemporary audiences could not have failed to notice that the author refuses to vilify the Indians for their determination to reclaim the diamond, even though they frighten decent English folk and murder the duplicitous Godfrey Ablewhite. Instead, Collins bookends his novel with a reversal of essentially the same situation—the first caused by imperialist greed and the second by personal greed—that allows a restoration of balance to occur both in England and in India. At the beginning, one Englishman kills three Indians, steals the diamond, and takes it to a foreign land; at the end, three Indians kill one Englishman (a relative of the first), steal the diamond, and restore it to its rightful place. Collins is prescient in suggesting that eventually, given time and circumstance, the Indians would prevail against their English oppressors. In the hybrid Jennings, "born, and partly brought up, in one of our colonies" (439), the author anticipates eventual cooperation between two disparate cultures as well as the biological mixing of the English with colonial indigenous peoples, a theme he had treated earlier in *Armadale*. Collins's "secret Dictate," then, was to inculcate his readers with an attitude of tolerance and acceptance rarely found in the work of his contemporaries but accomplished through his hybrid character, Ezra Jennings.

NOTES

1. Wilkie Collins, *The Moonstone* (Broadview Press, 1999), 479. All references are to this edition and are cited by page in the text.

2. Patrick Brantlinger, *Rule of Darkness: British Colonial Literature and Imperialism, 1830–1914*, 199. Subsequent references are cited by page in the text.

3. Jenny Sharpe, "The Unspeakable Limits of Rape: Colonial Violence and Counter-

Insurgency," 227. Subsequent references are cited by page in the text.

4. Christopher Hibbert, *The Great Mutiny: India 1857,* 213. Subsequent references are cited by page in the text.

5. Lyn Pykett, *The Sensation Novel: from* The Woman in White *to* The Moonstone, 1.

6. Ian Duncan, "*The Moonstone,* the Victorian Novel, and Imperialist Panic," 308. Subsequent references are cited by page in the text.

7. Margery Sabin, *Dissenters and Mavericks: Writings about India in English 1765–2000,* 105.

8. Cited in Lillian Nayder, *Unequal Partners: Charles Dickens, Wilkie Collins, and Victorian Authorship,* 4.

9. Cited in Lillian Nayder, "Class Consciousness and the Indian Mutiny in Dickens's 'The Perils of Certain English Prisoners,'" 3.

10. Jaya Mehta, "English Romance; Indian Violence," 618. Subsequent references are cited by page in the text.

11. Tamar Heller, *Dead Secrets: Wilkie Collins and the Female Gothic,* 190. Subsequent references are cited by page in the text.

12. Albert D. Pionke, "Secreting Rebellion: From the Mutiny to the Moonstone," 124.

13. Carolyn G. Heilbrun, introduction to *The Moonstone,* 493n3.

14. Homi K. Bhabha, "The Commitment to Theory," 2388. Subsequent references are cited by page in the text.

15. [Geraldine Jewsbury], "Unsigned review of *The Moonstone,*" 106, in *The Moonstone,* ed. Steve Farmer, 544.

16. Frances M. Mannsaker, "East and West: Anglo-Indian Racial Attitudes as Reflected in Popular Fiction, 1890–1914," 37.

17. Sue Lonoff, *Wilkie Collins and His Victorian Readers: A Study in the Rhetoric of Authorship,* 226.

- 20 -

WILKIE COLLINS'S GWILT-Y CONSCIENCE
Gender and Colonialism in Armadale

MONICA M. YOUNG-ZOOK

> The colonialist is an exhibitionist, because his preoccupation with security makes him remind the native out loud that there he alone is master.
> —Franz Fanon

Gender and Colonialism

WILKIE COLLINS'S subversive 1864–1866 serial novel *Armadale* challenges several nineteenth-century norms about race, class, and gender. What seems novel in this narrative (all puns intended) is the way Collins uses his characters Ozias Midwinter and Lydia Gwilt, both class, gender, and racial hybrids, to sensationally subvert the ideals of British nationalism and undermine dominant Victorian racial and gender ideologies. Collins's sensation novel is slightly flawed and overdetermined, yet it represents an attempt to "speak the truth" about certain gendered expectations in a colonial context.[1] In this essay, I will use various psychoanalytical and postcolonial approaches to describe how *Armadale* engages with the way economic class becomes racialized, race becomes gendered, and traditional Victorian masculine and feminine gender roles implode to strengthen a Britain weakened by the profligacy of her patriarchal colonists.

While Lillian Nayder has suggested that Collins displaces colonial tensions onto sexual tensions, subverting a discourse about race into a discourse about gender, I suggest that such displacements are not necessary.[2] Postcolonial theorist Anne McClintock finds that Victorian colonials configured race as already gendered and class markers as already racialized. According to McClintock, neither of these configurations are transmuted acts of racial hostility or romantic affection but of aggression within a global power structure.[3] Building upon this work, I argue, however, that in *Armadale* Collins's class and racial Others are the most compelling characters and as such subvert standard Victorian colonial discourses while pointing out the flaws therein.

Among the flawed discourses Collins will attack are those constructing masculinity in this novel. Through the gender confusion of the British colonial landscape, Collins's *Armadale* traces shifts in masculine power from the hierarchical patriarchy of the colonial station to the more fraternal professional brotherhood that saves the protagonists of this novel. It is through the strong bonds of brotherhood that Ozias Midwinter shows his worth as partner to the jolly yet intellectually challenged Allan Armadale. His superior nature as a fraternal figure also constructs him as a proper love object for the adventuress, Lydia Gwilt. Through Collins's manipulation of gender and racial discourse, we find standard Victorian gender roles insufficient to explain the appeal of his more tightly focused characters. The subversion here is not of a racial trauma turned for solution to a romance, but rather a class trauma resolvable only by fraternal associations.

British Colonial Patriarchy and Hierarchy

The novel features five Allan Armadales. The first is the grandfather who disowns his son (named Allan) for Matthew Wrentmore, who takes the name Allan Armadale as a condition of his inheritance. The first son, who renames himself Fergus Ingleby, vengefully steals Ms. Blanchard, the bride of the second, with the help of a young forger who will return later in the novel as Lydia Gwilt. In reaction to the loss of both woman and property, the second Allan drowns the first and moves to Barbados, where he marries a girl of mixed African and British descent and has a son whom he names—Allan Armadale. The stolen bride, Mrs. Armadale née Blanchard, ensconces herself in a small British seaside town where she bears a son whom she names yet again Allan Armadale! So there are five eponymous characters: Armadale the *grand-père*, two Armadale fathers, and their two sons. This entire history is revealed to the murderer's son via a letter his father dictates on his deathbed to the attorney Alexander Neal and which is given to the boy upon his eighteenth birthday. In a shock of inherited guilt, the young man renames himself Ozias Midwinter and sets himself about the world, accidentally finding his stepbrother Allan Armadale.

The misadventures of the Armadale family among these imperial places invoke what McClintock refers to as "Anachronistic space." In *Imperial Leather,* McClintock explores the aspects of Victorian literature that were driven by an audience fixated "on origins, with genesis narratives, with archaeology, skulls, skeletons and fossils" (40). She suggests that in establishing national hierarchies, Victorian

Britain focused on the virtues of domesticity, remarking that "the verb 'to domesticate' is akin to 'dominate,'" referring to the etymology of the Latin "*Dominus,* lord of the *dominum,* the home." McClintock argues that the verb "to domesticate" in current usage also means "to civilize" (35). Her studies in the Victorian relationship between race and gender suggest that in the British colonies, the mission station became a threshold institution for transforming domesticity rooted in visible British gender and class roles into domesticity as "civilizing" and controlling a colonized people. Through increasingly violent rituals of domesticity, resources, animals, and people were wrested from their "natural" yet, ironically, "unreasonable" state of "savagery" and inducted through the domestic progress narrative into a hierarchical relation to white men (35). Cultures become "children" of other cultures, allowing a moral excuse for imperial intervention, domination, and correction of less-mechanized peoples.

Collins's hero, Midwinter, is a racial hybrid. His father is the British Allan Armadale but his mother is described by Collins as a "woman of the mixed blood of the European and the African race with the northern delicacy in the shape of her face and the Southern richness in its colour" (14). She is "in the prime of her beauty," with "large languid black eyes" that bring Alexander Neal, for the first time in his life, "to his knees, a conquered man" (14). Neal, a Scotsman, and a kind of hybrid between Englishmen and their marginalized Celtic forbearers, once smitten, marries her. For his complicity in her husband's crime as a witness to the deathbed confession of murder, he atones by marrying (and thereby domesticating) her, and also perversely by beating her son.

Midwinter guiltily believes that he deserves this mistreatment. Many critics such as Natalie Schroeder, Jenny Bourne Taylor, and Peter Thoms have noted Midwinter's "nerves" and his interpellation of his father's guilt that turns him into a colonial subject who carries the guilt of the violent crimes of the colonizer.[4] He also carries the Anglocentric guilt of his position within the British colonial schema of racial hybridity of the colonized. Midwinter says:

> My mother knew what had really happened on board the French timber-ship, and my stepfather knew what had really happened, and they were both well aware that the shameful secret which they would fain have kept from every living creature was a secret which would be one day revealed to me. There was no help for it—the confession was in the executor's hands, and there was I, an ill-conditioned brat, with my mother's Negro blood in my face, and my murdering father's passions in my heart, inheritor of their secret in spite of them! (74)

Midwinter appropriates his father's guilt for the murder committed a generation earlier, but ascribes it in part to his "negro blood" (74), conflating an exterior racial marker and an inherited guilt for his dead father's criminal past.

Through his guilt, Midwinter becomes a Lacanian split subject.[5] As a child, Midwinter knows only that he is being beaten and assumes Neal is beating him for his racial otherness. Upon reading the letter from his father, he learns of his father's criminality and links the beatings with both causes, the exterior of his darkened skin and the interior that is marked by knowledge of his father's guilt. This is the first transference Collins contains in his narrative—that of criminal colonial behavior to the racial marker for the colonial native. Lacan writes of transference that it "does not refer to any mysterious property of affect, and even when it reveals itself under the appearance of emotion, it only acquires meaning by virtue of the dialectical moment in which it is produced" (225). Collins's transference is here driven by the Victorian colonial narrative that configures men of color as inherently flawed in their performance of proper British masculinity.

What makes McClintock's work important in reference to *Armadale* and Ozias Midwinter is that she associates gendered subject positions within the British Empire to racialized subject positions. She argues that "the rhetoric of *gender* was used to make increasingly refined distinctions among the different *races*. The white race was figured as the male of the species and the black race as the female" (55). Collins's racial hybrid Midwinter is given a number of feminine traits. As cited previously, Taylor mentions that "'Nerves' are a key term in defining Midwinter." She also points out that his "sensitivity" is "put forward in gender terms rather than class ones: his 'sensitive feminine organisation' coexists with resilience while remaining the sign of vulnerability; anxiety continually hovers on the brink of *hysteria*" (163). As a grown man, Midwinter is further split between his performance of British masculine business capability and aspects associated with his racial otherness: mysticism, precognitive dreams, visions, ascetic choices, and his "nerves"—his sensitivity to Allan and their troubled relationship. Midwinter, in carrying his own guilt of the past, also bears the guilt of inappropriately gendered behavior in his own performance of British manhood.

This feminizing of Midwinter ironically provides a possibility of sidestepping the Armadale masculine legacy of criminality, while allowing him an "Otherness" that corresponds with Gwilt's gender transgressions. In the Lacanian schema of desire, the subject desires the Other, the object which stands in as a "lack" in the subject. The Other also correlates to the unconscious Other, that part of the self that correlates to and communes with the reflection of one desired. Midwinter's effeminate masculinity and Lydia Gwilt's masculine femininity are both marked with that sense of "Otherness." Collins's narrative allows the hybrid hero son Midwinter to overturn the Lacanian Law of the Father in rebuking the Armadale legacy and building a fraternity that will eventually resolve the sins of the fathers.

That a landed, propertied gentleman like Allan Armadale is threatened by Lydia Gwilt suggests three things. First, the older squirearchy was built on paternal relationships that were threatened by the guilt of successive generations' mishandling of patriarchal power in England, Europe, and in the colonies. Secondly, though Collins's sympathies in this and other novels tend toward the bourgeois, the loss of these landed gentlemen who could maintain huge properties and the tenants who lived on them is an ambivalent loss configured through the effects on the simpleminded but sympathetic Allan. Third, and most important, those who know how to manage these estates are not the owners, but professional men of a different class altogether—a brotherhood of friends and professionals who will assist Allan with his patriarchal duties.

Liberty and Fraternity

British masculinity dictated that British men meet and domesticate "savage" people, and narratives frequently depict the British as bringers of order and proper Christian virtues. In *Armadale,* though, the British presence carries the criminal element usually allotted to the "savage" peoples of non-British countries and the only hope for redemption is in the mixed-blood son, Midwinter, and his particular brand of hybrid masculinity. Collins seems to construct his British heir, Allan, as the hero of *Armadale,* but the novel is driven by the danger the British fathers invoke with their murderous behavior and its effect upon their repatriated sons. Collins seems to be subverting his Anglocentric narrative with details of the hybrid characters. Midwinter's talents render him antithetical to the anxieties of miscegenation that appear to haunt Collins's other novels through characters like the wandering Indians of *The Moonstone* or Count Fosco in *The Woman in White*. Midwinter possesses the ability, awareness, thoughtfulness, and worldly experience Allan requires in managing the estates and his life and is the only friend Allan trusts.

Likewise, Midwinter's half-Barbadian mother is described as all loveliness and grace when Neal meets her at Wildbad. Her exotic mix of cultures, her innocence of her first husband's murder of Fergus Ingleby, and Matthew Wrentmore's mistreatment of her all make for a sympathetic character, though one so malleable as to allow her son to be beaten by her next husband. Collins's only critiques of her focus on her questionable choices of British husbands—the first doesn't love her and the second mistreats her innocent son. Neither man is described sympathetically, though Collins's portrait of the woman is as a benevolent and misused woman of virtue, grace, and beauty. Even the legally punctilious Alexander Neal is marked by a hardness of character. In this novel, the criminal evil comes through the British presence in the West Indies and Madiera, where Ms. Blanchard's family had repaired for reasons of her father's health.

Homi Bhabha writes that "Terms of cultural engagement, whether antagonistic or affiliative, are produced performatively. The representation of difference must not be hastily read as the reflection of pre-given ethnic or cultural traits set in the fixed tablet of tradition. The social articulation of difference, from the minority perspective, is a complex, on-going negotiation that seeks to authorize cultural hybridities that emerge in moments of historical transformation."[6] Collins participates in this transformative effect by returning the murdered Allan Armadale's son to inherit an estate, and the murderer's son to be beaten and starved. Collins subverts Victorian cultural discourse and his own narrative, though, by writing the young Allan Armadale as a happy-go-lucky but inept young man and the feminized racial hybrid Ozias Midwinter as an intelligent, aware, thoughtful, and capable presence who saves Allan from himself. This split between the next generation is important in the question of colonial metonymy through presence, but Ozias Midwinter is a fraternal presence, not a paternal one. All the fathers and surrogate fathers in the novel have died through misadventure. The paternal subject position, so tightly linked to colonial enterprises, is here either criminal or ineffectual. This "anachronistic space" hence becomes less about determining origins than repairing the fates of the surviving Armadale sons.

Collins problematizes the behavior of British landowners in the colonies and undermines the whole ideal of the British Empire not only by its affects on the colonized people themselves, but on Britain as a whole. Collins's subversion of the British colonial ideal suggests that he did not believe that the world is well ruled by British men. The colonial hybrid, Midwinter, with his half-sketched education and natural innate ability is more capable than Allan, and the symbiotic exchange of Midwinter's wits and abilities for Armadale's financial protection saves these brothers. The danger to British nationality and manhood in this novel comes not from the savage places that would contaminate colonizers with an otherness that weakens manhood, but a corrupt imperial manhood that threatens Britain with its recklessness. Of Collins's non-British characters in this novel, one is its loveliest woman—Midwinter's mother—and the other is its most loyal and capable man—Midwinter himself. Thus the novel sublimates these critiques into questions of friendship and proper romantic ties while simultaneously suggesting that the ideal of masculinity is not reckless and patriarchal but collective and fraternal, and not necessarily only British.

According to McClintock, the situation of class relationships within familial relationships was one epitomized in bourgeois writings about the working class and natives as "children" to be managed and reared into progressive society, trained out of non-British sexual and social habits, and taught the domestic talents that gave middle-class British women their dominion over the home. Imperial nineteenth-century Europe had its own interpretation in viewing primitive cultures as children of their more mechanized British counterparts. She also writes of a British imperial epistemology that positioned the Caucasian male in a paternal relationship to those they colonized (44). In a continuance of his ambivalent handling of paternal action and privilege, Collins's hybrid son Midwinter, brother to the Armadale and Blanchard heir, is Allan Armadale's only hope for success in his lordship over his estate Thorpe-Ambrose, and his only protection against the wiles of Lydia Gwilt.

In fact, if there is an ideal proposed by this narrative, it is of the kind of professional brotherhoods remarked upon by masculinities theorists James Sussman and Eli Adams.[7] These two critics suggest a shift in masculine performance from the strictly paternal to the fraternal as a natural outcome of the French Revolution and the committee-driven realm of scientific exploration and government solution-gathering associated with the work of Prince Albert in the nation's efforts toward medical and scientific solutions to complicated social problems. Resolving fraternity in this way posits the best brother, Midwinter, as the only proper love object for the novel's great adventuress, Lydia Gwilt.

Lydia Gwilt and the Racialization of Class

Much of *Armadale* is narrated by its antagonist, Lydia Gwilt. Whereas many critics focus on Gwilt's "psychosis" and "criminality"[8] or Midwinter's "sensitivity," "nerves," "loyalty," or "guilt,"[9] few critics except Lillian Nayder situate these characteristics within the political colonial context in which the novel takes place. Nayder's work with *Armadale* points out the way Collins conflates the otherness of race with the otherness of gender, situating Lydia Gwilt as a conduit for the novel's imperial and patriarchal guilt. Nayder argues that in the novel, the rage of the colonized peoples is translated to sexual jealousy, misplaced onto the anger of equally powerless women. I agree that Collins's ambivalent castigation of the colonial enterprise investigates the way women, specifically his adventuress Lydia Gwilt, are misused by colonial patriarchy. Nayder also writes that

> Collins wryly suggests that a wife's proper behavior may kill her. However, such insights do not keep him from sacrificing the emancipated women in his novel to an Imperial cause. Transforming them into docile and subservient figures, while also representing their subordination as natural and appropriate, he defuses the threat of native insurrection and assuages his sense of imperial guilt.[10]

I question, however, whether Collins represents Gwilt's subordination as "natural." Collins does not present her subordination to her husband, or anyone for that matter, as a natural state for Gwilt. Indeed, it is against Gwilt's subordination to traditional family structures through her love for (and marriage to) Ozias

Midwinter that she continuously struggles and by which she is eventually destroyed. Collins uses her inability to be docile and subservient to castigate the colonial projects, both abroad and at home, that would require her to be so. His authorial choice to give her half the novel bespeaks an appreciation of a character who will not conform to Victorian feminine ideals, while exploring and castigating the pressures that lead to her death.

Nayder focuses on Collins's equation of race and gender as an otherness that works in similar ways in this novel; building on this position, I must add the role of class through which Gwilt is racialized. Gwilt is introduced early in the novel as an orphaned English girl "of barely twelve years old, a marvel of precocious ability" (25), who becomes through her mistreatment an "adventuress of the worst class" (319). Matthew Wrentmore, the murderer who leaves the letter to his son, describes her even as a child to be a worthy adversary, suggesting that "No creature more innately deceitful and more innately pitiless ever walked the earth" (25). Yet he neglects to mention that her early efforts came at the behest of her young mistress, Ms. Blanchard, and that to Lydia, in the position of a friendless young girl employed halfway around the globe, her mistresses' orders were law. Lydia's colonial mistress requires Lydia's dissemblance to further her romantic project and must invoke a racialized colonial power relationship with her maid that relies on a colonial setting in order to achieve her designs.

Collins's Gwilt has been long troubled by abuse and necessity. Beginning life as a "beaten and half-starved child in the country" (25), she is appropriated by Ms. Blanchard because of her beauty and participates in the disastrous letter forging which leads to the murder of Fergus Ingleby. Afterward, she turns up at school where a teacher falls in love with her and, in a fit of shame and despair at his inappropriate protection of his student's virtue, shoots himself. Her reputation forever marred, she retires to a convent but does not take the veil. Left to her own devices, she falls among bad associates. They introduce her to a Mr. Waldron, who in the course of their relationship weds, beats, and abuses her. After her husband's untimely death by poison, of which she is accused, she is put on trial but released to manage as best she can but now penniless, friendless, and jobless.

Victorian Britain had no sufficient place of agency for its Lydia Gwilts. Women of talent but no means were to marry as best they could, become governesses, or open schools by which they would monitor their students' virtue. Gwilt's need for other professional options links her to racialized groups who were also denied the fruits of British national success and asked to endure their marginalized status with "goodness" and humility. Attempts to "civilize"—to domesticate—Lydia and the guilt she carries are the only hope the brothers have for their future safety. Yet, Collins presents the false binary of Lydia's choices—scheming temptress or virtuous housewife—as a pressure that destroys her and threatens the surviving Armadales.

Collins is at his most subversive in the racialization of Lydia's class situation. His narrative focuses on Lydia's plight and suggests an understanding of the social position of other racial groups and the class of public women (including working-class women in the public milieu and prostitutes). McClintock argues that the similarities link these two through similar subject positions. She writes that

> Prostitutes visibly transgressed the middle-class boundary between private and public, paid work and unpaid work, and in consequence were figured as "white Negroes" inhabiting anachronistic space, their 'racial' atavism anatomically marked by regressive signs: "Darwin's ear," exaggerated posteriors, unruly hair and other sundry "primitive" stigmata. (56)

Lydia Gwilt's association with the cruel and grasping Mrs. Oldershaw (a procuress) and her abortionist-physician associate, Dr. Downward, suggests an association with, if not an actual past in, prostitution. Her designs to marry Allan Armadale for his fortune bespeak the same—an exchange of sex for money. According to Victorian semiotics of dress and grooming, the "unruly" color of her flaming red hair also hints of some unspoken sin. According to Galia Ofek, in her essay included in this collection, "Gwilt's flamboyant hair and character (a poisoner, a forger, and a bigamist) were both a statement of unconventionality which challenged prevalent models of femininity on aesthetic, literary and social levels" (112). Gwilt's guilt, however, derives specifically from a class and gender position that led to her participation in the forgery of the letter for Ms. Blanchard. Ms. Blanchard then sets in motion the deceitful marriage to one Allan Armadale and his murder by the previously named Matthew Wrentmore. While Blanchard is protected by her wealth, Gwilt's participation in this crime removes her completely from any respectable or profitable position in society. She becomes an easily motivated accomplice for Mrs. Oldershaw and Dr. Downward, who eventually conspires with her to poison Allan while under Downward's care in a sanitarium. In this novel, unlike in *The Moonstone* and *The Woman in White*, it is not the racial hybrid (in this case, Midwinter) whose return represents a threat to England, but the class hybrid Lydia Gwilt. Yet by situating Gwilt's criminality in her class constructions, Collins effects a transference of her rage at her racialized class position into a love relationship that still cannot contain her un-British and unwomanly passion.

Thus, Gwilt is also a gender hybrid. She has her public persona—the epitome of feminine charm and wiles—and her private plans. Her cleverness is covered by a class drag as she passes herself off as an insipid governess. Her exquisite performance of middle-class domestic hyperfemininity belies her wits and abilities, rendering her yet more compelling and more dangerous to the Armadale brothers.

Both the way Collins depicts her and her letters of logistical plotting and planning to Mrs. Oldershaw reveal Gwilt's transgression of normative Victorian womanhood. She is not fainting in love to anyone, but planning and organizing a mercenary marriage to, and murder of, Allan Armadale.

The journal entry she writes upon her love marriage to Midwinter bespeaks the attempted closure of her masculine, plotting self to a domestic femininity Victorians would link to a sense of womanly virtue. It reads *"Sunday August 10th*—The eve of my wedding day—I close and lock this book, never to write in it, never to open it again. I have won the great victory; I have trampled my own wickedness underfoot. I am innocent" (504). Gwilt's loss of focus for monetary desire in lieu of domestic desire unhinges her plans to murder one of the Armadales; her happiness now rests in loving Midwinter. Gwilt, however, writes of a concern that "any unconscious disclosure of the truth escapes me in the close intimacy that now unites" her with Midwinter. She attributes this to "an unutterable Something left by the horror of my past life" (482). As a reformed vixen, she loses half of her drive, her desire flattens, and her character cannot adjust itself to this half-life where before there was such fire and brilliance. Collins associates Gwilt's not being suited to or satisfied by quiet domesticity with a criminal past inaugurated by her cleverness. She does not begin as a mad, scribbling woman, but ends up as such through the combined forces of "goodness" as a Victorian erasure of feminine identity and agency. As closely linked as domesticity is to British womanhood, her difficulty becomes not only a failure to properly perform her gender, but also her nationality. Hence the improperly gendered woman is an improperly British one—realized also by her lack of domestic desire.

Nayder sees Lydia's transgressions as a misplaced native aggression of racial rage onto gendered romantic aggression. The transference Collins evokes, however, from class anxiety to racialization, is directly linked to his narrator's appreciation of clever women and a castigation of a social system that will use them but give them no place in the social order. Collins grants his narrator a lavish appreciation of this racialized woman; yet in rendering her and her lover, Midwinter, as sympathetic characters, Collins points out both the nature of an already gendered racial colonial space and the way class interacts with gender to open another racialized space. This narrator, in his expression of mercy for her, frames Gwilt as someone to be pitied for her circumstances rather than despised for the character they produce.

Collins's relationship to that narrator is ambiguous; he wrote in the 1866 preface to the novel that readers may find that

> Armadale oversteps, in more than one direction, the narrow limits within which they are supposed to restrict the development of modern fiction—if they can. . . .

> Estimated by the claptrap morality of the present day, this may be a very daring book. Judged by the Christian morality that is of all time, it is only a book that is daring enough to speak the truth. (Preface)

This narrative effect is of course resolved upon Lydia Gwilt's death to save Midwinter from the poisoned room she had prepared for Allan. If Collins values his adventuress so highly, though, why does he kill her off? Because he has to if he is to "speak the truth." If his point is that the gendered national and colonial structures in which his characters are working are deeply flawed, there has to be a price. He cannot ask it of his hero, who must end happily ever after, but he asks it of the colonial hybrid, Midwinter, and he certainly asks it of his transgressive and highly problematic antagonist. Gwilt must be sacrificed in order for this novel to speak its truths. She cannot abide domesticity, has a criminal past that she cannot escape, and if she could be "reformed," within the context of the novel, not only would the novel lose its integrity, she would as well. She provides far too much insight into the problems of the Victorian colonial class, gender, and national schema for Collins to ruin her in that way. She speaks too loudly as a carrier for the guilt of the old paternal order that is being castigated and eliminated in the novel as an expression of Collins's ambivalence about the misuse and mishandling of colonial projects, misused classless women, and the similarities between these performances of British nationhood.

NOTES

1. Collins, in the 1866 preface to *Armadale* (Dover, 1977), claims that the novel is "daring enough to speak the truth." I will further discuss this claim later in my essay. All references are to this edition and are cited by page in the text.
2. See Lillian Nayder, "Agents of Empire in *The Woman in White*" and her chapter "Reverse Colonization and Imperial Guilt," in *Wilkie Collins*.
3. Anne McClintock, *Imperial Leather: Race, Gender and Sexuality in the Colonial Contest*. All further references are cited by page in the text.
4. Natalie Schroeder, "*Armadale:* 'A Book that Is Daring Enough to Speak the Truth,'" 5–17; Jenny Bourne Taylor, "*Armadale:* The Sensitive Subject as Palimpsest," 171; and Peter Thoms, *The Windings of the Labyrinth: Quest and Structure in the Major Novels of Wilkie Collins,* 119.
5. Jacques Lacan, *Ecrits: A Selection*. All further references are to this edition and are cited by page in the text. To Jacques Lacan, every child at a certain age realizes that he or she possesses both an interior and exterior self—one that feels, thinks, and watches and another that is perceived in its actions and agency. He calls this the "Mirror Stage" of the child's development. This develops from the child's understanding of interdictions on behavior upon growing out of infancy—the "Law of the Father"—resulting in a "Split Subject."
6. Homi Bhabba, *The Location of Culture,* 2.

7. See both James Eli Adams, in *Dandies and Desert Saints: Styles of Victorian Masculinities,* and Herbert Sussman, in *Victorian Masculinities: Manhood and Masculine Poetics in Early Victorian Literature and Art.*

8. Jonathan Craig Tutor, "Lydia Gwilt: Wilkie Collins's Satanic, Sirenic Psychotic," 37–55.

9. See Schroeder, "*Armadale:* 'A Book that Is Daring Enough to Speak the Truth'"; Taylor, "*Armadale:* The Sensitive Subject as Palimpsest"; and Thoms, *The Windings of the Labyrinth: Quest and Structure in the Major Novels of Wilkie Collins.*

10. Nayder, *Wilkie Collins,* 115.

WORKS CITED

Nineteenth-Century Periodicals

"Advertisement." *East London Observer* (November 26, 1864): 8.
[Austin, Alfred]. "Our Novels: The Fast School." *Temple Bar* 29 (May 1870): 177–94.
———. "Our Novels: The Sensational School." *Temple Bar* 29 (June 1870): 410–24.
———. "Our Novels: The Simple School." *Temple Bar* 29 (July 1870): 488–503.
"Authority." *Punch* (May 5, 1866): 183.
Banks, Linneas. "The Effingham." *Era* (October 20, 1867): 14.
Beard, Nathaniel. "Some Recollections of Yesterday." *Temple Bar* 102 (July 1894): 315–39.
[Black, William]. "Flirts and Flirtation." *Temple Bar* 26 (July 1869): 58–67.
[Bright, Henry Arthur]. Review of *Halves, and other Tales*, by James Payn. *Athenaeum* 2516 (January 15, 1876): 86.
———. Review of *Mad Dumaresq*, by Florence Marryat (Mrs. Ross Church) [later Lean]. *Athenaeum* 2406 (December 6, 1873): 729.
Buchanan, Robert. "Charles Reade." *Harper's New Monthly Magazine* 69, issue 412 (September 1884): 600–6.
[Butler, Arthur John]. Review of *Beauchamp's Career*, by George Meredith. *Athenaeum* 2514 (January 1, 1876): 18–19.
———. Review of *Fair to See*, by Laurence W[illiam] M[axwell]. Lockhart. *Athenaeum* 2299 (November 18, 1871): 653–54.
———. Review of *The Golden Bait*, by H[enry] Holl. *Athenaeum* 2259 (February 11, 1871): 173–74.
———. Review of *The History of a Week*, by L[ucy] B[ethia] Walford [née Colquhoun]. *Athenaeum* 3050 (April 10, 1886): 486.
———. Review of *Lady Judith*, by Justin M'Carthy. *Athenaeum* 2288 (September 2, 1871): 303.
———. Review of *Vanessa*, by the author of *Thomasina* [Margaret Agnes Paul (née Colville)]. *Athenaeum* 2455 (November 14, 1874): 636.
[Candy, (?)]. Review of *Caught in the Toils*, by Mrs. [Robert] Mackenzie Daniel. *Athenaeum* 2273 (May 20, 1871): 621.

[Chorley, Henry Fothergill]. Review of *Armadale,* by [William] Wilkie Collins. *Athenaeum* 2014 (June 2, 1866): 732–33.

———. Review of *Griffith Gaunt: or, Jealousy,* by Charles Reade. *Athenaeum* 2037 (November 10, 1866): 602–3.

———. Review of *Kingsford,* by the author of *Son and Heir* [Emily Spender]. *Athenaeum* 2037 (November 10, 1866): 603.

———. Review of *No Name,* by [William] Wilkie Collins. *Athenaeum* 1836 (January 13, 1863): 10–11.

[Collyer, Robert]. Review of *Checkmate,* by J[oseph Thomas] S[heridan] Le Fanu. *Athenaeum* 2260 (February 18, 1871): 207.

———. Review of *Fernyhurst Court,* by the author of *Stone Edge* [Frances Parthenope Verney (née Nightingale)]. *Athenaeum* 2288 (September 2, 1871): 303.

———. Review of *Jabez Oliphant; or, the Modern Prince,* [by John Holme Burrow]. *Athenaeum* 2220 (May 14, 1870): 640.

[Cosens, Frederick Williams]. Review of *Margarita, or the Queen of Night,* by Messrs Fernandez and Gonzales [Manuel Fernandez y Gonzalez]. *Athenaeum* 2211 (March 12, 1870): 351–52.

Dallas, Eneas Sweetland. "Lady Audley's Secret." *The Times,* November 18, 1862, 4. Repr. in Braddon, Mary. *Lady Audley's Secret,* ed. Natalie Houston. Peterborough, Ontario: Broadview, 2003.

[De Mattos, Katharine (née Stevenson)]. Review of *Like Lucifer,* by Denzil Vane [F. DuTertre]. *Athenaeum* 3059 (June 12, 1886): 775.

[Doran, John]. Review of *Alfred Hagart's Household,* by Alexander Smith. *Athenaeum* 1996 (January 27, 1866): 130.

———. Review of *For Ever and Ever: a Drama of Life,* by Florence Marryat [Church; later Lean]. *Athenaeum* 2032 (October 6, 1866): 427–28.

———. Review of *Thyra Gascoigne,* by Mrs. Edmund [Elizabeth Janet] Jenings. *Athenaeum* 1881 (November 14, 1863): 638–39.

[Eden, Lena]. Review of *Aurora Floyd,* by M[ary] E[lizabeth] Braddon [later Maxwell]. *Athenaeum* 1840 (January 31, 1863): 144–55.

———. Review of *East Lynne: A Story of Modern Life,* by Mrs. Henry [Ellen] Wood [née Price]. *Athenaeum* 1772 (October 12, 1861): 473–74.

———. Review of *Lady Audley's Secret,* 2nd ed., by M[ary] E[lizabeth] Braddon [(later Maxwell)]. *Athenaeum* 1826 (October 25, 1862): 525–26.

———. Review of *A Point of Honour,* by the author of *The Morals of May Fair,* &c [Annie Edward[e]s [née Edwards]. *Athenaeum* 1844 (February 28, 1863): 291–92.

———. Review of *Which Does She Love?* by Colburn Mayne. *Athenaeum* 1797 (April 5, 1862): 461–62.

[Hinton, James]. "The Fairy Land of Science." *Cornhill* 5 (1862): 36–42.

"Iota." *East London Observer* (December 3, 1864): 5.

[Jackson, Thomas Watson]. Review of *Man and Wife,* by [William] Wilkie Collins. *Athenaeum* 2228 (July 9, 1870): 45–46.

James, Henry. "Miss Braddon." *The Nation* 1 (November 9, 1865): 593–94.

[Jeaffreson, John Cordy]. Review of *Darkest before Dawn,* by the author of *The Cruelest Wrong of All. Athenaeum* 1933 (November 12, 1864): 633–34.

———. Review of *Foul Play,* by Charles Reade and Dion[ysius Lardner] Bou[r]cicault. *Athenaeum* 2119 (June 6, 1868): 792.

———. Review of *Janet's Home,* [by Anna Maria (Annie) Keary]. *Athenaeum* 1883 (November

28, 1863): 716.
———. Review of *John Marchmont's Legacy*, by the author of *Lady Audley's Secret* [Mary Elizabeth Braddon (later Maxwell)]. *Athenaeum* 1885 (December 12, 1863): 792–93.
———. Review of *Lady Flavia*, by the author of *Lord Lynn's Wife* [John Berwick Harwood]. *Athenaeum* 1969 (July 22, 1865): 110.
———. Review of *Lord Oakburn's Daughters*, by Mrs. H[enry (Ellen)] Wood [née Price]. *Athenaeum* 1927 (October 1, 1864): 428–29.
———. Review of *A Lost Name*, by [Joseph Thomas] Sheridan Le Fanu. *Athenaeum* 2115 (May 9, 1868): 657.
———. Review of *The Notting Hill Mystery*, compiled by Charles Felix from the papers of the late R. Henderson, Esq. *Athenaeum* 1955 (April 15, 1865): 520.
———. Review of *On the Recognition of the Southern Confederation*, by James Spence. *Athenaeum* 1817 (August 23, 1862): 232–33
———. Review of *Piebald: A Novel*, by R. F[rederick] Boyle. *Athenaeum* 2092 (November 30, 1867): 721.
———. Review of *The Trail of the Serpent; or, the Secret of the Heath*, by M[ary] E[lizabeth] Braddon [later Maxwell]. *Athenaeum* 1743 (March 23, 1861): 393–94.
———. Review of *Viola*, by the author of *My Son's Wife* [Emily Jolly]. *Athenaeum* 2190 (October 16, 1869): 494–95.
———. Review of *Wondrous Strange*, by the author of *Mabel* [Mrs. C. J. (Emma) Newby (née Barry)]. *Athenaeum* 1919 (August 6, 1864): 177–78.
———. Review of *The Wyvern Mystery: A Novel*, by J[oseph Thomas] S[heridan] Le Fanu. *Athenaeum* 2187 (September 25, 1869): 398–99.
[Jewsbury, Geraldine Endsor]. Review of *All in the Dark*, by G. [sic] J[oseph Thomas] Sheridan Le Fanu. *Athenaeum* 2018 (June 30, 1866): 860.
———. Review of *Altogether Wrong*, by the author of *The World's Furniture*. *Athenaeum* 1867 (August 8, 1863): 172.
———. Review of *The Cabinet Secret*, by Leigh Spencer. *Athenaeum* 2072 (July 13, 1867): 44.
———. Review of *Church and Chapel*, by the author of *High Church* [Frederick William Robinson]. *Athenaeum* 1863 (July 11, 1863): 46–47.
———. Review of *Cometh Up as a Flower: An Autobiography*, [by Rhoda Broughton]. *Athenaeum* 2060 (April 20, 1867): 514–15.
———. Review of *Common Sense*, by Mrs. C. J. [Emma] Newby [(née Barry)]. *Athenaeum* 1995 (January 20, 1866): 89.
———. Review of *Dacia Singleton*, by the author of *Altogether Wrong*, &c. *Athenaeum* 2040 (December 1, 1866): 710.
———. Review of *Dangerous Connexions*, by C[harles] Gibbon. *Athenaeum* 1920 (August 13, 1864): 209.
———. Review of *Emilia in England*, by George Meredith. *Athenaeum* 1905 (April 30, 1864): 609–10.
———. Review of *Guy Deverell*, by J[oseph Thomas] S[heridan] Le Fanu. *Athenaeum* 1982 (October 21, 1865): 536.
———. Review of *Hever Court*, by R[obert] Arthur Arnold. *Athenaeum* 2098 (January 11, 1868): 54.
———. Review of *The Lady's Mile*, [by Mary Elizabeth Braddon (later Maxwell)]. *Athenaeum* 2014 (June 2, 1866): 733.
———. Review of *Lynn of the Craggs*, by Charlotte Smith. *Athenaeum* 1947 (February 18, 1865): 233.

———. Review of *Miss Forrester: A Novel*, by Mrs. [Annie] Edward[e]s [née Edwards]. *Athenaeum* 1980 (October 7, 1865): 466.

———. Review of *Miss Jane, the Bishop's Daughter*, by John [Berwick] Harwood. *Athenaeum* 2066 (June 1, 1867): 720–21.

———. Review of *The Moonstone: A Romance*, by [William] Wilkie Collins. *Athenaeum* 2126 (July 25, 1868): 106.

———. Review of *Nature's Nobleman*, by the author of *Rachel's Secret* [Eliza Stephenson (née Tabor)]. *Athenaeum* 2145 (December 5, 1868): 750.

———. Review of *Olive Blake's Good Work: A Novel*, by John Cordy Jeaffreson. *Athenaeum* 1788 (February 1, 1862): 149–50.

———. Review of *One against the World; or, Reuben's War: A Novel*, by John Saunders. *Athenaeum* 1971 (August 5, 1865): 179–80.

———. Review of *Stella*, by Mrs. [Mary] Bennett. *Athenaeum* 1910 (June 4, 1864): 773–74.

———. Review of *Uncle Silas*, by Sheridan Le Fanu. *Athenaeum* 7 (January 1865): 16–17.

———. Review of *Woman against Woman*, by Florence Marryat (Mrs. Ross Church) [later Lean]. *Athenaeum* 199 (February 17, 1866): 233.

Jex-Blake, Sophia. "Speech for Admission to the Royal Infirmary of Edinburgh, 1871." In *The Englishwoman's Review* (April 1871), on *Women of Hastings and St. Leonards*. Web site by Helena Wojtczak, January 16, 2005. http://www.hastingspress.co.uk/history/19/sjbspeech.htm.

Linton, Lynn Eliza. "The Girl of the Period." *Saturday Review* 25 (1868): 339–40.

[Lush, William]. Review of *The Author's Daughter*, by Catherine Ellen Spence. *Athenaeum* 2138 (October 17, 1868): 494.

———. Review of *The Girls of Feversham*, by Florence Marryat (Mrs. Ross Church) [later Lean]. *Athenaeum* 2161 (March 27, 1869): 432.

———. Review of *Lucretia; or, the Heroine of the Nineteenth Century*, by the author of *The Owlet of Owlstone Edge* [Francis Edward Paget]. *Athenaeum* 2139 (October 24, 1868): 527–28.

———. Review of *The Man of Mark*, by the author of *Richard Langdon* [Janet Leith Story (née Maughan)]. *Athenaeum* 2027 (September 1, 1866): 266.

———. Review of *Married: A Tale*, by Mrs. [C. J. (Emma) Newby (née Barry)]. *Athenaeum* 2172 (June 12, 1869): 791–92.

———. Review of *Mrs. Hardcastle's Adventures*, by Lady Charles [Harriet Frances Thynne (née Bagot)]. *Athenaeum* 2165 (April 24, 1869): 565–66.

———. Review of *Never—For Ever*, by Russell Gray [Eleanor Frances Le Fanu]. *Athenaeum* 2085 (October 12, 1867): 460–61.

MacCarthy, Justin. "Novels with a Purpose." *Westminster Review* 26 (1864): 24–49.

[Maddyn, Daniel Owen]. Review of *Basil: A Story of Modern Life*, by W[illiam] Wilkie Collins. *Athenaeum* 1322 (December 4 1852): 1322–23.

[Mansel, Henry L.]. "Sensation Novels." *Quarterly Review* 113, no. 226 (April 1863): 482–514. January 17, 2004. http://gaslight.mtroyal.ca/sensnovl.htm.>

———. "Sensation Novels." *Quarterly Review* 113 (April 1863): 481–514. Excerpt in *Sensationalism and the Sensation* Debate, edited by Andrew Maunder, 1:32–56. *Varieties of Women's Sensation Fiction*. 6 vols. London: Pickering and Chatto, 2004.

[Noll, Theo]. Review of *Florence Manvers*, by Selina Bunbury. *Athenaeum* 1963 (June 10, 1865): 777–78.

Oliphant, Margaret. "The Byways of Literature: Reading for the Million." Blackwood's 84 (August 1858): 200–16. http://www.bodley.ox.ac.uk/cgi-bin/ilej/image1.pl?item=page&

seq=1&size=1&id=bm.1858.8.x.84.514.x.200.
———. *Salem Chapel.* New York: Garland Publishing, 1976.
———. "Sensation Novels." *Blackwood's Edinburgh Magazine* 91 (May 1862): 564–84.
———. "Novels." *Blackwood's Edinburgh Magazine* 102 (September 1867): 257–80.
Playbill. *The Black Doctor.* 1861. The British Library Playbills 397: Royal Effingham Saloon.
[Rae, W. Fraser]. "Sensational Novelists: Miss Braddon." *North British Review* 43 (September 1865): 180–204.
Review of *Cometh Up as a Flower. The Times,* June 6, 1867, 9.
Review of *The Master of Rylands,* by Mrs. G. Lewis [Lucy A.] Leeds. *Athenaeum* 3224 (August 10, 1889): 187.
Review of *Not Wisely but Too Well. Atheneaum* 2088 (November 2, 1867): 569.
Review of *Not Wisely but Too Well* and *Cometh Up as a Flower. The Spectator,* October 19, 1867, 1172–74.
Review of *Pauline,* by L[ucy] B[ethia] Walford [(née Colquhoun)]. *Athenaeum* 2607 (October 13, 1877): 465.
Review of *Vixen,* by Mary Elizabeth Braddon. *The Academy,* March 15, 1879, 233.
Review of *Vixen,* by Mary Elizabeth Braddon. *Athenaeum,* 2679 (March 1, 1879): 275.
Review of *Vixen,* by Mary Elizabeth Braddon. *Saturday Review,* March 1, 1879, 280–82.
Review of *Young Musgrave,* by Mrs. [Margaret] Oliphant, [(née Wilson)]. *Athenaeum* 2616 (December 15, 1877): 769–70.
[Romer, Robert]. Review of *Gwendoline's Harvest,* by the author of *Lost Sir Massingberd* [James Payn]. *Athenaeum* 2220 (May 14, 1870): 640–41.
———. Review of *Hilary St. Ives,* by William Harrison Ainsworth. *Athenaeum* 2228 (July 9, 1870): 47.
———. Review of *The Three Brothers,* by Mrs. [Margaret] Oliphant, [(née Wilson)]. *Athenaeum* 2229 (July 16, 1870): 78.
[Rumsey, Almaric (?)]. Review of *Denis Donne: A Novel,* by A[nnie Hall] Thomas [later Cudlip]. *Athenaeum* 1920 (August 13, 1864): 209.
———. Review of *Gaspar Trenchard: A Novel,* by [Samuel] Bracebridge Hemyng. *Athenaeum* 1937 (December 10, 1864): 781–82.
———. Review of *Percy Talbot,* by George Graham. *Athenaeum* 1945 (February 4, 1865): 160.
———. Review of *Sedgely Court: A Tale,* by the author of *Fanny Hervey* [Mrs. Stirling]. *Athenaeum* 1950 (March 11, 1865): 347.
———. Review of *Veronique: A Romance,* by Florence Marryat (Mrs. Ross Church) [later Lean]. *Athenaeum* 2186 (September 18, 1869): 367–68.
———. Review of *A Woman Against the World: A Novel,* [by William Gayer Starbuck]. *Athenaeum* 1911 (June 11, 1864): 804–5.
Teilleux. "Triple Infanticide." *Journal of Mental Science* 24 (1867): 555–57.
Unsigned Article. "Clitoridectomy." *British Medical Journal* 2 (1866): 664–65.
———. "Death from Starvation and Exposure." *East London Observer,* December 3, 1864: 2.
———. "Dr. Forbes Winslow's Evidence in the Townley Case." Quoted in the *Journal of Mental Science* 14 (1864): 295–97.
———. "Poisoning by Lead." *Shoreditch Observer,* November 26, 1864, 8.
———. "The Season and Local Charities." *East London Observer,* December 24, 1864, 2.
———. "The Theatres & c." *Era,* October 30, 1864, 10.
———. "Trade Murder or How to Expend Our Redundant Women." *East London Observer,* November 27, 1864, 6. S.
Unsigned Review. "The Drama that Never Fails." *Bioscope,* September 7, 1916, 923.

_____. "Dramatised Versions of Novels: *East Lynne* at the Surrey." *Sunday Times*, February 11, 1866, 8.
_____. "'Lady Audley.' On The Stage." *London Review*, March 7, 1863, 244–45.
_____. "Minor Theatres." *Era*, December 11, 1864, 10.
_____. "Our Sensation Novelists." *The Living Age* 78 (August 22, 1863): 353–54. January 10, 2003. <http://www.humanities.mcmaster.ca/~mactavis/vso/reviews/reviews.htm.>
_____."Review of Millais's Paintings." *Athenaeum* 1489 (May 10, 1856): 590.
_____. "Surrey Theatre." *The Times*, November 8, 1860, 6.
_____. "The Surrey." *Era*, February 11, 1866, 11.
_____. "The Theatres &c." *Era*, April 3, 1864, 10.
[Wilberforce, Edward]. Review of *Colonel Fortescue's Daughter*, by Lady Charles [Harriet Frances] Thynne [née Bagot]. *Athenaeum* 2120 (June 13, 1868): 827.
———. Review of *Waverney Court*, by George W. Garrett. *Athenaeum* 2158 (March 6, 1869): 338.

Other Primary and Secondary Sources

Allen, Emily. *Theater Figures: The Production of the Nineteenth-Century British Novel.* Columbus: Ohio State University Press, 2003.
Altick, Richard D. *The Presence of the Present: Topics of the Day in the Victorian Novel.* Columbus: Ohio State University Press, 1991.
Arata, Stephen D. "The Occidental Tourist: *Dracula* and the Anxiety of Reverse Colonization." *Victorian Studies* 33 (Summer 1990): 621–45.
Archer, J. W. *Marriage Bells, or, The Cottage on the Cliff.* Lord Chamberlain's Collection of Plays. British Library. Add Mss: 53259.
Archibald, Diana C. *Domesticity, Imperialism, and Emigration in the Victorian Novel.* Columbia and London: University of Missouri Press, 2002.
Auerbach, Nina. "Before the Curtain." In *The Cambridge Companion to Victorian and Edwardian Theatre*, 3–16. Cambridge: Cambridge University Press, 2004.
_____. *Communities of Women: An Idea in Fiction.* Cambridge: Harvard University Press, 1978.
_____. "The Power of Hunger: Demonism and Maggie Tulliver." In *Romantic Imprisonment: Women and Other Glorified Outcasts*, edited by Nina Auerbach, 230–49. New York: Columbia University Press, 1986.
Austen, Jane. *Pride and Prejudice.* London: Penguin, 1996.
Bachman, Maria K., and Don Richard Cox. "Introduction: The Real Wilkie Collins." In *Reality's Dark Light: The Sensational Wilkie Collins*, edited by Maria K. Bachman and Don Richard Cox, xi–xxviii. Knoxville: The University of Tennessee Press, 2003.
Baker, William. *Wilkie Collins's Library: A Reconstruction.* London: Greenwood Press, 2002.
Bakhtin, Mikhail. *The Dialogic Imagination: Four Essays.* Edited by Michael Holquist. Translated by Caryl Emerson and Michael Holquist. Austin: University of Texas Press, 1981.
Basch, Françoise. "Dickens's Sinners." In *Relative Creatures: Victorian Women in Society and the Novel, 1837–67*, translated by Anthony Rudolf, 210–28. London: Allen Lane, 1974.
Beebee, Thomas O. *The Ideology of Genre: A Comparative Study of Generic Instability.* University Park: Pennsylvania State University Press, 1994.
Beecher, Catharine, and Harriet Beecher Stowe. *The American Woman's Home.* New York: J. B. Ford & Co., 1870.

Beer, Gillian. "Sensational Women." *Times Literary Supplement,* March 11, 1994, 26.
Beigel, Hermann. *The Human Hair: Its Structure, Growth, Diseases and Their Treatment.* London, 1869.
Bellows, Donald. "A Study of British Conservative Reaction to the American Civil War." *Journal of Southern History* 51, no. 4 (November 1985): 505–26.
Bernstein, Stephen. "*Oliver* Twisted: Narrative and Doubling in Dickens's Second Novel." *Victorian Newsletter* 79 (Spring 1991): 27–34.
Bhabha, Homi K. "The Commitment to Theory." In *The Norton Anthology of Theory and Criticism,* edited by Vincent B. Leitch, 2377–97. New York: W. W. Norton, 2001.
———. *The Location of Culture.* London: Routledge, 1995.
Billi, Mirella. "Dickens as Sensation Novelist." In *Dickens: The Craft of Fiction and the Challenges of Reading,* edited by Rossana Bonadei, Clotilde de Stasio, Carlo Pagetti, and Alessandro Vescovi, 176–84. Milan, Italy: Unicopli, 2000.
Björk, Lennart A. *The Literary Notebooks of Thomas Hardy.* Vol. 1. London: Macmillan, 1985.
Blackett, R. J. M. *Divided Hearts: Britain and the American Civil War.* Baton Rouge: Louisiana State University Press, 2001.
Blackstone, William. *Commentaries on the Laws of England.* Vol. 1, bk. 1. Philadelphia: J. B. Lippincott, 1904.
Bland, Lucy. *Banishing the Beast: Sexuality and the Early Feminists.* New York: New Press, 1995.
Bodichon, Barbara Leigh Smith. "A Brief Summary, in Plain Language, of the Most Important Laws Concerning Women: Together with a Few Observations Thereon." In Tim Dolin, *Mistress of the House: Women of Property in the Victorian Novel.* Appendix. Aldershot: Ashgate, 1997.
Booth, Michael, and Joel H. Kaplan, eds. *The Edwardian Theatre.* Cambridge: Cambridge University Press, 1996.
Booth, Michael. "East-End and West-End: Class and Audience in Victorian London." *Theatre Research International* 2, no. 2 (1977): 98–103.
———. Melodrama and the Working Class." In *Dramatic Dickens,* edited by Carol Hanbery Mackay, 96–109. Basingstoke and London: Macmillan, 1989.
———. "The Metropolis on Stage." In *The Victorian City: Images and Realities,* edited by H. J. Dyos and Michael Wolff, 211–24. . London and Boston: Routledge & Kegan Paul, 1973.
———. *Theatre in the Victorian Age.* Cambridge: Cambridge University Press, 1991.
Bordo, Susan. *Unbearable Weight: Feminism, Western Culture, and the Body.* Berkeley: University of California Press, 1993.
Boucicault, Dion. *The Octoroon.* In *Plays by Dion Boucicault.* Edited by Peter Thomson. Cambridge: Cambridge University Press, 1984.
Bowen, Elizabeth. *Collected Impressions.* New York: Longmans Green & Co., 1950.
Boyle, Thomas. *Black Swine in the Sewers of Hampstead: Beneath the Surface of Victorian Sensationalism.* New York: Viking, 1989.
Bracebridge, Hemyng. "Prostitution." In Henry Mayhew, *London Labour and the London Poor,* edited by John d. Rosenberg. 4 vols. 4: 211–24. London: Dover.
Braddon, Mary Elizabeth. *Aurora Floyd.* Edited by P. D. Edwards. Oxford: Oxford University Press, 1996.
———. *Aurora Floyd.* Edited by P. D. Edwards. Oxford: Oxford University Press, 1999.
———. *Aurora Floyd.* Edited by Richard Nemesvari and Lisa Surridge. Peterborough, ON: Broadview Press, 1998.
———. *The Doctor's Wife.* Edited by Lyn Pykett. Oxford and New York: Oxford University Press, 1998.

———. *John Marchmont's Legacy.* Edited by Toru Sasaki and Norman Page. Oxford: Oxford University Press, 1999.
———. *Lady Audley's Secret.* Edited by David Skilton. Oxford: Oxford University Press, 1987.
———. *Lady Audley's Secret.* Edited by David Skilton. Oxford: Oxford University Press, 1998.
———. *Lady Audley's Secret.* Edited by Jenny Bourne Taylor. London: Penguin Classics, 1998.
———. *The Octoroon; or, The Lily of Louisiana.* Edited by Jennifer Carnell. Hastings: Sensation Press, 1999.
———. *Vixen.* 3 vols. London: Maxwell, 1879.
———. *Vixen.* New York: American Publishers Corp., 1899.
———. *Vixen.* Dover, NH: Alan Sutton, 1993.
———. *Vixen.* London: Sutton, 1993 (1879).
Brantlinger, Patrick. *The Reading Lesson: The Threat of Mass Literacy in Nineteenth Century British Fiction.* Bloomington: Indiana University Press, 1998.
———. *Rule of Darkness: British Colonial Literature and Imperialism, 1830–1914.* Ithaca, NY: Cornell University Press, 1988.
———. "What Is 'Sensational' about the 'Sensation Novel?'" *Nineteenth Century Fiction* 37 (1982): 1–28.
Bratton, Jacky, Jim Cook, and Christine Gledhill. *Melodrama: Stage, Picture, Screen.* London: British Film Institute, 1994.
Breuer, Josef, and Sigmund Freud. *Studies on Hysteria.* Translated by James Strachey. New York: Basic Books, n.d.
Bristow, Joseph. "'No Friend Like a Sister'? Christina Rossetti's Female Kin." *Victorian Poetry* 33 (1995): 257–81.
Broughton, Rhoda. *Cometh Up as a Flower.* Edited by Tamar Heller. Vol. 4b: 213–506. *Varieties of Women's Sensation Fiction.* 6 vols. London: Pickering and Chatto, 2004.
———. *Not Wisely but Too Well.* Dover, NH: Alan Sutton, 1993.
———. *Not Wisely but Too Well.* London: Tinsley Brothers, 1871.
Brumberg, Joan Jacobs. *Fasting Girls: The Emergence of Anorexia Nervosa as a Modern Disease.* Cambridge, MA: Harvard University Press, 1988.
Bucknill, John Charles, and Daniel H. Tuke. *A Manual of Psychological Medicine.* Philadelphia: Blanchard and Lea, 1858.
Burns, Wayne. *Charles Reade, a Study in Victorian Authorship.* New York: Bookman Associates, 1961.
Bushnan, J. S. "Private Asylums" Appendix to Charles Reade, *Hard Cash: A Matter-of-Fact Romance.* Boston: Fields, Osgood, & Co., 1869 (1863).
Carnell, Jennifer. Introduction to *The Octoroon; or, the Lily of Louisiana,* by Mary Braddon, edited by Jennifer Carnell, vii–xviii. Hastings: Sensation Press, 1999.
———. *The Literary Lives of Mary Elizabeth Braddon.* Hastings, East Sussex, UK: Sensation Press, 2000.
Carpenter, Mary Wilson. "'Eat Me, Drink Me, Love Me': The Consumable Female Body in Christina Rossetti's *Goblin Market.*" *Victorian Poetry* 29 (1991): 415–34.
Casey, Ellen Miller. "'Other People's Prudery': Mary Elizabeth Braddon." In *Sexuality and Victorian Literature,* edited by Don Richard Cox, 72–82. Knoxville: University of Tennessee Press, 1984.
———. "Weekly Reviews of Fiction: The *Athenaeum* vs. the *Spectator* and the *Saturday Review.*" *Victorian Periodicals Review* 23, no.1 (Spring 1990): 8–12.
Casey, Janet Galligani. "The Potential of Sisterhood: Christina Rossetti's 'Goblin Market.'" *Victorian Poetry* 29 (1991): 63–78.

Cerullo, John J. "Swedenborgianism in the Works of Joseph Sheridan Le Fanu: Desocialization and the Victorian Ghost Story." In *Swedenborg and His Influence,* edited by Erland Brock. Bryn Athyn: Academy of the New Church, 1988.
City University, London. *The Athenaeum Index of Reviews and Reviewers: 1830–1870.* <http://web.soi.city.ac.uk/~asp/v2/home.html.>
Clarke, Edward H. *Sex in Education; Or, A Fair Chance for the Girls.* 1873. Reprint. Salem, NH: Ayer Company Publishers, 1972.
Cobbe, Frances Power. "Criminals, Idiots, Women, and Minors." In *Criminals, Idiots, Women, and Minors: Victorian Writing by Women on Women.* Edited by Susan Hamilton. 2nd ed. Peterborough: Broadview Press, 2004.
Collins, Philip. *Dickens and Crime.* 3rd ed. New York: St. Martin's Press, 1994.
Collins, Wilkie. *Armadale.* London: Penguin 1995.
_____. *Armadale.* Edited by John Sutherland. New York: Dover, 1977.
_____. *Armadale.* London: Oxford University Press, 1989.
_____. *Basil.* Edited by Dorothy Goldman. Oxford: Oxford University Press, 1990.
_____. *The Dead Secret.* Edited by Ira B. Nadel. London: Oxford University Press, 1997.
_____. *Man and Wife.* Edited by Normal Page. London: Oxford University Press, 1995.
_____. *The Moonstone: A Romance.* Edited by Sandra Kemp. London: Penguin, 1998.
_____. *The Moonstone.* Edited by Steve Farmer. Peterborough: Broadview Press, 1999.
_____. *The Moonstone.* Edited by Carolyn G. Heilbrun. New York: Modern Library, 2001.
_____. *Man and Wife.* London: Chatto and Windus, 1907.
_____. *No Name.* London: Oxford University Press, 1986.
_____. *The Woman in White.* Edited by John Sutherland. Oxford: Oxford University Press, 1996.
_____. *The Woman in White.* New York: Penguin, 1985.
_____. *The Woman in White.* New York: Signet, 1985.
Conrow, Margaret. "Wife-Abuse in Dickens's Fiction." *Dickens Studies Newsletter* 14, no. 2 (June 1983): 43–47.
Cornwell, Neil. *The Literary Fantastic: From Gothic to Postmodernism.* Hempstead: Simon and Schuster, 1990.
Cox, R. G., ed. *Thomas Hardy: The Critical Heritage.* London: Routledge & Kegan Paul, 1970.
Craft, Chrisopher. *Another Kind of Love: Male Homosexual Desire in English Discourse, 1850–1920.* New Historicism, no. 30. Berkeley: University of California Presss, 1994.
Crosland, T. W. H. *The Suburbans.* London: John Long, 1905.
Curtis, Jeni. "The 'Espaliered' Girl: Pruning the Docile Body in *Aurora Floyd.*" In *Beyond Sensation: Mary Elizabeth Braddon in Context,* edited by Marlene Tromp, Pamela K. Gilbert, and Aeron Haynie, 77–92. Albany: SUNY Press, 2000.
Cvetkovich, Ann. "Ghostlier Determinations: The Economy of Sensation and *The Woman in White.*" *Novel* 23 (1989): 24–43.
_____. *Mixed Feelings: Feminism, Mass Culture, and Victorian Sensationalism.* New Brunswick, NJ: Rugers University Press, 1992.
Davidoff, Leonore. "Class and Gender in Victorian England." In *Sex and Class in Women's History,* edited by Judith L. Newton, Mary P. Ryan, and Judith R. Walkowitz, 17–71. London: Routledge and Kegan Paul, 1983.
Davis, Jim. "The East End." In *The Edwardian Theatre: Essays on Performance and the Stage,* edited by Michael R. Booth and Joel H. Kaplan, 201–18. Cambridge and New York: Cambridge University Press, 1996.
_____. "The Gospel of Rags: Melodrama at the Britannia 1863–74." *New Theatre Quarterly* 7 (1991): 369–89.

———, and Victor Emeljanow. *Reflecting the Audience: London Theatregoing 1840–1880.* Ames: University of Iowa Press, 2001.

———. "Victorian and Edwardian Audiences." In *The Cambridge Companion to Victorian and Edwardian Theatre,* 98–108. Cambridge: Cambridge University Press, 2004.

Day, Gary, ed. *Varieties of Victorianism: The Uses of a Past.* Basingstoke: Macmillan, 1998.

Deane, Bradley. *The Making of the Victorian Novelist: Anxieties of Authorship in the Mass Market.* New York: Routledge, 2003.

Debenham, Helen. "Not Wisely but Too Well and the Art of Sensation." In *Victorian Identities: Social and Cultural Formations in Nineteenth-Century Literature,* edited by Ruth Robbins and Julian Wolfreys, 9–24. Hampshire: Macmillan; New York: St. Martin's, 1996.

Dellamora, Richard. *Masculine Desire: The Sexual Politics of Victorian Aestheticism.* Chapel Hill: University of North Carolina Press, 1990

de Mann, Paul. Introduction. *Towards and Aesthetic of Reception,* by Hans Robert Jauss. Translated by Timothy Bahti, vii–xxv. Minneapolis: University of Minnesota Press, 1982.

Derrida, Jacques. *Writing and Difference.* Translated by Alan Bass. Chicago: University of Chicago Press, 1978.

Dickens, Charles. *Dombey and Son.* New York: Modern Library, 2003.

———. *Dombey and Son.* Oxford: Clarendon, 1974.

———. *Martin Chuzzlewit.* New York: Penguin Books, 1995.

———. *Oliver Twist; or, the Parish Boy's Progress.* New York: Signet Classic, 1961.

———. *Sketches by Boz.* The New Oxford Illustrated Dickens. Vol. 19. New York: Oxford University Press, 1957.

———. *A Tale of Two Cities.* Oxford: Oxford University Press, 1998.

———. *A Tale of Two Cities.* Ware: Wordsworth Editions, 1993.

Dolin, Tim. *Mistress of the House: Women of Property in the Victorian Novel.* Aldershot: Ashgate, 1997.

Doyle, Arthur Conan. *Through the Magic Door.* Garden City, NY: Doubleday, Page, & Co., 1923.

Duncan, Ian. "*The Moonstone,* the Victorian Novel, and Imperialist Panic." *Modern Language Quarterly* 55, no. 3 (1994): 297–319.

Dyos, H. J. *Victorian Suburb: A Study of the Growth of Camberwell.* Leicester: Leicester University Press, 1973.

———, and D. A. Reeder. "Slums and Suburbs." In *The Victorian City: Images and Realities,* edited by H. J. Dyos and Michael Wolff, 359–86. London and Boston: Routledge & Kegan Paul, 1973.

———, and Michael Wolff, eds. *The Victorian City.* 2 vols. London: Routledge, 1973.

Edwards, Peter David. *Dickens's 'Young Men': George Augustus Sala, Edmund Yates and the World of Victorian Journalism.* Brookfield: Ashgate, 1997.

———. "Introduction." *Aurora Floyd.* Oxford: Oxford University Press, 1996, vi–xxii.

———. *Some Mid-Victorian Thrillers. The Sensation Novel, Its Friends, and Its Foes.* St. Lucia: University of Queensland Press, 1971.

Ellison, Mary. *Support for Secession: Lancashire and the American Civil War.* Chicago: University of Chicago Press, 1972.

Eliot, George. *Daniel Deronda.* Edited by Barbara Hardy. London: Penguin Classics, 1986.

———. *The George Eliot Letters.* Edited by G. Haight. Vol. 4: 309–10. New Haven, CT: Yale University Press, 1954.

Eliot, T. S. "Introduction." *The Moonstone.* 1928. London: Oxford University Press, 1966.

Ellis, Sarah Stickney. *The Mothers of England: Their Influence and Responsibility.* New York: D. Appleton, 1844.
Elwin, Malcolm. *Charles Reade: A Biography.* London: Jonathan Cape, 1931.
———. *Old Gods Falling.* New York: Macmillan, 1938.
Epstein, Deborah Nord. *Walking the Victorian Streets: Women, Representation, and the City.* Ithaca, NY, and London: Cornell University Press, 1995.
Esquinol, Jean Étienne Dominique. *Des malades mentales, Considérées sous les rapports médicals, hygiéniques et médico-légal* (1838). Translated by E. K. Hunt as *Mental Maladies: A Treatise on Insanity.* Philadelphia: Lea and Blanchard, 1845.
Faderman, Lillian. *Surpassing the Love of Men: Romantic Friendships and Love between Women from the Renaissance to the Present.* 1981. New York: Quill, William Morrow, 1998.
Finkelstein, David. "A Woman Hater and Women Healers: John Blackwood, Charles Reade, and the Victorian Women's Medical Movement." *Victorian Periodicals Review* 28, no. 4 (Winter 1995): 330–52.
Fisch, Audrey. *American Slaves in Victorian England.* Cambridge: Cambridge University Press, 2000.
Fishman, Robert. *Bourgeois Utopias: The Rise and Fall of Suburbia.* New York: Basic Books, 1987.
Fitzgerald, Percy Hetherington. *Memooirs of an Author.* London: R. Bentley and Son, 1895.
———. *The Woman with the Yellow Hair and Other Modern Mysteries.* London: Saunders 1862.
Fladeland, Betty. *Abolitionists and Working-Class Problems in the Age of Industrialization.* Baton Rouge: Louisiana State University Press, 1984.
Flaubert, Gustave. *Madame Bovary.* Edited by Leo Bersani. Translated by Lowell Bair. New York: Bantam Books, 1989.
Flint, Kate. *The Woman Reader, 1837–1914.* Oxford: Oxford University Press, 1993.
Foner, Philip S. *British Labor and the American Civil War.* New York: Holmes & Meier Publishers, 1981.
Forster, John. *The Life of Charles Dickens.* London: Cecil Palmer, 1928.
Foucault, Michel. *Abnormal: Lectures at the Collège de France 1974–1975.* New York: Picador, 2003
———. *The History of Sexuality, Volume 1: An Introduction.* New York: Pantheon Books, 1978.
———. "The Order of Things." In *Literary Theory: An Anthology.* Edited by Julie Rivken and Michael Ryan. Oxford: Blackwell, 1998.
———. *Power/Knowledge: Selected Interviews and Other Writings 1972–1977.* New York: Pantheon, 1980
———. "What Is an Author?" Translated by Joseph V. Harari. In *The Foucault Reader,* edited by Paul Rabinow, 101–20. New York: Pantheon, 1988.
Frederic, Kenneth C. "The Cold, Cold Hearth: Domestic Strife in *Oliver Twist.*" *College English* 27 (March 1966): 465–70.
Freud, Sigmund. "The Psychogenesis of a Case of Homosexuality in a Woman." In *The Standard Edition of the Complete Psychological Works of Sigmund Freud,* edited and translated by James Strachey. Vol. 18: 147–71. London: Hogarth, 1953–1974.
Frierson, William Coleman. *The English Novel in Transition, 1885–1940.* Norman: University of Oklahoma Press, 1942.
Fryckstedt, Monica Correa. *Geraldine Jewsbury's* Athenaeum *Reviews: A Mirror of Mid-Victorian Attitudes to Fiction.* Stockholm: Uppsala, 1986.
Garnett, Robert R. "*Oliver Twist*'s Nancy: The Angel in Chains." *Religion and the Arts* 4, no. 4 (2000): 491–516.

Gaylin, Ann. *Eavesdropping in the Novel from Austen to Proust.* Cambridge: Cambridge University Press, 2002.

Gilbert, Pamela K. "Braddon and Victorian Realism: *Joshua Haggard's Daughter.*" In Tromp and Gilbert, 183–95.

———. *Disease, Desire and the Body in Victorian Women's Popular Novels.* Cambridge: Cambridge University Press, 1997.

———. "Ingestion, Contagion, Seduction: Victorian Metaphors of Reading." In *Scenes of the Apple: Food and the Female Body in Nineteenth- and Twentieth-Century Women's Writing,* edited by Tamar Heller and Patricia Moran, 65–86. New York: State University of New York Press, 2003.

Gilbert, Sandra M., and Susan Gubar. *The Madwoman in the Attic: The Woman Writer and the Nineteenth-Century Literary Imagination.* 2nd ed. New Haven, CT: Yale University Press, 2000.

Gitter, Elisabeth. "The Power of Women's Hair in the Victorian Imagination." *PMLA* 99 (1984): 936–54.

Gledhill, Christine, *Home Is Where the Heart Is: Studies in Melodrama and the Woman's Film.* London: BFI, 1987.

Haines, Lewis F. "Reade, Mill, and Zola: A Study of the Character and Intention of Charles Reade's Realistic Method." *SP* 40 (1943): 463–80.

Hardy, Thomas. "General Preface to the Novels and Poems." *Thomas Hardy's Personal Writings.* Edited by Harold Orel. London: Macmillan, 1967.

Harrison, Antony H. *Christina Rossetti in Context.* Chapel Hill: University of North Carolina Press, 1988.

———. *Victorian Poets and the Politics of Culture: Discourse and Ideology.* Charlottesville: University Press of Virginia, 1998.

[Hazleton, Harry]. *The Woman with the Yellow Hair: A Romance of Good and Bad Society.* N.pub., 1865.

Heilbrun, Carolyn G. "Introduction." *The Moonstone,* by Wilkie Collins. New York: Modern Library, 2001.

Heller, Lee F. "Frankenstein and the Cultural Uses of the Gothic." In *Frankenstein,* by Mary Shelley, edited by Johanna M. Smith, 325–41. Boston: St. Martin's Press, 1992.

Heller, Tamar. *Dead Secrets: Wilkie Collins and the Female Gothic.* New Haven, CT: Yale University Press, 1992.

———. Introduction. *Cometh Up as a Flower,* by Rhoda Broughton. In *Varieties of Women's Sensation Fiction: 1855–1890.* Vol. 4: xxxiii–xliv. London: Pickering & Chatto, 2004.

———. "The Vampire in the House: Hysteria, Female Sexuality, and Female Knowledge in Le Fanu's 'Carmilla.'" In *The New Nineteenth Century: Feminist Readings of Underread Victorian Fiction,* edited by Barbara Leah Harman and Susan Meyer, 77–95. New York: Garland, 1996.

Heywood, Christopher. "Miss Braddon's *The Doctor's Wife:* An Intermediary between *Madame Bovary* and *The Return of the Native.*" *Revue de littérature comparée* 38 (1964): 255–61.

Hibbert, Christopher. *The Great Mutiny: India 1857.* New York: Viking Press, 1978.

Hill, Jen. "Examining Women: Charles Reade's *A Woman Hater,* Lesbian Contagion, and the Debate on Medical Education for Women." Unpublished paper presented at the Victorians Institute Conference, Columbia: University of South Carolina, 2000.

Hoeveler, Diane Long. "*Jane Eyre* through the Body: Food, Sex, Discipline." In *Approaches to Teaching Brontë's* Jane Eyre, edited by Diane Long Hoeveler and Beth Lau, 116–23. New York: MLA Press, 1993.

Holder, Heidi J. "The East End Theatre." In *The Companion to Victorian and Edwardian Theatre*, 257–76. Cambridge: Cambridge University Press.
Hollington, Michael. "Dickens the Flâneur." *Dickensian* 77 (Summer 1981): 71–87.
Hughes, Winifred. *The Maniac in the Cellar: Sensation Novels of the 1860s*. Princeton, NJ: Princeton University Press, 1980.
Hyde, James. *A Bibliography of the Works of Emanuel Swedenborg, Original and Translated*. London: Swedenborg Society, 1906.
Irigaray, Luce. "Commodities among Themselves." In *This Sex Which Is Not One*, translated by Catherine Porter and Carolyn Burke. Ithaca, NY: Cornell University Press, 1985.
James, Henry. "Miss Braddon." *Notes and Reviews*. Cambridge, MA: Dunster House, 1921.
———. *Notes and Reviews*. 1921. Reprint. Freeport, NY: Books for Libraries, 1968.
Jauss, Hans Robert. *Toward an Aesthetic of Reception*. Translated by Timothy Bahti. Minneapolis: University of Minnesota Press, 1982.
Jenkins, Philip. "Into the Upperworld? Law, Crime and Punishment in English Society." *Social History* 12 (January 1987): 93–102.
Johnson, Edgar. *Charles Dickens: His Tragedy and Triumph*. Virginia: Penguin Books, 1952.
Joyce, Patrick. *Work, Society, and Politics: The Culture of the Factory in Later Victorian England*. New Brunswick, NJ: Rutgers University Press, 1980.
Katz, Stanley N. Introduction. *Commentaries on the Laws of England*, by William Blackstone, iii–xiii. Chicago and London: University of Chicago Press, 1979.
Keating, P. J. *Into Unknown England 1866–1913: Selections from the Social Explorers*. Manchester: Manchester University Press, 1979.
Kellett, J. R. "The Railway as an Agent of Internal Change in Victorian Cities." In *The Victorian City: A Reader in British Urban History, 1820–1914*, edited by R. J. Morris and Richard Rodger, 181–208. London and New York: Longman, 1993.
Kendrick, Walter M. "The Sensationalism of *The Woman in White*." *Nineteenth Century Fiction* 32, no.1 (June 1977): 18–35.
Kennedy, George E., II. "Women Redeemed: Dickens's Fallen Women." *Dickensian* 74 (January 1978): 42–47.
Korobkin, Laura Hanft. "Silent Woman, Speaking Fiction: Charles Reade's *Griffith Gaunt* (1866) at the Adultery Trial of Henry Ward Beecher." In *The New Nineteenth Century: Feminist Readings of Underread Victorian Novels*, edited by Barbara Leah Harman and Susan Meyers, 45–62. New York and London: Garland, 1996.
Kushnier, Jennifer S. "Educating Boys to Be Queer: Braddon's *Lady Audley's Secret*." *Victorian Literature and Culture* 30 (2002): 61–75.
Lacan, Jacques. *Ecrits: A Selection*. Translated by Alan Sheridan. Norton: New York, 1977.
Langbauer, Laurie. *Women and Romance: The Consolations of Gender in the English Novel*. Ithaca, NY: Cornell University Press, 1990.
Langland, Elizabeth. *Nobody's Angels: Middle-Class Women and Domestic Ideology in Victorian Culture*. Ithaca, NY, and London: Cornell University Press, 1995.
Ledwon, Lenora. "Veiled Women, the Law of Coverture, and Wilkie Collins's *The Woman in White*." *Victorian Literature and Culture* 22 (1994): 1–22.
Le Fanu, Sheridan. "Carmilla." In *In a Glass Darkly*, edited by Robert Tracy, 243–319. New York: Oxford University Press, 1993.
———. *In a Glass Darkly*. Herefordshire: Wordsworth Editions, 1995.
———. *In A Glass Darkly*. London: John Lehman, 1947.
———. *The Poems of Joseph Sheridan Le Fanu*. Edited by Alfred Percival Graves. London: Downey & Company, 1896.

———. *Uncle Silas: A Tale of Bartram-Haugh*. Edited by Victor Sage. New York: Penguin Books, 2000.
Le Fanu, William R. *Seventy Years of Irish Life*. London: Edward Arnold, 1907.
Levin, Amy. *The Suppressed Sister: A Relationship in Novels by Nineteenth- and Twentieth-Century British Women*. Lewisburg: Bucknell University Press, 1992.
Loesberg, Jonathan. "The Ideology of Narrative Form in Sensation Fiction." *Representations* 13 (Winter 1986): 115–38.
Lonoff, Sue. *Wilkie Collins and His Victorian Readers: A Study in the Rhetoric of Authorship*. New York: AMS Press, 1982.
Lord, Hazel D. "Husband and Wife: English Marriage Law from 1750: A Bibliographic Essay." *Southern California Review of Law and Women's Studies* (Fall 2001): 1–65. <http://web2.westlaw.com>.
Lovett, R. M., and H. S. Hughes. *The History of the Novel in England*. New York: Houghton Mifflin, 1932.
Lynch, Eve M. "Spectral Politics: M. E. Braddon and the Spirits of Social Reform." In Tromp and Gilbert, 235–76.
Mackay, Carol Hanbury, ed. *Dramatic Dickens*. London: Macmillan, 1989.
McClintock, Anne. *Imperial Leather: Race, Gender and Sexuality in the Colonial Contest*. New York: Routledge, 1995.
McCormack, W. J. *Dissolute Characters: Irish Literary History through Balzac, Sheridan Le Fanu, Yeats and Bowen*. Manchester: Manchester University Press, 1993.
———. *Sheridan Le Fanu and Victorian Ireland*. New York: Oxford University Press, 1980.
Mannsaker, Frances S. "East and West: Anglo-Indian Racial Attitudes as Reflected in Popular Fiction, 1890–1914." *Victorian Studies* (Autumn 1980): 33–51.
Martineau, Harriet. *History of the Peace: Being a History of England from 1816 to 1854*. Vol. 4. Boston: Walker, Wise, and Company, 1865–66.
May, Leila Silvana. *Disorderly Sisters: Sibling Relations and Sororal Resistance in Nineteenth-Century British Literature*. Lewisburg: Bucknell University Press, 2001.
Mayer, David. "Encountering Melodrama." In *The Cambridge Companion to Victorian and Edwardian Theatre*, 145–62. Cambridge: Cambridge University Press.
Mayhew, Heney. *London Labour and the London Poor*. 4 vols. London: Constable, 1968.
Mehta, Jaya. "English Romance; Indian Violence." *Centennial Review* 39, no. 3 (1995): 611–57.
Menke, Richard. "The Political Economy of Fruit: Goblin Market." In *The Culture of Christina Rossetti: Female Poetics and Victorian Contexts*, edited by Mary Arseneau, Antony H. Harrison, and Lorraine Janzen Kooistra, 105–36. Athens: Ohio University Press, 1999.
Michie, Helena. *Sororophobia: Differences among Women in Literature and Culture*. Oxford: Oxford University Press, 1992.
Miller, D. A. "*Cage aux Folles:* Gender and Sensation in Wilkie Collins's *The Woman in White*." In *The Making of the Modern Body: Sexuality and Society in the Nineteenth Century*, edited by Catherine Gallagher and Thomas Laqueur, 107–36. Berkeley: University of California Press, 1987.
———. "*Cage aux folles:* Sensation Fiction and Gender in Wilkie Collins's *The Woman in White*." *Representations* 14 (Spring 1986): 107–36.
———. "Cage aux Folles: Sensation and Gender in Wilkie Collins's *The Woman in White*." In D. A. Miller, *The Novel and the Police*, 46–91. Berkeley: University of California Press, 1988.
Miller, J. Hillis. *Charles Dickens: The World of His Novels*. Cambridge, MA: Harvard University Press, 1958.

Millgate, Michael, ed. *The Life and Work of Thomas Hardy, by Thomas Hardy.* London: Macmillan, 1984.

_____. *Testamentary Acts: Browning, Tennyson, James, Hardy.* Oxford: Clarendon, 1992.

Millingen, John Gideon. *The Passions; or Mind and Matter* (1848). In *Embodied Selves: An Anthology of Psychological Texts, 1830–1860*, edited by Jenny Bourne Taylor and Sally Shuttleworth, 169–70. Oxford: Oxford University Press, 1998. .

Mintz, Steven. *A Prison of Expectations: The Family in Victorian Culture.* New York: New York University Press, 1983.

Montwieler, Katherine. "Marketing Sensation: Lady Audley's Secret and Consumer Culture." In Tromp and Gilbert, 43–61.

Morley, Henry. *Diary of a London Playgoer.* Leicester: Leicester University Press, 1974.

Morrison, Ronald D. "'Their Fruits Like Honey in the Throat/But Poison in the Blood': Christina Rossetti and *The Vampyre.*" *Weber Studies* 14 (1997). http://weberstudies. weber. Edu/archive/archive%20B%20Vol.%2011–16.1/Vol.%2014.2/14/2Morrison.htm. Accessed March 29, 2003.

Mumm, Susan. *Stolen Daughters, Virgin Mothers: Anglican Sisterhoods in Victorian Britain.* London: Leicester University Press, 1999.

Murphy, Patrick, ed. *The Tempest: Critical Essays.* London: Routledge, 2001.

Nayder, Lillian. "Agents of Empire in *The Woman in White.*" *Victorian Newsletter* 83 (1993): 1–7.

_____. "Class Consciousness and the Indian Mutiny in Dickens's 'The Perils of Certain English Prisoners.'" *Studies in English Literature* 32, no. 4 (1992): 17. *Ebsco Host.* Blackwell Library, Salisbury University. February 3 2004 <http://web 18. Epnet.com/citation.asp?an =9301031635&db=aph>.

_____. "Rebellious Sepoys and Bigamous Wives: The Indian Mutiny and Marriage Law Reform in *Lady Audley's Secret.*" In Tromp and Gilbert, 31–42.

_____.*Unequal Partners: Charles Dickens, Wilkie Collins and Victorian Authorship.* Ithaca, NY: Cornell University Press, 2002.

_____. *Wilkie Collins.* London: Prentice Hall, 1997.

Nemesvari, Richard. "Robert Audley's Secret: Male Homosocial Desire and 'Going Straight' in *Lady Audley's Secret.*" In *Straight with a Twist: Queer Theory and the Subject of Heterosexuality*, edited by Calvin Thomas, 109–21. Chicago: University of Illinois Press, 2000.

_____. "The Mark of the Brotherhood: The Foreign Other and Homosexual Panic in *The Woman in White.*" *English Studies in Canada* 28, no. 4 (December 2002): 603–27.

———, and Lisa Surridge. "Introduction" to *Aurora Floyd,* by Mary Elizabeth Braddon. Peterborough, Ontario: Broadview Press, 1998.

Newey, Katherine, and Veronica Kelly, eds. *East Lynne. Dramatised by T. A. Palmer.* Queensland: Australasian Drama Studies Association, 1994.

Norton, Caroline. *Caroline Norton's Defense: English Laws for Women in the Nineteenth Century.* Chicago: Academy Chicago, 1982.

Norwood, Robin. *Women Who Love Too Much.* New York: Pocket Books, 1986.

Ofek, Galia. "Medusa's Head: The Representation of Maggie's Head of Hair in the Mill on the Floss." *Q/W/E/R/T/Y* 12 (October 2002): 85–89.

_____. "'Tie Her Up by the Hair': Dickens's Retelling of the Medusa and Rapunzel Myths." *Dickens Quarterly* 20, no. 3 (September 2003): 184–99.

O'Neill, Philip. *Wilkie Collins: Women, Property and Propriety.* Basingstoke: Macmillan, 1988.

O'Shea, Edward. "Modernist Versions of *The Tempest*: Auden, Woolf, Tippet." In The Tempest: *Critical Essays,* edited by Patrick M. Murphy, 543–59. New York and London: Routledge,

2001.
O'Toole, Fionn. "Introduction." *Vixen.* Dover, NH: Alan Sutton, 1993, vii–xi.
Page, Norman. "Introduction." *John Marchmont's Legacy,* by Mary Elizabeth Braddon. Oxford: Oxford University Press, 1999.
———. *Wilkie Collins: The Critical Heritage.* London: Routledge & Kegan Paul, 1974.
Paroissien, David. *The Companion to* Oliver Twist. Edinburgh: Edinburgh University Press, 1992.
Pavis, Patrice. *The Intercultural Performance Reader.* London: Routledge, 1996.
Pedlar, Valerie. "The Woman in White: Sensationalism, Secrets and Spying." In *The Nineteenth-Century Novel: Identities,* edited by Dennis Walder, 48–68. London: Routledge, 2001.
Peters, Catherine. *The King of Inventors.* Princeton, NJ: Princeton University Press, 1991.
Pietz, William. "The Origin of the Fetish II." *RES* 13 (1987): 23–45.
Pionke, Albert D. "Secreting Rebellion: From the Mutiny to the Moonstone." *Victorians Institute Journal* 28 (2000): 109–40.
Pizer, Donald. *Twentieth-Century American Naturalism: An Interpretation.* Carbondale and Edwardsville: Southern Illinois University Press, 1982.
Pollard, Arthur. "*Griffith Gaunt:* Paradox of Victorian Melodrama." *Critical Quarterly* 17 (1975): 221–27.
Poovey, Mary. "Forgotten Writers, Neglected Histories: Charles Reade and the Nineteenth-Century Transformation of the British Literary Field." *ELH* 72.2 (2004): 433–53.
———. *Uneven Developments: The Ideological Work of Gender in Mid-Victorian England.* Chicago: University of Chicago Press, 1988.
Powell, Kerry, ed. *The Cambridge Companion to Victorian and Edwardian Theatre.* Cambridge: Cambridge University Press, 2004.
———. *Women and Victorian Theatre.* Cambridge: Cambridge University Press, 1997.
Prichard, James Cowles. *A Treatise on Insanity and Other Disorders Affecting the Mind.* Philadelphia: Haswell, Barrington, and Haswell, 1837.
Punter, David. *The Literature of Terror: A History of Gothic Fictions from 1765 to the Present Day.* New York: Longman, 1980.
———. *The Gothic Tradition.* Vol. 1 of *The Literature of Terror: A History of Gothic Fictions from 1765 to the Present Day.* New York: Longman, 1996.
Pykett, Lyn. "Afterword." In Tromp and Gilbert, 277–80.
———. "Introduction." *The Doctor's Wife,* by Mary Elizabeth Braddon, edited by Lyn Pykett, vii–xxv. Oxford and New York: Oxford University Press, 1998.
———. *The "Improper" Feminine: The Women Sensation Novel and New Woman Writing.* London: Routledge, 1992.
———. "The Newgate Novel and Sensation Fiction, 1838–1868." In *The Cambridge Companion to Crime Fiction,* edited by Martin Priestman, 19–40. Cambridge: Cambridge University Press.
———. *The Sensation Novel: From* The Woman in White *to* The Moonstone. Plymouth, England: Northcote House, with British Council, 1994.
———, ed. *Wilkie Collins: New Casebooks: Contemporary Critical Essays.* New York: St. Martin's, 2002.
Rance, Nicholas. *Wilkie Collins and Other Sensation Novelists: Walking the Moral Hospital.* Rutherford: Fairleigh Dickenson University Press, 1991.
———. *Wilkie Collins and Other Sensation Novelists: Walking the Moral Hospital.* Basingstoke: Macmillan, 1991.
Reade, Charles. "Androgynism; or Woman Playing at Man." *English Review* 9, nos. 1–2 (August–September 1911): 10–29, 191–212.

_____. *Christie Johnstone*. Boston: Fields, Osgood, & Co., 1869.
_____. *The Cloister and the Hearth, or Maid, Wife, and Widow*. Boston: Fields, Osgood, & Co., 1869.
_____, with Dion Boucicault. *Foul Play*. [1868]. In *Works of Charles Reade*. Vol. 4. New York: Collier, n.d. .
_____. *Griffith Gaunt; or, Jealousy*. Boston: Fields, Osgood, & Co., 1869.
_____. *Griffith Gaunt*. In *The Works of Charles Reade*. Vol. 7. New York: Peter Fenelon Collier, 1895?.
_____. *Hard Cash: A Matter-of-Fact Romance*. Boston: Fields, Osgood, & Co., 1869.
_____. *It Is Never Too Late to Mend: A Matter-of-Fact Romance*. 1856. Boston: Fields, Osgood, & Co., 1869.
_____. "Propria Quae Maribus" ("The Bloomer"). [1857]. In *Works of Charles Reade*. Vol. 4. New York: Collier, n.d.
_____, *Readiana: Comments on Current Events; Bible Characters*. London: Chatto & Windus, 1896.
_____. *A Simpleton: A Story of the Day*. [1873]. New York: P. F. Collier & Son, n.d.
_____. *A Terrible Temptation, a Story of the Day*. [1871]. New York: P. F. Collier & Son, n.d.
_____. *The Wandering Heir*. Boston: Fields, Osgood, & Co., 1872.
_____. *A Woman-Hater: A Novel*. [1877]. New York: Norman L. Munro Publisher, n.d.
Reade, Charles L., and Compton Reade. *Charles Reade . . . : A Memoir*. New York: Harper Brothers, 1877.
Reed, John R. "English Imperialism and the Unacknowledged Crime of *The Moonstone*." *Clio* 2 (1973): 281–90.
Riddell, Charlotte. *The Race for Wealth*. 1866. London: Elibron, 2003.
Ridding, Lady Laura. "What Should Women Read?" *Woman at Home* 37 (1896): 29.
Robb, George. *White-Collar Crime in Modern England: Financial Fraud and Business Morality, 1845–1929*. Cambridge: Cambridge University Press, 1992.
Rosenman, Ellen Bayuk. "'Mimic Sorrows': Masochism and the Gendering of Pain in Victorian Melodrama." *Studies in the Novel* 35 (Spring 2003): 22–37.
Rossetti, Christina. "Goblin Market." In *Poems and Prose*, edited by Jan Marsh, 162–76. North Clarendon, VT: Charles E. Tuttle, 1994.
Russett, Cynthia Eagle. *Sexual Science: The Victorian Construction of Womanhood*. Cambridge, MA, and London: Harvard University Press, 1989.
Sabin, Margery. *Dissenters and Mavericks: Writings about India in English 1765–2000*. Oxford: Oxford University Press, 2002.
Said, Edward. *Culture and Imperialism*. New York: Vintage Books Edition, 1993.
_____. *The World, the Text, and the Critic*. Cambridge, MA: Harvard University Press, 1983.
Sala, George Augustus. *Gaslight and Daylight*. London: Chapman and Hall, 1858.
_____. *The Seven Sons of Mammon*. 3 vols. London, 1862.
Schlicke, Paul. *Oxford Reader's Companion to Dickens*. Oxford: Oxford University Press, 1999.
Schlossberg, Linda. "Consuming Images: Women, Hunger, and the Vote." In *Scenes of the Apple: Food and the Female Body in Nineteenth- and Twentieth-Century Women's Writing*, edited by Tamar Heller and Patricia Moran, 87–106. New York: State University of New York Press, 2003.
Schmitt, Cannon. *Alien Nation: Nineteenth Century Gothic Fictions and English Nationality*. New Cultural Studies. Philadelphia: University of Pennsylvania Press, 1997.
Schor, Hilary. *Scheherezade in the Marketplace: Elizabeth Gaskell and the Victorian Novel*. Oxford: Oxford University Press, 1992.

Schroeder, Natalie. "Feminine Sensationalism, Eroticism, and Self-Assertion: M. E. Braddon and Ouida." *Tulsa Studies in Women's Literature* 7 (1988): 87–103.

———. "*Armadale:* 'A Book that Is Daring Enough to Speak the Truth.'" *Wilkie Collins Society Journal* 3 (1983): 5–10.

Shanley, Mary. *Feminism, Marriage, and the Law in Victorian England, 1850–1895.* Princeton, NJ: Princeton University Press, 1989.

Sharpe, Jenny. "The Unspeakable Limits of Rape: Colonial Violence and Counter-Insurgency." In *Colonial Discourse and Post-Colonial Theory,* edited by Patrick Williams, 221–43. New York: Columbia University Press, 1994.

Shattock, Joanne, ed. *Women and Literature in Britain.* Cambridge: Cambridge University Press, 2001.

Showalter, Elaine. *A Literature of Their Own: British Women Novelists from Brontë to Lessing.* Princeton, NJ: Princeton University Press, 1977.

———. "Desperate Remedies: Sensation Novels of the 1860s." *Victorian Newsletter* 49 (1976): 1–5.

Sigtstedt, Cyriel O. *The Swedenborg Epic: The Life and Works of Emanuel Swedenborg.* New York: Bookman Associates, 1952.

Silver, Anna Krogovoy. *Victorian Literature and the Anorexic Body.* Cambridge: Cambridge University Press, 2002.

Silverstone, Roger, ed. *Visions of Suburbia.* London and New York: Routledge, 1997.

Small, Helen. *Love's Madness: Medicine, the Novel and Female Insanity, 1800–1865.* Oxford: Oxford University Press, 1996.

Smiles, Samuel. *Self-Help, the Art of Achievement Illustrated by Accounts of the Lives of Great Men.* 1859. Centenary edition introduced by Asa Briggs. London: John Murray, 1958.

Smith, Ashley. "Dangerous Sexuality in *Not Wisely but Too Well.*" Unpublished essay, University of Cincinnati, 2004.

Smith, Elton E. *Charles Reade.* Boston: G. K. Hall & Co., 1976.

Sparks, Tabitha. "Fiction Becomes Her: Representations of Female Character in Mary Braddon's *The Doctor's Wife.*" In Tromp and Gilbert, 197–209.

Spurr, David. *The Rhetoric of Empire: Colonial Discourse in Journalism, Travel Writing, and Imperial Administration.* Durham, NC: Duke University Press, 1993.

Stodart, M. A. *Female Writers: Thoughts on Their Proper Sphere, and on Their Powers of Usefulness.* London: R. B. Seeley and W. Burnside, 1842.

Surridge, Lisa. "Unspeakable Histories: Hester Dethridge and the Narration of Domestic Violence in *Man and Wife.*" *Victorian Review* 22 (1996): 161–85.

Sutcliffe, Emerson Grant. "Psychological Presentation in Reade's Novels." *SP* 38 (1941): 521–42.

Swedenborg, Emanuel. *The Animal Kingdom.* Translated by J. J. Wilkinson. Bryn Athyn: Swedenborg Scientific Association, 1960.

———. *Arcana Caelestia.* Translated by John Clowes. West Chester: Swedenborg Foundation, 1998.

———. *Heaven and Hell.* Translated by George Dole. West Chester: Swedenborg Foundation, 2000.

Swinburne, Algernon Charles. "Charles Reade." In *The Complete Works of Algernon Charles Swinburne.* Bonchurch Edition, Vol. 14: 346–75. New York: Russel and Russel, 1925.

Taylor, Jenny Bourne. "*Armadale:* The Sensitive Subject as Palimpsest." In *Wilkie Collins,* edited by Lyn Pykett, 149–76. New York: St. Martin's Press, 1998.

———. *In the Secret Theatre of Home: Wilkie Collins, Sensation Narrative, and Nineteenth Century Psychology.* London: Routledge, 1988.

———. "Introduction." *Lady Audley's Secret,* by Mary Elizabeth Braddon. London: Penguin

Classics, 1998.
Thomas, Ronald. *Detective Fiction and the Rise of Forensic Science.* Cambridge: Cambridge University Press, 1999.
Thomas, Tammis Elise. "Masquerade Liberties and Female Power in Le Fanu's *Carmilla.*" In *The Haunted Mind: The Supernatural in Victorian Literature,* edited by Ed. Elton E. Smith and Robert Haas, 39–66. Lanham, MD: Scarecrow Press, 1999.
Thompson, Nicola. "'Virile' Creation versus 'Twaddlers Tame and Soft': Gender and the Reception of Charles Reade's *It Is Never Too Late Too Mend.*" *Victorians Institute Journal* 23 (1995): 193–218.
Thoms, Peter. *The Windings of the Labyrinth: Quest and Structure in the Major Novels of Wilkie Collins.* Athens: Ohio University Press, 1992.
Thomson, Peter, ed. *Plays by Dion Boucicault.* Cambridge: Cambridge University Press, 1984.
Todorov, Tzvetan. *Genres in Discourse.* Translated by Catherine Porter. Cambridge: Cambridge University Press, 1990.
Trodd, Anthea. *Domestic Crime in the Victorian Novel.* New York: St. Martin's Press, 1989.
———. "Introduction" *The Moonstone,* by Wilkie Collins. Oxford and New York: Oxford University Press, 1982.
Tromp, Marlene. *The Private Rod: Marital Violence, Sensation, and the Law in Victorian Britain.* Charlottesville and London: University Press of Virginia, 2000.
———, Pamela K. Gilbert, and Aeron Haynie, eds. *Beyond Sensation: Mary Elizabeth Braddon in Context.* Albany: State University of New York Press, 2000.
Trudgill, Eric. *Madonnas and Magdalens: The Origins and Development of Victorian Sexual Attitudes,* 277–306. New York: Holmes and Meier, 1976.
The University of Ghent. *The Athenaeum Index of Reviews and Reviewers (1872–1886).* http://catserv.rug.ac.be:8505/ALEPH/6751660602C2979B1325A54EA180C68B-00599/start/ath01.
Vicinus, Martha. *Independent Women: Work and Community for Single Women 1850–1920.* Chicago: University of Chicago Press, 1985.
Wadsworth, Darryl. "'A Low Born Labourer Like You.' Audience and Victorian Working-Class Melodrama." In *Varieties of Victorianism: The Uses of the Past,* edited by Gary Day, 206–19. Houndsmill, Basongstoke, Hampshire: Palgrave Macmillan, 1998.
Wagner, Tamara S. *Longing: Narratives of Nostalgia in the British Novel, 1740–1890.* Lewisburg: Bucknell University Press, 2004.
———. "Overpowering Vitality: Nostalgia and Men of Sensibility in the Fiction of Wilkie Collins." *Modern Language Quarterly* 63, no. 4 (2002): 473–502.
Walker, Lenore. *Battered Women.* New York: Harper & Row Publishers, 1979.
Ward, Mary Augusta (Mrs. Humphrey). *Robert Elsmere.* Edited by Rosemary Ashton. 1888. Oxford: Oxford University Press, 1987.
Wills, Adele. "Witnesses and Truth: Juridical Narratives and Dialogism in Wilkie Collins' *The Moonstone* and *The Woman in White.*" *New Formations: A Journal of Culture/Theory/Politics* 32 (Autumn–Winter 1997): 91–98.
Winslow, Forbes. *On the Obscure Diseases of the Brain and Disorders of the Mind.* Rev. ed. 1860. London: John Churchill and Sons, 1868.
Wojtczak, Helena. "Sophia Jex-Blake: Determined to Be a Physician." In *Notable Women of Victorian Hastings* Web site, January 16, 2005. <http://www.hastingspress.co.uk/history/19/jex.htm.>
Wolff, Robert Lee. "Devoted Disciple: The Letters of Mary Elizabeth Braddon to Sir Edward Bulwer-Lytton, 1862–1873." *Harvard Library Bulletin* 22 (1974): 1–35, 129–61.

_____. *Nineteenth-Century Fiction: A Bibliographical Catalogue Based on the Collection Formed by Robert Lee Wolff.* 5 vols. New York: Garland, 1981.

_____. *Sensational Victorian: The Life and Fiction of Mary Elizabeth Braddon.* New York and London: Garland Publishing, 1979.

Wolfreys, Julian, and William Baker, eds. *Literary Theories.* London: Macmillan, 1996.

Wollstonecraft, Mary. *A Vindication of the Rights of Woman.* Edited by Carol Poston. 2nd ed. New York: Norton, 1988.

Wood, Marilyn. *Rhoda Broughton: Profile of a Novelist 1840–1920.* Stamford: Paul Watkins, 1993.

Wynne, Deborah. *The Sensation Novel and the Victorian Family Magazine.* Houndsmills, Basingstoke: Palgrave, 2001.

Young, Mrs Henry. *Jessy Ashton; or the Adventures of a Barmaid; a Drama in Four Visions.* British Library. Lord Chamberlain's Collection of Plays. Add. Mss: 53013.

Young, Robert J. C. *Colonial Desire: Hybridity in Theory, Culture, and Race.* London: Routledge, 1995.

Zola, Emile. "The Experimental Novel." 1880. Repr. in *Documents of Modern Literary Realism.* Edited by George J. Becker. Princeton, NJ: Princeton University Press, 1963.

_____. "Naturalism in the Theatre." 1880. Repr. in *Documents of Modern Literary Realism.* Edited by George J. Becker. Princeton, NJ: Princeton University Press, 1963.

LIST OF CONTRIBUTORS

Editors

Kimberly Harrison is associate professor of English and director of Undergraduate Writing at Florida International University. Her publications include *Contemporary Composition Studies: A Guide to Theorists and Terms* (with Edith Babin, Greenwood Press, 1999) and *A Maryland Bride in the Deep South: The Civil War Diary of Priscilla Bond* (Louisiana State University Press, 2006). Her research now focuses on women's rhetoric during the American Civil war. She teaches courses in composition, women's writing and rhetoric, and sensation fiction.

Richard Fantina teaches English at the University of Miami. He is the author of *Ernest Hemingway: Machismo and Masochism* (Palgrave Macmillan, 2005) and editor of *Straight Writ Queer: Non-Narrative Representations of Heterosexuality in Literature*, forthcoming from McFarland (2006). In 2003, he was awarded fellowships from the Northeast Modern Language Association and the Hemingway Society.

Contributors

Diana C. Archibald is an associate professor of English and director of Gender Studies at the University of Massachusetts Lowell. Her book, *Domesticity, Imperialism, and Emigration in the Victorian Novel* (University of Missouri Press, 2002), examines the image of the "angel in the house" in an age of mass migration from the English imperial center to New World peripheries. Her other work focuses both on Victorian womanhood and on Charles Dickens.

Ellen Miller Casey is professor of English and Distinguished University Fellow at the University of Scranton. Her much-cited essay, "Other People's Prudery: Mary Elizabeth Braddon," appeared in *Sexuality and Victorian Literature,* edited by Don Richard Cox

(University of Tennessee Press, 1984). She is a recognized authority on Victorian periodicals and has published widely on this subject, including "'Boz Has Got the Town by the Ear': Dickens and the *Athenaeum* Critics," *Dickens Studies Annual* 33 (2003). Her work has appeared in *Studies in American Fiction, Victorian Studies,* and the *Dickens Studies Annual.*

Lindsey Faber is currently pursuing her graduate degree in English and Comparative Literature at the University of Cincinnati.

Catherine J. Golden is professor of English at Skidmore College, where she teaches courses in Victorian literature and women writers. She is author of *Images of the Woman Reader in Victorian British and American Fiction* (University Press of Florida, 2003) and editor of Charlotte Perkins Gilman's *The Yellow Wall-Paper: A Sourcebook and Critical Edition* (Routledge, 2004); *Book Illustrated: Text, Image, and Culture 1770–1930* (Oak Knoll Press, 2000); *The Mixed Legacy of Charlotte Perkins Gilman* (with Joanna Zangrando, University of Delaware Press, 2000); *Unpunished* (with Denise D. Knight, The Feminist Press 1997); and *The Captive Imagination: A Casebook on "The Yellow Wallpaper"* (The Feminist Press, 1992).

Tamar Heller, associate professor of English and Comparative Literature at the University of Cincinnati, is author of *Dead Secrets: Wilkie Collins and the Female Gothic* (Yale, 1992), and coeditor of both *Approaches to Teaching Gothic Fiction* (MLA, 2003) and *Scenes of the Apple: Food and the Female Body in Nineteenth- and Twentieth-Century Women's Writing* (SUNY, 2003). She has also edited Rhoda Broughton's *Cometh Up as a Flower* for Pickering and Chatto's *Varieties of Women's Sensation Fiction* (2004).

Andrew Mangham is a research postgraduate and part-time lecturer in Victorian literature at the University of Sheffield, UK. He specializes in sensation fiction and nineteenth-century science (especially medicine). His current project is on legal, medical, and fictional representations of violent women in mid-Victorian culture. He has written interdisciplinary articles for the *Wilkie Collins Society Journal* and *Critical Survey.*

Andrew Maunder is a lecturer at the University of Hertfordshire, UK. His previous publications include an edition of *East Lynne* (2000), and he is the author of *Bram Stoker* (Northcote House, 2004). He is one of the editors of the journal *Critical Survey* and is also general editor of the series *Varieties of Women's Sensation Fiction 1855–1890* (Pickering and Chatto, 2004).

Lillian Nayder is professor of English at Bates College, where she teaches courses on nineteenth-century British fiction. Her books include *Wilkie Collins* (Twayne, 1997) and *Unequal Partners: Dickens, Wilkie Collins, and Victorian Authorship* (Cornell University Press, 2002). She is writing a biography of Catherine Dickens.

Richard Nemesvari is associate professor of English at St. Francis Xavier University. He has published articles and reviews on Thomas Hardy, Mary Elizabeth Braddon, Wilkie Collins, Emily Brontë, and Joseph Conrad in such journals as *Studies in the Novel, English Studies in Canada, Victorian Studies, JEGP,* and the *Victorian Newsletter.* His edition of Hardy's *The Trumpet-Major* was published by Oxford University Press. His coedited text of Braddon's *Aurora Floyd* and his edition of *Jane Eyre* were both published by Broadview Press. He is currently working on a book entitled *Disproportioning Realities: Thomas Hardy and Sensationalism.*

Galia Ofek received her D. Phil from Oxford University and is a Golda Meir postdoctoral Research Fellow at the Hebrew University of Mount Scopus, Jerusalem. She is currently writing a book about Victorian representations of women's hair in literature, art, and science.

Albert C. Sears is assistant professor at Silver Lake College in Wisconsin. His publications include "H. Rider Haggard," in *Biographical Dictionary of Literary Influences: The Nineteenth Century, 1800–1914,* edited by Derek Blakeley and John Powell (Greenwood, 2000); "The Politics and Gender of Duty in Frances Power Cobbe's *The Duties of Women,*" *Nineteenth-Century Feminisms* 1, no. 2 (2000); and "Male Novel Reading of the 1790s, Gothic Literature, and *Northanger Abbey,*" *Persuasions: The Jane Austen Journal* 21 (1999).

Jennifer Swartz is assistant professor of English and director of the Writing Center at Kent State University, Salem campus. Her areas of specialization are the law in literature and Victorian studies.

Dianna Vitanza is associate professor of English at Baylor University. She teaches courses in both Victorian poetry and the Victorian novel and has written on the novels of Charles Reade, George Eliot, and Charlotte Brontë and on the poetry of Robert Browning and Elizabeth Barrett Browning. Much of her career has been devoted to academic administration, and she has served as director of Undergraduate Studies in English, associate dean of the College of Arts and Sciences, and vice provost for Academic Affairs at Baylor University. She is coeditor of two books on church-related higher education.

Tamara S. Wagner is assistant professor of English Literature at the School of Humanities and Social Sciences (HSS) at NTU in Singapore. She is the author of *Occidentalism in Novels of Malaysia and Singapore, 1819–2004: Colonial and Postcolonial "Financial Straits"* (2005). Her previous publications include articles and chapters on nostalgia, occidentalism, and the functions of commerce in fiction. Wagner's latest projects are a book-length study of the myths, or fictions, of speculation in Victorian literature and the editing of a collection of essays on eighteenth- and nineteenth-century consumption.

Nancy Welter earned her master's degree from the University of Toledo in 2000. She now teaches at Wayne State University in Detroit, where she is currently working on her Ph.D.

Vicki Corkran Willey is an instructor of English at Salisbury University and a Ph.D. candidate at Indiana University of Pennsylvania. Her interests include fiction of the British Raj and nineteenth-century American women's fiction.

Monica M. Young-Zook is assistant professor of English at Macon State College. Her article, "Sons and Lovers: Tennyson's Fraternal Paternity," was published in *Victorian Literature and Culture* (2005). Her continuing work with psychoanalytic criticism, history, and Victorian gender roles has led to numerous conference papers. She is currently working on a book that investigates the shifting masculinities in the mid- to late nineteenth century and the effect on paternal roles in the poetry and novels of the period.

Devin P. Zuber is completing his dissertation on Romantic aesthetics and Emanuel Swedenborg at the City University of New York. He is the recipient of a teaching fellowship at Queens College where he currently teaches courses in American Studies and English literature. His publications include articles on aesthetics and visuality for *American Quarterly* and the Swiss journal *Variations,* and a forthcoming chapter contribution to a volume on Jonathan Edwards.

INDEX

Abercrombie, John, 116
abolitionism, 213, 215, 216
Abrahams, Morris, 176
Academy, The, 51
Adams, James Eli, 240, 244n8
advice books, 31, 215
Ainsworth, Harrison: *Hilary St. Ives*, 9; *Jack Sheppard*, 54, 174, 179; *Newgate Calendar*, 54; *Rockwood*, 54
Alcott, Louisa May, 91; *All the Year Round*, 161; *Little Women*, 150
Allen, Emily, 199n7
Altick, Richard, 112–13
American Civil War, 154, 212–24
Anderson, James, 178
anorexia nervosa, 90–91, 96–98
Archer, J.: *Marriage Bells*, xx, 177–87
Archibald, Diana C., 132, 136n20
Athenaeum, 3–14, 51, 74, 77, 91, 228
Auerbach, Nina, 100n10, 150–52, 155, 159n7, 186n9
Austen, Jane, 91, 149; *Northanger Abbey*, xiv; *Pride and Prejudice*, 150–51, 155, 159n8
Austin, Alfred, 6

Bachman, Maria K., xiii, xxiin17
Baker, William, 125n2
Bakhtin, Mikhail, 17–18, 27n4
Balzac, Honoré de, 75

Banks, Linneas, 176, 187n19
Barker, Joseph, 216
Basch, Françoise, 57
Beard, Nathaniel, 113n5
Beebee, Thomas, 19, 24, 28n10
Beecher, Catharine, 31
Beer, Gillian, 45, 52n16
Beigel, Hermann, 114n23
Bellows, Donald, 223n7
Bentley's Miscellany, 54
Bentley, George, 173
Bentley, Richard, 74
Bernstein, Stephen, 62n11
Bhabha, Homi K., 229, 231, 233n14, 238–39, 244n7
bigamy, 5, 9, 25, 112, 193–94
Billi, Mirella, 53, 57, 62n1
Björk, Lennart, 28n19
Blackett, R. J. M., 224nn23–24
Blackstone, William, xvi, 161, 168n4; *Commentaries on the Laws of England*, 161
Blackwood's Edinburgh Magazine, 15, 29, 100n2, 113n6, 134, 214
Bland, Lucy, 98, 101n27
Bodichon, Barbara Leigh Smith, 161
Booth, Michael, 175, 179, 186n13, 187n17n30
Bordo, Susan, 99, 101n31
Boucicault, Dion, 41, 130, 213, 221–22,

271

223nn5–6, 224n26; *Foul Play,* 41–42, 130–31; *The Octoroon; or, Life in Louisiana,* 213, 221–22
Bowen, Elizabeth, 84n17
Boyle, Thomas, xxiin14, 53, 62n2
Braddon, Mary Elizabeth, xvi–xvii, 10, 21–25, 29–52, 65, 74, 126, 129, 188–99, 212–24; *Aurora Floyd,* xx, 10, 21, 44, 46–47, 50, 108, 173, 188–99; *Cloven Foot,* 51; *Doctor's Wife,* xiv, 21–23, 29–40, 44, 107, 210; *Eleanor's Victory,* 21; *Garibaldi,* 8; *Henry Dunbar,* 21, 23; *Ishmael,* 30; *John Marchmont's Legacy,* 3–4, 21, 22, 109; *Joshua Haggard's Daughter,* 30, 42, 44; *Lady Audley's Secret,* xiii, ix, xi, xv, xix–xx, 3–4, 10, 16, 18, 21, 29–30, 41, 42–43, 49, 51, 103, 105, 106–11, 135, 150, 173–74, 212, 214, 218, 221, 224n21; *Lady's Mile,* 5, 9; *Octoroon; or, The Lily of Louisiana,* xx, 212–24; *Only a Clod,* 21; *Trail of the Serpent,* 8; *Vixen,* xiv, 41–52
Brantlinger, Patrick, xiii, xxiin15, 3, 5, 7, 12n1, 13n64, 17, 74, 83n3, 214, 223n8, 225–27, 232n2
Breuer, Josef, 101n29
Brewster, Patrick, 216
Briggs, Asa, 224n13
Bristow, Joseph, 141, 148n8
British Medical Journal, 117
Brontë, Anne, xxiin7
Brontë, Charlotte, xxiin7, 89, 92–94, 100, 100n19, 142; *Jane Eyre,* xvii, 34, 92–96, 151
Broughton, Rhoda, x, xi, 45, 46, 52n19, 87–101, 149–59; *Belinda,* 99; *Cometh Up as a Flower,* xvii, 87, 89, 99, 149–59; *Dear Faustina,* 99; *Good-bye Sweetheart,* 99; *Not Wisely but Too Well,* xvii, 48, 87–101
Brown, Isaac Baker, 117–18
Browning, Elizabeth Barrett, 75
Brumberg, Joan Jacobs, 101n28
Bucknill, John, 116, 125n4
Buckstone, John: *Luke the Labourer,* 179
Bulwer-Lytton, Edward, 29, 35, 39, 43–44, 54; *Zanoni,* 37

Burns, Wayne, 64–65, 73n, 136n3
Butler, Arthur, 5
Byron, George Gordon Lord, 35; *Cain, a Mystery,* 22; *Sardanapalus, A Tragedy,* 22; *Two Foscari, a Tragedy,* 22

Carnell, Jennifer, xi, 212, 223n2, 224n18
Carpenter, Mary Wilson, 141–42, 148n14
Casey, Ellen Miller, x, xvii, xxiin1, 45, 52n14
Casey, Janet Galligani 142, 140, 148n7n10
Cawnpore, 225
Chambers, Ross, 24
Chapman & Hall, 25
Chorley, Henry Fothergill, 6, 10–11, 12, 13n45, 114n29
City of London Theatre, 175
Clarke, Dr. Edward H., 31
Clarkson, Thomas, 216
class, x, xii, xix, xx–xx, 165, 168, 173–87, 193, 234–45
Cobbe, Frances Power, 161
Coleridge, Samuel Taylor, 75
Collins, Philip, 62n7
Collins, Wilkie, ix–x, xv, 10, 17, 24, 30, 50, 63nn30–31, 65, 74–75, 100n11, 103, 115–25, 126, 160–69, 200–211, 225–33, 234–45; *Armadale,* xvi, xix–xx, xxi, 6, 45, 111–13, 229, 232, 234–45; *Basil,* xiii, ix, xx, 5, 200–211; *Dead Secret,* xv; *Evil Genius,* xviii; *Heart and Science,* xviii, 204; *Law and the Lady,* xvi; *Man and Wife,* xv, xviii, 5, 59; *Memoirs of the Life of William Collins,* 228; *Moonstone,* xvi, ix–x, xi, xx–xxi, 11, 75, 120, 160–69, 210, 225–33, 238, 242; *No Name,* xv–xvi, xix, 10, 45, 157–58; "Sermon for Sepoys," xx, 227; *Woman in White,* xi–x, xv–xviii, 3–4, 16, 18, 46–47, 81, 90, 115–25, 135, 150, 165, 167, 173, 201, 203, 210, 227, 238, 242
Collyer, Robert, 8, 12n3, 13n43
colonialism, xx, 93, 136, 234–45
Conrow, Margaret, 62n12
Contagious Diseases Act, 98
Cornhill Magazine, 115, 125n1
Cornwell, Neil, 74

Cosens, Frederick, 6, 13n
Couttes, Angela, 58
coverture, 161, 163–65
Cox, Don Richard, xiii, xxiin17
Craft, Christopher, 148n22
Criminal Law Amendment Bill, 134
Crosland, T. W. H., 210n5; *The Suburbans*, 202
Curtis, Jeni, 199n5
Cvetkovich, Ann, xi, xvii, xxiin29, 3, 4, 12n1, 13n64, 17, 18, 27n7, 210n2

D. A. Reeder, 211n12
Dallas, Eneas Sweetland, xxiin18
Darwin, Charles, 64–65; *The Origin of Species*, 65
Davidoff, Leonore, 91, 100n14
Davis, Jim, 175, 183, 187n20
de Mann, Paul, 18, 27n8
De Mattos, Katharine, 4
Debenham, Helen, 101n25
Defoe, Daniel: *Robinson Crusoe*, 225–26
Dellamora, Richard, 130, 136n14
Derrida, Jacques, 78, 83n12
Dickens, Charles, x, xi, 29, 40n17, 73n3, 75, 105, 161; *Bleak House*, 133, 175; *David Copperfield*, 34, 37, 38, 209; *Dombey and Son*, 34–36, 40n17, 103, 204, 209; *Great Expectations*, 15–16; *Hard Times*, 184; *Oliver Twist*, xiii, 34–35, 53–63; *Our Mutual Friend*, 38, 103; "Perils of Certain English Soldiers," xx, 227; *Tale of Two Cities*, 102, 113n2
Divorce Act 1857, 106
Dolin, Tim, 161, 168n5
domestic violence, 58–63
Doran, John, 5, 8–9, 13n23
Doyle, Arthur Conan, 132, 135, 136n17
Dreiser, Theodore, 66
Dublin University Magazine, 87, 105
Duncan, Ian, 226, 230, 233n6
Dyos, H. J., 211n12

East London Observer, 179, 182, 187n37
Eden, Lena, 4, 5, 10, 13n12
Edwards, P. D., x, xxiin7, 9, 13n57, 46, 52n18, 114n12

Effingham Theatre, xx, 174, 176–87
Egan, Pierce: *Life in London*, 58
Eliot, George, ix, xxiin4, 18, 63n32, 64, 89, 100, 102, 126; *Adam Bede*, 15–16; *Middlemarch*, 39, 149; *The Mill on the Floss*, 15–16, 103; *Silas Marner*, 103, 185
Eliot, T. S., x, xxiin5
Elliot, Jeanne, xvii
Ellis, Sarah Stickney, 31
Ellison, Mary, 223n4
Emeljanow, Victor, 187n25
empire, xii, xix, xx–xxi
Engels, Friedrich, 181, 184
Epstein, Deborah Nord, 63n12
Era, 173, 177, 178, 186n2
Esquirol, Jean, 116–18, 125n37

Faderman, Lillian, 128, 130, 136n10
Fantina, Richard, 30
Felix, Charles: *The Notting Hill Mystery*, 3
feme covert, 163–65
feme sole, 161–65, 168
feminism, xvi–xvii, 93–94, 133–36
Finkelstein, David, 137nn24–25
Fisch, Audrey, 212–13, 223n3
Fishman, Robert, 202, 205, 210n6
Fitzgerald, Percy, 105–6, 114n9; *Woman with the Yellow Hair and Other Modern Mysteries*, 105–6
Fladeland, Betty, 224n16
Flaubert, Gustave, 35; *Madame Bovary*, 22, 30, 32–33, 36–37, 39, 40n6
Flint, Kate, 29, 40n2
Foner, Philip S., 223n4
Forster, John, 63n31
Foucault, Michel, 43, 52n6, 84n15, 127–28, 132; *Abnormal*, 136n8; *History of Sexuality*, 127, 136n7
Fanon, Franz, 234
Frederick, Kenneth C., 59, 63n13
French Revolution, 240
Freud, Sigmund, 83, 99, 101n29, 148n18; "The Pyschogenesis of a Case of Homosexuality in a Woman," 143
Frierson, William Coleman, 65, 73n11
Fryckstedt, Monica Correa, 100n4; *Garibaldi*, 177

Garnett, Robert R., 57, 63n16
Gaskell, Elizabeth, 99–100; *Mary Barton,* 184
Gaylin, Ann, 199n3
genre, xi, xiii, xiv, xxii, 3, 15–28
Gilbert, Pamela K., 42, 44, 52n4, 91, 100n7n15
Gilbert, Sandra, 100n10, 116, 142, 148n17
Gissing, George: *The Workers in the Dawn,* 184
Gitter Elizabeth, 106, 114n13
Glasgow Medical Journal, 118–19
Gledhill, Christine, 187n31
Gobineau, Joseph, 221, 224n25
Golden, Catherine, 40n1n18, 42, 223n8
gothic novel, 27, 200–211
Graves, Caroline, xv
Gubar, Susan, 100n10, 116, 142, 148n17

Haines, Lewis F., 65, 73n13
hair, women's, 102–14
Halfpenny Journal, 212, 213, 214, 216
Hardy, Thomas, xi, xiv, 25–27, 28n17; *Desperate Remedies,* 25–26; *Far From the Madding Crowd,* 25; *Hand of Ethelberta,* 26; *Jude the Obscure,* 25; *Laodicean,* 26; *Pair of Blue Eyes,* 26; *Poor Man and the Lady,* 25; *Return of the Native,* 25; *Tess of the d'Urbervilles,* 25; *Trumpet-Major,* 26; *Two on a Tower,* 26; *Under the Greenwood,* 25; *The Well-Beloved,* 26
Harrison, Antony H., 141, 148n11
Harrison, Kimberly, 30
Harwood, John: *Miss Jane, the Bishop's Daughter,* 7
Hazelwood, C. H., 178; *Jeannie Deans,* 178
Hazleton, Harry, 114nn7–8; *The Woman with the Yellow Hair,* 104
Heilbrun, Carolyn G., 233n13
Heller, Lee F., 31, 40n9
Heller, Tamar, xi, xiii, xvii, xxiin16, 101n33, 148n24, 150, 159n5, 201, 208, 210n2, 211n16, 227–28, 233n11
Hemyng, Bracebridge, 176, 187n18
Hibbert, Christopher, 226, 233n4
High Church novel, 27
Hinduism, xx

Hoeveler, Diane Long, 100n10
Holder, Heidi J., 187nn16, 32
Holl, Henry: *The Golden Bait,* 5
Hollington, Michael, 211n13
Homer, Winslow, 32
homosexuality, x, xviii, 128–31, 133–4, 138–48
Horne, R. H., 54
Horton, Augustus, 217
Household Words, xx, 227
Howells, William Dean, 132, 135
Hughes, H. S., 65, 73n12
Hughes, Winifred, xii, x, xxi, xxiin10, 3, 12n1, 13n64, 15, 17, 27n2, 62n10, 63n29, 65, 73n14, 84n14, 132, 135, 136n19, 147n3
hybridity, xi, xiv, xvii, xxi–xxii, 75, 91–92, 229, 231, 234–45
Hyde, James, 83n7

imperialism, xix, xxi, x, 225–26. *See also* colonialism; empire
India, xx, 225–33
Indian Mutiny, xix–xx, 219, 225–26. *See also* Cawnpore; Sepoy Rebellion
inheritance law, 161
insanity, 5, 29, 115–25
Ireland, xxi, 74–84
Irigaray, Luce, 138–48; "Commodities among Themselves," 138

Jackson, Thomas, 5
James, Henry, xiii, xxiin19, 64, 73n4, 74, 108, 114n19, 126; *Portrait of a Lady,* 35; *Turn of the Screw,* 83
Jauss, Hans Robert, 18–19, 24, 27n6
Jeaffreson, John Cordy, 3–14; *Olive Blake's Good Work,* 3
Jenings, Elizabeth: *Thyra Gascoigne,* 9
Jerrold, Douglas: *Black Ey'd Susan,* 179
Jewsbury, Geraldine, 3–14, 74, 77, 83n4, 87, 100n4, 228, 233n15
Jex-Blake, Sophia, 134
Johnson, Edgar, 63n21
Jones, Avonia, 173
Journal of Mental Science, 117
Joyce, Patrick, 223n11
Jung, Carl, 83

Katz, Stanley, 168n3
Keating, P. J., 187n43
Kellett, J. R., 204, 211n10
Kelly, Veronica, 173, 186n1
Kennedy, George E., 57, 63n13
Korobkin, Laura Hanft, 132, 135, 136n22
Kushnier, Jennifer S., xviii, xxiin25, 137n28

Lacan, Jacques, 237, 244n6
Langbauer, Laurie, 184, 187n45
Langland, Elizabeth, 169n11
Le Fanu, Sheridan, Joseph, x, xi, xiii, xviii, xxi, 9, 74–84, 143–48, 210n7; *All in the Dark,* 6; *Carmilla,* xviii, 79, 138, 143–48; "Green Tea," 78–79, 82–83, 203, 205; *In a Glass Darkly,* 76, 79, 203; *Uncle Silas,* 74–84; *Wyvern Mystery,* 10–11
Le Fanu, William R.: *Seventy Years of Irish Life,* 84n16
Ledwon, Lenora, 165, 167, 169n10
Leeds, Mrs. G. Lewis: *The Master of Rylands,* 4
lesbianism, xviii, 128–30, 134, 138–48
Levin, Amy, 158n4
Lewis, Matthew, 174
Linton, Elizabeth Lynn, 114n30
Loesberg, Jonathan, xii, xix, xxiin8nn11, 17
Lonoff, Sue, 232, 233n17
Lovett, R. M., 65, 73n12
Lush, William, 6–7, 12n16, 13nn27–28, 14n65
Lynch, Eve M., 223n10
MacCarthy, Justin, 17, 19, 27n5
Maddyn, Daniel Owen, 5, 13n
Magdalen College, Oxford, xv
Mannsaker, Frances M., 233n16
Mansel, H. L., xiii, ix 19–22, 27, 28n11, 100n6
Married Woman's Property Act, xvi, 106, 161
Marryat, Florence, xi; *For Ever and Ever,* 8; *Veronique,* 9
Martineau, Harriet, 224n18
Marx, Karl, 181, 184
Masonic orders, 75

Matrimonial Causes Act of 1857, xvi
Maunder, Andrew, xi, xii, xix, xxiin9, 100n6
Maxwell, John, xv, 29, 52n2, 105, 212
May, Leila Silvana, 150, 159n6
Mayer, David, 178, 187n29
Mayhew, Henry: *London Labour and the London Poor,* 176
Maynard, Jessica, 187n34
McCarthy, Justin, 112–13
McClintock, Anne, 234–37, 239, 242, 244n3–4
McCormack, W. J., 76, 83n8
Mearns, Andrew: *A Bitter Cry of Outcast London,* 184
Mehta, Jaya, 169n13, 227–28, 233n10
melodrama, xii, 18, 173–87, 214
Menke, Richard, 141, 148n9
Meredith, George, 17; *Beauchamp's Career,* 6
Michie, Helena, 157, 158n1
Millais, John, 111, 114n27
Miller, D. A., x, xviii, 101n21, 137n29
Miller, J. Hillis, 62n12
Millgate, Michael, 28n14
Millingen, John, 116, 125n8
Mintz, Steven, 209, 211n20
miscegenation, xx–xxi, 212–24
Mitchell, Sally: *The Fallen Angel,* x
Montwieler, Katherine, 114n15
Morant Bay Rebellion, xix
Morley, Henry, 186n6
Morrill tariff, 217
Mumm, Susan, 101n26
murder, 5, 25, 55–56, 191

naturalism, xiii, 27, 64–73
Nayder, Lillian, xi, xvii, xx, xxiinn30–31, 62n8, 133, 135, 137n23, 201, 210n1, 233nn8–9, 234, 240–41, 243, 244n2
Nemesvari, Richard, xviii, 137n28
New Surrey Theatre, 173, 176, 178, 184–85
New Woman, 98, 129
Newby, Emma, 9; *Common Sense,* 6; *Wondrous Strange,* 8, 10–11
Newey, Katharine, 173, 186n1
Newgate Calendar, 20, 54–56

Newgate fiction, xii–xiii
Newgate novel, xiii, 15, 20, 27, 31, 53–56, 61
Newgate Prison, 54
Norris, Frank, 66, 70
North British Review, 21, 23
Norton, Caroline, 167
Norwood, Robin, 63n22

O'Neill, Philip, 209, 211n19
O'Shea, Edward, 175, 186n12
O'Toole, Fionn, 45, 52n15
Ofek, Galia, 113n3, 242
Oliphant, Margaret, xxiin13, 15, 19, 27n1, 29, 40n3, 41, 42–43, 52n1, 63n32, 87, 89, 100n2, 103, 113n6, 214, 223n9; *Three Brothers,* 7; *Young Musgrave,* 10
Ouida, 47
Oxenford, John, 173, 184

Page, Norman, xxiin6, 114n29
Parent-Duchâtelet, Alexandre, 57
Paroissien, David, 57, 62n9, 63n15n18
Pater, Walter, 130
Pavis, Patrice, 187n47
Pedlar, Valerie, 62n2
penny dreadfuls, 29
penny press, 212–16, 218
Peters, Catherine, xi, xvii, xx, xxiin23
Phelps, Samuel, 178
Pionke, Albert D., 228, 233n12
Pizer, Donald, 70, 72, 73nn20–21
Pollard, Arthur, 64, 73n6
Poovey, Mary, 126, 136n4, 169n14
postmodernism, 27
Powell, Kerry, 175, 186n11
Pre-Raphaelite Brotherhood, 110–13
Prichard, James: *Treatise on Insanity,* 117, 125n10
Pullan, Matilda, 32, 40n12
Punch, 110, 114n24
Punter, David, 74, 83n1, 147n2
Pykett, Lyn, xi, xxiin7n13, 3, 12n1, 17, 35, 40n14, 44, 108, 114n18, 160, 168n1, 223, 224n27, 226, 233n5

Quarterly Review, 19, 100n6

race, x, xii, xix, 93–94, 212–24, 234–45
Radcliffe, Ann, 50; *Mysteries of Udolpho,* 83
Rae, W. Fraser, 21–24, 27, 28n12, 107, 114n17
Rance, Nicholas, 74, 83n5, 210n3
Reade, Charles, x, xi, xv, 20, 29–30, 50, 64–73, 126–37; "Androgynism; or Woman Playing at Man," xviii, 128–29, 132; "Bloomer," 131, 133; *Christie Johnstone,* 133; *Cloister and the Hearth,* xv, 64, 126, 130, 135; *Foul Play,* xviii, 41–42, 130–31, 136; *Griffith Gaunt,* xiii, 10, 64–73, 126, 132–33, 134, 135, 136; *Hard Cash,* xv, xviii, 126–27, 130, 133, 135–36, 203; *It Is Never Too Late to Mend,* xviii, xxi, 127, 136; *Simpleton,* xxi, 131, 136; *Terrible Temptation,* xv, 135; *Wandering Heir,* xviii, 129–30; *Woman-Hater,* xviii, 131–34
Reade Charles L.: *Charles Reade . . . A Memoir,* 73n2
Reade, Compton: *Charles Reade . . . A Memoir,* 73n2
realism, 27, 44, 61
Reform Bill of 1832, xix, 213
Reform Bill of 1867, xix
Reynold's Miscellany, 212
Rhys, Jean, 93
Rich, Adrienne, 128
Richardson, Samuel, 174
Riddell, Charlotte, 204, 210n8; *City and Suburb,* 204; *Race for Wealth,* 204
Ridding, Lady Laura, 31–32, 40n11
Ritchie, Anne Thackeray, 40n15
Robb, George, 209, 211n17
Robin Goodfellow, 218
Romanticism, 20
Romer, Robert, 7, 9, 13n39
Roscoe, William, 216
Rosenman, Ellen Bayuk, xviii, xxiin26, 137n28
Rosicrucianism, 75
Rossetti, Christina, 114n14, 147, 150; "Goblin Market," xviii, 138–42, 147, 150
Rudd, Martha, xv
Rumsey, Almaric, 3, 13n7
Russett, Cynthia, 162, 168n7

Sabin, Margery, 226–27, 233n7
Said, Edward, xxi, xxiin33
Sala, George Augustus, 105–6, 114n11, 177, 187n23; *The Seven Sons of Mammon,* 105–6
Saturday Review, 25, 51
Saussure, Ferdinand de, 83
Schlicke, Paul, 62n3
Schlossberg, Linda, 101n30
Schmitt, Cannon, 139, 147n4
Schor, Hilary, 99, 101n34
Schroeder, Natalie, xviii, xxiin27, 137n28, 236, 244n5
Scott, Walter, 74, 174; *Bride of Lammermoor,* 35; *Waverley,* 15
sentimentalism, 44
Sepoy Rebellion, 225, 227–29
sexuality, xiv–xv, xvii, xix, 108, 112, 123–25, 127
Seymour, Laura, xv
Shakespeare, William, 64, 126; *Othello,* 92
Shanley, Mary, 168n6
Sharp, Granville, 216
Sharpe, Jenny, xxiin28, 225–26, 228, 232–33n3
Shelley, Mary, 174
Shelley, Percy Bysshe, 33, 35
Shoreditch Observer, 187n35
Showalter, Elaine, xvi, 52n5; *A Literature of Their Own,* x, 42–43
Sigstedt, Cyriol, 83n9
silver fork novel, 27
Silver, Anna Krugovoy, 90, 100n13
Silverstone, Roger, 211n9
Sixpenny Magazine, 218
Skene, Felicia, xi
slavery, 212–24
Small, Helen, 125n15
Smiles, Samuel, 215, 224n14; *Self-Help,* 215
Smith, Ashley, 101nn22–23
Smith, Elton E., 132, 136n5
somatophobia, 92, 96–98
Southworth, E.D.E.N., 178
Sparks, Tabitha, 23, 28n13, 44, 52n13
Spectator, 89, 100n8
Spence, Catherine: *Author's Daughter,* 7

Spence, James: *On the Recognition of the Southern Confederation,* 4
Spender, Emily: *Kingsford,* 12
Spurr, David, 221, 224n25
Starbuck, William: *Woman against the World,* 3
Stodart, Mary, 198, 199n6
Stoker, Bram: *Dracula,* 143, 145
Stowe, Harriet Beecher, 31; *Uncle Tom's Cabin,* 174, 178, 213, 217
Suburban Gothic, 202
suffragettes, 99
Surridge, Lisa, 59, 63nn23–24
Sussman, Herbert, 240, 245n8
Sutcliffe, Emerson Grant, 65, 73nn17–18
Swedenborg, Emanuel, xiii, 74–84; *Arcana Caelestia,* 76; *Heaven and Hell,* 75–77, 79–80; *Regnum Animale,* 76
Swinburne, Algernon Charles, 126, 136n1

Taylor, Jenny Bourne, 210n3, 224nn21–22, 236, 244n5
Taylor, T. P.: *Bottle; or, The Drunken Doom,* 178; *Wild Tribes of London; or, Life in the East and West,* 178
Teilleux, Dr., 117, 125n9
Temple Bar, 6, 105, 113, 116, 125n5
Tennyson, Alfred Lord, 36; *In Memoriam,* 40n19
Thackeray, William Makepeace, 29, 40, 55–56, 60; *Vanity Fair,* 34–35
Thomas, Annie: *Denis Donne,* 9
Thomas, Tammis Elise, 144, 148n20
Thompson, Nicola, 132–133, 135, 136n21
Thoms, Peter, 236, 244n5
Thomson, Peter, 223n6
Thucydides, 20
Thynne, Harriet: *Colonel Fortescue's Daughter,* 7
Tillotson, Kathleen, x
Times, 156, 174–175, 186n6
Todorov, Tzvetan, 19, 27n9
Toronto Globe, 135
Trent Affair, 217
Trodd, Anthea, xx, xxiin32, 199n4
Trollope, Anthony, xxiin, 6, 61, 102; *Three Clerks,* 209

Tromp, Marlene, 60–61, 63n27, 160, 168n
Trudgill, Eric, 63n17
Tuke, Daniel, 116, 125n4
Tutor, Jonathan Craig, 245n9

vampirism, 138, 143–48
Vane, Denzil: *Like Lucifer*, 4
Vicinus, Martha, 98, 101n26
Victorian realism, x, xii, xiv, 19, 25

Wadsworth, Darryl, 175, 186n14
Wagner, Tamara S., 211n15
Walford, Lucy: *The History of a Week*, 9
Walker, Lenore, 63n22
Ward, Mary: *Robert Elsmere*, 202
Waterston, R.C., 31, 40n10
Webber, Andrew Lloyd, ix
Welter, Nancy, 114n14
Wesleyan-Methodist Magazine, 33
Westminster Review, xxiin3, 17, 19, 25
Wilberforce, Edward, 7
Williams, Raymond, 185
Wills, Adela, 166, 169n12
Winslow, Forbes, 115–16, 118–19, 125n3; *On the Obscure Diseases of the Brain and Disorders of the Mind*, 115
Wojtczak Helena, 137n26
Wolff, Robert Lee, 29–30, 40n20, 43–45, 52n10, 212, 223n1
Wollstonecraft, Mary, 92, 95, 100n20; *A Vindication of the Rights of Woman*, 93–94
Wood, Ellen (Mrs. Henry), xvii, 173–87; *East Lynne*, x, xvii, xx, 5, 16, 18, 91, 173–87
Wood, Marilyn, 100n1, 150, 158n3
Wynne, Deborah, 3, 12n1, 14n64, 16, 27n3

Yonge, Charlotte, 31
Young, Mrs. Henry, 178, 179, 183, 187n41; *Desolation*, 183; *Jessy Ashton or the Adventures of a Barmaid*, 183; *Left Alone; or the Footsteps of Crime*, 183
Young, Robert, 219, 224n23
Young-Zook, Monica, 229

Zola, Émile, xiii, 64–66, 73n; *Le Roman experimental* ("The Experimental Novel"), 64–66

www.ingramcontent.com/pod-product-compliance
Lightning Source LLC
Chambersburg PA
CBHW021137230426
43667CB00005B/146